AT HOME WITH MUSIC

Books BY SIGMUND SPAETH

AT HOME WITH MUSIC

FUN WITH MUSIC

FIFTY-FIVE ART SONGS

MAXIMS TO MUSIC

THEY STILL SING OF LOVE

STORIES BEHIND THE WORLD'S GREAT MUSIC

THE FACTS OF LIFE IN POPULAR SONG

MUSIC FOR EVERYBODY

MUSIC FOR FUN

A GUIDE TO GREAT ORCHESTRAL MUSIC

GREAT PROGRAM MUSIC

GREAT SYMPHONIES

AMERICAN MOUNTAIN SONGS

GENTLEMEN, BE SEATED

READ 'EM AND WEEP

WEEP SOME MORE, MY LADY

THE ART OF ENJOYING MUSIC

WORDS AND MUSIC

BARBER SHOP BALLADS

THE COMMON SENSE OF MUSIC

MILTON'S KNOWLEDGE OF MUSIC

At Home With Music

BY SIGMUND SPAETH

DOUBLEDAY & COMPANY, INC.

GARDEN CITY, NEW YORK 1946

PRINTED AT THE COUNTRY LIFE PRESS, GARDEN CITY, N. Y., U. S. A.

To Butler Sumner,
a good friend and helpful companion
in making others at home with music

PREFACE

The suggestion for this book came originally from Mr. Frank Freimann, a pioneer in supplying music to an ever-growing public. He felt, as do many others today, that with the enormous increase of general interest in music there is more than ever a need for some perfectly simple and practical guide to the things that every inexperienced listener would like to know, free from confusing technical terms or possibly baffling illustrations in musical notes.

The new audience for good music is being developed largely through radio and phonograph records, and since Mr. Freimann is a vice-president of the Magnavox Company, which manufactures instruments combining the best features of both, it is quite natural that he should wish to co-operate with this potentially unlimited audience in every way possible. His interest is responsible also for the inclusion of a beautiful series of pictures in color, from the unique Magnavox collection, and these pictures, with their human stories, add enormously to the value of the book.

Acknowledgments are made also to Whittlesey House, New York, and the Garden City Publishing Company for permission to use and revise some of the material that appeared in the author's earlier books, such as *The Art of Enjoying Music*, *Music for Fun* and *Stories behind the World's Great Music*. Some of the opera plots may be found in *Fun with Music*, now published by the Handibook Library and Greenberg, New York, and there are occasional parallels also in *Music for Everybody*, the former Leisure League booklet, whose new edition is distributed by Sentinel Books, New York. The chapter on music for parents and children originally appeared as an article in *Parents' Magazine*, later enlarged as a premium for the Magnavox Company, and there are a few brief excerpts from contributions to *Life Story* and other journals.

Essentially, however, this is a new book, and it goes further than any previous work by the author in a series of honest attempts to reach the vast army of potential music-lovers who have been so easily and habitually frightened away by the insistent obscurities, technicalities and superiorities of well-intentioned scholars who still fail to realize how few people actually know anything at all about music. The so-called "appreciation" books, presumably addressed to the traditional "layman," generally presuppose a well-established enthusiasm and often a detailed knowledge which seldom exist in fact. They reach the recognized devotees of music, but not the self-styled outsiders, whose aesthetic inferiority complex has been nursed by years of snobbish contempt for a taste whose possibilities of development are just beginning to be realized. Far too many potential amateurs of music, participants as well as listeners, have been not only discouraged but definitely antagonized by the attitude of those who apparently could not conceive of a state of mind so far removed from their own.

So this book is addressed both to those who already have some acquaintance with music, which they would like to see ripen into intimacy, and to those who have not yet trusted themselves to take even the first steps toward such an acquaintance. It presupposes only a sense of hearing, which is certainly not too much to expect. It assumes that most people have access to records and the radio rather than to concert halls and opera houses, and it takes advantage of every bit of co-operation afforded by those enormously practical and efficient aids to musical understanding. There is reason to believe that the music of the future will depend more and more upon science for its universal distribution, yet without ever neglecting the human equation. If a reader of these pages occasionally feels insulted, that is too bad. But such a risk must be taken if our audience is measured in millions rather than mere thousands or even hundreds. So great an art and so rich a treasury of happiness must surely be worth every possible effort toward a completely sincere and appreciative enjoyment. Here is your music!

SIGMUND SPAETH

Westport, Conn.
May 1, 1945.

CONTENTS

ILLUSTRATIONS

AT HOME WITH MUSIC

CHAPTER I YOUR TASTE IS NOT BAD

IT SEEMS there was a man who had heard the now famous Tschaikowsky Piano Concerto in several of its sixteen jazz versions (all the way from *Tonight We Love* to *Boogie de Concerto*), and he finally discovered a record of the original composition, with Toscanini conducting the orchestra and Horowitz at the piano. This man's enthusiastic comment was, "That's the best arrangement of that piece I ever heard!"

There is plenty of music just as melodious as that Tschaikowsky theme, or even more so, and just as exciting in its orchestration, waiting to be discovered by anyone wishing to listen to a record or the radio or, if possible, a concert performance. Much of it has already become familiar through popular arrangements, like those of "the Concerto" itself. Music-lovers have known about such pieces for a long time. They have taken their attractiveness for granted, while moving on toward other material, which eventually might prove equally attractive and perhaps even more worth while.

SCIENCE IS A HELP

Radio and records have made it possible to hear such music over and over again, thus arriving at that pleasant feeling of recognition, without requiring the first aid of a more obvious jazz arrangement. If you want to discover music of permanent interest, without being baffled by apparent difficulty or ugliness or dullness, the best way to start is by listening to what might be called "the sure-fire classics," many of which may already be old friends in a popular form.

Band leader Freddy Martin's records made millions of people aware of a Tschaikowsky tune whose appeal had long been recognized by the serious music-lovers of the world. A little later he performed a similar operation on the Piano Concerto of Edvard Grieg, which needed it even less, for its melodies have always been irresistible. Today it figures prominently, along with other Grieg music, in the successful operetta, *Song of Norway*, and appears also on the screen, played and conducted in its original form by José Iturbi, in the film well called *Music for Millions*. Another successful film, *A Song to Remember*, has Iturbi, off screen, playing the music of Chopin, whose popularity is now equally apparent.

Tschaikowsky, once considered a melancholy Russian with an unpronounceable name, has become one of the star composers of Tin Pan Alley. They even wrote a song that pointed out how everybody made money out of his tunes except the composer himself. If you heard the popular *Moon Love*, you were actually listening to the slow theme from Tschaikowsky's fifth symphony, whose opening strain, incidentally, may have influenced that older hit, *Digga, Digga Doo*.

Another modern hit song, *Our Love*, came right out of Tschaikowsky's *Romeo and Juliet* Overture, where its romantic melody has exactly the same significance. *On the Isle of May* is the second theme in the *Andante Cantabile* or slow movement of Tschaikowsky's String Quartet.

Dave Rose's *Holiday for Strings* owes most of its pizzicato technique (plucking instead of bowing the violins) to the Scherzo of Tschaikowsky's fourth symphony, whose Finale is built on a combination of Handel's down-the-scale hymn tune, *Joy to the World*, and a Russian folk-song generally known as *The Birch Tree*. The Tschaikowsky Violin Concerto has also contributed to popular music, and it was not so long ago that Sigmund Romberg appropriated his *June* Barcarolle for the middle part of *Lover, Come Back to Me*. By the time these lines appear in print, our popular composers will probably have discovered several more potential hits in the melodic inventions of Russia's great symphonist. (Alec Templeton definitely has one up his sleeve.)

THIS IS ONLY A START

There are lots of other pieces in the symphonic literature that have either produced currently popular tunes or possess easily remembered characteristics, with a guaranteed response either way. It is no longer news that Romberg found the *Song of Love* (*Blossom Time*) in Schubert's *Unfinished Symphony*, and he had a perfect right to use this fine cello theme in an operetta dealing with the life of Schubert himself. (The beginning of that popular symphony shows a melodic line that was followed closely by *Limehouse Blues.*) The song, *Goin' Home*, often regarded as a Negro spiritual, is actually the Largo from Dvorak's *New World Symphony*, with words by William Arms Fisher. The last movement of that Bohemian-American work echoes the refrain of our folk-song, *Peter Gray*, and deliberately introduces a brief imitation of *Yankee Doodle* itself. The great fifth symphony of Beethoven has an opening motto now identified with the telegraphic rhythm representing V for Victory, and its Finale is an unmistakable march of triumph, to which everyone inevitably keeps time. Beethoven's ninth has a choral Finale whose words are an *Ode to Joy*, and this melody is again suggested at the close of the first symphony of Brahms, who also has a tune in his lighter number two which may have influenced the popular *Play, Fiddle, Play*.

England sings *Land of Hope and Glory* to the main melody of Edward Elgar's march, *Pomp and Circumstance*, and there are words also to the broad, patriotic strain of the Sibelius *Finlandia.* Most of us are familiar with such minor parallels as that of Debussy's *Reverie* with its jazz version, the fox-trot *Marta* with its operatic ancestor by Flotow, the derivation of *The Lamp is Low* from Ravel's *Pavane, My Moonlight Madonna* from Fibich's *Poeme*, and the transmigration of a Mozart Piano Sonata into Raymond Scott's *In an Eighteenth Century Drawing Room.*

TRY THESE ON YOUR EAR

Most of this music is of the "light classic" type, and none of it could fail to attract the attention of even a novice at a first hearing. If you can recognize such pieces through their popular parallels or echoes, you should find it equally easy to spot the familiar *Pilgrims' Chorus* at the start of Wagner's *Tannhäuser* Overture and perhaps the *Prize Song* in his *Meistersinger* Prelude, the "Heigh-ho, Silver" quickstep in Rossini's *William Tell*, possibly even the Bach *Prelude* that supplies the accompaniment for Gounod's *Ave Maria*.

Discovering great music is largely a matter of getting started, and different individuals almost necessarily start at different points. The admirer of Tschaikowsky's Piano Concerto might have received his first thrill from the original instead of a more obvious jazz version. The important point is that his response was honest in each case. Some people sincerely like a piece of extreme modernism, without knowing anything about it, and who shall criticize or condemn their taste? Some prefer folk-music—the simple, down-to-earth material that is particularly strong on masculine appeal.

It is human nature to follow the line of least resistance, and this applies to music as well as other things. For some people this obvious appeal comes most easily through rhythm; for others it lies in a haunting melody; still others have a strong preference for harmony, perhaps even of the barbershop type. The fascination of instrumental color may be the drawing-card, which is a possible explanation of the success of "swing." Extraordinary skill, as such, will always find sincere admirers, and this is a strong element in the appeal of the brilliant coloratura soprano, the dazzling violinist or pianist, or the prima-donna conductor of an orchestra. Finally there may be some to whom the purely intellectual qualities of music are of immediate interest, including the technical details of form and the mathematical properties of tone and acoustics in general.

With so many facets to the jewels of its treasury, there can be no surprise at the ever increasing demand for good music. Radio and the phonograph have unquestionably been the greatest factors in creating and developing that demand, and they will doubtless continue to enjoy that distinction for a long time to come, perhaps sharing it with the screen and with television.

LET'S BE HONEST FOR A CHANGE

We have definitely graduated from that artificial state of the past when it was considered fashionable to listen to music and talk about it with hypocritical, parrotlike enthusiasm, when a piano in the home was believed to be a mark of social distinction, regardless of its neglect or abuse, and when high-sounding technical terms and clichés were accepted as evidences of extreme refinement and culture. We have thrown off also the crippling tradition that music was in some strange way a feminine pursuit, beneath the notice of able-bodied he-men. Today it is taken as a matter of course by the male population as well as the female, and there is far more honesty in its pursuit than ever before. Athletes like Bill Tilden and movie stars like Fredric March are proud of their collections of records, and many a businessman finds his greatest relaxation in listening to the music of his combined radio and phonograph.

But even though we are marching steadily forward in our discovery of great music, we still need some guidance, and there is still the danger of trying to progress too rapidly, perhaps accepting the advice of confirmed and well-intentioned music-lovers without realizing that they are a little too far ahead of us and unaware of our own handicaps and limitations. Too often such advice results in a totally unnecessary setback, and sometimes these bland assurances of the dyed-in-the-wool fanatics have actually stopped the willing novices in their tracks.

DOWN TO EARTH IN RECORDS

A list of musical compositions is offered below, all available on outstanding records, which are guaranteed to please the great majority of potential listeners. Many of them are already associated with familiar melodies, and others possess clear marks of identification and recognition. They are by no means cheap or obvious or merely transient in their appeal; this is permanent music, as proved by the unerring test of time. It need not be your entire listening repertoire, but it is a good foundation for any home library of records.

These albums, even after many hearings, should convince you that the enjoyment of good music is not a difficult or complicated matter, but a normal human experience. If they do not live up to this recommendation, you can always go back to a more obviously popular music; and if they fail to satisfy your soul for long, you may be sure that there is a wealth of still more significant material waiting to be discovered. Here is your music, in a sure-fire list of recorded classics:

WHAT EVERY MUSIC-LOVER SHOULD KNOW

(Available in albums of records. C, Columbia; D, Decca; V, Victor)

BEETHOVEN: *Symphony No. 5*–CM. 498; VDM. 640
BIZET: Selections from *Carmen*–CX. 144; DA. 366; V. 6873-4
BRAHMS: Hungarian Dances–C. 17352-D; DA. 89; V. 4321
Academic Festival Overture–CX. 200; V. 12190
CHOPIN: Waltzes–CM. 390; DA. 185; VM. 863-4
FRANCK: *Symphony in D minor*–CM. 479; VDM. 300
GOUNOD: Waltzes from *Faust*–C. 69031-D; V. 10-1009
GRIEG: *Piano Concerto*–CM. 313; VDM. 900
Peer Gynt Suite–CX. 180; DA. 169; VM. 902
HAYDN: *Surprise Symphony*–CM. 363; VDM. 55
HUMPERDINCK: Prelude to *Hänsel and Gretel*–CM. 424; V. 11929
LISZT: *Les Préludes*–CX. 198; VDM. 453
MENDELSSOHN: Overture to *A Midsummer Night's Dream*–CM. 504; VDM. 57
Incidental Music to *A Midsummer Night's Dream*–CM. 504; VDM. 57
Violin Concerto–CM. 190; VDM. 531
MOZART: *Symphony in G minor*–CM. 316; VDM. 631
Overture to *The Magic Flute*–C. 67660-D; V. 15190
PONCHIELLI: *Dance of the Hours*–C. 11621-D; V. 11833
PROKOFIEFF: *Classical Symphony*–CX. 166; V. 7196-7
Peter and the Wolf–CM. 477; DA. 130; VDM. 566
RACHMANINOFF: *Piano Concerto No. 2*–VDM. 58
RAVEL: *Bolero*–CX. 174; D. 18515; V. 7251-2
RIMSKY-KORSAKOFF: *Scheherazade*–CM. 398; DA. 162; VDM. 269
ROSSINI: Overture to *William Tell*–CX. 60; DA. 157; VDM. 605
Overture to *The Barber of Seville*–C. 70704-D; V. 7225
SAINT-SAËNS: *Danse Macabre*–C. 11251-D; V. 14162
SCHUBERT: *Unfinished Symphony*–CM. 330; VDM. 319
Ballet Music from *Rosamunde*–CM. 343; V. 1312
SCHUMANN: *Spring Symphony*–VDM. 655
SIBELIUS: *Finlandia*–C. 11178-D; V. 7412
JOHANN STRAUSS: Waltzes–CM. 364; DA. 5, 318, 392; V. 8580
RICHARD STRAUSS: Waltzes from *Rosenkavalier*–C. 11542-D
TSCHAIKOWSKY: *Nutcracker Suite*–CM. 395; DA. 23; VDM. 265
Romeo and Juliet–CM. 478; VDM. 347
Symphony No. 4–CM. 468; VDM. 880

Symphony No. 5—CM. 470; VDM. 828
" *No. 6*—CM. 558; VDM. 337
Piano Concerto No. 1—CM. 318; VDM. 800
Violin Concerto—CM. 413; VDM. 356
Overture, 1812—CX. 205; VDM. 515
VERDI: Selections from *Aida*—C. 71401-D; VDM. 54
Prelude to *La Traviata*—C. 69064-D; V. 18080
WAGNER: Prelude to *Die Meistersinger*—CM. 549; VDM. 731
Overture to *Tannhäuser*—CX. 123; V. 9161
Prelude to *Lohengrin*—CM. 549; VDM. 731
Overture to *The Flying Dutchman*—CX. 107; VDM. 979
Prelude to Act III, *Lohengrin*—CM. 549; V. 9005
WEBER: *Invitation to the Dance*—C. 11481-D; V. 15192
Overture to *Der Freischütz*—C. 11817-D; V. 12040
" " *Oberon*—C. 69410-D; V. 12043

MUSIC YOU ENJOY

(Twenty-four single discs, selected by the author as chairman of the National Committee on Music Appreciation, with the help of leading artists in the fields of concert and opera. These records were made by the Columbia Symphony Orchestra, Howard Barlow conducting, and are distributed by the organization known as Music You Enjoy, 420 Lexington Avenue, New York City.)

1. (a) *Blue Danube Waltz*, STRAUSS; (b) *Tales of the Vienna Woods*, STRAUSS.
2. *Serenade*, *Moment Musical* and Ballet Music from *Rosamunde*, SCHUBERT.
3. *Peer Gynt Suite*, GRIEG.
4. Overture and Entr'actes from *Carmen*, BIZET.
5. *Spanish Caprice*, RIMSKY-KORSAKOFF.
6. *Midsummer Night's Dream* Overture, MENDELSSOHN.
7. *Finlandia*, SIBELIUS.
8. *William Tell* Overture, ROSSINI.
9. *Dance of the Hours*, PONCHIELLI.
10. *Second Hungarian Rhapsody*, LISZT.
11. (a) *Ride of the Valkyries*, WAGNER; (b) Prelude to Act III, *Lohengrin*, WAGNER.
12. (a) *Rakoczy March*, BERLIOZ; (b) *Coronation March*, MEYERBEER.
13. *Magic Flute* Overture, MOZART.
14. *Oberon* Overture, WEBER.

15. *Minuet in G, Turkish March* and *Country Dances*, BEETHOVEN.

16. Triumphal March and Ballet Music from *Aida*, VERDI.

17. *Danse Macabre*, SAINT-SAËNS.

18. (a) *Pomp and Circumstance*, ELGAR; (b) *Londonderry Air* (Irish Tune).

19. Ballet Music from *Faust*, GOUNOD.

20. *Air, Bourrée, Gavottes, Gigue*, BACH.

21. (a) *Melody in F*, RUBINSTEIN; (b) *Gopak*, MOUSSORGSKY; (c) *March*, IPPOLITOFF-IVANOFF.

22. *Academic Festival* Overture, BRAHMS.

23. *Träumerei*, *Abendlied*, *The Poet Speaks*, SCHUMANN.

24. *Nutcracker Suite*, TSCHAIKOWSKY.

CHAPTER II YOUR CHILDREN ARE MUSICAL

PARENTS IN GENERAL are likely to ask three leading questions regarding music and their children:

1. How early should a child be exposed to music and when should lessons begin?

2. Are all children sufficiently musical to be worth training to some extent?

3. If a child shows extraordinary musical talent, even genius, what shall we do about it?

The answers to these questions are fairly obvious, even though they have been so consistently ignored as to produce a race whose musical ability and understanding must still be considered far below normal. Those of the present generation who look back with horror at the drudgery of music lessons, mixed with regret over the unsatisfactory results, can blame careless parents as much as bad teachers, with perhaps a little left for themselves. The common complaint is, "I wish I had worked at music when I had the chance," generally adding the false assumption, "Now it is too late."

AN IMPORTANT PROBLEM

Since parents are presumably more efficient today than in the past, and certainly better equipped in many ways, it may be worth their while to give some honest and serious consideration to this whole problem of music. With all the practical advantages offered by modern science, music need not remain the mystery it once was. If it is admitted that people who enjoy music and use it for self-expression are happier than those who do not, then surely the subject deserves careful study.

The first two questions are so closely related that they may well be treated together. Briefly and bluntly, every child should be "exposed" to music as early as possible, just as he is exposed to human speech. Actual music lessons can be started whenever the *child* (not the parent) shows a desire to learn, which might be at any time from the age of three on. An inherent love of music, with some instinct for its expression, may be assumed in every normal child, and even the exceptional "tone-deaf" individuals can be trained to considerable enjoyment and even some participation in music.

The whole thing becomes very simple if you think of music in the same terms as language and treat it accordingly. We take it for granted that every child learns first to understand, then to speak, and eventually to read, write and spell his own language. There is no reason on earth why the same should not be true of the language of music. Granting that some human beings are musically more talented than others, it is also true that some children learn to talk, read and write more quickly than others, and that a literary talent may be as marked as a gift for music.

MUSIC AND LANGUAGE

We teach our children the English language without any thought of their becoming authors or orators or actors, even though that may occur in a few isolated cases of special ability. Why should we not similarly expect every child to know something of music, without necessarily thinking of a career as composer or performer? And why should not the universal language of music be taught in exactly the same way as the limited language of our own people?

Children learn English "by ear." They understand many words and phrases long before they themselves have learned to speak. By the time they are ready for school, they have acquired a considerable vocabulary. They are neither inarticulate nor illiterate, and the teacher merely has to show them how to read, write and spell the language with which they are already familiar.

Compare this commonly accepted situation with that of the child presumably starting to take music lessons. In most cases he is thrown to the teacher without any musical experience of his own, completely ignorant of the simplest principles of rhythm, melody or harmony.

When a child is taught to spell "cat," he at least knows the word as applying to a familiar object. He has seen, heard and felt an actual cat. But when he meets the musical scale, it is usually as a dark and mysterious riddle, with no relation to any past experience with tones or time.

Therefore the question of early exposure to music and the possible start of musical training must be answered through the obvious analogy with language itself. Let the child hear music practically from the day of his birth, and let him begin to make music as well whenever he shows an inclination to do so.

LISTENING COMES FIRST

This part of a child's musical education is the responsibility of his parents, just as definitely as the first steps in speech. With the phonograph and radio co-operating, there should be no difficulty in selecting, for infant listening, music whose permanent effect can hardly be measured. It is greatly preferable, however, that parents should make this introduction themselves if possible. "But I am not musical myself," says the average parent, "and know very little about music. What can I do?" The answer is quite simple. Why not use the child as an excuse for a bit of musical self-education? Anybody at all can learn to sing the nursery rhymes and folk-tunes of the world, and this is the material that is obviously best for young children. What difference does it make if the performance is not very good? The baby is too young to check up on musical standards, and by the time he has grown old enough to be aware of pitch and time and quality, perhaps the parents themselves will not be so bad. Many an adult might find a stimulus to musical performance, instrumental as well as vocal, in the opportunity to play and sing with an enthusiastic child, enjoying a parallel development of taste and ability.

The music of infancy is necessarily simple and direct. It should have a strongly marked rhythm and a melody that is easily remembered. Words of the Mother Goose type have long proved their popularity, and there is no limit to such material.

EARLY SONG AND RHYTHM

By the time a child can talk, he can also sing, and in many cases children have shown the ability to carry a tune even before they became articulate. The sense of rhythm has also expressed itself in many cases before a child could walk. If the child has heard music constantly during the inarticulate years, partly through mechanical aids and partly from the parents themselves, he will be more than ready to participate as soon as he enters the walking and talking stage.

Now he can learn to sing the little songs with which he is already familiar and to keep time to the rhythmic tunes. Some of his earliest toys can also be musical. Even a rattle has rhythmic possibilities, which may be discovered by infants as well as their parents. The old-fashioned music box requires only the turn of a handle. When creeping leads to toddling, the wheeled toys that are pulled or pushed on the floor can just as easily give out musical sounds, even if it is only a pattern of bells. Donald Duck and his colleagues, as well as the old Mother Goose characters, are available in a variety of musical forms, and their example is quite likely to stimulate primitive imitation.

FIRST SIGNS OF PARTICIPATION

As soon as this desire has been clearly expressed, a toy piano or trumpet or a set of bells may be substituted or added to the toys that automatically produce music of a sort. Eventually the day will come when any child, facing a real piano for the first time, will instinctively pound on the keys for the sheer pleasure of making a noise.

Now is the time to find out whether a child has any special musical talent, without waiting for any of those elaborate tests or the verdict of a teacher. If the child can be interested in patterns of any kind, melodic, harmonic or even rhythmic, it is permissible to assume an individual gift above the average. Try melody first, using some familiar phrase, perhaps the three successive tones of *Three Blind Mice*. (If a child does not recognize such a tune at a very tender age, blame it on the parents.) Sing the words and the melody, striking the keys, E, D, C, in the middle of the keyboard. Then do the same thing, pressing down the keys with the child's own index finger. It may seem like teaching a puppy a new trick, but if within a reasonable time the child succeeds in playing such a pattern by himself, the mutual satisfaction will be enormous. Once this stage is reached, Papa or Mamma can add a harmony to Baby's melody, perhaps carrying out the complete round, and it will sound like a real piece, with Baby still playing only three notes.

Similar experiments can be made with the first half of *Au Clair de la Lune* or the start of *Yankee Doodle*, using the same three notes. If the child's hands are large enough, the harmony pattern of C, E, G can be tried, perhaps with the left hand playing a C for the bass, and this one chord is enough to accompany the singing of *The Farmer in the Dell* or such a round as *Row, Row, Row Your Boat.* If melody and harmony patterns are still too difficult, try letting the child play just one note in time, as accompaniment to any rhythmic melody played by the parents.

THE SIMPLEST TEST OF TALENT

Such experiments will soon determine the musical nature of a child. Mozart began playing in just that way at the age of three, picking out the patterns for himself. If a child of five or six cannot be interested in turning mere noise into logical combinations of sound, the likelihood of exceptional talent may be automatically dismissed. That is no reason, however, for discontinuing the exposure to music, at least as a listener, or the encouragement to join with others in song.

While it is entirely true that every child can be taught to sing by ear (just as he is taught to speak) and later to read and write music just as easily as his own language, there is no reason to expect any precocious ability to play upon an instrument. Any such attempts must be considered merely as a game, to be continued only as long as the child enjoys it. If there is no sign of particular interest or ability, it is better to return to the listening stage and the use of mechanical instruments.

MUSIC IS FUN

Even when regular lessons are started, which may be at any age from three or four up, the recreational spirit should continue to be emphasized. There is no sense whatever in turning music into drudgery at any time. If a child has to be forced to practice by threats or bribes, the chances are that he should not be playing at all. A good teacher can turn the early lessons into a series of games, consistently making pleasant music and letting the scales and exercises wait until a real enthusiasm has developed. Parents can also do their share of making the practice period a real pleasure.

The truly talented child does not have to be urged to practice unless he happens to be exceptionally lazy as well. In that case a musical career is out of the question, and the only concern of teachers and parents alike is to encourage a reasonable proficiency and hope for the best. The old-fashioned music teacher who treated every pupil as a potential concert artist and insisted upon technical facility at all costs often created a permanent hostility to music rather than a love of the art. *Nine tenths of the scales and exercises of the past were completely wasted, failing to produce creditable performers while killing off potential music-lovers in general.*

DON'T BLAME THE TEACHER

The responsibility falls ultimately upon the parents rather than the teachers. If the parents have started early to encourage interest and participation in music, the later education of their children will present no problems. Music will have become either a game that is fun and easy to play, or an absorbing passion that laughs at drudgery and surmounts all obstacles.

In either case the parent is the gainer. An honest enthusiasm for music is the simplest and best road to the constant entertainment demanded by normal children. If the phonograph habit is formed early, hours of time can easily be passed in merely listening to records. Children have been known to develop a special affection for certain pieces and to pick out the discs by some secret means of identification long before they could possibly read the labels. Many a mother has found it possible to get a lot of work done while keeping the children quiet with a steady succession of attractive records, at the same time laying the foundation for permanent listening habits. Such habits are actually as desirable as the ability to give an impressive performance, and far more easily attained.

USING THE PHONOGRAPH

A list of pieces is given at the end of this chapter, indicating how the family phonograph can be used progressively to supplement the early musical attempts of both parents and children. This of course is merely a suggestion, barely scratching the surface of the available material, and not to be taken too literally. It may be guaranteed, however, that every composition mentioned in that list has a potential appeal to children. The order of acquaintance can be varied according to circumstances.

All the companies manufacturing records have brought out numerous albums and individual discs that are definitely intended for children, and most of these recordings excellently serve their purpose and should be made the basis of every home library. The Victor catalogue, for instance, lists all of the better-known Mother Goose songs, interpreted by such artists as Louis James, Clifford Johns and James Harkins, plus Uncle Mac's *Nursery Rhymes*, Vaughan De Leath's *Jolly Songs for Jack and Jean*, settings of Stevenson's *Child's Garden of Verses*, Milne's *Winnie the Pooh* and *Christopher Robin*, William Woodin's *Raggedy Ann Songs*, *Lullabies of Many Lands* and *Songs from Shirley Temple Pictures*. There are also children's operettas, like *Robin Hood* and *The Bumblebee Prince* (to Rimsky-Korsakoff's music), dramatizations like *America Grows Up*, singing and guessing games and tunes of youthful appeal played by the popular bands.

The Columbia list balances this with a number of albums, including such titles as *Adventures of Bubble and Squeak*, *Captain Kidd's Cats*, *Cherub the Chick*, *Edward, the Dignified Monkey*, *Herman, the Littlest Locomotive* and *Mike, the Tough Little Tug-Boat*, besides comprehensive collections from the Birchard *Singing School Music Series* and Silver Burdett's *Music Hour*, *a Nonsense Alphabet Suite*, *Music Fairy Stories*, Lullabies, Folk-Dances, etc.

The Decca records for children make use of both Bing Crosby and Frank Luther as vocalists, with instrumental effects by Victor Young and others. Judy Garland interprets *The Wizard of Oz* and Ireene Wicker, "the Singing Lady," takes care of the Lullabies. Cliff Edwards ("Ukulele Ike") is heard in his own version of the Walt Disney *Pinocchio*, and there are French folk-songs, Christmas music, *Gulliver's Travels* and instrumental novelties.

The writer happens to have had a hand in selecting the material for a set of miniature records known as *Little Masters*, based upon the adult series called *Music You Enjoy*, and to have co-operated in preparing the children's discs issued by the same company, in which the voice of Milton Cross delivers charming stories over an orchestral accompaniment conducted by the late Erno Rapee, of Radio City Music Hall.

FUN WITH RECORDS AT HOME

There are many ways of using phonograph records besides merely listening to them. The possibility of singing with a record has been amply demonstrated by that early morning favorite, Lois January, on the air. Playing an occasional chord on the piano, in harmony with the phonograph, lends a fascinating touch of co-operation to those who can do it.

The potentialities of a rhythmic accompaniment are endless. A young man who is now editor of a leading musical magazine, and writing an authoritative column on jazz and swing, started by simply drumming with records, gradually building up an elaborate set of traps and learning all the tricks of the professional skin-beaters.

There is also the limitless game of pretending to be a conductor and beating time while a record is played. That is how the prodigious Loren Maazel began his career with the baton, and by the time he was ten years old he had conducted some of the greatest symphony orchestras of America in person. Children like to play at conducting, and since their sense of time is generally good, they can entertain themselves for hours with such a game.

When developing your child's musical appreciation in this way, the selection of a radio-phonograph becomes doubly important. Be careful not to dull the keenness of his ears by subjecting them to an inadequate instrument. You'll want a radio-phonograph that reproduces music as the composer and conductor intended it to be.

Those who can really play the piano or the violin or the cello will enjoy performing with the so-called Add-a-Part records, in which one instrument is omitted, but with the notes supplied so that an actual musician can fill the gap. This requires considerable skill, but gives corresponding satisfaction to the player and perhaps the listener as well.

After children have heard a number of records repeatedly, a musical memory test makes an excellent game. Short snatches of melody can be played on records specially marked for the purpose, and prizes can be given to those who guess them correctly. This plan has been used successfully in schools and for adults as well as children in connection with the band concerts of Edwin Franko Goldman in the New York parks.

More ambitious perhaps is the recognition of themes in symphonies or other major instrumental works. This can be simplified by supplying words to fit the tunes, which are thus likely to become literally unforgettable. (The author has provided plentiful material for this innocent trick in two books, *Great Symphonies* and *Great Program Music*.)

MUSICAL INSTRUMENTS FOR BEGINNERS

It is a mistake to think of the piano as the only possible instrument for the musical novice. Sometimes there is none available, and often it would be far better if a child were given some opportunity for choice among various possibilities for making his own music.

A most practical instrument, closely related to both piano and organ, is the piano accordion, which has the same keyboard on a smaller scale. Its tones are produced by reeds, suggesting the quality of saxophones or clarinets in harmony. The greatest asset of the piano accordion is that a set of buttons controls a series of chords, making it very easy to accompany a melody played by the right hand. There is a twelve-bass accordion which is ideal for beginners, permitting the use of six different keys in common chords and bass notes. When this comparatively simple instrument is mastered, it is not difficult to change to a more elaborate accordion, permitting additional keys as well as minor chords, etc., gradually working up to the almost orchestral outfit of 120 buttons and several octaves of keyboard.

The tone of a harmonica or mouth organ is similar to that of an accordion, and it is also a reed instrument. Certainly it is the easiest of all the wind family to play, a modern representative of the original Pan pipes which began the whole process of blowing on reeds. The advantage of the harmonica is that you can immediately play a scale by merely running your mouth along the holes and alternately

The Bach family had fun with music

THERE HAVE BEEN many families in history showing special musical gifts, but none to compare with the immortal tribe of Bach. For nearly two hundred years the music of Europe was enriched by one or more composers of that name, with Johann Sebastian Bach himself as the climax. His own talents were inherited from several ancestors and passed on to at least five of his twenty children.

The great Bach could relax with music, besides practicing it as a profession. He liked nothing better than to sit at the keyboard, surrounded by members of his family, armed with various instruments, or using their voices to good effect, all making music spontaneously and for the pure fun of it.

So skilled were the Bach boys and girls that any one of them could start a tune, improvised on the spur of the moment, and have the rest join in immediately in perfect harmony and counterpoint. Here was a family literally "at home with music," centuries before science and art had combined to bring great performances of the classics into every household.

An unusual gift for the creation or interpretation of music is often the result of such heredity and environment, and there is no questioning the permanent influence of early habits of listening (and perhaps participation) in the development of sincere music-lovers, even where no special talent exists. Every normal human being can have fun with music, without expecting to approach the attainments of the famous Bach family.

breathing in and out, which is the natural fashion. Boys and girls have been known to become expert harmonica players at a tender age, and the concert possibilities of this humble instrument have been amply demonstrated by such artists as Larry Adler and John Sebastian. It has been one of the most popular of all purveyors of music for our men at the front, when pianos and other instruments were no longer available.

There are other wind instruments almost as simple as the harmonica: the ocarina or "sweet potato" and its near relative, the tonette, played like an end-blown flute, by covering certain holes with the fingers, the tin whistle, even easier to manipulate, the ancient recorder, which is truly musical in its effects, and the trombone flute or slide whistle, which at least affords plenty of amusement. These are more than mere toys, and may easily create the ambition to play on a more serious wind instrument, like the saxophone or clarinet, perhaps leading eventually to the undeniable difficulties of the oboe and bassoon.

A toy trumpet may be the forerunner of an ordinary bugle, familiar to Boy Scouts and campers in general, and from there the step to a cornet or trumpet is almost inevitable, with the trombone and French horn still a potential challenge for the future.

Stringed instruments can be similarly progressive. The ukulele presents perhaps the smallest problem for a mere strumming of chords, but the guitar, banjo and mandolin are not much harder, particularly if a simple accompaniment for singing is desired. A mandolin is tuned like a violin, and it may in time encourage the young performer to try the far more exacting instrument, along with its relatives, the viola and cello and perhaps the bass viol. When youngsters arrive at an adequate command of such instruments, they are sure to be in constant demand for school orchestras and the unique delights of ensemble playing—thus sharing with others the enjoyment they derive from music.

PERCUSSION AS A BASIC PRINCIPLE

Drums of all kinds are of course the commonest and most practical of all musical instruments. The instinct for rhythm appears to some extent in all human beings, and it represents the first musical response of the savage, the child and the untutored adult.

Everybody has a tendency to drum, if only through the nervous movements of the fingers in a telephone booth, while waiting for an answer. Children love to strike a resounding surface, the louder the better. Toy drums and other primitive noise-makers can easily lead to percussion instruments of greater complexity, perhaps with some melodic significance.

Bells, tuned to the intervals of the scale, have already been mentioned. They can be had in sets of three and five, producing fundamental patterns of melody and harmony. The progress to a full scale can be gradual, with the xylophone, glockenspiel and marimba as future ideals. There are books of musical games in which a set of metal bells plays an important part, and through these a child may actually learn to read notes, while developing a good ear for pitch and a memory for tunes.

When regular percussion instruments are not available they can be created on the spot. Spoons tapped on plates have the making of a rhythm band, and a pencil on a lamp shade may take the place of actual drumsticks on parchment. If a variety of pitch is desired, just fill some glasses with water at different levels and check the resulting intervals of the scale. The higher the water, the lower the pitch.

Now the entire family is equipped to make its own music, and again the phonograph can be called in to supply a truly satisfactory background. Haydn's *Toy Symphony* was built on exactly the same basis. Homemade music readily progresses from such primitive experiments to a surprisingly effective ensemble, with no particular talent required from anyone concerned, yet providing hours of musical enjoyment for the entire family.

THE PRECOCIOUS YOUNG GENIUS

But if a child turns out to be a musical prodigy, there is still no reason for parental worry. The responsibility for good training of the genius or near-genius should be taken more seriously than with the average child, and every effort should be made to give such exceptional gifts unlimited opportunity for development. There need be no fear of overworking such a child or letting him advance too rapidly. If music is his chief diversion, let it be enjoyed to the utmost. Practice is fun for such a prodigy, and the child knows best how much he can stand.

The public exploitation of such talents, however, should not be encouraged. It is not generally realized that practically all the great musicians of modern times were infant prodigies, most of them showing an astonishing skill by the time they were eight, nine or ten years old. But if their careers were wisely guided, they seldom appeared in public before the age of fourteen or fifteen, when they could be considered fairly mature artists.

At the moment there are many exceptional talents all over America, but most of them are being wisely developed to the point where it will be unnecessary for critics to qualify their superlatives with the damning phrase, "for a child." Actually it is impossible for even the most precocious child to have an emotional grasp of the great works of musical literature. It is only after a complete technical equipment has been attained that the deeper problems of interpretation can be solved. But this equipment may well reach astonishing proportions long before maturity is reached.

There is also the financial problem to be considered, for no concert career can be launched today without considerable expenditure of money. If the family of a genius can take care of the preliminary expenses, it is usually possible to find one or more "angels" to provide the big investment, assuming that future possibilities are by that time well established.

MAKING A LIVING OUT OF MUSIC

At best, the life of a professional musician can be recommended only when it is clearly inevitable. It demands far more than musical ability as such. There must be personality, tremendous concentration, indefatigable industry, dependable health, and, perhaps of the most vital importance, a raw courage, a self-confidence amounting almost to effrontery, that refuses to accept defeat. Such a combination is so rare as to be almost negligible.

Professionalism has been one of our greatest handicaps to musical development. There are far too many professional musicians and not nearly enough amateurs in America today. A concert career should be the ambition of only a few specially chosen souls; but a sane and practical participation in music as a recreation and a normal pleasure is within the reach of every human being.

THE FINAL RESPONSIBILITY

It is the parents who must decide in what way and to what extent music will affect the lives of their children. They cannot afford to wait for the teachers, any more than they would wait for kindergarten or school days to decide whether their children shall speak and understand their own language. If adult participation in music can be encouraged by the obvious interest of our children, so much the better. There is no need of repeating the mistakes of the past, which created a thoroughly unmusical generation that is just beginning to recover from its inferiority complex in relation to music.

If parents are willing to inflict baby talk on their offspring, they may as well try their hand at baby music also. With steady progress on both sides, it is entirely possible that parents and children alike will eventually discover for themselves some of that permanent beauty which is most easily revealed through the universal language of music and which adds inevitably to the enduring satisfactions of life.

MUSIC RECOMMENDED FOR YOUNG CHILDREN

Mother Goose Rhymes and Nursery Jingles
The Star-Spangled Banner
Three Blind Mice
Row, Row, Row Your Boat and other Rounds
Mary Had a Little Lamb
Good-night Ladies
Frère Jacques
Au Clair de la Lune
Malbrouck (He's a Jolly Good Fellow)
Oh, Where, Oh, Where Has My Little Dog Gone? (*Lauterbach*)
The Lorelei
Oh, Susanna! and other Foster Songs
Polly, Wolly Doodle
Glow Worm
Frog Went a-Courtin'
Shortenin' Bread
Sourwood Mountain
La Paloma
Turkey in the Straw
The Arkansas Traveler
Pop Goes the Weasel
The Mermaid
There Is a Tavern in the Town

Clementine
Dixie
Shoo, Fly, Don't Bother Me
The Wearing of the Green
Brahms' Lullaby
Old McDonald Had a Farm
Billie Boy
Now the Day Is Over
Home on the Range
Mighty Lak a Rose (*Nevin*)
Long, Long Ago
Sweet and Low
Baby's Boat
Kentucky Babe
Silent Night
Abide with Me
The Irish Washerwoman
Green Sleeves
Moment Musical (*Schubert*)
Golliwogg's Cakewalk (*Debussy*)
Waltzing Doll (*Poldini*)
Santa Lucia
Songs from *Snow White* (*Churchill-Disney*)
The Stars and Stripes Forever (*Sousa*)
God Bless America (*Berlin*)
America the Beautiful
Tramp! Tramp! Tramp!
Battle Hymn of the Republic
Rally Round the Flag, Boys (The Battle Cry of Freedom)
Nutcracker Suite (*Tschaikowsky*)
Turkish March (*Beethoven*)
Für Elise (*Beethoven*)
Scenes from Childhood and Album for the Young (*Schumann*)
Emmett's Lullaby
Rousseau's Lullaby
Rock-a-bye, Baby
The Girl I Left Behind Me
The Campbells Are Coming
Alouette
Minuet (*Paderewski*)
Minute Waltz (*Chopin*)
Spinning Song (*Mendelssohn*)
Jeux d'Eau (*Ravel*)
Hark, Hark, the Lark (*Schubert*)
Skaters' Waltz (*Waldteufel*)
Yankee Doodle
America
Auld Lang Syne
Old Hundred
My Bonnie
Blue Danube Waltz (*Strauss*)
Babes in Toyland (*Herbert*)
Cielito Lindo
Surprise Symphony (2d Movement) (*Haydn*)
Dance from Orpheus (*Gluck*)
Aloha Oe
Dance of the Will-o-the-wisps (*Berlioz*)
Gnomenreigen (*Liszt*)
To a Wild Rose (*MacDowell*)
Estrellita
Marche Militaire (*Schubert*)
Marche Lorraine (*Ganne*)
Inventions (*Bach*)
Minuet in G (*Beethoven*)
Minuets (*Mozart*)
Ballad for Americans
Songs of the North and South (*Luther*)
Brazilian Songs (*Elsie Houston*)
Carry Me Back to Old Virginny
Oh, Dem Golden Slippers
In the Morning (*Bland*)
In the Evening (*Bland*)
Turkish Rondo (*Mozart*)
Gypsy Rondo (*Haydn*)
Siegfried Idyl (*Wagner*)

Selections from Gilbert and Sullivan
The Cat and the Mouse (*Copland*)
Animal Pieces (*Ganz*)
Waltzes (*Brahms*)
Adventures in a Perambulator (*Carpenter*)
Berceuse (*Grieg*)
Papillon (*Grieg*)
Papillons (*Schumann*)
Little Sandman (*Brahms*)
Through the Looking-Glass (*Taylor*)
Midsummer Night's Dream Overture (*Mendelssohn*)
Waltzes (*Schubert*)
Parade of the Wooden Soldiers
Swinging on a Star
Old Man River
Prelude to Hänsel and Gretel (*Humperdinck*)
Funiculi-Funicula
Peter and the Wolf (*Prokofieff*)
Country Gardens (*Grainger*)
Shepherds' Hey, Molly on the Shore, Mock Morris (*Grainger*)
Country Dances (*Beethoven*)
Volga Boat Song
La Cucaracha
La Colomba
O Sole Mio
Irish Tune from County Derry
Dutch Song of Thanksgiving
The Quilting Party
Love's Old Sweet Song
Hail, Columbia
Juba Dance (*Dett*)
I Got Rhythm (*Gershwin*)
Songs without Words (*Mendelssohn*)
Norwegian Dance (*Grieg*)
Praeludium (*Järnefelt*)
Coppelia (*Delibes*)
L'Arlesienne Suites (*Bizet*)
The Sorcerer's Apprentice (*Dukas*)
Pastoral Symphony (*Beethoven*)
Carnival of the Animals (*Saint-Saëns*)
Unfinished Symphony (*Schubert*)
Clock Symphony (*Haydn*)
Toy Symphony (*Haydn*)
Pizzicati (*Delibes*)
Song without Words (*Tschaikowsky*)
Scarf Dance (*Chaminade*)
España Rhapsody (*Chabrier*)
Slavic March (*Tschaikowsky*)
Sylvia and Naila Waltzes (*Delibes*)
Pomp and Circumstance (*Elgar*)
March of the Dwarfs, Sailor's Song (*Grieg*)
On the Trail (*Grofé*)
Largo (*Dvorak*)
Dance of the Hours (*Ponchielli*)
Humoresque (*Dvorak*)
Largo (*Handel*)
March from Aida (*Verdi*)
Lullaby (*Gretchaninoff*)
Flight of the Bumble Bee (*Rimsky-Korsakoff*)
Song of India (*Rimsky-Korsakoff*)
Rustle of Spring (*Sinding*)
Ride of the Valkyries (*Wagner*)
William Tell Overture (*Rossini*)
Anitra's Dance and Hall of the Mountain King (*Grieg*)
Now Is the Month of Maying (*Morley*)
Light Cavalry Overture (*Suppé*)
Poet and Peasant Overture (*Suppé*)
Zampa Overture (*Herold*)
Rakoczy March (*Berlioz*)

Minuet (*Boccherini*)
Orientale (*Cui*)
Fury over a Lost Penny and Dance of the Dervishes (*Beethoven*)
Pavanne (*Gould*)
Dances from Prince Igor (*Borodin*)
Reverie (*Debussy*)
The Harmonious Blacksmith (*Handel*)
Bourrée, Gigue, Loure, etc. (*Bach*)
La Campanella (*Paganini-Liszt*)
Jingle Jangle (*McBride*)
Fugato on a Well-Known Theme (*McBride*)
Children's Corner (*Debussy*)
Finale of Eroica Symphony (*Beethoven*)
Scherzo, Fourth Symphony; 2d Movement of Fifth and 3d of Sixth (*Tschaikowsky*)

(A list of Special Records for Children will be found near the end of this book, with catalogue numbers representing Columbia, Decca and Victor.)

CHAPTER III A SIMPLE APPROACH TO MUSIC

IT IS EASY ENOUGH to rhapsodize about music, to throw exaggerated similes and poetical expressions about in all directions, to read hidden meanings into innocent compositions, and to create epigrams on the importance of music as compared with such necessities as food and sleep. It is even easier to write pages of technical and utterly unintelligible comment that even a trained musician can scarcely follow. But it is a very difficult matter to make music intelligible to the average person without indulging in technical terms and without descending to mere "soft-soap."

Many music-lovers, and particularly musicians, take music too hard. They put it on such a high pedestal that they never actually get close to it. One is inclined to resent the reverential, unctuous tones with which radio announcers salute any composition that has been labeled "classical" (which means almost any piece that is not a ready seller in the music stores). One wishes they would make some distinction between a really great masterpiece and a pleasing little potboiler that has caught the public fancy. If only the public would realize the vast gulf between talent and genius, or even between talent and the ordinary ability to put notes on paper, as anyone can put words on paper, and have them make sense! Above all else, people should have the courage to say what they really think about music, and not be so eternally worried over what somebody else may think and say.

The success of our popular music is founded upon a sincerity of taste plus a highly developed commercial system. If everybody had been encouraged to be equally sincere about "good" music, instead of being tempted to play the hypocrite and pretend an interest that often did not exist, and if the better type of music had received the commercial attention lavished upon popular hits of the day, we might now be in a very different state musically.

WE HAVE IMPROVED

It is true, however, that hypocrisy and insincerity are not so rampant as they were before two World Wars destroyed all our pet illusions. If people today really like a thing, they are inclined to say so, even though their liking may have been engineered by forces of which they are unaware. It is true also that there are more opportunities to hear good music well performed than there have ever been in the past. We no longer compel our young to practice at the piano in order to be deemed socially correct, which may be unfortunate in view of the undoubted decrease in piano-playing of any kind. On the other hand, we find a surprising number of adults today regretting that they threw away the musical opportunities of their youth, or that they were handled so absurdly by their teachers and parents that nobody could have expected them to make any real progress, and trying now to make up for lost time by at least finding out something about music, and perhaps even attempting a little musical performance of their own.

The music mentioned in this book is mostly material that is likely to be heard on the radio or to be available on records. There is no point in trying to create interest in something which is utterly inaccessible. We need touch only lightly on music which, while historically significant, seems to have no particular aesthetic appeal for the modern listener; it seems a waste of time to dwell on works of art whose chief virtue is their historic or scientific interest.

HOW DO YOU LISTEN?

Even regular concert-goers are surprisingly vague as to the things that they are listening for in music or the reason for their response to a performance, good or bad. They sit generally in a comfortable coma, a luscious lethargy, out of which they stir themselves to polite applause at the proper moments, often aided by a professional claque. The music affects them as a mild stimulant at the most, or perhaps an opiate, and they dream through a concert with vague sensations of pleasure, largely influenced by the sensuous beauty of what they are hearing, but with little real grasp of what is going on. No one would wish to substitute for this the purely intellectual attitude of those scholarly appreciators who arm themselves with a complete score and follow every note of the music with the eye as well as the ear. But somewhere between the two there is a happy medium, whereby the listener can secure a most satisfying and sensuous enjoyment, and at the same time have a fairly clear idea of what it is all about.

The enjoyment of music is primarily an instinct, and no one can be stopped from having that experience, except perhaps by the insistence on turning the whole thing into a horrible task. But just as creative instincts can be developed into actual art, through the study of what others have discovered in the past, so the enjoyment of music or any other art may itself become an art by adding to instinctive human reactions the experience of others. If to this art of enjoyment can be added some small ability as a performer of music, so much the better, for a true appreciation of musical values, interpretive as well as creative, comes most surely through the actual experience of personal participation in music. If anyone can sing in a local chorus, or play a little on the piano, or take part in any instrumental group, the opportunity should never be overlooked. It is not necessary to aim at showing off and astonishing the neighbors, or to turn a natural talent to commercial account, for the real object of such personal performance is that of recreation and self-expression and a more intimate communion with beauty for its own sake.

The general reader is advised to use this book as a check on his instinctive reactions to music, absorbing only those portions of it that make listening in general an easier and more logical matter. If he is seriously interested in the pursuit of the art, then a detailed study of certain compositions, guided by the analytical material in these pages, will be found helpful. But it would be a mistake to try to read the book right through without hearing any of the music with which it deals. In fact, more will always be accomplished by listening than by reading. Repeated hearing of the best music is the surest path to good musical taste, and even after such a taste has been formed, in accordance with traditional values, the most important question is still, "Do you like this piece?" and perhaps the next is, "Why?" If the answer to that Why is made at all easier by any of these pages, the book as a whole will be amply justified.

SO WHAT IS MUSIC?

Music is made of Tones in Time. The tones are the result of vibration. If you stretch a rubber band (holding one end in your teeth) and then start it vibrating by twanging it with your fingers, it will produce a musical tone of a sort. The tighter you stretch it, the higher the tone will be.

You can also make a tone higher by reducing the length of the vibrating surface (as the violinist does when he holds down the string with his finger).[1] So you arrive quite simply at these two principles:

Longer and looser makes a tone lower.
Tighter and tinier makes it high-tonier.

The vibration (or shaking) of an actual surface, such as a string, drumhead, reed or metal tube, is transferred directly to the air itself, and it is vibrating air that we actually hear when we listen to music.

Prove this to yourself by the familiar act of whistling. Your lips (vibrating) set the air in motion, and the resulting sound is a very pure tone. The looser and larger the lips are in starting the vibration, the lower will be the tone. Conversely, the more tightly you purse them the higher the sound becomes.

Air vibrations can be amplified by resonators or by electricity (as proved by radio). In a piano the resonator is the sounding board, made of wood, which is a fine amplifier. In a violin or cello it is the wooden body of the instrument. For the human voice we get resonance through the nose, the lips and various cavities of the head and chest.

Regular vibration produces a musical tone. Irregular vibration produces noise. You can prove this by striking a piece of tin with a hammer. The vibrations are irregular, and the result is noise. But strike the key of a piano, which sets the strings vibrating regularly, and the result is a musical tone.

Tone is generally considered musical only when it has a definite

[1]If you look at the strings in a piano you will notice that the lower tones are produced by strings that are longer, looser and larger in size than those producing the upper tones.

pitch, and this pitch or height of tone depends on the number of vibrations per second. The faster the vibrations, the higher the resulting tone. (Obviously a shorter or tighter string will vibrate more rapidly than a longer or looser one.)

TONE COLOR OR QUALITY

Musical tones vary not only in pitch but in quality (also known as color or *timbre*). Every tone is composed of a fundamental tone, which sets the pitch, and a number of "overtones," which affect the quality. Overtones are really other tones sounding in harmony with the fundamental tone and seemingly a part of it. This becomes very evident if you strike a bell or a gong, where the overtones can be clearly distinguished from the fundamental.[2] As the tone dies away, the overtones gradually disappear, until only the fundamental tone is heard.

Tone color or quality is governed by friction or interference at the point of production and by the nature of the resonator, which emphasizes the overtones. Thus the tone of a violin depends partly on the friction between the bow and the string and partly on the wood, varnish and shape of the resonance chamber or body. The tone of a flute has less color than that of an oboe, because the latter uses vibrating reeds, creating more evident overtones.

(The voices of different musical instruments can be distinguished as easily as the actual voices of friends on the telephone, and it is their tone color or quality that makes them individual. But it is much more fun to pick out the various strings, wood-winds or brasses in an orchestra than to answer a call that begins with "Guess who this is.")

Think of music as a practically continuous stream of sound constantly affected by both pitch and quality. The individual tones are regulated as to length and frequency by the measure of Time. Without the element of time, it is difficult to think of a regular melody, and certainly of a complete composition.

Time, in its broadest sense, determines how fast the individual tones are played or sung, how long they are sustained, which ones are accented and which unaccented, and what pauses or rests come be-

[2]In most bells or gongs there are also some irregular vibrations, producing noises, which conflict with the musical tones and overtones, the final result being an obviously mixed tone often of uncertain pitch.

tween them. Tones and time, therefore, are actually the entire material of music. The variations of pitch, in progressions of tones, create melody. The combinations of tones of various pitches, sounding simultaneously, create harmony (and sometimes discord, depending partly on the ear of the listener). The variations and combinations of instrumental or vocal quality create tone color in the larger sense. The fundamental beats of time and distribution of accents create rhythm. The patterns of time, tune, harmony and tone color, logically combined, create the form of a complete composition.[3]

HERE IS A BASIC DEFINITION

From these facts it is easy to arrive at a comprehensive definition of music as the Organization of Sound toward Beauty.

This definition can be applied to any of the other arts by simply changing the name of the raw material. Beauty is always the goal of the artist, and it should be noticed that the definition says "*toward* beauty," not "*to* beauty." The artist can at least be working *in the direction of* beauty, even though he may not always attain it.

The raw material of music is Sound.[4] A painter uses color as his raw material, and a sculptor clay, marble or bronze. An architect uses stone, wood and other building materials, and a writer uses words. Behind the technical organization of all these materials lie the thoughts, moods and emotions of the artists.

An artist is a person who succeeds in transferring his own thoughts, moods and emotions to other people. If beauty and truth are the same, as has been claimed, then an artist arrives at beauty by expressing his own feelings in such a way that others will recognize their truth.

Insincerity is generally easy to detect in art. But sincerity alone does not make an artist. There must also be the command of a medium of expression that will inevitably transfer the feelings of the artist to others.

Anyone can have a thought, a mood or an emotion. Too often this

[3]It is well to form the habit immediately of thinking of music in terms of patterns. The patterns of music are as easy to follow, after a little experience, as the patterns of wallpaper or carpets or curtains.

[4]The simplest organization of sound is the mere regulation of vibrations, producing a musical tone.

universal human trait is confused with art itself. A child, pounding on the keys of a piano, may be sincerely expressing the joy of life, but unless it means something more than an atrocious noise to others, it can hardly be called art.

The artist must know how to organize the raw materials of his art in the direction of a beauty which will at least be generally recognizable, perhaps not immediately, but certainly in time. If it is great art, it must pass the test of permanence. That is, over a period of years, a number of people must recognize it as beautiful or true, or both in one.

HERE ARE THE ORGANIZING FACTORS

If music is recognized as the Organization of Sound toward Beauty, it is not difficult to pick out the organizing factors: Time or Rhythm;[5] Tune or Melody; Harmony; Tone Color or Quality; and Form. It is quite possible to enjoy music without knowing anything about its organizing factors, for human instinct recognizes these factors unconsciously and gets an emotional pleasure out of an emotional stimulus, even when it is unexplainable.

But just as it is more fun to watch a football or baseball game if you know something of the rules, so it is more fun to listen to music if you have some idea of what it is all about. The appreciation of music does not necessarily mean a technical knowledge of music, either practical or theoretical. It simply means the *enjoyment* of music, and if this enjoyment includes a little understanding of basic principles, it is just that much more worth while.

Remember the five fundamental factors that organize sound toward beauty: Rhythm, Melody, Harmony, Color and Form. They can be found in every composition, from a popular song to a symphony, and the interest of that composition to the listener will depend on one or more or perhaps all of them. For the great, permanent music of the world contains all of these factors in a high degree, and its significance depends on the way its composer made use of them.

These principles are universal, and fall easily into stock patterns and traditional formulas that quickly grow tiresome if they are not

[5]The terms Time and Rhythm are here used interchangeably, although certain distinctions will later be made between them.

touched with genius. It is almost impossible for anyone to invent absolutely new musical material, except perhaps by upsetting human standards and outraging human instincts for beauty. But any really great artist, whether creative or interpretive, can inform old materials with new life and individuality, making the results entirely and unmistakably his own.[6]

Therefore the enjoyment of music should include not only the ability to recognize basic principles and factors of organization, but also a discriminating taste for the ways in which composers (and to a certain extent interpreters) can stamp their individual personalities on the material they present.

The following chapters will point out the ways in which the organizing factors of rhythm, melody, harmony, color and form affect great music (and some not so great), and also the individual manifestations of talent and occasionally genius that give life and zest to the most fascinating of all the arts.

[6]Music is often called "the universal language," and a comparison with actual, articulate language is fairly obvious. The English language follows certain patterns and formulas which every writer uses. There are trite expressions that appear again and again, and it is impossible to avoid the use of the same words and phrases and the same principles of sentence structure. But the writer who has something to say manages to do so in his own style, and his work is judged by the importance of his thoughts and emotions as well as his technical command of expression. So in music the great composer has something worth while to express, in addition to the means of expressing it.

A composer's life is saved by a button

ONE OF THE strangest duels in history was fought between two musical friends, George Frederick Handel and Johann Mattheson. They had met in Hamburg, where Mattheson was already well established, and he showed a sincere and unselfish interest in the young genius from Halle.

Their disagreement arose from an absurd combination of circumstances and ended even more absurdly. Mattheson was conducting the orchestra for his own opera, *Cleopatra,* in which he also played the part of Antony. Handel, his understudy at the clavecin, insisted that the actor-composer should not return in full costume to the orchestra after having been killed on the stage, and backed up his opinion by staying at the keyboard and refusing to move. An old-fashioned fist fight resulted, with a formal duel as the logical consequence.

They joined in mortal combat in the Hamburg market place, and since both were good swordsmen it was quite a battle while it lasted. Suddenly Mattheson lunged forward, his sword about to pierce the young man's chest. But to the astonishment of all, it snapped off short. The point had struck a large button on Handel's coat, and a very important life was saved. Simultaneously the friends embraced and burst into tears.

Handel lived to the ripe age of seventy-four and won immortality with his *Messiah* and other oratorios, as well as operatic airs, concertos, and sonatas. His *Largo* is one of the most popular melodies of all time; piano students still play his variations on a theme known as *The Harmonious Blacksmith,* and discriminating music-lovers find pleasure in such orchestral works as the *Water Music.* Today the appeal of Handel's music is practically unlimited.

BUEHNE

CHAPTER IV RHYTHM COMES FIRST

EVERY NOTE OF MUSIC, played or sung, is affected by three outstanding factors: Time, Pitch and Quality. The pitch, determined by the rapidity of vibrations, gives it a relatively high or low position as compared with other tones in a melody or harmony. The quality, or color, determined chiefly by overtones (but also affected somewhat by the comparative loudness or softness), gives it its vocal or instrumental individuality. The time element affects the length or shortness of the tone, its relative position in a group of tones forming a rhythmic pattern, and the amount of emphasis it receives in that group through a natural or artificial accent.

It is impossible to play or hear any musically significant group of tones without certain definite accents, just as it is impossible to think of any intelligible sentence in the English language that does not emphasize certain words and syllables more than others. Metrical poetry insists on a regular beat, with the accents coming at definite intervals, and practically all music does the same thing. But even prose has its accents, although not so marked or so regular as those of poetry, and some examples of prose can be credited with a fairly definite rhythm.[1]

The simplest way to grasp the significance of time in music is by direct comparison with poetry. If you read any conventionally metrical line of verse, you cannot help giving it the proper accents and quantities. Take for instance the opening of Longfellow's *Psalm of Life:*

Tell me not in mournful numbers
Life is but an empty dream.

[1]There are some passages in music, generally called "recitative," and fairly common in opera and oratorio, which correspond to prose, as compared with the metrical character of most music. But even these have obvious accents, resulting from the necessary emphasis on certain syllables of the words themselves.

It is impossible to read those two lines without accenting the syllables *tell, not, mourn, num, life, but, emp* and *dream.* If a musician were reading a corresponding line of melody, he would recognize the accents by the length of the notes and their position in the grouping. Read the two lines of Longfellow's verse again, and you will notice that the syllables group themselves naturally in pairs, with the first of a pair always accented and the second unaccented. The first line has four such groups, and if it were set to music it would normally have four measures, each containing one accented and one unaccented tone.

DOWN-BEAT AND UP

In music the first tone in a measure invariably carries the strongest accent. If there are two beats to the measure, as in this line, the first is a down-beat and the second an up-beat. That is the way a conductor would actually beat the time with his stick, down for the accented note and up for the unaccented.

But music is more flexible than poetry, and while this line seems normally to be in march time (one-two, one-two, or down-up, down-up, or left-right, left-right), it might also be set in waltz time, with three beats to a measure. In that case, the first or accented syllable would carry two beats, while the second syllable would carry the third beat. (In written music it would be easy to indicate that the first note is twice as long as the second in each measure; or the second beat of the measure could be represented by a "rest," which would still give the measure three beats, one down, or accented, and two up, or unaccented.)

Prove this to yourself by the simple test of singing the line to the tune of the *Merry Widow Waltz.* It is at once evident that there are three beats to a group, and that the first syllable of each pair actually lasts twice as long as the second.

If Longfellow's lines were being scanned in an English class, the accents and measures (or feet) would be indicated like this:

—v/—v/—v/—v/
—v/—v/—v/—

It is unnecessary to mark these accents or groupings in a printed poem, because the reader's knowledge of the language makes him do the right thing, but music requires a system of notation whereby every tone has an absolute indication of not only its pitch but also its duration in beats or the fraction of a beat. (Theoretically, one tone can last for an unlimited number of beats, and each beat can also carry an unlimited number of notes.)

The important thing at this point is to be able to hear the fundamental beats of time in all kinds of music. You noticed above how easily a line of poetry falls into groups of two beats each, and how the same line, considered as music, could have its beats grouped in twos or in threes, with one real accent to a group, always on the first tone of that group. You will soon discover, in listening to music, that *all* fundamental time-beats run in twos or threes. Even the supposedly irregular 5-4 time is merely the alternation of twos and threes, and all "compound time" (such as 6-8, 9-8, 12-8, etc.) runs in multiples of two or three.

THIS IS A UNIVERSAL PRINCIPLE

There is a law of Nature behind this fact, for Nature is full of rhythmic time-beats. The commonest is the beating of the human heart. A healthy pulse is always regular, the beats running in pairs, with one accented and the other unaccented. A clock ticks the same way, and this is of course the mechanical demonstration of time itself. A sleeping baby (and sometimes an adult) breathes rhythmically, with the intake corresponding to the accented beat in a group of two.

The walk of a human being (or any other animal) is naturally rhythmical, with the steps going in pairs, and usually showing a slight accent. This accent is emphasized when marching is accompanied by music, or even a drumbeat, and it is customary to mark this accent with the left foot. Such a rhythmic accompaniment compels regularity in the act of walking, and thereby makes it much easier, which is the reason for all military bands, fifes, drums and bugles. When soldiers or Boy Scouts have no music to play for them, they can supply their own by singing on the march, and this organization of rhythm more than makes up for the loss of breath in the process. (Primitive music really developed through the discovery that physical labor of any kind was made easier by a rhythmic accompaniment, as witness the work songs in every type of folk-music, sailors' chanties for pulling on ropes, the *Volga Boat Song*, etc.)

Most of Nature's time-beats run in pairs, but the canter or gallop of a horse is distinctly in waltz time, which has three beats to a measure. Since only the first of these beats is accented, one easily gets the impression of hearing a form of two-beat time, in which the first beat is twice as long as the second. There is an interesting theory that cowboy songs are patterned rhythmically according to the gait of the horse, from the slow walk, in evenly paired beats, to the triple time of a canter or gallop. (When the horse gets to running too fast, the cowboy naturally stops singing.)

The law of balanced time-beats extends even to the major operations of Nature. The movements of the tides are essentially rhythmic, and the entire activity of the solar and planetary system can be similarly considered, on the largest possible scale. The ancient philosophers worked this all out, with some pretty fanciful results, such as the "music of the spheres," but it is a fact, not a mere theory or myth, that Nature tends to express itself rhythmically. The beating of waves on the shore, the patter of raindrops, the flow of a brook or the rush of a waterfall, these all have definite rhythmic values and can be measured in terms of time. When the forces of Nature are harnessed by machinery, all the way from a mill wheel to the explosions of a gasoline engine, the regular beat of time becomes even more apparent.

So music is really proving its universal truth when it insists upon a definite rhythmic beat. And since this is its closest relation to Nature, it is logical that the time element should be the most primitive and the most widely recognized. Rhythm forms the skeleton of music, but that skeleton becomes a complete body only when the flesh and blood of melody and harmony have been added.

RHYTHM'S PRIMITIVE APPEAL

The first attempts of the savage to make music are nothing more than time-beats, and the same is true of a child. Rhythm is almost entirely a physical stimulus, and the response of the feet is practically a reflex action. (The foot-listeners of the world are still in the great majority, but at least they are taking a step in the right direction.) Practically everybody can keep time to a rhythmic beat. (The ability to *beat* time is something quite different.) Even where there is no evidence of a "musical ear," or where one finds it difficult or even impossible to "carry a tune," the instinctive reaction to a regular time-beat is likely to assert itself.

Test your sense of time immediately by listening to several pieces of music (preferably marches) that have a strongly marked fundamental beat in twos.[2] Keep time with the music, either by stamping the feet alternately, with the left foot taking the accented beat, or marching around the room, or clapping the hands (making the down-beat the louder of the two), or actually beating time with the right hand or with a stick.

Fast marches, or one-steps, are written in 2-4 time, which means that there are two beats to a measure, each representing the length of a quarter-note, which is the commonest unit of written music. Slower marches have a time-signature of 4-4 (often called "common time"), which is really only an extension of 2-4 time and means that there are four beats to a measure (the equivalent of four quarter-notes).[3]

Marches can also be written in 6-8 time, but this merely represents two groups of three eighth-notes (or their equivalent) in each measure, and can be beaten as though it were 2-4 time, with a down-beat on the first note of the measure (as always) and an up-beat to start the second group. The fact that each beaten group contains three actual beats (like the galloping of the horse) encourages a skipping step such as people danced when *Valencia* was popular.[4]

If you are beating march time, move the stick or your right hand down for the accented beat and up for the unaccented. This applies to 2-4 and 6-8 time, counting the latter as two beats to a measure. With a slower march, or fox-trot, written in 4-4 time, beat down for the first, to the left for the second, to the right for the third (carrying the secondary accent) and up for the fourth.

Practice these beats at home with phonograph records or the radio.

[2]Schubert's *Marche Militaire* and Sousa's *Stars and Stripes Forever* are good samples for a start.

[3]Examples of marches in 4-4 time are the Priests' March from Mendelssohn's *Athalia,* the Coronation March from Meyerbeer's *Prophet* and the Triumphal March from Verdi's *Aida,* all of the slow, stately type. Elgar's *Pomp and Circumstance,* although written 2-4, is of the same type.

[4]Other examples of 6-8 march time are *Up the Street,* the *Marche Lorraine* and Sousa's *Washington Post.*

Beat upon an imaginary level, not lower than the waistline, and preferably a little higher, using a light stick or a long pencil, and you will soon have the pleasant sensation of leading an orchestra yourself. You should be able to figure out the proper beat by listening for the accents.

Get the feeling of the fundamental beat firmly into your consciousness, so that you are thinking in terms of time, not merely responding to a rhythmic stimulus. Don't let any accumulation or disarrangement of tones interfere with your steady realization of this fundamental beat, which is always in twos or threes. The secret of the fascination of jazz, which uses a distorted rhythm, inherited from "ragtime" (literally tearing the music to tatters), is that the listener or dancer sticks to the fundamental beat in spite of all syncopation or false accenting, and has the subconscious satisfaction of saying to himself: "You can't fool me. I'm coming down on that beat no matter *what* you do to throw me off."

GROUPING NOTES IN TIME

While the fundamental beats of time can always be grouped in twos or threes, the musical results of such grouping show a wide variety, depending partly on the speed or slowness of tempo[5] and partly on the distribution of accented and unaccented tones over the fundamental beat. March music is by no means limited to two, four or six notes to a measure, nor waltz music to three, even though these may be the fundamental beats, and with only one or two accents to a measure. Each beat of time may carry anywhere from one to thirty-two, possibly even sixty-four, actual notes (theoretically there is no limit), and these groups may exhibit various minor accents within themselves.

Popular music nowadays runs chiefly to fox-trots and waltzes, with an occasional tango, rumba or other example of individual rhythmic structure. But within these limitations it has developed a surprising variety of time effects, through syncopation (which is the artificial delaying or anticipating of accents), the slow dragging of tempo,

[5]The word "tempo" has become quite common in the English language, through its use in the movies and by dramatic critics. It is merely the Italian word for "time," and, strictly speaking, refers only to the rate of speed at which a piece of music is performed.

the shifting emphasis of "blues," and the liberal use of three tones against two beats.

The more serious music of the world, however, has developed an infinitely greater versatility of rhythm. This is chiefly because popular music is intended primarily for dancing, whereas there are no such restrictions on the symphonies, operas, oratorios and chamber music of the past and present.[6]

Symphonic music may show various forms of two-beat, three-beat, four-beat or six-beat time (occasionally also five-beat), and if you watch any good conductor, you will notice that he is always beating in one of those groupings, usually with a decided indication of the fundamental twos and threes. A skilled composer often disguises the bald count that is the basis of his music by the use of rests, shifting accents and cross-rhythms, while a good conductor can do even more to prevent a rhythmic monotony, such as we have in most popular music, by varying the tempo, deliberately retarding or accelerating the music for short stretches, and sometimes holding on to a single note or chord far longer than the fundamental beat calls for. Such "expression" is sometimes indicated by the composer and more often supplied by the imagination or musical sense of the interpreter, and it is this factor that makes it difficult for the average listener to follow the exact time-beats in an elaborate piece of music.

But they are there, nevertheless, and can be discerned by any good ear. It will also be found that serious composers have actually made dance music the basis of many forms of instrumental composition, often maintaining the rhythm quite strictly, and preserving the original names even when there is no thought of using the music for an actual dance. An outstanding example of this is the Minuet, which occurs as a movement in many symphonies and string quartets, without any conscious relation to the stately, rhythmic steps once performed in the costumes and powdered wigs of colonial days.

MARCH AND WALTZ TIME

The march may be considered the standard of duple time, and the waltz of triple. With these two as starting-points, it is a simple mat-

[6]Chamber music, broadly speaking, is meant for performance in a small room, by a limited number of instruments or voices, as compared with the more elaborate music designed for large concert halls or opera houses.

ter to place any other significant forms based on the same fundamental time-beats.

To understand what is meant by triple time, it is best to make another direct comparison with metrical verse. A quotation from Longfellow will again serve as an example. The poem *Curfew* begins as follows:

Solemnly, mournfully, dealing its dole,
The curfew bell is beginning to toll.

As in the quotation from *Psalm of Life*, it is practically impossible to give wrong accenting to these lines. Obviously, the accents must come on the syllables *Sol, mourn, deal, dole, cur, bell, gin* and *toll.* But where the other lines naturally grouped the syllables in pairs, this couplet exhibits mostly three syllables to a foot or measure. The words "solemnly" and "mournfully" are perfect examples of such grouping, with a natural accent on the first syllable, and an utter impossibility of accent on either of the others. The two lines therefore scan thus:

—vv/—vv/—vv/—
v/—v/—vv/—vv/—

THREE BEATS TO A WALTZ

While the lines from *Psalm of Life* could be given the musical value of triple time (by simply making the first syllable in each foot carry two beats), the lines from *Curfew* cannot possibly be considered as in duple time. The first two words inexorably demand a triple beat, and cannot be read in any other way. Therefore the lines provide a natural example of waltz time in poetry. Try setting them to music. You will find it quite easy, for they practically sing themselves.

Remember that waltz time in music has only one real accent to a measure, and this comes, as always, on the first note of the measure. The other two are both considered up-beats. (They may, of course, carry as many notes as a composer desires.) There are always three beats to the waltz measure, and a single tone may extend over two of them, as in the *Merry Widow Waltz*, or even over all three, as at the start of *My Hero*, from *The Chocolate Soldier*.

Try keeping time to a waltz, by clapping your hands, loudly on the first beat and softly on the other two. You cannot march to a waltz unless it is played so fast that it becomes practically 6-8 time and you take one step to each group of three beats.

To beat waltz time, move the stick or your right hand down on the first beat of each group of three. Move it to the right for the second beat and upward for the third beat. This fixes things so that you will always make a definite downward motion on the first or accented beat of a measure.

There is a peculiar snap to Viennese waltzes (used also by Victor Herbert, who preserved the Viennese tradition), which comes from a slight artificial accent on the second beat, and this is sometimes emphasized by playing the note or accompanying chord just a shade ahead of the actual beat.[7]

OTHER FORMS OF TRIPLE TIME

The Minuet (also known as Menuet and Menuetto) is in triple time, but slower than a waltz, and with all three beats equally accented. This is not literally true, for it is impossible to avoid a conscious or unconscious emphasis on the first beat of a measure. But a true minuet gives the effect of three equally important beats in each measure, and the dignified dance once performed to such music consistently carried out that idea.

Many composers, notably Haydn and Mozart, used the minuet as the third movement of a symphony, and it is a regular part also of the suites which came before the symphony and which were actually sets of dance pieces. The best minuets for practice are those of Mozart, particularly the ones from his symphonies in G minor and E-flat, and the one from the opera, *Don Giovanni.* Beethoven wrote a familiar *Minuet in G,* which is fairly easy to play on the piano. Others worth trying are the popular *Minuet* of Paderewski and the old-fashioned one by Boccherini, which has a rather tricky, syncopated rhythm.

The Mazurka, made famous by the piano music of Chopin, is also

[7]Good waltzes on which to practice beating or keeping time are the *Beautiful Blue Danube* of Johann Strauss, the *Merry Widow* and *My Hero,* already mentioned, Herbert's *Kiss Me Again, Valse Bleu,* and the old *Skaters' Waltz,* which is always played for trapeze performers at the circus and for jugglers in vaudeville. Schubert wrote some charming waltzes, which are easy to follow, but the waltzes of Chopin are for playing rather than for dancing, and their complexities may prove difficult for a novice.

in triple time, but usually rather faster than a waltz, and with an artificial accent on the third beat of each measure, which produces a unique effect. Any of the mazurkas of Chopin are good material for practice, and they are all beautiful music. (Probably the most familiar of all mazurkas is Ganne's *La Czarina.*)

The Polonaise is another Polish dance in triple time, but quite slow and stately. It is used for court processions and seems therefore to present an exception to the rule that marches must be in duple time. But actually the marchers in a polonaise do not keep strict time, or else they do not mind shifting the accent from one foot to the other. The tempo is so slow that it would also be possible to march with two steps to each beat of the triple time.

The best polonaise music is again that of Poland's greatest composer, Frederic Chopin, particularly the one called *Military* and the one in A-flat. Edward MacDowell, the American composer, wrote an excellent polonaise, and there is a fine, original one in Moussorgsky's opera, *Boris Godounoff*.

Another very slow form of triple time is the Sarabande, coming originally from Spain, but no longer in use as a dance. The finest examples of such music are to be found in the suites of Johann Sebastian Bach. The same composer is responsible for some splendid Gavottes (there are good modern examples in the *Mignon* of Thomas and *Manon* of Massenet), Bourrées, and Loures.

These all figured in the old-fashioned suites, along with the Allemande (of German origin, in 4-4 time), Courante, Galliard, Gigue and Passepied, all triple time, and sometimes the Branle and Pavane (both 4-4). The pavane originated in Padua, but supposedly got its name from the slow, stately step, which suggested the walk of a peacock. There is a beautiful modern example by Ravel.

Later Spanish dances included the Bolero (also immortalized by Ravel), Fandango, Jota and Seguidilla, all in triple time, and the Habañera and Tango, in 4-4. The opera *Carmen* contains the best-known examples of the Habañera and Seguidilla. Arthur Sullivan, in *The Gondoliers*, composed a Cachucha, which refers also to the Fandango and Bolero, all in lively triple time. The Italians have a fast dance in 6-8 time called the Tarantella, traditionally caused by the bite of the tarantula. The typical Hungarian dance is the Czardas, consisting of a slow section (Lassu) and a fast one (Friss). The ancient Gigue is now spelled Jig (3-4) and figures in folk-music with the Reel (4-4) and Rigadoon (2-4) (French Rigaudon). A favorite ballroom dance of past generations was the Schottische, in 2-4 time, and another was the Polka (originally Polish) in 4-4 time, which has enjoyed something of a modern revival stimulated by such examples as the popular *Roll Out the Barrel,* a favorite with all the Allied armies of the second World War.

TIME AND RHYTHM

The words "time" and "rhythm" are generally used quite loosely, and there is considerable disagreement as to their exact meaning. "Time" strictly applies only to the number of beats in a measure. It is convenient to call it duple time when the beats run in twos, and triple time when they run in threes. According to these fundamental beats, it is possible to speak of "march time," "waltz time," etc., and, more specifically, 2-4 time, 4-4 time, 6-8 time, etc.

When the word "time" is used as a translation of the Italian "tempo," it means the rate of speed at which the music is played or sung, and nothing else. So it is possible to speak of fast or slow time, regardless of the fundamental beat. When there has been a retarding or accelerating of time, and a composer wants to get back to the regular speed, he marks the music *a tempo,* meaning that it is to be played "in time," as it was before the slowing or speeding up occurred.

ANALYZING RHYTHM

Rhythm, as distinguished from time, has to do with the distribution of long and short tones, accented and unaccented, over the fundamental beat, and this distribution of tones easily creates a definite pattern, which may be repeated again and again in a piece of music, just as it would be in a piece of wallpaper. The rhythm of a composition, in the larger sense, is governed by such patterns rather than by the fundamental time-beats, and this of course permits an infinite variety of effects. A skillful dancer feels this larger rhythm rather than the mere count of one-two, one-two-three or one-two-three-four. With a singer or instrumentalist, this feeling for rhythm expresses itself in "phrasing," which is a logical division of the music into rhythmic and melodic patterns. Anyone reading a poem does the same thing instinctively, with the help of the division into lines and the various marks of punctuation.

It would be literally impossible to describe, or even suggest, all the potential patterns of rhythm. But it is not difficult to recognize some of the commonest combinations, and once you get the habit of hearing rhythmic similarities, you will have no difficulty in picking out the rhythmic patterns in any piece of music.

Once more it is easier to find rhythmic patterns in popular music than in the classics. The demands of the dancers, for whom all popular music is written, encourage the composers, or adapters, to stick to a fairly obvious arrangement of tones in rhythmic phrases. If this continues right through a chorus, it makes the tune just that much easier to remember, which is the first and last desideratum of all popular music.

The simplest way to analyze rhythmic patterns is to start with the even time-beats. The most obvious pattern, of course, is one which has a note on every beat of the time. There is an old A-B-C tune, attributed to Mozart, whose rhythmic pattern consists of six evenly balanced notes in a row, followed by a seventh which is twice as long as any of the others. Essentially the pattern represents a note to a beat, and it runs without change through the entire melody, which is one of the simplest in the world.

Instead of the letters of the alphabet, you will sometimes hear this little tune sung with the words "One, two, three, four, five, six, seven, All good children go to Heaven," which emphasizes the number of notes in the rhythmic pattern. It is worth noting that exactly the same rhythmic pattern is used by Haydn in his *Surprise Symphony*.

Another interesting parallel of rhythmic patterns occurs in Chopin's *Funeral March* and, paradoxically, the *Wedding March* from Wagner's *Lohengrin.* Both are built on a slow 4-4 time, and both have four notes in a repeated rhythmic pattern. This amusing identity of rhythmic patterns, in two pieces of such widely different intentions, can best be brought out by tapping the rhythm of either tune on a table, or by clapping the hands, and then filling in the notes of each melody at the piano.

A fascinating game can be played, either by two individuals or by a group of any size, by having the one who is "it" tap out a rhythmic pattern representing some familiar piece of music, and letting the others guess what it is. It is surprising to find how often more than one tune will be found to fit practically the same rhythmic pattern.

This is a further indication of the limitations of rhythm in music, and of the importance of melody and harmony in giving real individuality to any organized sounds.

The rhythmic pattern of one long note followed by two short ones (each representing half the length of the first) is quite common. It occurs in a fast duple time in Schubert's *Marche Militaire*, and the same pattern, played slowly, runs through practically all of the old song, *Long, Long Ago*, as well as some hymn tunes.

The corresponding pattern in triple time has one long note and one short one, as at the start of the *Merry Widow Waltz.* Most compositions contain several rhythmic patterns, sometimes quite a number, and it is the arrangement of these patterns that creates the rhythmic pattern of the whole piece.

CHAPTER V MELODY FOR REMEMBRANCE

IN THE ORGANIZATION of sound toward beauty, rhythm is the first and most primitive step. The savage must have discovered very early that he could imitate the rhythmic sounds of Nature by beating on a hollow log. The regularity of such beats must have fascinated him, and he probably soon gave them a religious significance. They became a part of his ritual and were applied to various purposes, including the incitement to battle (for which they are still used), protection against evil spirits, a request for rain, and the healing mysteries of the medicine man.

Just how early the practical value of rhythm as an aid to manual labor was discovered, it is hard to say; but it certainly had its place almost from the outset as a stimulator of the dance and a help to physical exercise in general. Moreover, the savage probably found out very soon what could be accomplished by stretching a piece of skin over the end of the hollow log and thus manufacturing the first crude drum.

Most of the musical instruments of savage tribes today are still drums of different kinds, and the favorite music of the civilized savage, or foot-listener, is that which has plenty of percussion, supplied by drums, gourds, rattles, banjos, cymbals and tin-pan pianos.

When the savage discovered that a higher tone was produced by stretching the skin tighter over the end of the hollow log, he took an important step toward the discovery of melody. His first attempts in that direction consisted of letting one drum, of lower pitch, play the fundamental beat, while another, with a higher note, produced rhythmic patterns in the same time. (This custom is still found in most primitive music.)

Drums, however, cannot go very far in the creation of actual melody (even the kettledrums of the modern orchestra rarely play more than three or four different tones in the course of a composition), and it required the invention of stringed and blown instruments to achieve what might be fairly termed a tune. (The human voice may have tried to sing in the very early days of music, but judging by even the modern examples of savage singing, the results were mostly noise, without any definite pitch.)

Ancient myths make much of the discovery of the lyre and the flute, for with these instruments it became possible to sound many different notes in quick succession, and the immediate result was a variety of melody. The invention of the lyre was credited to either Apollo or Mercury, the story being that the god found a dried-up turtle on the beach, whose insides, tightly stretched across the shell, produced musical tones when they were touched. The rather prettier story of the flute was that when Pan pursued the nymph Syrinx to the water's edge, she was turned into a reed for her protection, whereupon the goat-god manufactured from the reed a set of pipes on which he blew sweet melodies. (You can see the modern representative of the Panpipes in the pipes of an organ. The older generation used to buy them in candy stores, made of licorice.)

A DEFINITION OF MELODY

Melody, as already suggested, is a logical progression of tones, at various levels of pitch. A single melody may contain an indefinite number of tones (although it is difficult to make it sound logical after a certain distance has been covered), and as few as only two tones may be called technically a tune.

For example, we find in Nature a real suggestion of melody in the song of birds, and the two bird calls that have the most definite pitch, those of the cuckoo and the bobwhite or quail, are limited to two tones. The cuckoo's two-toned melody has been adopted by the whole world as a "come-hither" whistle and is in constant use today, as complete and logical as any combination of tones in written music.

This of course is a reduction to the absurd, but it can fairly be argued that any combination of two or more tones, of different pitch, is potentially a melody, or the pattern for a melody. A single tone, even though repeated, can hardly be called a melody. It is true that Peter Cornelius composed a song called *Ein Ton* (Monotone), in which the voice sings the same tone throughout, but the cleverness of the song lies in the definite melody carried by the accompaniment against the monotone of the voice, without which the words might just as well be spoken.[1]

Ultramodern music seems to decree that any progression of pitches, no matter how fantastic, must be recognized as legitimate melody. But such music has a very limited audience, and the tradition of both serious and popular composition still insists that there should be some logic to a melodic progression. Just why certain progressions should seem logical and others illogical is difficult to explain, and it may be admitted that it is probably largely a matter of habit. Certainly the melodies that gain the quickest and easiest popularity are those which follow well-established formulas.

When people object to the apparent aimlessness of much of the ultramodern music, it is easy to answer that Wagner and other composers were considered completely unmelodic in their day, whereas now their compositions are melodically quite intelligible. Unquestionably the human ear can develop an appreciation and enjoyment of more and more subtle and unusual melodic progressions, but whether such development is potentially unlimited is open to argument.

It is perhaps significant that our popular composers of recent years, as well as the writers of more serious music, have consistently produced less and less obvious melodies. George Gershwin was certainly many miles ahead of *After the Ball*, just as the melodies of Richard Strauss, Debussy and Wagner are more exciting than the simpler patterns of Haydn, Mozart and Schubert. But it is worth remembering that each kind of music was thoroughly satisfying to the public of its own day.

For the beginner in music, it is best to analyze the appeal of melody

[1]The Amen sung at the end of a prayer or a hymn often consists of two chords having the same tone in the melody part, yet this combination would not have the effect of a complete composition if it were not for the change in harmony, which means that the inner voices provide the necessary variety of pitch. About the nearest thing to a one-tone melody is the "ta-da" played by a vaudeville orchestra when a performer comes out to take a bow, or the same chord as it is heard when the interlocutor in a minstrel show says, "Gentlemen, be seated."

in its traditional forms. If, after such a background has been created, an honest interest in the newer melodic experiments should develop, it is entirely possible for every individual to follow his or her inclinations, perhaps even arriving at ways and means of distinguishing the sincere and occasionally inspired creators of music in a new idiom from the fakers and charlatans, which has thus far proved a difficult matter.

PATTERNS OF MELODY

A pattern of melody may have as few as two tones, like the familiar cuckoo call. It is quite surprising how much of an actual tune can be built on such limited material. (This pattern is frequently found in the cries of savages and in primitive melodies, such as those of the American Indian.)

The commonest three-tone pattern is the bugle call. In addition to such calls as Reveille, Taps, etc., complete marching tunes can be made out of these three tones and their octaves.

The three bugle tones are very common in the national anthems of the world (possibly because of their martial significance), and obviously represent practically all the trumpet calls of operatic music. Played from the top down and then up again, the three-tone bugle pattern creates the opening of the *Star-Spangled Banner*. A slightly different arrangement of the same tones produces the German *Watch on the Rhine*, also used as *Bright College Years* at Yale. They are prominent near the start of the old Russian anthem (reappearing as *Hail, Pennsylvania* and a hymn tune) and the French *Marseillaise*.

America's patriotic song writers have also featured the three-tone pattern as the opening of the *Long, Long Trail*, *Over There* (almost a complete bugle tune) and *Dixie* (in which two scale passages follow, to introduce another succession of bugle tones). The familiar hymn *Holy, Holy, Holy* opens with the same pattern, sounding each note twice. The *Blue Danube Waltz* does almost the same thing, using the pattern for practically all of its first section.

The three-tone pattern is now commonly heard on a certain type of automobile horn and can be found also in the ordinary set of dining-room chimes, as well as those made familiar by radio. Trumpet calls using this pattern include the famous offstage signal which appears in Beethoven's *Fidelio,* as well as the overture to that opera known as *Leonore No. 3,* and in Wagner's *Lohengrin* and *Meistersinger,* to name only outstanding examples. Wagner uses a number of other trumpet patterns in his operas, particularly the Nibelungen cycle, although the actual horn of Siegfried contains far more notes than those of the bugle. (It starts always with the three-tone pattern, however, and then picks up the rest of the scale.) The well-known March in *Tannhäuser* starts with the three trumpet tones, and the Pilgrims' Chorus has a similar pattern. The call of the *Flying Dutchman* requires only two of the three tones. Beethoven's *Die Ehre Gottes aus der Natur* (The Worship of God in Nature) builds its fine melody on the same fundamental tones, and Grieg provides another interesting example in his *Folk-Song.* The final melody in Beethoven's *Pastoral Symphony* is largely a three-toner.

Another common three-tone pattern can be found by simply playing the first three notes of the scale, upward or downward. Its most familiar example is the start of the round, *Three Blind Mice.* Rousseau's *Lullaby* is largely built on these three tones, and Foster's *Swanee River* starts with the same material.

When we sing *Good Night, Ladies,* we start with a three-tone bugle pattern, and then change to the three scale tones in succession for "Merrily we roll along," first down, then up.

The old French round, *Frère Jacques,* starts with these three tones, going through them twice, and then repeating the process on another three-tone combination higher up. (Its whole structure is similar to that of *Three Blind Mice.*) Another fine old French melody, *Au Clair de la Lune* (*In the Moonlight*), uses only three tones for its entire first half, with only a short contrasting section on another pattern, ending with a repetition of the same three tones. A very familiar use of these three scale tones is the ribald whistling signal generally given the words *Over the fence is out.*

FOUR TONES THAT SHAKE THE WORLD

For a good four-tone pattern, listen to the Westminster Chime, as played by Big Ben in London, and reproduced in thousands of clock towers and grandfathers' clocks all over the world. (Handel is generally credited with inventing this progression.) A clearly deliberate borrowing of the pattern is in the popular waltz of some years ago, *Three O'clock in the Morning.*

But the greatest number of melodic descendants from this four-tone pattern follow the tones from the bottom up. If you play them in that order, you almost automatically supply the words *How dry I am.* (Actually the melody of that lament is the hymn, *O Happy Day.*) Another fine hymn, starting with the same pattern, is *Lead, Kindly Light,* and still another, which begins the same way, is taken directly from the slow movement of Beethoven's *Second Symphony.*

There is an old French song, *Plaisir d'Amour,* starting thus, and also a *Song without Words* by Mendelssohn. Franz Lehar used this four-tone pattern both for his *Merry Widow Waltz* and for the tune of *Vilia* in the same operetta. *Sweet Adeline* merely changes the order of the tones, and following the pattern from the top down produces two other old-time favorites of the harmonizers, *Say au revoir, but not good-bye* and *Oh, I don't know.* Other classic examples of the pattern, in various arrangements, are Mozart's *Voi che sapete,* and *Isis und Osiris,* the hymn *Adeste Fideles* and the *Soldiers' Chorus* from *Faust.*

A pattern very common in the folk-music of the world is the five-tone scale, which is likely to suggest immediately the once popular fox-trot, *Stumbling,* or possibly the start of Berlin's *Always* chorus.

The five-tone pattern can be found very easily on the keyboard of the piano by simply playing the black keys, starting with the lower of a pair and going right up through those two and the three above. This may be an explanation of why so many people think it is easier to play on the black keys than on the white. (The list includes such successful composers as Irving Berlin himself and the late Charles K. Harris, of *After the Ball* fame, both of whom, however, equipped themselves with "transposing pianos," whereby they could shift a melody into the proper key by merely pulling a lever, always playing in the strange key of G-flat themselves.)

BACK TO THE SCALE

Any melody pattern containing more than five different tones almost necessarily follows the scale itself, and many of the world's best tunes are actually built on adjoining tones. Even five tones in a row produce a passable melody. That is the tune played by Papageno in Mozart's *Magic Flute*, and it also represents the limits of the old Pan-pipe. The chief melody in Liszt's *Hungarian Fantasie* (a folk-tune) runs up the scale for six tones and back again, getting its effect mainly by a syncopated rhythm.

Following the scale from the top down we find the hymn *Joy to the World*, paralleled at the start of the Finale in Tschaikowsky's *Fourth Symphony*, and the popular tune of long ago, *Tickle Toe*, in which passing notes were inserted between the scale tones, but without destroying their regularity.

Among the classics, one of the finest scale tunes is Handel's *Largo*, which has a very close parallel in the slow movement of Bach's Concerto for two violins. The *Largo* starts at various points in the scale, but almost invariably follows its pattern for several tones, up or down, particularly in the long introduction. The old tune of *Robin Adair* is chiefly a scale progression, imitated by the modern college song, *Fordham Ram*.

Chromatic scale tunes are easily recognized by the fact that their important tones lie only half a tone apart. Godard wrote a *Valse Chromatique*, which is really a study in chromatic melody, but the classic examples of the style are the famous aria from Saint-Saëns' *Samson and Delilah*, My Heart at Thy Sweet Voice, which comes down the scale, mostly in half-tone steps, and Rimsky-Korsakoff's *Song of India*, popularized as a fox-trot, in which the scale figures are almost entirely chromatic. This tune was definitely imitated by the waltz *Beautiful Ohio*, and there is a suggestion of similar chromatic treatment in such other popular tunes as the *Missouri Waltz*, *Carolina Moon*, *When the moon comes over the mountain*, and the Italian *Ciribiribin*, not to speak of such old-timers as *Dardanella* and *Egyptian Ella* (copied from Grieg's chromatic *March of the Dwarfs*).

CHAPTER VI HARMONY FOR EVERYBODY

JUST AS MELODY came out of rhythm, so harmony comes out of melody. If you play the opening tones of the *Star-Spangled Banner* (Oh, say, can you see?) and then sound them all together, the result is a perfect major chord. Harmony is created whenever two or more related tones are sounded together, producing a pleasant or satisfying or even interesting effect.[1]

While the perfect major chord never leaves any doubt as to its rightness, many other combinations are open to argument, and the extremists of modern music insist that any tone can be made to harmonize with any other tone.

The earliest harmony was really a combination of melodies. It was found that by singing or playing the same melody simultaneously at two different levels of pitch, a new effect resulted. Later it was discovered that the sounds were pleasanter if two different melodies were joined together, and this led gradually to the whole structure of polyphonic or many-voiced music. The principle can be very simply illustrated by singing simultaneously the tunes of *The Long, Long Trail* and *Keep the Home Fires Burning*, which was a very common trick of community singing at the time of the first World War. *Swanee River* and Dvorak's *Humoresque* fit together quite well, as do *Solomon Levi* and *The Spanish Cavalier*. You can even make *Yankee Doodle* and *Dixie* harmonize throughout the first part of their melodies, adding *Home, Sweet Home* if able.

[1]Scholarly and popular opinions have constantly varied as to harmony and discord. It is a mistake to lay down hard-and-fast rules, and most of the so-called "laws" of harmony are mere conventions for the naming and spelling of chords. Today each individual ear has a right to accept or reject combinations of tones as harmonies or discords.

When people sing a round, they are making a melody harmonize with itself, by overlapping, the tune being so constructed as to fall naturally into three or four parts, all of which harmonize with each other. By bringing in the voices one at a time, on the right beats, an effect of harmony is created, although the parts are continually moving.

ACCENTUATE THE HARMONY

There has been much talk about the good old days when everybody could read music at sight, and any social gathering included some general music, with all the guests sitting around a table, singing from books handed out by the host, in six or more parts, or taking their share of a "chest of viols," for similar instrumental experiments. This may have been a very popular game, as it should be today, but there is no way of proving that the musical effect was particularly pleasant.

On the other hand, even an impromptu bit of "close harmony," with four or more singers managing to keep in tune with each other, and avoiding a raucous quality of tone, may sound quite lovely, especially to those who are producing it, chiefly because of the fascination of hearing a sustained combination of different tones that in some mysterious fashion seem to blend into one. (Hence the insistent cry of "Hold it!")

Just why this should be so, it is hard to say. A purely scientific explanation is not enough, for only a few intervals of the scale have an exact relationship of vibrations, calculated to produce harmony. Even the overtones that blend with the fundamental in creating a single musical sound are not necessarily pleasant when actually played or sung in harmony with that tone. About all that can be said is that certain combinations of tones sound "comfortable" to the human ear, and that this comfort is a variable factor, depending on habit and experience. It is quite possible to believe that the obvious harmonies of the commonest chords are less pleasing to many modern ears than the unconventional and even discordant combinations that have become characteristic of so much of our music.

The word "harmony," in the original Greek sense, meant simply system or organization, and the word was often applied to the actual scales or "modes." "Symphony" was first used in the modern sense of "harmony" and later referred to an actual band of players or singers performing together. The rhythm of a drumbeat, which in savage music accompanies a similar unison singing or playing, is really the most primitive form of harmony, as we know it, and even in the modern orchestra the kettledrums play tones that are definitely in harmony with what the other instruments are playing.

MAJOR AND MINOR

One of the difficult things to explain in music is the peculiar effect of minor harmonies. Actually the difference between a major and a minor chord is simply that the interval of the third is sounded half a tone lower in the minor than in the major.

The major chord has a bright, cheerful, optimistic sound, whereas the minor is by comparison dull, melancholy, pessimistic. Funeral marches are generally written in minor key. This difference between major and minor is by no means absolute, and there are plenty of cheerful pieces written in minor key, while many a composer has succeeded in expressing melancholy in the major. In general, however, the distinction is a good one, and in the long run the ear can judge very quickly whether it is hearing music in major or minor key.

The original Greek "modes" or scales were all in minor keys, corresponding roughly to the white keys of the modern piano, without sharps or flats, and they were imitated by the later ecclesiastical modes, used in early church music, and sung in unison, without harmony. The distinction between major and minor is therefore basically a distinction of mode or "mood," rather than of key or melody. Lovers of "close harmony" often speak affectionately of "barbershop chords," which actually had their origin in the barbershops of the South, where Negro quartets first flourished. The term refers chiefly to a type of harmonizing in which three voices move around a fourth, which remains stationary.

KEEP IT PRACTICAL

To the layman, the subject of harmony will always remain something of a mystery, and this is largely because musicians have chosen to surround it with a nomenclature that is purely artificial, and, in the light of modern practice, almost meaningless. Harmony is something that should appeal to the ear, not the eye, and if one can learn to harmonize a melody by ear, and to sing a part in a quartet the same way, it is of more practical value than to be able to call a great many chords by their right names. If later one succeeds in writing out practical parts for four voices or instruments, or for both hands on the piano, so much the better. But a baby should learn to talk before it is taught to spell, read and write, and the same is true of music. The conventional subject of harmony is nothing more than the correct spelling of chords, and it seems logical to become thoroughly familiar with these chords by ear before trying to spell or write them.

It is always possible at least to recognize interesting harmonies in listening to music, and this is one of the most fascinating angles in the enjoyment thereof. Listen to Chopin's *Prelude in C Minor* for the piano and see how marvelously he makes his chords progress in a logical yet always novel and interesting fashion. Or listen to that extraordinary example of Russian ecclesiastical music, *Lord God, Have Mercy upon Us,* by Lvovsky, in which the one sentence is repeated throughout, but with such constant variety of harmony, up and down the scale, that there is no suggestion of monotony. There is a fascination too in the accompaniment which Peter Cornelius wrote to his song *Ein Ton* (Monotone) in which the melody stays on one note all the way, with only the harmony to give it variety. For simpler examples of excellent harmonizing, try Barnby's familiar *Sweet and Low,* or the popular evening hymn, *Now the day is over.* A lovely harmonizing of three voices will be found in the female chorus, Lift Thine Eyes, in Mendelssohn's *Elijah.*

CHAPTER VII TONE COLOR FOR QUALITY

IN MODERN MUSIC the most important factor in the organization of sound toward beauty is Tone Color. This has already been defined as the quality of a tone, sometimes called the *timbre*, and its underlying causes indicated.

Its importance in modern music is due to the fact that the resources of melody, rhythm and harmony have been so nearly exhausted, whereas the possibilities of instrumentation and the invention or discovery of new effects of color seem to be infinite. It is no longer easy to be original in rhythm, melody or harmony unless one goes in for absurdly illogical progressions and combinations (which seems the deliberate practice of some of the more extreme exponents of the modern style). But with tone color there are always new opportunities for experimentation, and there are many effects in music today that were undreamed of only a few years ago.

For the enjoyment of music one should have the ability not only to recognize patterns of rhythm, melody and harmony, but also to distinguish the tone color or quality of individual instruments and various types of human voices, and eventually to analyze their effects in combination. In some respects the ability to recognize tone color is the easiest of all to acquire, for most musical instruments have quite a definite quality of tone, while the difference between male and female voices, and even between soprano and alto or tenor and bass, is fairly obvious.

It has been stated that tone color depends on the friction or interference at the point where the vibrations of the air are started, in order to produce a musical tone, and also on the nature of the resonators amplifying the tone. Every musical tone consists of a fundamental (which determines the recognizable pitch) and a series of overtones, in harmony with the fundamental, but not audible, as a rule, except in so far as they affect the color of the complete, compound tone. The more the overtones are evident, the more color the complete tone is likely to have.

There are three ways of generating musical tone, which might be called, freely, striking, rubbing and blowing. In order to make the air vibrate, some tone-producing surface must first be set in vibration. This may be accomplished by a blow, like that of a drumstick, or by continuous friction, like that of a bow across a string, or by the mere passage of air through a tube, as in various wind instruments.

Actually, it all comes down to a definite contact between two surfaces or between a surface and a controlled column of air, and the impression of a continuous tone is easily created by what is essentially a series of forcible contacts. The hum of a gasoline engine makes one forget that one is actually hearing a series of explosions, and the roll of a pair of drumsticks may produce as steady and continuous a tone as the passage of a bow across a string.

THIS IS LITERALLY STRIKING

Percussion is the simplest and most primitive method of producing a tone, and every musical tone can be reduced to a percussion of some sort, or to a series of percussions. Singers often speak of "the stroke of the glottis"; and the attack of the breath upon the vocal cords, which are the tone-producing vibrators of the human voice, is like a real blow, although frequently a very gentle one.

The human voice is a wind instrument, and the vocal cords are like the vibrating reeds that are placed in the mouthpiece of some actual members of the wood-wind family. The color of the resulting tone depends partly on the vocal cords themselves, as on the instrumental reeds, and partly on the resonators that amplify the tone.

People who sing or speak badly try to make their vocal cords do all the work. Their voices sound "in the throat," and they obviously strain to create more volume. In a very short time they become hoarse, for the throat makes desperate efforts to protect itself and its vocal cords against the strain, and the result is a "frog."

The resonators are most important in this whole matter of tone color, and their quality makes all the difference between a good and a bad instrument. A good singer makes use of resonating chambers in the nose, the mouth (including the bell-like formation of the lips), the cavities in the bones of the head, the chest, and to some extent the entire body. It is recognized also that a singer will secure additional resonance by standing on a board surface instead of a carpet, and still more by eliminating any heavy curtains in the background and possibly using an actual sounding-board, such as is found in many pulpits.

If you watch a canary singing, you will notice that the whole body vibrates, while the little bird achieves astonishing range and volume by a remarkable tone production. Phonograph records have been made of bird song (one of a nightingale is actually used in a modern orchestral piece, Respighi's *Pines of Rome*), and here the artificial resonance of the machine adds to that of the bird itself. Today we add electrical amplification to that of the old-fashioned horn or resonating chamber of the phonograph, and the tone color is definitely affected by such treatment, just as a voice coming over the radio or from a record or the talking screen is almost bound to have its quality slightly altered.

The tone of a small tuning-fork is almost inaudible. But when the base of the fork is placed against a wooden surface, the added resonance immediately makes the tone clear and beautiful. A piano would have very little tone without its wooden sounding-board. Drums have their volume and quality affected by the size and shape of their resonating chambers, and so do the members of the viol family, harps, etc. Wind instruments depend upon the size and shape of their tubes and the formation of the opening from which the tone emerges. A pipe organ takes in a great variety of resonating chambers, with a consequent versatility in its command of tone color.

FROM DRUMS TO LYRES

Percussion is the starting-point of all tone, and from the drums of different pitches to the strings of a lyre or harp is a logical progression. A taut string is simply a reduced section of drumhead, with far greater possibilities of tonal beauty and accuracy of pitch. Actually the earliest stringed instrument must have been a monochord, or some sort of box covered with a single string. It is possible that progress was first made by stretching several strings on a frame or over a box, gourd or shell, drawing them to various degrees of tightness and therefore producing a different pitch with each string. But the discovery must also have been made quite early that by stopping a string with the finger, halfway down its length, the tone became an octave higher, and that intermediate tones could be produced by merely shifting the stopping-point. This could be done with the monochord, and also with several strings running above a neck against which the strings could be pressed.

From the primitive harp and lyre were developed the dulcimer (the first instrument to be played with hammers for melodic effect), the zither, the cymbalom of the gypsies, the lute, mandolin, guitar, banjo and ukulele, the xylophone, marimba, glockenspiel and celesta, the Russian balalaika, all the members of the viol family, and the modern pianoforte, with its ancestors, the clavichord, harpsichord, spinet, virginal, etc. A distinction is generally made between bowed instruments and those which are plucked by the fingers or with a plectrum, or struck with hammers. But essentially they all belong to the percussion family.

BLOWING COMES NEXT

Wind instruments were the commonest purveyors of melody in its early stages, and this classification naturally includes the human voice. The mere sound of the wind through the trees, the Aeolian harp of Nature, must have suggested to primitive man the possibilities of creating his own flutes and pipes, and he must have discovered quite early the variety of pitch and quality that could be produced by his own voice.

The earliest horns and trumpets probably had no definite pitch, but were made from shells or the horns of animals, chiefly to serve as signals or to inspire terror. In fact, the real control of trumpet tones is a fairly modern development in music, resting on the discovery that the column of air in a tube can be shortened exactly as a string is shortened, by piercing the tube with holes at various points (as in a flute) and then stopping certain ones with the fingers, or by sliding one tube into another (as with a trombone) or by bending the tube into several sections, which can then be shut off from each other by valves or pistons.

The whole mechanism of wind instruments has been developed from the scientific fact that a tone-producing tube, tuned at any pitch, will give out at least five natural tones by mere variation in the force of the breath. Here is the law of Nature that created the pattern of the bugle tones and made it so significant in music. As with the stopping of strings, so also with the air in a tube, the process of shortening produces a higher tone, and thus a complete scale can be worked out by the various ways of controlling the length of the tube, with the possibility of securing higher octaves by "overblowing."

IDEALS OF PURITY

The flute produces the purest tone of all wind instruments, simply because the method of blowing permits no interference whatever, and thus practically eliminates the awareness of overtones. The human breath blows across a hole in the tube, directly setting the air in vibration. There is practically no friction at the point of tone production, and the resulting tone might almost be called colorless, although undeniably charming. Poets have referred to the "silvery" tone of the flute (regardless of the metal of which it is often made), and other fanciful listeners have credited the instrument literally with a light blue color of tone.

The distinctive mark of all of the wood-wind family, with the exception of the flute itself (which was originally made of wood), is the reed or pair of reeds used for producing the tone. In a pure flute, the human lips actually take the place of this reed, and the ordinary act of whistling, whose tone is similar to that of a flute, represents perhaps the simplest possible production of musical tone, but generally with limited range or volume.

In the category of reed instruments, the clarinet and bass clarinet are played with a single reed, set in a chisel-shaped mouthpiece. This reed is actually a flat piece of cane or some other light wood, set in vibration by the breath. (The principle is the same as that of blowing upon a piece of grass held between the two hands.)

The double-reed instruments have no mouthpiece, but expose the two reeds directly to the lips, which by the passage of the breath set them vibrating against each other, producing a more strident, possibly a harsher and certainly a more colorful tone than the single reeds. The oboe is the most important of the double-reed instruments, and it is to be found in quite ancient forms, represented also by the hautboys of the Middle Ages (literally *haut bois* or "high wood"). Its alto or tenor counterpart is to be found in the "English horn," which is neither English nor a horn, but merely a lower-voiced oboe, with a cup-shaped end opposite the mouthpiece, which curves up to the reeds. The bassoon is the bass of the double-reed family, with its tube doubled up for the sake of a lower register, and a mouthpiece extending from the side. There is also a contra-bassoon, which can play a whole octave lower.

The saxophone, while not generally recognized by the symphony orchestra, has proved a most practical instrument in smaller combinations, and can be made to take the place of some of the regular wood-winds when players of these difficult instruments are not available. It is really a metal clarinet with a single reed and a special quality of tone by no means unpleasant when well produced, getting its volume and timbre chiefly from the large bowl, suggestive of a Dutchman's pipe.

Among the recognized brass instruments, the French horn has the most beautiful tone color and is also closest to the real horn of tradition, used originally for hunting and signaling purposes. The Germans call the instrument a *Waldhorn* or "forest horn," and its shape, with the wide bell and curved tube, suggests the old prints of actual hunting scenes. There is also the trumpet, with its close relative, the cornet, and for the lower registers we have the alto horn (used mostly in brass bands), the trombone and the tuba, which is the real bass of the brass. It should be remembered that the pipe organ is a wind instrument, producing many of the effects of brass and wood-wind. The harmonium, or parlor organ, is a reed instrument, with a different reed for each tone. The harmonica, or mouth organ, also uses reeds, as do the accordion and concertina.

The modern members of the viol family are the violin, viola, violoncello (generally abbreviated to "cello") and double-bass or bass-viol. Among their ancestors were the viola d'amore, viola da gamba, the rebeck, the Welsh crwth or crowder, and the ancient Chinese fiddle. All have the common characteristic of being played with a bow, thus producing a tone color that is quite different from that of plucked or hammered strings or of wind instruments.

POSSIBILITIES OF TONE COLOR

The great variety of possible tone color can be imagined when it is realized not only that there are many different instruments, of various families, but that each instrument has a certain individuality of tone, like the individual human voice, and finally that each instrument and each voice presents a wide variety of colors within its own range. The lower tones of a flute are quite different from the higher. The G string of a violin has an absolutely different quality from that of any of the other three; and even the average human voice shows a wide range of color, both in speaking and in singing.

Beyond all this diversity of individual timbre, there are almost endless possibilities of multiplying musical instruments and human voices and of combining them harmoniously, excitingly, and sometimes discordantly. Twenty violins playing in unison produce a tone that is absolutely unlike the tone of a solo violin, quite apart from the difference in volume, and when several hundred male voices sing softly together, a completely new tone color is produced, having nothing in common with the more familiar types of singing. The possibilities of the symphony orchestra were scarcely realized before the time of Wagner, and such composers as Richard Strauss, Tschaikowsky, Debussy and Stravinsky have literally created tonal coloring of which Haydn, Mozart and even Beethoven did not dream.

The natural qualities of many of the musical instruments have been further augmented by such devices as muting, the playing of harmonics (overtones), striking the strings with the stick of the bow, playing close to the bridge, etc., often producing weird and unearthly noises, occasionally complicated still further by mere "sound effects," such as the wind machine that Strauss brought into his *Don Quixote*, to represent flying through the air.

Realizing, then, the enormous range of simple and compound tonal coloring that is possible in modern music, and admitting the obvious limitations on the side of rhythm, melody and harmony, it is only natural that the average listener should find the greatest fascination in analyzing instrumental and vocal effects, and observing closely the

The father of the symphony had his troubles

A HARD-WORKING COMPOSER like Franz Joseph Haydn could hardly be expected to remain calm when he found his wife cutting up his manuscripts to make herself some curl papers! She was nine years his senior, and a shrew; but Haydn had the satisfaction of outliving her by those same nine years, in a cottage which she had persuaded him to buy "for her widowhood."

Marriage was only one of Haydn's troubles. He had to serve his musical apprenticeship as valet to a bad-tempered singing-teacher, Niccolo Porpora. During the thirty years that he spent as orchestral conductor and composer in the employ of Prince Esterhazy, he wore the livery of a lackey and ate his meals with the servants.

But Franz Joseph Haydn had a sense of humor and was also blessed with a deeply religious nature. These qualities made him superior to all his troubles.

Some of Haydn's jokes became famous. There was the *Surprise* symphony with its crashing chord "to wake up the audience." There was also a *Farewell* symphony, in which the musicians left the stage two by two as a hint to the Prince that a Christmas vacation was in order.

It was Mozart who gave his friend and teacher the affectionate title of "*Papa*," which stuck to Haydn throughout his long life. Today he is known as "the father of the symphony" and credited with perfecting the sonata form, which has become so significant in orchestral music.

Haydn's oratorio, *The Creation*, is a supreme expression of his devout sincerity, and another work of similar type, *The Seasons*, indicates his deep love of nature. The number of his quartets, trios, and symphonies is prodigious, but his best-known melody is the *Emperor's Hymn*, now supplied with sacred as well as patriotic words.

part played by skillful arrangement and orchestration in the final appeal of every significant composition.

PATTERNS OF TONE COLOR

Just as the patterns of harmony are likely to run in groups of four tones (the conventional chord), so one may speak freely of patterns of tone color, also grouped in foursomes. Actually, these patterns are far less accurate than those of rhythm, melody or harmony, yet the quartet combination is one of the fixed traditions of music, and it produces a definite, composite tonal coloring, much as the harmonizing of a single tone in four parts provides that tone with a distinctly new color.

The mixed quartet of human voices consists of soprano, alto, tenor and bass. Its parallel in instrumental music is the string quartet, in which violins take the parts of soprano and alto, with the viola as tenor and the cello as bass. When the string quartet, with each instrument duplicated many times, becomes the major portion of a symphony orchestra, a fifth part is added in the double-basses, which theoretically support the lighter-voiced cellos by doubling the bass part an octave lower, but actually supply the groundwork for the whole orchestral harmony, leaving the cellos free for significant parts of their own, often including the command of important melodic passages.

But the orchestra includes several other quartets in addition to the strings. Within the wood-winds alone, several complete quartets can be assembled, using various combinations of flutes, clarinets, oboe, English horn, bassoon and contra-bassoon or bass clarinet. The four French horns of the symphony orchestra are a complete quartet in themselves (listen to them in the Prayer from Weber's *Freischütz*, for example), but they also combine admirably with various patterns of the wood-wind choir and are usually seated close to that section.

The real brass quartet of the orchestra consists of first and second trumpets, a trombone and a bass tuba. But again it is possible to have a complete quartet of trombones alone, and separate trombone or trumpet parts are very common.

The French horns can also be combined with other members of the brass section, while in a brass band the soprano part is likely to be played by clarinets, flutes and cornets (or trumpets), separately or in unison, with alto horns corresponding to the alto voice, trombones acting as tenors, and the tuba or Sousaphone as the bass.

Even the percussion section of a symphony orchestra may have four or more instruments playing simultaneously, with tympani or kettledrums, bass and side drums, triangle, cymbals, bells, tambourine, castanets and xylophones available, and while these do not in any sense harmonize, being mostly without definite pitch, they produce a wide variety of tone color. (It is only necessary to hear the bass drum alone, and then with the cymbals added, to realize the enormous difference made by so simple a combination.)

With so many possible quartet patterns in the full-sized symphony orchestra, it is worth remembering also that the entire instrumental body divides naturally into four sections, the strings, wood-winds, brass and percussion. It is not therefore merely fanciful to say that the pattern of four parts, which is the essence of harmony, appears again in the logical combinations of instrumental and vocal tone color.

With the commonest and most practical of the stringed instruments, the four-part tonal coloring persists, through the number of the strings themselves. Each member of the string quartet has four strings, and each of these strings has its individual quality of tone.

MEMBERS OF THE STRING QUARTET

The violin, perhaps nearest to the human voice among instruments, can sing a very high soprano on its E string. The color of this upper string of the violin is clear and brilliant, leaning more and more toward a whistle as the tones become higher.

The A string of the violin, lying to the left of the E string, has a mellower quality, and this is intensified in the D string, next below. The lowest and most heavily colored tones of the violin are produced by the G string, whose quality resembles that of a cello rather than a violin. While all four of the violin strings are made of gut, the G string is wrapped with metal wire (silver or gold), and this additional resistance to the bow naturally emphasizes the overtones. Interesting effects of tonal coloring are produced by deliberately playing high up on the G string so as to maintain the darker quality even in tones of the upper register.

It should be remembered that the quality of violin tones is influenced by the friction of the bow on the string, the touch of the left hand in stopping the string, and the combination of wood and varnish to be found in the body (which is the chief resonator), the bridge, etc.

While the left hand can be trained to a mechanical perfection in stopping the strings for notes of different pitch, the individual genius of violin-playing lies in the right or bowing hand and arm. The control of the bow by the right wrist, fingers and forearm is responsible for all the finer shadings of tone color, even though a human quality is imparted also by the left hand, often intensified (sometimes unduly) by a "vibrato" or shaking of the finger controlling the pitch. It is this combination of human control of tone, emanating from both the left and the right hands, with perhaps even a sympathetic vibration of the player's body as the instrument is held between the chin and the left shoulder, that makes the sound of the violin so completely personal. The bow, which is made of horsehair stretched over a tapering stick, can make some horrible sounds when not properly managed, and the left hand not only has to combat the tendency to play out of tune (with no guide but the ear and the instinctive sense of touch), but must guard against stopping the strings too lightly or incompletely, which at once produces raucous or whistling tones. In the hands of a master, the violin can be the most beautiful of all instruments. In the hands of a beginner it can create some of the most agonizing sounds in human experience.

The second violin in a quartet is exactly the same as the first, merely playing a different part. But the viola is distinctly larger in body and lower in range. Its top string is tuned to the A of the violin's second string, and to the D string and G string below it adds a still lower C string. The tone color of the viola is dark throughout, sometimes suggesting the quality of wood-wind, and it varies with the different strings, of which the lower two are wire-wrapped.

The viola is seldom heard as a solo instrument, but is a very important member of the string quartet, and the viola group in a symphony orchestra is often given beautiful parts to play. The slow movement of Beethoven's *Fifth Symphony* begins with a famous melody played by the violas and cellos together, and there are fine rapid passages for the violas in Wagner's *Tannhäuser* Overture, representing the Venusberg. A familiar and effective piece exhibiting the solo viola is the section of Ippolitoff-Ivanoff's *Caucasian Sketches* called *In the Village*. There is also an excellent viola solo in the *Algerian Suite* of Saint-Saëns (*Rêverie du Soir*).

STRINGS OF LOWER PITCH

The violoncello, or cello, has the same tuning as the viola, but an octave lower. It has a great range and a wide variety of tone color, mostly dark, but of great richness. Romance, temperament and emotion are well expressed by the cello, and it is easy for a mediocre artist to abuse these qualities with exaggerated effects of expression. The performer on a cello has to sit down to his work, letting the instrument stand upright between his knees, supported on a peg whose point keeps it from slipping. The bow moves across the strings in the opposite direction from that of a violinist, with the highest string farthest to the left. The two lower strings are both wire-wrapped and much thicker than those of the violin or viola.

Because of its size, the cello cannot perform the feats of dexterity that are possible on the higher stringed instruments, and rapid passages are likely to sound unpleasantly like sawing wood. But it shows a surprising flexibility in the hands of an expert, with some high tones and harmonics that suggest a robust violin. It is popular as a soloist, highly important in the string quartet, and most effective as a group in the orchestra. The most familiar of cello solos is the rather hackneyed *Swan* of Saint-Saëns, which Pavlowa immortalized with her dance. But it has also elaborate concertos and sonatas in its repertoire.

A quartet of cellos is used effectively by Wagner in the first act of his *Valkyrie*, to accompany Siegmund's love music, and Puccini makes similar use of four cellos in harmony at the start of the last act of *Tosca*. Rossini also gives the cellos a beautiful passage at the start of his *William Tell* Overture. Beethoven shows the possibilities of cellos in unison, not only in the slow movement of his *Fifth Symphony*, where they have the help of the violas, but also in the Finale of the *Ninth Symphony*, to introduce the melody that eventually serves for the choral *Ode to Joy*.

Beethoven was the first composer to realize the possibilities of the double-bass in the orchestra, and this huge, unwieldy instrument is today an important factor in tonal coloring, both in serious and in lighter music. It looks like a large-sized cello, and has to be played standing up, or sitting on a high stool. Its range is an octave lower than that of the cello, and the music has to be written an octave higher than it is actually played. There are four strings, tuned a fourth apart (because of the greater distance between notes on one string), and sometimes a fifth string is added, to take care of unusually low notes.[1] While the double-bass has been used for solos (Koussevitzky, the conductor of the Boston Symphony Orchestra, was formerly a virtuoso on the instrument), its chief function is as the groundwork of the orchestral string section. Beethoven's rapid passages for the double-basses in his *Fifth Symphony* were called by Berlioz "the happy gambols of an elephant." He used similar effects in his *Leonore* Overture, No. 3, and in the *Ninth Symphony* the double-basses play an almost human role in arguing over the possible theme for the choral Finale.

All of the bowed instruments can be played "pizzicato," that is, by plucking the strings with the fingers instead of using the bow, and this effect is a valuable addition to string tone color, particularly in the two lower viols of the group, which can thus emphasize a rhythmic bass.[2] Muting is accomplished by slipping a metal or ebony clamp over the top of the bridge, deadening some of the overtones, as well as decreasing the volume of sound. A "tremolo" effect (also called "agitato") is produced by having the bow quiver very rapidly back and forth across the string, using only a small portion of its own length. In the lower strings this produces weird sounds, the suggestion of a storm, etc.

STRIKING AND BLOWING

The advantage of a bowed over a plucked or hammered string instrument is that the tone can be sustained and even swelled after it starts, whereas in a true percussion instrument, such as the harp or

[1]There are also three-stringed bass-viols.

[2]Listen to the Scherzo of Tschaikowsky's *Fourth Symphony* as an example of continued pizzicato by all the strings. Plucking and slapping the string-bass has become one of the commonest effects of jazz, particularly in the style known as "boogie woogie."

the piano, it begins to die away the moment after the string is struck. This robs the percussive type of stringed instruments of much of their potential tone color and is the chief reason for the comparative insignificance of such minor instruments as the mandolin, banjo, guitar, etc.

The piano derives its variety of color largely from its complex tonal combinations, and from the use of the pedals, which permit a versatile command of overtones. There is a great range of volume as well as of pitch, but the player has practically no control of the color of an individual tone once it has been created by the mechanical dropping of a hammer upon the strings.

The harp is still further handicapped, although its strings are set in vibration directly by the hands instead of through hammers. It has a certain variety of color, largely dependent on pitch and volume, with special effects of harmonics. But it is dynamically limited because of the lack of resonators, as compared with the piano and its sounding-board. The xylophone, marimba, celesta, glockenspiel, etc., all show similar limitations, although each has a distinctive tone color within its own range.

Wind instruments in general show a more decided tone color than do the strings. The flute, as already indicated, emphasizes overtones less than the other wood-winds or the brass, but its lower tones have an individual coloring, while the small flute known as the piccolo (one half the length of the regular flute, and therefore sounding exactly an octave higher) produces shrill and often piercingly unpleasant tones. The composite tone color of three flutes is well illustrated in the *Danse des Mirlitons*, from Tschaikowsky's *Nutcracker Suite.* There are solo pieces for flute by Bach and other composers, and it is often heard as an obbligato to the florid arias for coloratura soprano, whose voice it is supposed to resemble.

The double-reed instruments, oboe, English horn, bassoon and contra-bassoon, all have something of a nasal quality, making their tones very penetrating and also sometimes unpleasant or comical in their effect. The bassoon in particular has served as the comedian of the orchestra, being used for grotesque passages in Wagner's *Meistersinger* Prelude and in the *Sorcerer's Apprentice* of Paul Dukas.

Beethoven used the oboe for its gay quality in the Scherzo of his *Pastoral Symphony*, and for a melancholy effect in the Funeral March of the *Eroica*. Tschaikowsky makes good use of it in his *Fourth Symphony*, and Richard Strauss has some beautiful oboe passages in his tone poem, *Don Juan*.

The alto oboe, or English horn, plays a famous solo at the start of the last act of Wagner's *Tristan und Isolde*, representing a shepherd's pipe, and its slow melody in Dvorak's *New World Symphony* is also well known (partly because of its vogue as a song, *Goin' Home*). César Franck gives the English horn (*cor anglais*) a beautiful solo in the slow movement of his *D minor Symphony*, accompanied by pizzicato strings and harp.

The clarinet has a more mellow voice than any of the double-reed instruments and has proved very practical in smaller instrumental combinations, where it can play the soprano part with almost any pattern of wood-wind, strings or brass. It plays a beautiful theme in the first movement of Tschaikowsky's *Pathétique Symphony*, and was popular with Liszt in his tone poems. Richard Strauss gives the theme of Sancho Panza in his *Don Quixote* to the bass clarinet, which is usually a mere filler at the bottom of a chord.

THE BLARE OF BRASS

If the flutes can be fancifully credited with such colors as silver or light blue, with perhaps various shades of brown in the reed instruments, the brass would logically run to various shades of red, reaching a bright scarlet in the trumpets themselves. A famous trumpet solo is the one played offstage in Beethoven's opera, *Fidelio*, appearing also in the second and third *Leonore* overtures. The French horns are milder and more mellow in quality, although they can produce exciting effects, as in the direct suggestions of hunting calls by Wagner and Strauss.

The trombones have a definite blaring sound, easily distinguished by ear, in addition to the dramatic action of their sliding technique. Comedy effects, such as the hyena laugh, etc., have been introduced into modern popular music for the trombone. The tuba is important chiefly as a sustainer of the bass in the brass choir or band. Wagner makes splendid use of the brass in all his operas, particularly the Siegfried Funeral March in *Götterdämmerung*, the Pilgrims' Chorus in *Tannhäuser*, and some of the solemn moments in *Parsifal*. He uses the tuba effectively to represent the snoring of the dragon, Fafner, in *Siegfried*.

By carefully listening for the different instruments, singly and in combination, one may learn to distinguish a great variety of tone colors, and the whole subject will be found endlessly fascinating. It was believed at one time that the seven colors of the spectrum definitely corresponded to the seven steps of the diatonic scale, and even in modern times interesting experiments have been made in combining actual colors and tones, as in the *Prometheus* of Scriabin, and the practical "color-organ" of Thomas Wilfred.

While any discussion of tone color must necessarily be in somewhat vague terms, as compared with the more accurate patterns of rhythm, melody and harmony, the very fact that it leaves so much to the imagination and direct investigation of the listener adds enormously to the general appeal of the entire subject.

CHAPTER VIII THE SYMPHONY ORCHESTRA

THEY TELL ABOUT a rural poet who was asked to write about a symphony orchestra. He had never seen or heard such a thing, but the instruments represented something tangible, and he began to ask questions. He was told about the various combinations of wood and brass—that the fiddlestrings were made of catgut, and that horsehair was used for the bows.

When he wrote his poem, it began like this:

A noise arose from the orchestra, as the leader drew across
The intestines of the agile cat the tail of the noble hoss.

That is one way of looking at a symphony orchestra. What is yours? Are you one of those people who sit in that "comfortable coma," allowing the music to envelope you, physically and emotionally, without in the least caring what it is all about? Do you belong to the great army of foot-listeners, who are satisfied so long as they have a good, snappy rhythm to keep time to? Or the heart-listeners, whose highest aesthetic ideals are summed up in goose-pimples? Worst of all, are you one of those utterly utter head-listeners who think entirely in technical terms, follow the music with a printed score, evidently in the hope that somebody will miss a note, and firmly believe that their reactions must be intellectual at all costs?

You have not fully enjoyed the performance of a symphony orchestra until you have arrived at a happy combination of all three methods of listening—the physical, the emotional and the intellectual; but you can have a lot of fun developing into such a triple threat, and even a first hearing is by no means wasted, so long as you keep your ears open and stay awake.

A piece of symphonic music is like a cathedral. There must be a first impression, perhaps of the vaguest and most general sort, after which every return visit means the discovery of new beauties, details that you would never have suspected on chance acquaintance.

So, first of all, never judge either yourself or a symphony by a single hearing. Keep your mind and your ears and your heart open, and find out, frankly and honestly, what the combination of a composer, a conductor and a group of performers can do to you.

THE CONDUCTOR'S ROLE

The man who conducts a symphony orchestra is not nearly so important in actual performance as in the long hours of preliminary rehearsal. He has established all the details of interpretation in advance—the exact tempo of every measure, the "expression" created by gradual or sudden changes in volume, the balance of parts needed to bring out the intentions of the composer. If the practice sessions have done their work, the concert itself is no more than a series of reminders by the man who swings the baton. He may indulge himself in some fancy gestures and poses if he wishes. Naturally he must keep firm control of his forces at all times. But spontaneous inspiration in front of an audience is practically non-existent, even with full credit to personality and showmanship, which occasionally are permitted to obscure more important musical qualities.

It is fun to watch a good conductor and a well-drilled orchestra. But there can be almost as much fun in following symphonic music by the ear alone, particularly on records, which can be played over and over again. Listen first of all for tunes. They are the Gothic arches and the rose windows of your musical cathedral. And never let anyone tell you that symphonies are unmelodious. Every great piece of music contains melody, for it is by its melodies that a composition is remembered, and without the appeal to memory there can be no permanence in art of any kind, least of all music.

A symphonic theme is not likely to be so obvious as a popular tune. It may not last for more than a few measures or even a few notes at a time. But it is always recognizable, and that pleasure of recognition is the first step toward appreciation, or, preferably, enjoyment of good music.

There is a particular excitement in discovering a piece of music that grows more fascinating with each successive hearing—particularly if the listener finds each time new beauties that he had not suspected before. This is the real explanation of the attitude of the confirmed music-lover, and it may explain also why so many people would rather hear something they already know than to experiment with unfamiliar material, no matter how good.

Of course there must be a first time for everything, and the listener is fortunate if a new piece is introduced in the presence of someone who has heard it before and can therefore build a proper predisposition to enthusiasm. It always helps to be placed in a receptive mood, and if the novelty then turns out to be honestly enjoyable, the pleasure is all the greater.

Every great composition can stand practically unlimited repetition, following the well-known law of the survival of the fittest. Whatever is cheap and obvious and commonplace, even though it may exert an immediate appeal, fails when put to the test of permanence.

The average popular song is a good example. Its very nature demands that it be quickly and easily remembered; but it is often just as quickly and easily forgotten, after being subjected to constant repetition. Six months is about the limit of its activity, and six weeks will sometimes be enough to kill it completely. The average listener makes these decisions himself, showing thereby a fundamental appreciation of the things that are not transient but permanent.

THERE ARE DIFFICULTIES

But how shall the person totally inexperienced in music discover for himself the things that are permanent? Unfortunately, if he is exposed to them without preparation or a preliminary build-up, they are likely to sound merely dull, and the enthusiasm of a confirmed music-lover may be completely wasted. Try to interest a novice directly in a Bach fugue, a Beethoven sonata, a Brahms symphony or a Wagner opera, regardless of interpretation, and see how much progress you will make. It simply cannot be done. The people who love and appreciate those great classics today forget that they first went through various stages of enjoying lighter pieces, including perhaps some downright trash. They listened to plenty of bad music and some that was only fairly good, and they gradually eliminated from their listening repertoire everything that did not pass the test of time—at least as far as they were concerned.

This matter of permanence in music presents curious problems. The giddy, scatterbrained jitterbug is ready to accept any hot record by a popular dance band as the last word in significant music. At the other extreme, the ultramodernist is no longer sure that the accepted classics of the "three B's" are really the climax of absolute music, or that Wagner went about as far as possible on the dramatic side.

Permanence seems to be a relative term after all, except insofar as it represents practically a unanimity of opinion over a considerable period of time. But one man's permanence in music may be another man's passing fancy.

The person who has become engrossed in the pursuit of music, either as a listener or as a performer, will not be satisfied with compositions which to the dilettante or the frankly unmusical observer may seem the ultimate in musical beauty. A great many listeners, obviously, have never gone beyond the platitudes and clichés of popular music. Some have stopped at Grieg, MacDowell, Nevin, Chaminade, perhaps Dvorak. To still others, permanence represents the lighter works of the greatest masters, and beyond this there is still the bulk of the real music-lovers, the hidebound classicists, the modernists and the ultramodernists.

IF THIS BE TREASON

Now here is a heretical thought, which is uttered deliberately and in all sincerity. Take it for what it is worth, and let it cure your inferiority complex, if any: *You can have just as much fun with the music of Grieg and Nevin and Chaminade as a highbrow has with that of Bach, Beethoven and Brahms.* Actually you may enjoy it even more, for your pleasure will be direct and natural, unhampered by intellectual considerations.

There are only certain people who have the time, the inclination and the innate gifts to develop a sincere enjoyment of music that to the average listener sounds extremely complicated, hopelessly difficult and perhaps downright dull. It would be absurd to try to bring everybody up to that level of intelligent appreciation, even though it may be entirely possible for anyone willing to make the effort.

The point is that anybody honestly enjoying any kind of music, from a popular song to a classic symphony, is going through somewhat the same process—part physical, part emotional, part intellectual. The fundamental stimuli may be quite different, but the sensations of pleasure are likely to possess a definite similarity.

The pleasure derived from music is at best not accurately definable. You yourself are the only one who knows if you have it, and so long as you are satisfied, that is all that really matters. It is far better to feel the thrill of honestly enjoying some comparatively insignificant music than to pretend to like something that secretly bores you to death.

If you like the music of some of the minor composers, and keep on listening, the chances are that you will eventually discover the major ones also, and possibly develop for them the same sincere enjoyment. The various lists of recommended records included in this book may prove helpful in this development.

RECORDS TO THE RESCUE AGAIN

Here are some short pieces, guaranteed easy on the ear, representing a transition from the most obviously appealing music to something perhaps a little better:

Arensky's *Waltz for Two Pianos;* Beethoven's *Turkish March* and *Für Elise;* Boccherini's *Minuet;* Brahms's *Lullaby;* Chaminade's *Scarf Dance* and *Pas des Amphores;* Delibes' *Coppelia* and *Sylvia* ballet music; Dett's *Juba Dance;* Dvorak's *Humoresque* and *Slavonic Dances;* Elgar's *Salut d'Amour;* Fibich's *Poeme;* Gardner's *From the Cane Brake;* Edward German's *Dances from Henry VIII;* Godard's *Berceuse from Jocelyn;* Gounod's *Funeral March of a Marionette;* Grainger's *Country Gardens, Shepherds' Hey* and *Molly on the Shore;* Grieg's *Last Spring, Erotik, Nocturne* and *To Spring;* Herbert's *Al Fresco, Babillage* and *Punchinello;* Järnefelt's *Praeludium;* Kreisler's *Caprice Viennois, Tambourin Chinois, The Old Refrain, Liebesfreud, Liebesleid* and *Schön Rosmarin;* Liadoff's *Music Box;* Liszt's *Liebestraum;* MacDowell's *To a Wild Rose, Scotch Poem* and *Witches' Dance;* Mendelssohn's *Spring Song;* Moszkowski's *Serenade* and *Spanish Dance;* Nevin's *Narcissus* and *A Day in Venice;* Offenbach's *Barcarolle;* Paderewski's *Minuet;* John Powell's *Banjo*

Picker; Rachmaninoff's *Prelude in C-sharp minor;* Rimsky-Korsakoff's *Flight of the Bumble Bee;* Rubinstein's *Melody in F* and *Kamenoi-Ostrow;* Schubert's *Serenade* and *Ave Maria;* Schumann's *Träumerei* and *The Happy Farmer;* Cyril Scott's *Lullaby;* Sibelius' *Valse Triste;* Suppé's *Poet and Peasant* Overture; Tschaikowsky's *Humoresque, Song without Words* and *June Barcarolle;* Wagner's *Song to the Evening Star.* One might add Borodin's Dances from *Prince Igor;* Chabrier's *España Rhapsody;* Glazounoff's *Autumn;* Goldmark's *Sakuntala* Overture; Nicolai's Overture to *The Merry Wives of Windsor;* the Gavotte from Thomas' *Mignon;* some of the Waldteufel Waltzes; Wieniawski's *Souvenir de Moscow* and the Intermezzo from Wolf-Ferrari's *Jewels of the Madonna.* The list would still represent only a few steps on the fascinating way to the discovery of permanent music.

CHAPTER IX A MATTER OF FORM

THE ORGANIZING FACTORS of rhythm, melody, harmony and tone color all enter into every musical composition of real importance. The principles of Form co-ordinate them into a complete work of art.

Form in music is similar to form in athletics. It means the attainment of the greatest results with the least waste of effort.

Strength and energy alone will not make a good golfer or tennis player, or a football star. A command of form is required to make the most of an athlete's natural resources.

So the great composer, having created a melody in a certain rhythmic pattern, and having harmonized it and given it to certain instruments or voices, for effective tonal coloring, applies form as his final organizing factor, and only through form can he arrive at a complete and logical composition.

All of the principles already discussed are necessary factors in form. But form goes beyond all of these factors as an organizing force, and therefore has an independent significance.

It is possible for a musician to be a master of form without the creative inspiration to give it real importance, and this is true also of painters, writers and other artists. It is also possible for a human being with vast creative instincts to fail in the achievement of true art because of neglecting the technique of form.

Rhythm, melody and harmony are all to a certain extent instinctive, although their command may be developed through experience and training. Form also may be largely instinctive (as it appears in the better types of folk-music), but as a rule it is acquired through study and practice, and it may be an entirely artificial attainment.

The hero was only human after all

BEETHOVEN dedicated his Third Symphony to Napoleon Bonaparte, the hero who was to save the world from tyranny. But when Napoleon himself assumed dictatorship by taking the title of Emperor of France, the disillusioned composer tore off the dedicatory page and trampled it under foot.

When the symphony was published, in 1806, it was called simply *Eroica,* with an inscription, in Italian, "to the memory of a great man." For Beethoven, Napoleon was dead, an idol who had succumbed to the human lust for power and missed a glorious opportunity. The second movement of the *Eroica* is one of the greatest funeral marches in all music.

Ludwig van Beethoven was the rugged individualist among composers. He resented the artificial superiority created by noble birth or inherited wealth, even though he was generally dependent on just such people for support. He criticized his friend Goethe for tipping his hat to a nobleman, and when his own brother signed his name as "Property owner," Beethoven promptly countered with "Brain owner."

The great Fifth Symphony of Beethoven, with its opening motto that is now interpreted as V for Victory, expresses man's uncompromising struggle with Fate. Its Finale is an ecstatic march of triumph. His choral ninth ends with an *Ode to Joy,* and his opera *Fidelio* deals with the circumvention of villainy through unswerving loyalty and courage. The third *Leonore* Overture is a complete drama in itself, summing up this entire opera. Such other Overtures as *Coriolanus* and *Egmont* deal with the eternal struggle for fairness among human beings.

The uncompromising honesty of Beethoven's music is today appreciated by an ever growing audience.

AS TO SIZE AND GREATNESS

The great composer, naturally, is the one who possesses unusual creative ability and combines with it a highly developed command of form. This form is not necessarily elaborate, although a complicated piece, of large proportions, is potentially more significant than a brief and simple melody. Similarly, a book is likely to prove more important than a short story or newspaper paragraph; a portrait or landscape makes a deeper impression than a rough sketch or cartoon, and a cathedral certainly represents more art than a bungalow or a garage. Yet each of these more modest structures may exhibit a form that is distinctive, and within its limitations decidedly worth while, and it would be a mistake to suggest that mere size is in any way admirable. (This mistake, however, is frequently made in every branch of art.)

A bad symphony is perhaps worse than a bad song, simply because its pretensions are so much greater, and a bad opera is worse than either. But a correctly made symphony or opera deserves no particular credit beyond that of honest workmanship, and if its composer happens to be utterly uninspired, as is often the case, there is no reason for glossing over the fact with hypocritical praise of his technique. Anybody can learn to write a symphony, exactly as anybody can learn to write a book. But how many books are really worth reading? And how many symphonies are really worth listening to?

Stephen Foster had an instinctive command of form, as indicated by practically all his songs. Their permanence in the hearts of human beings should be sufficient proof of their unique qualities of inspiration. A Foster song may be considered more significant than an uninspired symphony; but when it is compared with a truly great example of a larger form, the simple song necessarily fades into the background. Such comparisons are dangerous in any case, if not odious. They are like the comparison of a tiger with an elephant, or a forget-me-not with a chrysanthemum. It is safer to say at the outset that every type of music has its own possibilities of form, and that great inspiration plus a fine technique will inevitably produce a highly significant composition in whatever style the composer may have selected.

FORM IS PRACTICALLY JUSTIFIED

The necessity of form in music is practical as well as artistic. A melody soon becomes monotonous if repeated over and over again, and this is the early fate of most popular music. A song of any kind must at least have its own limited form, and if within those limitations it achieves permanence, that is all the more a tribute to its inherent qualities of inspiration.

But even supposing that a melody is a great one, there would be little pleasure in hearing it played over and over, without a stop. Even the practical music of the dance floor is always arranged so as to avoid complete monotony, usually by the combination of several tunes, with interludes, and frequent changes of key and instrumentation. A composer in the larger forms does all these things far more elaborately and logically, often with less melodic material to start with.

The basic principle of all form in art is that of *contrast*. That is the best way to avoid monotony, and when contrasting material is followed by a reminder of what had previously been presented, the effect on the observer is most satisfying. So the basic pattern of form may be called threefold, consisting of Statement (Exposition), Contrast (Development) and Reminder (Recapitulation).

This is the basis of form not only in music, but in a play or a novel. The author brings on his characters and states the situation that makes his story possible. If then he has nothing happen, but merely keeps the whole scene and its characters in a static condition, he fails in his purpose. It is necessary for him to introduce some problem, some contrasting or hostile force that will create suspense and enlist the interest and sympathy of his audience. This is the plot of the play or novel, corresponding to the development of musical themes.

But if the playwright or novelist fails to solve his problem and arrive at a happy or at least a logical ending, he has again disappointed his audience and upset the principles of form. He must leave a final reminder that everything is as it should be, and similarly the musical composer ends with a recapitulation or reminder of his most important themes, creating satisfaction in the minds of his listeners.

Reduced to its simplest terms, this common pattern of form may be called A-B-A. The A represents the leading thematic material, which is repeated at the close, with B representing the contrasting material. While this is the essential principle of statement, contrast and reminder, it has many possible variations. The A section, for instance, is frequently repeated before the B section begins. This would make the pattern A-A-B-A, which is the commonest form of the modern popular chorus and of many folk-songs.

THE COMMONEST PATTERN

It is fairly safe to look for some variation of the A-B-A form in practically all music. While the reminder of the first section will not always be found, it is almost inevitable that there should be contrast of some sort. This necessity for contrast is exhibited even in the lesser details of form.

A melody almost always occupies an even number of measures, usually a multiple of four. These sets of four can in turn be divided into groups of two, and these groups will generally be found to have a contrasting effect, in the manner of a question and an answer. (Sometimes this effect is given even in two measures, the first acting as a question, and the second as an answer.)

So the form of music enters into every step of construction, from a simple pattern of only a few tones to the complex architecture of a symphony. One or two measures may constitute a phrase, just like a few words of spoken language. When an answering phrase is added, we get a clause, perhaps a musical sentence. If this clause ends in a perfect cadence, it is called a "period," just as a complete sentence in English ends in a punctuation mark of the same name. (The word "strain" is loosely applied to such a period, and sometimes to a complete melody.)

Some of our popular tunes are excellent examples of economy in arriving at the necessary number of measures for a recognizable chorus. Nowadays it is considered proper and almost necessary to have thirty-two measures in such a chorus, with the verse perhaps half that length. (This is partly due to the convenience of timing such choruses on the radio.)

But the structure of a melody is only a small part of form in the larger sense. Where folk-song and popular music are satisfied with the obvious and easily remembered material of a single tune, the great composer almost always builds further, combining several themes or melodies in one composition, breaking them up into their component parts, changing the rhythm, the harmony, the key and the instrumental coloring, possibly turning them upside down, and even letting two or more of them sound simultaneously.

The intricacies of classical and modern form are many, yet it is all quite likely to come down to some variation of the principle of statement, contrast and reminder. In the long run, form achieves unity through variety, which is a well-established axiom of art in general. Unity is meaningless if it represents nothing more than identity. But when an artist has combined seemingly antagonistic elements and arrived at a recognizable unity in spite of their contrasting qualities, he has put the stamp of individuality on his work, regardless of the originality of his basic materials.

SONATA, RONDO, VARIATIONS

The climax of the simple song form is found in Sonata form, which is of such importance in the symphonic and chamber music of the world that it demands detailed study and discussion later. It is enough to indicate at this point that it is the most elaborate flowering of the A-B-A principle, permitting every conceivable treatment of melodic materials, and resulting in some of the most sublime creations of musical genius. It follows roughly the technique of the playwright, with A serving as the exposition (statement of themes), B as the development or plot, and A once more, though often greatly changed, as recapitulation, restatement, reminder–in short, the happy ending.

Simpler than sonata form, but more elaborate than the song form, are the Rondo, the various dance forms, and the common structure of variations on a theme.

Polyphonic or many-voiced music shows great complexity of form, often within a small compass, with the fugue as its outstanding example.

The rondo, as its name implies, is based on a round dance, using a principal theme (A) and two or more subsidiary themes (B, C, etc.) which are presented in rotation, always alternating with the main theme. A rondo may end with its A theme or with a "coda," literally a "tail," tacked on merely for a finish, and made of either old or new material. The form would thus be A-B-A-C-A, possibly continuing with a D theme, etc., and ending with a coda. The tempo is usually fast, and this makes the rondo a popular form for a symphonic or sonata movement.

Of the dance forms, the most important in serious music is the Minuet, which also figures in many symphonies and sonatas. A slow, stately dance, in triple time, it usually has a definite form, consisting of a first section (A) in two parts, each of which is repeated, followed by a trio (B) representing the contrasting section, also repeated, and finally a repetition of the two parts of A.

An excellent example of a rondo will be found in the Finale of Haydn's *Trio in G major*, generally known as the *Gypsy Rondo.* Some of the finest minuets are in the symphonies of Mozart, particularly the G-minor and the E-flat.

Variations on a theme may constitute an entire composition (like those written by Brahms on a theme by Haydn or Handel or Paganini) or the movement of a symphony or sonata, usually in slow time. The Andante of Beethoven's *Fifth Symphony* is a classic example, and the slow movement of his *Kreutzer Sonata*, for the violin, is also famous, both for its theme and for its variations. Schubert wrote some fine variations on his own theme of the song, *Death and the Maiden*, in a string quartet, and another of his compositions (a quintet) has a movement built on the theme of his livelier song, *Die Forelle* (The Trout). Bach, Haydn, Mozart, Schumann and Chopin all wrote variations that have become famous.

Variations on a theme can be of many different kinds. The commonest merely add extra notes to the melody itself, disguising it only slightly. Changes of rhythm are also common, and it is a simple matter to turn the key from major to minor or vice versa. Sometimes the theme is put in the bass, with new melodies and harmonies to disguise it still further. It is generally recognized that a variation should follow some definite pattern throughout, so as to give the hearer a fair chance to figure out the melody for himself. Modern swing, incidentally, consists of improvised variations on popular tunes.

SONG AND DANCE FORMS

It should be realized that much music appears in the song form that is not intended for singing. Similarly, there are many compositions bearing the names of dances that have nothing to do with dancing as such. Even the waltzes of Chopin are not intended for actual dancing, while such names as minuet, rondo, gavotte and polonaise have become established in serious music, with little to remind one of their original significance.

But actual songs and dances are worthy of careful analysis because of the larger forms that they created, and obviously it is far easier to study form itself in its simplest manifestations. The practical songs of the world have been governed largely by the nature and rhythm of their words, while the dance music is fundamentally dependent on the steps and figures that it accompanies. But in spite of such restrictions, both songs and dances have developed an astonishing variety even in their simpler forms, while the outgrowth of their primitive models has reached amazing proportions in the great compositions of musical literature.

It is well to remember, therefore, that the most elaborate piece of music may exhibit a form that is essentially related to the simple A-B-A of statement, contrast and reminder, as found in song itself, and that most of the melodies of the world, whether fast or slow, exhibit rhythmic patterns that go back to actual dance measures. If the ear has once become accustomed to hearing the fundamental divisions of form in the simpler styles, it will gradually acquire the habit of following the formal outlines of more elaborate compositions, so that eventually an entire symphony or fugue may become as clear to the listening mind as would the plot of a story or play.

It is an interesting game to analyze the form of folk-songs, or even the average popular chorus, and then gradually to apply the same principles to the more complicated "art songs" and to instrumental music in general. It will be found that all folk-songs having more than one stanza use the same tune for each stanza, no matter what the variation of the words may be. This is called the "strophic" style of song writing, and is found also in all of the modern popular music (which is really an up-to-date form of folk-song). The art song, on the other hand, usually has its music follow the words closely throughout, striving to fit their spirit as well as their meter, and naturally developing a far more elaborate type of melody, which in some modern songs hardly seems a melody at all.

Some strophic songs have a chorus or refrain, which may present a different pattern from that of the stanzas. There are examples of folk-music also in which the voices of an actual chorus interrupt after each line, perhaps with meaningless syllables, like the "hey nonny nonny" of the English madrigals, or the "fol-de-rol" that figures in some college songs. The Negro music is full of such "burdens," and sometimes the choral undercurrent may be heard right through the stanzas themselves.

A clear comprehension of simple song forms will make it far easier to follow the more complicated structure of sonata form and other types to be found in larger compositions such as the symphony, sonata, overture, concerto, etc. In many cases it will be found that a symphonic movement (particularly a slow movement) is actually in an elaborate song form.

The early "sonatas" had little relation to the elaborate examples of form eventually produced under the same name. Originally, a sonata was merely a piece to be played ("sounded"), as compared with a cantata, which was meant to be sung ("chanted"). Sonata form is of such importance in music that it deserves some special attention in its simpler as well as its more complicated phases. Before looking into it further, it is well to remember that "absolute music" (which means music without any words or descriptive material to make its meaning clear) depends largely upon form for its effect, since this is the chief factor in making it coherent and, in a sense, articulate; and sonata form has been the most successful development of absolute music in that direction.

SONATA FORM

It is easy to see how an inspired composer of music would soon grow dissatisfied with letting words do half his work for him, as in a song, or with merely fitting notes to the rhythm of dance steps. He might of course write a "Song without Words," a melody of strongly dramatic or romantic character, and by giving it a title, such as Elegy, Romance, Serenade, Spring, or Funeral March, make it fairly easy for his hearers to guess his meaning. (It is a habit of humanity to attach such meanings to absolute music, even when the composer gave no hint as to his intentions.)

But the more music broke away from the support of words and

dance steps, the more elaborate became the attempts of serious composers to develop a form that would actually take the place of a program, a form that would allow pure music to speak for itself, without benefit of even a descriptive title, and would make that musical speech logical, sufficiently varied to be continually interesting, and with some appeal to the emotions as well as to the intellect.

From the time of Haydn, sonata form was applied not only to the sonata itself (which by that time had become definitely a composition for a solo instrument) but to the symphony, the concerto, and sometimes to the operatic overture. It should be remembered, therefore, that "sonata" is really a family name, properly applied by itself only to a piece of absolute music for a solo instrument (with piano accompaniment if needed), usually in three movements, at least one of which is technically in sonata form. A concerto is a sonata for a solo instrument with orchestral accompaniment; a string quartet, trio or quintet is a sonata for the combination indicated; and a symphony is a sonata for orchestra alone (usually in four instead of only three movements).

The most important characteristic of sonata form is the "development," which represents the second section in the basic principle of statement, contrast, reminder. While a simple song melody states a theme (A) possibly with a repetition, then introduces a contrasting theme (B) and ends with a reminder of A, the structure of sonata form uses at least two contrasting themes for its A section, developing them with all the technique of musicianship into a complex B section, and restating them, perhaps in different keys, or even in combination, as a closing reminder of A.

While this general pattern of A-B-A (exposition, development, recapitulation) is the essence of sonata form, there are infinite possibilities for variety of detail, in addition to the highly individual treatment of the development section. The earlier sonatas or symphonies of Haydn are quite modest in their development sections, whereas Beethoven makes this contrasting material the actual plot of his sonata movements, possibly more important even than the themes themselves.

In any case, the development provides the best opportunity for a composer to display his real command of musical resources. Anyone may invent an effective melody, and completely untaught musicians are constantly doing this very thing, as in the folk-music of the world and the popular songs of today. But it takes an experienced musician, with something more than melodic invention, to develop such material into a completely symphonic movement. Again, the well-taught musician may have all the technical tricks at his command and still fail to create real interest because of the lack of individuality or inspiration in his work.

So there is every reason for the almost reverent attitude of experienced music-lovers toward a well-made symphony, and since the sonata form is so vital a part of such a musical creation, it is well worth the unceasing attention and study of all those listeners who want to enjoy music to the fullest extent. The best way to study sonata form is by the analysis of a few outstanding examples, not too complicated to begin with.

A GENERAL SUMMARY

It will be found that there is often an introduction, having little or nothing to do with the melodies that follow, and actually going back to the habit of striking a few chords to get the attention of the audience. (The modern conductor does this by beating on a music stand with his stick, and sometimes it takes longer than it should for the chatter to stop.)

But with or without an introduction, the first theme or "subject" is announced in a clear and definite fashion, quite early in the movement, and in the key selected by the composer as the tonic. This melody may be slightly developed or discussed before the second subject is announced, or there may be an interlude of some additional melodic material. But the second subject must eventually be announced quite as definitely as the first. It should be of contrasting character and in a different key.

The second subject may also receive some slight development or discussion, and it is quite common to find both the first and second subjects repeated before the actual development section begins. This part of a movement in sonata form is almost unmistakable, if only because it is the hardest for the listener to follow. Thus far he has been hearing well-defined melodies, but now he is plunged suddenly into a maelstrom of imitations, contrasts of tone color, changes of rhythm and key, snatches of both melodies, tossed back and forth in bewildering fashion, possibly even fugal passages in which parts of both themes appear.

The more interesting a composer makes this development section, and the more logically and ingeniously he handles his materials, the greater will be the ultimate significance attached to the entire movement. If it were not for the development section, the sonata form would not differ materially from an enlarged song form, and there are plenty of movements in the sonatas and symphonies of the world that do not deserve the term sonata form, simply because they overlook the opportunities of this important and individual part.

The recapitulation conventionally consists of a restatement of both of the subjects of the first part, in new keys. There may be a coda at the close, and this coda often assumes an importance of its own, running to considerable length, and building upon the materials of the earlier themes.

A PRACTICAL APPLICATION

Now apply these principles to one of the best loved of all symphonic movements, the first of Schubert's *Unfinished Symphony*, in B minor, using phonograph records for illustration. It begins with an introduction, in triple time, played, without harmony, by the bass strings. But this is no mere noise to attract attention, for the material is to be heard later in some very important development. Four measures of interlude (in the manner of a popular vamp) introduce the first subject, a plaintive minor melody, played by oboe and clarinet over quivering strings, with a rhythmic pattern in the pizzicato bass.

The beautiful second melody enters on the bows of the cellos, the other strings playing a syncopated accompaniment. This is the tune that Sigmund Romberg made the basis of his *Song of Love* in *Blossom Time*, the modern operetta that had Franz Schubert himself as its hero.

To start the development or B section, Schubert first lets his pizzicato strings carry the key from B minor to E minor and then plays the introductory theme in that key. It is developed slowly and at first very softly, with a constant tremolo in the bass, gradually growing louder and louder, as the minor melody is turned upside down, until the rage of the orchestra seems to be spent.

Evidently the first and second subjects are to be practically ignored until the recapitulation sets in, and this tentative suggestion is finally made by the dulcet, pacifically minded clarinet. The flute takes it up with seeming approval, and suddenly we are back in B minor, with the strings quivering out their soft vamp over the pizzicato rat-a-tat of the basses. A long, sustained horn tone once more announces the modulation to the second subject, again with the cellos carrying the melody against the syncopated accompaniment.

Technically there is nothing very remarkable about this movement, unless it be the clearness of the workmanship. But as a piece of pure melodic invention, carried out with consistent charm and unabated interest for the listener, it stands almost unrivaled in musical literature. It is by far the most pleasant and satisfying introduction to symphonic music, and once its whole scheme is grasped, it will make other compositions in sonata form seem easy also.

MORE SONATA FORM

Sonata form is of such importance that it will be worth while to analyze at least two more first movements of famous symphonies at this point, and to listen carefully to any other examples that may be available. Remember that sonata form is characteristic of the opening movement of most symphonies, sonatas, concertos and such chamber music as trios, string quartets, quintets, etc., therefore it is not difficult to find plenty of specimens. Again the constant use of records is recommended.

One of the loveliest pieces of sonata form, most compact and logical in its structure, yet most graceful and charming in its musical content, is the first movement of Mozart's *Symphony in G minor*.

The fascinating thing about this symphonic movement, aside from the beauty of his melodic invention, is the way he makes a small amount of material go a long distance without ever becoming monotonous, and this, after all, is the essence of good form in music. The basic patterns of his first subject, both rhythmic and melodic, are surprisingly simple, concentrating largely on two-tone combinations.

The movement opens with no more introduction than three quick beats of the first measure, with the strings at once establishing their predominating accompaniment pattern. The first subject is naturally in the key of G minor, the tonic of the symphony, and its repetition soon develops into a transitional theme. This is a sturdy, vigorous tune, which is to assert itself more and more as the movement progresses. It stops for the moment on two chords, and after a measure of rest, the second subject softly announces its chromatic pattern.

A repetition of this little melody, with more wood-winds adding color, leads to a passage in which the opening two-tone pattern can be distinctly heard, played slowly, with an overlapping answer of the same pattern turned upside down.

Early in the development section, the cellos, double-basses and bassoon play the first subject in octaves, while the flute, oboe, clarinet and horns suggest the second. Meanwhile, the violins are providing a decorative filigree, which is promptly imitated by the clumsier but equally sportive basses. It becomes a regular game of give and take, with the first subject appearing alternately at the top and at the bottom of the orchestra, and the wood-winds soon trying their hand at an imitation of the transitional theme, which also works in very nicely.

Now comes a genial interlude of pure conversation between the violins and the wood-winds, each giving an individual version of that little two-tone pattern that has by now become so significant. They go on alternating in confidential fashion until the violas and cellos suddenly break in rather impatiently, mocking at this insistence on trivial talk, while the wood-winds echo with questioning inversions of the little pattern, until the whole orchestra comes in with violent reminders of the sturdier parts of the transitional theme. The basses and cellos continue to mutter the two-tone motif down below, while the violins experiment with it above, twisting it about in various ways, without arriving at any satisfactory conclusion.

The wood-wind choir finally presents the main patterns of both the first and second subjects in alternation, emphasizing their close melodic relationship, and the recapitulation is allowed to begin with the first subject in its original key, exactly as at the start.

Mozart also lets the second subject be heard in G minor, the basic key of the symphony. The coda begins with the violins alternating in bits of the first subject, as though looking for a way out, and when the wood-winds show a tendency to start all over again in octaves, the full orchestra hastily overrules the suggestion, going into a series of chords to prove that it is all really over, with a final set of four good thumping ones on the tonic to make sure you will not forget the key.

BEETHOVEN'S CONTRIBUTION

One more example of sonata form may well be noted at this time in the first movement of Beethoven's *Fifth Symphony*, more involved and fuller of emotional content than the work of either Mozart or Schubert, yet built with a clarity of structure that makes it equally easy to follow. Here there is no gentle dalliance with light and pleasant melodies, developed for their own sake, but a serious and profound approach to life itself in musical terms.

Beethoven almost put his *Fifth Symphony* into the class of "program music" by admitting that the insistent motto of the first movement (three short notes and a long one) represented Fate knocking at the door. Even if he had not given us this hint, it would be permissible to read such a significance into the music, for the emotional mood is unmistakable.

Yet this movement may be regarded as absolute music also, remembering always that Beethoven dramatized life as did no other symphonic composer, with a fiercely independent and personal attitude that was almost unique in the world of art. So this great opening of a great symphony inevitably connotes a struggle, a battling with the unseen forces of Fate, and it is a battle in which Beethoven himself eventually emerges as the victor.

The announcement of the motto, twice over, a tone apart, serves as introduction to the movement. This motto has only two melody tones. Its rhythmic pattern (three introductory short notes and a long, accented one) definitely imitates an actual knocking, and this is made more portentous at the outset by holding the sustained note to an extra length.

With this basic pattern established, the first subject grows right out of it. It is really nothing more than a series of experiments with the motto, at different levels of pitch, but so arranged as to form a logical melody.

The motto is heard again, half a tone higher than before, with an added octave above, this time only once. Again the melody picks it up, as though trying to interpret its meaning, proceeding in the same experimental vein as before, and ignoring the rhythmic warnings in the bass, until nearly sixty measures have been covered. Then the horns break in and insist upon a new theme.

It is immediately supplied by the strings, a beautiful melody of distinctly lyric quality, suggesting an almost naïve security in the face of hostile elements. Even during its first statement, the bass continues to reiterate the warning rhythm of the motto, until the whole orchestra breaks in with a transitional theme.

After a complete repetition of this rather brief exposition, the development section begins with another warning from the horns and an answer from the whole orchestra. This starts the first subject on its way in a new key, and it proceeds through a maze of modulation and instrumental alternation to a violent shaking out of dissonant chords, till agreement is finally reached on the rounding out of the motto as first suggested by the horns.

The recapitulation begins with the first subject in its original key, but with a smoothly flowing bass that gives it a gentler and less menacing character. A curious little solo by the oboe adds to this feeling of sympathy, but soon the struggle is on again, with the same development that had been heard in the first exposition of the theme.

A battle of tonality follows, with further defiant shaking of tremendous chords. The tonic C minor is the winner, and its unison reminder of the motto in that key rides roughshod over protesting figures in the violins. The struggle degenerates into an exchange of mere shouts of defiance, and a last attempt to suggest the beauty of that second subject is drowned out with inexorable chords. The fight is practically over when the motto takes a hand once more, this time riding to a crashing climax on an unexpected chord. There is a short coda, in which the motto tiptoes in very softly, building up a little fugal effect as other instruments come in with it. This is the last sign of mercy or peace. Fate wins out, and its final beatings are expended on innocent chords in C minor, a brutal finish if ever there was one.

But don't forget that there are three more movements to this *Fifth Symphony* of Ludwig van Beethoven.

THE REST OF THE SYMPHONY

It has already been stated that such movements of a symphony as are not in sonata form may appear as mere elaborations of the song form (which is really what sonata form itself turns out to be) or as a rondo or minuet, going back to the dance forms, or finally a theme with variations. The last-named is a common structure for the slow movement, which usually stands second among the four parts of a symphony, and, as it happens, the slow movement of Beethoven's *Fifth Symphony* is essentially nothing more than a set of variations on a theme.

This theme, however, really has two distinct parts, which might be considered as first and second subjects, but their development is almost entirely in the manner of variations, and there is nothing to suggest the three-part division of sonata form. The melody itself has an interesting history, for this is one of the themes that Beethoven developed most painstakingly in his famous notebooks, those personal records that he always carried with him for jotting down stray musical thoughts and inspirations. According to the notebook, the slow melody of the *Fifth Symphony* was a long time in taking shape, first occurring to the composer in one of the forms that he later relegated to a mere variation.

Its evolution was in the direction of simplicity and nobility of utterance, and when it emerged in its final form, it had discarded all non-essentials of decoration. The first part of this great melody is announced by the violas and cellos in unison, over a pizzicato bass, in a slow (but not too slow) triple time. (Again the reader is advised to use phonograph records if this analysis is to be followed.) The tones of the major chord are prominent in this theme.

The second half (or second subject, as preferred) shows a basic melody pattern of two introductory tones and a simple series of three tones right up the scale.

Each variation of these basic melodies becomes more complicated, finally arriving at an almost jazzy effect of breaking up of the accompaniment in soft chords. The first subject becomes a plaintive "blue" tune (shockingly similar to the modern saxophone treatment). It is picked up by the cellos with a little further distortion, while the oboe utters grace-note comments up above. The melody becomes more recognizable as it gets back into the original key, and then comes the final surprise of the movement, the touch for which every lover of this symphony waits expectantly. The familiar closing strain of that first subject starts once more, but this time instead of the conventional drop to the keynote, a heart-rending change carries the melody all the way up to the major seventh—one of those stabs of genius that create involuntary shudders of delight.

After that there is nothing more to be said. The coda is a mere arrangement of the tones of the major triad, which have been so prominent all the way through the movement.

COMPLETING BEETHOVEN'S FIFTH

If you have become interested in this battle between Beethoven and Fate, it may be just as well to hear the two remaining movements of the *Fifth Symphony* immediately. The slow movement may have indicated quiet confidence, or perhaps a temporary resignation. But the fast movement that follows is defiant, sardonic, almost blasphemous in its contemptuous treatment of the Fate motto.

Yet it is unmistakably a dance movement, almost like an unwieldy minuet in form. A sepulchral phrase rises from the basses at the outset, in triple time, answered naïvely and unsuspectingly by the woodwinds above and strings. The combination is repeated almost literally, and that is as far as it gets for the moment.

Like the fist that Beethoven shook at heaven on his deathbed, a mocking version of the four-note motto is shaken out by the horns, all on the same tone, and with an insistence on the triple time that suggests an unwilling giant being forced to dance. But this piece of monumental sarcasm develops into a real theme before it gives way to the opening question and answer once more. A slight development leads to another display of defiance with the distorted motto, an octave higher than before.

A strange co-operation soon begins between the first and second subjects, developing into an actual dance that is as close to lighthearted gaiety as this curious Scherzo ever comes. The noisy monotone of the motto interrupts and brings the section to a quick close.

What would be the trio of a minuet begins with a boisterous theme introduced by the basses and carried on in fugal style by other instruments. The passage is repeated, and then the counterpoint becomes more and more involved, until the orchestra wearies of all this rough play and permits the first section to return in its original key.

A variety of treatment is secured by the simple process of letting the strings play the sepulchral phrase pizzicato instead of with the bows, and immediately the whole atmosphere brightens. One can already scent approaching victory as the plucked strings carry on into a repetition of the lighthearted dance of the first section.

The last lingering doubt is expressed in a long-sustained soft tone by the strings, as the death rattle of the fateful motto sounds on a monotonous C. Confidence returns in a series of experiments with the material of the opening phrase, which soon drown out the motto and become more and more clearly a desperate, indefatigable struggle to get into the martial key of C major. It is accomplished at last in a tremendous crescendo, and without a pause the march of triumph begins.

BEETHOVEN'S GREAT FINALE

An amazing march in C major, a veritable frenzy of triumph, yet broad and sane and human in its gloating over a conquered Fate, constitutes the Finale of the symphony, a piece of gigantic effrontery such as had not been heard in music up to that time and has seldom been equaled since. It is impossible to describe this victory parade, and a mere quotation of its chief melodies would give only a faint idea of the actual content. Obviously, it gets its effect once more from that universal pattern of the major triad, followed by equally universal scale progressions. It soon runs into a lighter dance rhythm, with triplets suggesting that of the previous movement and possibly a final mockery of the rat-a-tat of Fate.

Beethoven is prodigal with his tunes by this time, and he introduces yet another, this time broad and confident, as though smiling with satisfaction, and again following the scale downward (as in the familiar hymn, *Joy to the World*). He insists on a repetition of the whole march of triumph, and then proceeds to develop the dancing passage in triplets, with much calling back and forth among the instruments, like a good-natured crowd after a football game. And now it becomes evident that the composer was actually mocking the Fate motto in these triplets, for it is heard in pitiful protest, only to receive another good shaking as the full orchestra rushes on to a series of chords which seem about to bring back the march melody.

But Beethoven changes his mind with astonishing suddenness. It is his whim to exhibit that Fate motto once more, in a completely tamed condition, like a dancing bear that has learned not to resist. In a soft minor, and a fairly slow triple time, the subdued motto penitently follows his orders, going through several tricks of modulation and finally permitting itself to be lashed into a crescendo that brings back the march melody for the last time.

It is given a complete hearing, including the dancing triplets, and the broad scale melody, with some development of this and the triplets. Tonic and dominant chords seem to announce a finish, but the end is not yet. A variation of the second strain occurs to Beethoven, with an imitation still higher, and this proves interesting enough for a repetition, developing into more and more excited dance modulations.

Only a coda remains, and it starts with a presto change to fast time on the broad scale theme, which, however, is merely an introduction to still more excitement, and with a hasty reminder of the triad that started the triumphal march, the symphony settles down to a thorough mastication of the C-major chord, worrying it like a happy animal, playing its tones up and down, singly and with tremolo, all on a fortissimo level that shouts to the world, "This is going on until I choose to stop!" And it takes eight closing chords before it does.

It will now be worth while to listen to all three of these important symphonies, Mozart's in G minor, Beethoven's in C minor, and Schubert's Unfinished in B minor, of which the first is a fine example of how a minor key can sound happy, while Beethoven gets the same effect by going into the corresponding major. There are plenty of opportunities of hearing all of these symphonies in the concert hall as well as on records and via radio. Each of them should be heard many times, until at least the outstanding melodies and the chief details of form and instrumentation are quite familiar.

CHAPTER X STORY AND PICTURE MUSIC

THE PRECEDING DISCUSSIONS and analyses of symphonic music (which should be read only in connection with actual hearings of the compositions on records) have given some indication of a general distinction between absolute and program music. In the broadest sense of both terms, the former refers to any music that receives no help whatever toward its interpretation by the listener in the form of a descriptive title, detailed explanation or actual words, while all music that receives any such help may legitimately be classed as having a program.

Freely speaking, therefore, all opera, all songs, cantatas, oratorios, etc., whose words convey a definite meaning which the music merely amplifies, are obviously program music, as well as all instrumental pieces that have even a definite title of more than a merely formal significance. (Such titles have often been supplied without the intention or even the consent of the composer, sometimes after his death, and the habit of trying to read into music stories and pictures of which its creator never dreamed is a common one. The ballet and motion pictures have done much to add compulsory programs to absolute music, often with fantastic results.)

Technically, however, the term "program music" is limited to instrumental compositions (without words) for which the composers voluntarily supplied either a descriptive title or explanatory notes. Such music may be narrative in character (telling a definite story) or merely descriptive or pictorial (dealing with a scene from Nature or an actual picture), and it may contain passages that are frankly imitative of sounds outside the realm of recognized man-made music, such as birdcalls, rain, wind and thunder, a babbling brook, etc. In a few cases, such imitation has been accomplished by means that are not considered legitimately musical.[1]

As a general rule, program music is easier to grasp at a first hearing than is absolute music, and conversely it may be argued that it is likely to have less significance, for the very reason that it has so much to lean upon. If people are told in advance that a piece of music represents a certain picture or story, they will accept almost anything in good faith, and the same obvious effects may serve for an outburst of human temper or a thunderstorm, the lament of a grief-stricken mother or a passionate love song, the rushing of a stream or a ride on a merry-go-round. The system is reduced to absurdity in such familiar tricks as the story of the *Three Trees*, in which the same combinations of tones at the piano always represent the same dramatic "realism." It is the favorite form of attack upon music in general, and the easiest way of making it ridiculous. (Countless vaudeville acts, some of them very funny, have been built upon this simple principle.)

While admitting the obviousness of much program music (and the more complete the program, the more insignificant the music is likely to be), it should not be overlooked that most of the great composers indulged occasionally in such relaxation, quite aside from the use of actual words, or the still greater support of operatic scenery and costumes.

There are some very early sacred sonatas, for organ and clavier, presumably describing such Biblical scenes as *The Combat of David and Goliath*, *The Sickness and Recovery of Hezekiah* and *The Marriage of Jacob*. An old French composer, Daquin, wrote a piano piece called *Le Coucou*, built on the pattern of the cuckoo's song, and still played. Domenico Scarlatti composed a *Cat's Fugue*, and the great Bach left a *Capriccio on the Departure of a Beloved Brother*, in which the postilion's horn is imitated.

Other early attempts at program music included various *Combats of the Birds* (always a popular subject) and noisy battle scenes. *The Battle of Prague* was much played at one time (there was also an early American description of the Battle of Trenton) and one of the weakest large works ever written by Beethoven was his *Battle*

[1]The spectacular example is still the wind machine in the *Don Quixote* of Richard Strauss.

Symphony, although it contained such good tunes as the French *Malbrouck* (*We won't go home until morning*), *God Save the King* and *Rule, Britannia.*

Haydn composed an amusing symphony about chickens (*La Poule*), and there were similar descriptive and imitative effects in the early music of Lully, Rameau and others. Beethoven jokingly gave one of his rondos the title *Wrath Over a Lost Farthing*, but he was not responsible for the labeling of his *Moonlight Sonata*, which had nothing whatever to do with moonlight or the love story so commonly read into it. On the other hand, Beethoven produced some of the finest and most legitimate program music in his *Pastoral Symphony* (No. 6) which includes definite and well-marked descriptions of scenes in the country, birdcalls (with the cuckoo again prominent), a storm, and the subsequent calm and thanksgiving of the peasants. (It has now reached the screen in *Fantasia.*)

Beethoven called his third symphony *Eroica*, and on its original title page announced that his hero was Napoleon, but later eliminated this in disappointment over his fallen idol. This "hero" symphony is one of his greatest (some critics place it at the very top of the list of nine) and contains a remarkable funeral march. The seventh Beethoven symphony was called by Wagner "the apotheosis of the dance," and has received a number of other titles gratuitously, none of them particularly apt. But the Fate motto of the fifth may be considered a legitimate "program," and the ninth eventually resorts to actual words in its choral Finale, preceded by an equally realistic debate among the orchestral instruments as to what the melody for this Ode to Joy shall be. There are definite programs also in the incidental music to *The Ruins of Athens* (including the popular *Turkish March* and *Dance of the Dervishes*) and the overtures to *Fidelio* (*Leonore*), *Egmont* and *Coriolanus.*

Beethoven gave one of his piano sonatas the title of *Farewell*, and recognized others as *Pathétique* and *Appassionata*, descriptive terms which are justified by the mood of the music, but such names as Waldstein and Kreutzer are merely of historical significance, and with all possible respect for Tolstoy's book, *The Kreutzer Sonata*, it cannot be said to have a thing to do with the actual music, which is a far from sensual piece of absolute composition.

ROMANTIC PROGRAM MUSIC

Robert Schumann, one of the first Romanticists of music, naturally wrote much in the program style, and his meaning was generally quite clear. He filled his piano music with references to his own life and that of his friends, calling himself by such fanciful names as Florestan and Eusebius, and imagining a secret fraternity called the Davidsbündler, whose mission it was to battle against the Philistines in art. Schumann's *Carnaval* is a charmingly imaginative set of short pieces, all in the program style, with descriptive titles, including an imitation of Chopin, suggestions of Harlequin and Columbine, and a final *March of the Davidsbündler against the Philistines.*

There is a whole series of *Davidsbündler Dances,* as well as *Kreisleriana,* named for the *Kapellmeister* (conductor) Kreisler of the stories of E. T. A. Hoffman. *Papillons* (Butterflies) resembles the *Carnaval* in its musical pictures of gay scenes and characters, and some of the same melodic material appears in both pieces. There are also the famous *Scenes from Childhood* (*Kinderszenen*) and an *Album for the Young,* containing the familiar *Träumerei* (Dreaming) among other little gems of program music. Schumann's orchestral music includes three program overtures, *Genoveva, Faust* and *Manfred.*

Another composer of the romantic school who wrote much program music was Mendelssohn, best remembered today for such short piano pieces as the *Spring Song, Spinning Song, Consolation* and other "Songs without Words." But his orchestral compositions also leaned toward the program style, perhaps the finest being his youthful *Midsummer Night's Dream,* a fascinating musical description of Fairyland, with some outstanding realism in the scene of Nick Bottom's metamorphosis, expressed by unmistakable brays from the orchestra. The Mendelssohn *Wedding March* (played for the exit, not the entrance) is part of the incidental music to this Shakespearean play. This same composer wrote symphonies which he labeled *The Reformation, Italian* and *Scotch,* and overtures describing *Calm Sea and a Prosperous Voyage, The Fair Melusina* and *Fingal's Cave* in the Hebrides Islands. (Listen for the regular wash of the waves in the last.)

Chopin wrote much program music for the piano, although most of his pieces had such noncommittal titles as Etude, Waltz, Prelude, etc. One of his best-known études or studies has the name of *Butter-*

fly, and there is also the famous "waltz of the little dog chasing his tail," likewise called the *Minute Waltz*, because of the supposed length of time required to play it. There is a prelude known quite properly as *The Raindrop*, and a polonaise equally well called "military." One of the Chopin sonatas contains the most famous of all funeral marches; there is a beautiful Nocturne that describes a solitary evening on the island of Majorca, with a sailor's song heard above the rippling of the water.

Hector Berlioz went in heavily for program music, calling one of his symphonies *Fantastic*, another *Romeo and Juliet* and another *Harold in Italy*, all with elaborate descriptive material. (Not satisfied with his own descriptive, narrative and pictorial music, he insisted on reading special meanings into the absolute music of other composers, some of which did not turn out so convincingly.) An overture called *Roman Carnival* is still popular on the concert stage.

THE MODERN ATTITUDE

But program music has received the greatest attention from the more modern composers, who have also achieved the best results with this popular style of composition. Franz Liszt tended instinctively toward the dramatic and the realistic, and his imagination was the first to create "symphonic poems" with such subjects as Orpheus, Tasso, Francesca da Rimini, Mazeppa and the Battle of the Huns. *Les Préludes* is an impressive musical picture of approaching death, and there are two choral symphonies entitled *Faust* and *Dante*. Among his smaller piano works are the familiar *Liebestraum* (Dream of Love), *Waldesrauschen* (*Murmuring Woods*), the *Loreley* (not the popular melody, but a more elaborate instrumental treatment), *St. Francis Preaching to the Birds*, *St. Francis Walking on the Waves*, *Dance of the Gnomes*, a *Mephisto Waltz* and an étude bearing the title *Un Soupir* (A Sigh).

Wagner wrote a *Faust* overture, but his great contribution to program music is in the preludes to his operas, all of which have found a permanent place in the orchestral concert repertoire. The preliminary music of the *Flying Dutchman*, *Rienzi*, *Lohengrin*, *Tannhäuser* and *Die Meistersinger* tells the whole story of those dramatic works, while the *Vorspiel* to *Tristan und Isolde* remains the greatest expression of human love in the literature of music. For religious exaltation the *Vorspiel* to *Parsifal* is similarly outstanding, with the *Good Friday Spell* generally combined with it in concert performance. All this actually becomes absolute music of the highest type when separated from its operatic background, and deserves a hearing for its own sake, quite apart from any program. The same is true of the beautiful *Siegfried Idyl*, written as a birthday present for Wagner's wife, Cosima, the daughter of Liszt, and there are instrumental interludes such as the Torchlight Procession from *Lohengrin*, or the Rhine Journey from *Siegfried*, or even the Ballet from *Tannhäuser*, well worthy of independent performance as program music.

French composers have been both prolific and successful with descriptive and pictorial compositions. Gounod's *Funeral March of a Marionette* is still widely played, and there is a popular little violin piece called *The Bee* by François Schubert (not the song writer), now permanently associated with Jack Benny.

Saint-Saëns specialized in program music, winning success with his tone poems, *Phaëton, Le Rouet d'Omphale* (The Spinning Wheel of Omphale) and the realistic *Danse Macabre* (Dance of Death) in which, after the striking of midnight, the xylophone represents skeletons keeping time with their bones upon tombstones, while Death plays the tune upon his fiddle (with a flat E string) and the whole ghostly scene is brought to a close by a reassuring "cockadoodledoo" at dawn, with the dancers scurrying back to their graves. A far more cheerful piece of program music is the Saint-Saëns *Carnival of the Animals*, which contains not only the famous *Swan*, played as a cello solo, but humorous musical descriptions of turtles, lions and even critics.

Debussy has made thousands happy with his delightful *Children's Corner*, including the *Golliwogg's Cake-walk* (a piece of French ragtime), *Jimbo's Lullaby* (obviously referring to an elephant), *The Snow Is Dancing* and *The Little Shepherd.* His *Prelude to the Afternoon of a Faun* contains unique beauties of the impressionistic school, based upon a poem by Mallarmé, and there is realism as well as beauty in such other orchestral works as *La Mer* (The Sea) and the two Nocturnes, *Nuages* (Clouds) and *Fêtes.* In his piano music of a more serious nature than the *Children's Corner*, Debussy includes many picturesque titles such as *The Girl with the Flaxen Hair, Goldfish, Gar-*

dens in the Rain, The Submerged Cathedral, Moonlight (*Clair de lune*), etc.

Other French program music worth mentioning is the *Sorcerer's Apprentice* of Paul Dukas, a popular tone poem for orchestra (immortalized by Mickey Mouse in Walt Disney's *Fantasia*), Vincent d'Indy's *Istar* symphony, Maurice Ravel's spectacular *Bolero* (a most interesting study in an elaborately monotonous rhythmic pattern, with extraordinary instrumentation), and Honegger's musical description of a locomotive, *Pacific 231*.

THE RUSSIAN STYLE

Among the Russians Tschaikowsky leads the way in program music, with his fourth, fifth and sixth (*Pathétique*) symphonies, all supplied with explanatory material of some sort, in addition to one which he called *Manfred*. The popular *Pathétique* lives up to its title by ending with a movement of abject melancholy, after a triumphal march almost as optimistic as that of Beethoven's fifth Finale. Tschaikowsky's fifth also has a program concerned with the human struggle against Fate, this time resulting victoriously, with the minor "motto" of the start reappearing in major at the close, in an exultant march time that again harks back to the spirit of Beethoven. The fourth is perhaps the most interesting of the three, particularly in its third (Scherzo) movement, largely a continuous pizzicato by the strings, representing the bustle and stir of a crowd, and in the Finale, built upon a Russian folk-song, *The Birch Tree*.

Some of Tschaikowsky's finest orchestral writing is to be found in his Fantasy Overture called *Romeo and Juliet*, which was planned as part of an opera, and contains a vivid balcony scene, as well as other details of the drama. His *Francesca da Rimini* is also excellent program music, and most popular of all is the *Nutcracker Suite*, a fairy story in music, with dances by all sorts of fascinating toys and sweetmeats, and a final *Waltz of the Flowers* that is one of the best of its kind. Tschaikowsky's *Ballet of the Seasons*, containing the well-known *June Barcarolle* (cf. *Lover come back to me*) and such piano pieces as the *Troika* (cf. *Horses*) are perhaps also worth mentioning.

That older realist of Russian music, Moussorgsky, wrote a convincing nature study, *A Night on Bald Mountain*, as well as *Pictures at an Exposition*, and his pupil, Rimsky-Korsakoff, contributed the justly popular symphonic poem, *Scheherazade*, with its glamorous tales from the *Arabian Nights* (all strung together by a violin theme representing the fair storyteller herself), as well as the brilliant *Flight of the Bumblebee*, the *Russian Easter*, etc.

Rachmaninoff has given us a musical picture of *The Island of the Dead*, after the famous painting by Böcklin, and his piano compositions, particularly the hackneyed *Prelude in C-sharp minor*, have been burdened with programs, mostly not of his own choosing. Scriabin's symphonies are programmatic, especially the *Prometheus*, which was supplied with a definite part for the "color-organ." Much of Stravinsky's ballet music, such as *The Fire Bird*, *Petrouschka* and the *Sacre du Printemps* (Rites of Spring), has become established in the orchestral repertoire, and may be considered legitimate program music, even without stage effects. The *Caucasian Sketches* of Ippolitoff-Ivanoff and Glazounoff's *Seasons* are fairly obvious but attractive pieces of the same sort, on a smaller scale.

Smetana's musical description of the river Moldau and his string quartet *Aus meinem Leben* are characteristic program music of Bohemia, to which may be added the *New World Symphony* of Dvorak and his *American Quartet*, both employing Negro melodies. Brahms composed mostly absolute music, but his *Edward Ballade*, for the piano, is a fine bit of dramatic realism. Gustav Mahler attempted to give some of his symphonies elaborate programs, including choral effects and solo voices, but his results were not always equal to his intentions.

The best composer of them all, for real program music, is Richard Strauss. His symphonic poems go far beyond the models of Liszt or Saint-Saëns, and will probably be remembered as supreme works of their kind. *Till Eulenspiegel* is a good one for a first hearing, with its fantastic story of the medieval clown whose tricks land him eventually on the gallows. The genius of the composition lies in the amazing way in which Strauss has used a basic motif of an impish, almost vulgar character to represent Eulenspiegel himself and then transformed it into a melody of spiritual beauty for the apotheosis of his hero in death.

Don Juan, based upon the poem of Niklaus Lenau, convincingly describes the desperate search of the classic libertine for a pure and perfect love, and is a remarkable piece of instrumentation, full of melodic inspiration as well. *Tod und Verklärung* (Death and Transfiguration) is an elaboration of the idea first used by Liszt in *Les Préludes,* but on a far higher plane of creative genius. Here also the melodies must be called inspired. *Don Quixote* has already been mentioned. There is a philosophical and rather difficult *Also sprach Zarathustra* (Thus Spake Zarathustra) and finally the glorious *Heldenleben* (A Hero's Life) which may be considered largely autobiographical. The hero and his wife are both given beautiful themes; there is much instrumental bickering on the part of the hero's enemies, and a brutally realistic battle scene, in which the sardonic march is worth a whole treatise on disarmament. Toward the close, Strauss brings in quotations from several of his own works, including the lovely song, *Traum durch die Dämmerung* (Dream in the Twilight).

When program music reaches such levels as this, it can hold its own with any of the world's absolute music.

MUSIC IN MOTION PICTURES

The modern screen has developed into a most important medium for program music, with almost unlimited possibilities for the future. Motion pictures make use of music in two ways, first as a background to the action and dialogue, and second as actual subject matter, with the film illustrating a definite piece of music, instead of merely using it for atmosphere.

The "background music" of Hollywood has been produced largely by a group of composers who specialized in this type of work, all excellent musicians, with particular aptitude and experience in fitting their scores to the needs of the screen. Their chief problem is to keep the music unobtrusive, while at the same time utilizing its full possibilities for emphasizing dramatic climaxes or supplying a variety of atmosphere. Occasionally there are difficulties due to the necessity for cutting a film, with consequent damage to musical continuity.

The Hollywood musical specialists include such outstanding composers as Erich Korngold, Alfred Newman, Max Steiner, Franz Waxman, Dimitri Tiomkin, Herbert Stothart, Miklos Rozsa, Roy Webb, Victor Young and Scott Bradley. Recognized composers, not necessarily specializing in film music, are often called in for particularly significant assignments, and these have almost invariably proved highly successful. In this group one finds such well-known names as Louis Gruenberg, Werner Janssen, Aaron Copland, Virgil Thomson, Alexander Tansman, Gail Kubik, Richard Hageman and Bernard Herrmann.

But the screen's greatest contribution to music is in the direct presentation of masterpieces, which thus find a new and enormous audience under the most favorable conditions. The lives of various composers have been filmed, sometimes with the aid of Technicolor, and we may look forward to a practical presentation of grand opera on the screen. Admittedly the most effective illustration of individual compositions has been in cartoon form, as in Walt Disney's popular *Fantasia*, with still more significant things now on the way.

CHAPTER XI SOMETHING ABOUT SONGS

THE MOST OBVIOUS program music, of course, is that which includes words, leaving no doubt whatever as to the meaning of a composition. Such program music may take the form of a single song, for one or more voices, or a combination of vocal numbers strung together (perhaps with instrumental connecting links) as an opera, an oratorio, a cantata, or some other kind of religious music, possibly even a music-drama of the Wagnerian type, in which the entire structure is more elaborate and closely knit than in any other style of vocal music.

The principles of the simple song form are the same as those of the larger combinations of words and music, and it is easiest to analyze them within the smaller frame. The distinction between folk-song and art-song has already been made. The former is valuable for its honesty, its directness, and often for its melodic invention, which may be the result of an actual evolution by way of constant repetition with slight variations. But it is a mistake to think of folk-song as the product of organized community effort. It begins always with a single composer (generally unidentified), and merely has the advantage of being passed on by word of mouth and thus gradually achieving a permanently popular version.

Folk-song is inevitably strophic in form, the same tune serving for each stanza, no matter how much the meaning of the words may vary. This means that a successful folk-song must have a very good tune, and should preferably be sung by people who can make that tune express many different things. Folk-song exposes the absurdity of arguing that any melodic progression of tones has a definite meaning all its own. The same tunes have been used with equal success not only for the different stanzas of one song, but for various other texts of different kinds. Some of the finest hymns in the world were originally folk-songs, often with distinctly vulgar words.

A tune usually has a fairly definite character of seriousness or gaiety, depending on its major or minor mode, and on the speed of its tempo. But beyond this, the words are of tremendous importance in establishing the final effect of the music. Try the experiment of singing the *Battle Hymn of the Republic* in the dignified and spiritual style that befits the original text by Julia Ward Howe. Then sing *John Brown's Body* to the same tune. Finally sing the popular nonsense verses, *One grasshopper jumped right over the other grasshopper's back,* and compare the results. The tune is always the same, but the effects are entirely different, depending on the words.

Similar comparisons can be made by singing any two or more accepted sets of words to the same tune. A splendid example is the *Irish Tune from County Derry,* also known as the *Londonderry Air,* which is equally effective, although in rather different ways, with the words "Would God I were the tender apple blossom" and "Danny Boy." The Irish love song, *Believe me if all those endearing young charms,* becomes a stately anthem as *Fair Harvard,* and the ribald *To Anacreon in Heaven* has more than thirty other sets of words, of which the best known and most dignified are those of *The Star-Spangled Banner.*

Art-song is the reverse of folk-song in almost every way.[1] Where folk-song establishes a melody, which may then be fitted with a variety of words, art-song begins with a definite poem, striving to fit it with music that will express every detail of its meaning. Often several composers have been inspired by the same poem, and the results are decidedly interesting. Rudyard Kipling, Goethe and Heinrich Heine are among the poets whose work has lent itself so naturally to music that the same texts were made to serve again and again, sometimes with little to choose between equally successful but quite different settings.

[1]The writer's recent collection of *Fifty-five Art Songs* (C. C. Birchard & Co., Boston) contains some of the best examples of this form of music.

ANALYZING ART-SONG

While an art-song may be strophic, and often is (although this type of setting is generally called "folk-like") the technique of its form almost demands a more thorough and detailed following of the words. The Germans call this style *durchkomponiert,* literally "composed throughout," and while there is no English equivalent for the term, as the opposite of strophic, the word "thorough" may conveniently serve the purpose. The very nature of such composition implies a more elaborate, a more subtle, a more refined creative art, although perhaps with less obvious melodic appeal. Unfortunately, art-song also permits an utterly uninspired composer to make a fairly impressive showing with nothing more than the ability to follow the metre and perhaps the meaning of a poem in a fashion that makes musical sense. Such an artificial setting is so easy to compose, with all the inspiration supplied by the poem, that many a sincere craftsman in music actually deceives himself into imagining a real talent of his own, where none exists.

The great composers of art-song (and there have been many) were never satisfied to set a poem with a merely conventional set of musical phrases corresponding to the accents of the text. They insisted on a basic melody of independent value and form, fitting the mood and emotional content of the poem as well as its metrical outlines, and they built this up with a carefully wrought accompaniment, a subtle combination of keys and harmonies, and a delicate use of modulation that produced the effect of a new and complete work of art.

Some verses, such as the swinging rhythms of Kipling, practically sing themselves, and almost any kind of a tune would do, since the listeners are primarily interested in the words. It may almost be argued that some of the greatest and most familiar poems in literature are not well adapted to art-song, and have never been successfully set to music. On the other hand, a great many minor poems, some of them by distinctly minor poets, have resulted in exquisite songs, if only because the words did not overwhelm the music with their importance.

Composers of the German *Lied,* which remains the model of modern art-song, were well aware of this, and did not hesitate to use text material of seemingly small importance, often by obscure poets of

Only twenty cents for music that is immortal

THROUGHOUT HIS SHORT LIFE of only thirty-one years, Franz Schubert never received an adequate financial return for any of his music. He was unquestionably the most prolific composer of all time, the one who most nearly approached the popular conception of pure and spontaneous genius, producing masterpieces without an effort. His songs alone total over six hundred, and many of these are perfect examples of their kind.

Schubert sometimes wrote as many as six songs in a day, putting them away in a drawer and forgetting about them as soon as he had finished. Some of them were sold later for as little as twenty cents apiece. His friends used to say that he could set anything to music; and he actually wrote the melody of *Hark, Hark, the Lark*, on the back of a bill of fare in a restaurant, where the inspiration seized him immediately on reading Shakespeare's poem.

Even though he lived in abject poverty, Franz Schubert was not unhappy. He had a gay, carefree disposition, and he was amply satisfied with expressing himself in music and talking and playing with a small circle of intimate friends. He began composing as a small boy, when he had no money even for the purchase of music paper. By the time he was eighteen he had written the great *Erlking* and several other important songs. Music leaped full-grown from his heart, his brain, and his fingers, and his chief problem was to write it down fast enough.

Obviously such a haphazard technique was often open to criticism; but the spirit was always there, regardless of the form. Today the whole world loves Schubert's *Serenade*, his *Ave Maria*, his *Marche Militaire*, and his *Unfinished Symphony*. A growing public is becoming familiar also with his larger works and his piano and chamber music. Schubert sold his pieces for a few pennies, but his immortality is beyond price.

their personal acquaintance. The word *Lied* really means nothing more than "song," but it has become almost a technical term in music to describe the romantic, typically German style of song writing, immortalized by Schubert, Schumann, Franz, Brahms, Hugo Wolf and Richard Strauss. A hearing of the outstanding songs of these composers is the best possible introduction to art-song in general, and it will be found that much of the finest song writing of other countries (excepting of course the folk-songs themselves) is built upon the foundation of the *Lied.*

EARLY MASTERS OF ART-SONG

Franz Schubert is still considered by many authorities the greatest of all song writers, partly because of his amazing productiveness (he turned out over six hundred songs, in addition to a wealth of instrumental music, in his tragically short life of thirty-one years), partly because he was the first composer to give the art-song its proper importance, and partly because of the many and varied manifestations of genius that are constantly evident in his work. It would be foolish to say that all of Schubert's songs were good, for this is decidedly not the case. He was not nearly critical enough of the texts he selected (it was said of him that he could set a bill of fare to music), and sometimes perhaps not sufficiently self-critical either. His friends accused him of working too fast and being too often satisfied with a first draft of any composition, and since he was perhaps the most purely inspirational composer that ever lived, he rather resented this criticism.

Schubert was by no means the first composer to write *Lieder.* Johann Sebastian Bach wrote a deeply moving love song, *Bist du bei mir* (If thou art with me), and his son, Karl Philipp Emanuel Bach, was responsible for some dignified settings of Gellert's *Geistliche Oden* (Sacred Odes). Haydn was represented by some lovely songs, of which the best known today are *The Mermaid* and *My mother bids me bind my hair.* Mozart's dainty music to Goethe's *Das Veilchen* (The Violet) is still deservedly popular.

Beethoven made some interesting experiments in the song form. His *Adelaide* is a classic of the frankly sentimental type, far more elaborate than most of the songs of its day, and with a characteristic beauty of melody and accompaniment. His setting of Goethe's familiar song of Mignon, *Kennst du das Land?* (Knowest thou the land?) is one of the simplest yet most effective of the many that have graced that poem. But his greatest contribution to song literature was in the creation of the first real cycle of art-song, *An die ferne Geliebte* (To the Distant Loved One). These songs are definitely linked together by piano interludes, and there is a reminder of the opening melody at the close, giving the whole series a unity of music as well as of thought.

Beethoven's sketchbook shows that he planned a setting of the famous *Erlkönig* (Erlking), one of the prodigious achievements of Schubert, later also set to music by Carl Loewe, essentially a composer of ballads. (Loewe's best song was the old English *Edward*, but his *Erlking* has dramatic power, even though it lacks the inspiration of Schubert's.)

SONGS BY A PRODIGY

Schubert's *Erlking*, written when he was only eighteen, and still one of his most popular songs, remains one of the miracles of music and as fitting an example as may be found of its composer's individual genius. The words are by Goethe, always an inspiration to the musicians of his time, and the thrilling story of the father riding through the forest at night, with a sick child in his arms, invites realistic treatment.

Schubert immediately suggests the galloping of the horse in his piano introduction (octaves played in triplets), and the portentous notes of the bass create an atmosphere of horror, with the moaning of the wind through the trees. After the narrator has briefly described the scene, a dramatic dialogue occurs between the father and his terror-stricken child, who thinks he sees the Erlking following them. (The name of this ghostly creature has never been translated, but literally it means the "king of the alders.") Suddenly, the voice of the Erlking himself is heard, in an enticing whisper, promising the child joy and riches if he will come with him.

The cries of the boy become more anguished, and the father tries in vain to quiet him. As the Erlking's voice is heard again, the accompaniment changes to a harplike serenade. Once more the child's discordant shrieks answer (with the voice and accompaniment only half a tone apart, a daring but completely effective dissonance) and again the father's soothing tones are of no avail. The final attack of the Erlking changes suddenly from blandishment to the threat of violence, and the climactic outcry of the child (each time a half tone higher than before) indicates that the threat has been carried out. From there to the end of the song there is a feeling of desperate hurry and impending tragedy. As the horse finally gallops into the courtyard of the inn, the rhythm of the hoofbeats slows down. A single line of recitative, spoken rather than sung, finishes the story with brutal suddenness. The child is dead.

The *Erlking* was published as op. 1 among the works of Schubert, but actually it was preceded by *Gretchen am Spinnrade* (Marguerite at the Spinning-Wheel), the song from Goethe's *Faust.* This is another specimen of incredible precocity in a boy of seventeen, showing an astonishingly mature grasp of the tragic text and an instinctive musicianship which gives the setting that stamp of inevitability that only a few masterworks possess. Just as the *Erlking* achieved realism through the galloping accompaniment, so the song of Marguerite indicates the constant whirring of the spinning-wheel. The minor melody follows the words with dramatic fidelity. When the climax arrives with the memory of the lover's kiss, the wheel stops for a moment, then resumes its whirring gradually, almost wearily. Another climax is reached in the melody before the hapless Marguerite finally lets both her voice and the spinning-wheel die out.

It is impossible to give here much more than the mere titles of Schubert's most significant songs. They must be heard for the enjoyment of their spontaneous melodic invention, the consistent rightness of their accompaniments, the logic of their form, and their fidelity to the spirit and letter of the text. Many are now available on records.

Some of the finest of the Schubert *Lieder* are contained in his three cycles, *Die schöne Müllerin* (The Beautiful Maid of the Mill), *Winterreise* (Winter Journey) and *Schwanengesang* (Swan Song). The first two are real cycles, with a continuous story, while the last is a series of unrelated songs, having in common only the fact that they represented the final creative work of his short life.

The *Müllerlieder* not only refer to the miller's daughter and her disconsolate lover, but owe their words to Wilhelm Müller, a friend of Schubert. Their story is told in twenty songs, beginning with the arrival of the young apprentice, who follows the brook to the mill, and ending with his suicide in the same brook, which throughout has been his confidant and the recipient of his woes.

OTHER CYCLES BY SCHUBERT

The *Winterreise* cycle consists of twenty-four songs, most of them meeting the highest musical standards. The lover this time begins with a dejected farewell and continues through various stages of depression, ending, however, less drastically than in suicide.

Among the fourteen numbers of the *Swan Song* collection, the first, *Liebesbotschaft* (Love's Message), is remarkable for another melody and brook-like accompaniment of the *Müllerlieder* type. The beloved *Serenade* is the fourth in the series, a thoroughly sentimental melody of such enormous appeal that it has resisted every attempt to sing and play it to death. *Aufenthalt* (My Dwelling Place) shows dramatic power and a typical appreciation of Nature, and *Der Atlas* gives a classic representation of the mythological figure supporting the world on his shoulders.

Another folk-like melody appears in *The Fisher Maiden* (*Das Fischermädchen*), and the brief musical picture of *The Town* (*Die Stadt*) is followed by still another favorite, *Am Meer* (By the Sea), drenched in sentimentality, but again irresistible in its melody, harmony and form. Number 13 is the famous *Doppelgänger* (The Phantom Double), which conveys with a few snatches of recitative over sustained, gloomy chords, a terrific portrayal of one who meets his own ghost, lamenting before the window of a lost love. (Try to imagine Heine's words to a conventional folk-tune and you will at once appreciate the difference between folk- and art-song.)

Among other masterpieces of song created by Franz Schubert, mention should be made of the charming *Heidenröslein* (The Wild Rose), which has become practically a folk-song in Germany; the great *Wanderer*, with its unforgettable dramatization of the simple word *Wo?* (Where?); *Death and the Maiden* (*Der Tod und das Mädchen*), with its dramatic dialogue and the calming melody that later served as a theme in a string quartet; *Sei mir gegrüsst* (My Greeting), another melody of the inevitable type; *Frühlingsglaube* (Faith in Spring), of similar charm; *Die Forelle* (The Trout), literally sparkling in its musical suggestion of the flashing water and the fish within its depths; *Die Junge Nonne* (The Young Nun), another powerful piece of dramatic writing, with strong religious feeling; *Ave Maria*, originally a setting of Ellen's Prayer from Scott's *Lady of the Lake*, but today known all over the world as a great melody, regardless of its vocal significance; *Du bist die Ruh'* (Thou art my rest), almost as popular for its sustained melodic beauty and ethereal calmness; Mignon's Song, *Nur wer die Sehnsucht kennt* (None but the longing heart), which should be compared with Tschaikowsky's setting of the same words; *Auf dem Wasser zu singen* (To be sung on the water), once more translating Nature into music, and famous through the piano transcription of Liszt; the *Wanderers Nachtlied* (Wanderer's Night Song); the two inimitable songs from Shakespeare, *Hark, Hark, the Lark* and *Who Is Sylvia?* (of which the former was written on the back of a bill of fare in a restaurant, and later also turned into a brilliant piano composition by Liszt); the first of the *Songs of the Harper*, from Goethe's *Wilhelm Meister; Die Liebe hat gelogen* (Love has lied); *Nacht und Träume* (Night and Dreams), a slow melody of ineffable beauty; *Die Allmacht* (Omnipotence), one of the stateliest and most sublime expressions of religion in music; *An die Musik* (To Music), which, in a perfect melody, expresses the same reverence for music itself; a tender *Wiegenlied* (Lullaby); a *Litany for All Souls' Day*, again baffling in its inevitability; the Ossian songs; the classic *Ganymede;* the sprightly *Musensohn* (Son of the Muses), and finally a little gem, too seldom heard, *Nähe des Geliebten* (Nearness of the Beloved), amazing in the modulations of its accompaniment, and unerring in its direct and simple appeal.

SONG WRITERS AFTER SCHUBERT

Art-song received its greatest stimulus from Schubert, but some later composers actually surpassed him in the emotional quality and musical impressiveness of their work, although none ever equaled his versatility, his pure melodic inspiration or the astonishing volume of his creations. Schumann, Franz, Brahms, Hugo Wolf and Richard Strauss have been mentioned as the great developers of the *Lied* tradition, and they belong with Schubert in setting a standard of song writing for all time. There were other important composers of art-song both in Germany and elsewhere, but these five should be considered first.

Robert Schumann went beyond Schubert in his expression of the romantic and sentimental through music. He was of a less naïve nature, a profound philosopher and critic as well as a creative genius. Most of his great songs were written under the influence of Clara Wieck, one of the finest pianists among women, who became his wife.

Schumann received much of his poetic inspiration from Heinrich Heine, whose deeply sensitive but sardonic nature was most congenial to him. On the technical side, his songs show an elaboration of the accompaniment, often a greater individuality of melody, and a more careful workmanship throughout, with no loss in spontaneity.

Like Schubert, he wrote cycles as well as individual songs. One was called *Myrthen* (Myrtles), containing twenty-six songs dedicated to his beloved Clara. Another was entirely devoted to the poetry of Heine (*Liederkreis von Heine*). A third had the title *Frauenliebe und Leben* (Woman's Love and Life) and the final cycle was the famous *Dichterliebe* (A Poet's Love). All of these cycles contain treasures of song writing which should be heard many times.

From *Myrthen* comes the great *Widmung* (Dedication), whose ecstatic expression of whole-souled sentiment has seldom been equaled in music. The contrast between the unrestrained passion of the first section (repeated at the close) and the slow middle melody (with the reminiscent words, *Du bist die Ruh'*) makes the entire composition a perfect example of song form (A-B-A).

The same cycle included *Der Nussbaum* (generally translated specifically yet guardedly as The Almond Tree), a song of the purest Schubertian melody, yet unmistakably Schumannesque in its treatment. *Die Lotosblume* (The Lotus Flower) is similar in spirit, a quiet Nature study, incredibly lovely in both melody and harmony, with only a slight blemish in the musical division and accenting of the words in the opening sentence (*ängstigt sich*).

Du bist wie eine Blume (Thou art like a flower) is another song from the *Myrthen* cycle that has gained world-wide popularity, again with the clear stamp of Schumann's personality upon every note. (The Schumann setting of these words should be compared with those of Liszt and Rubinstein later.) *Stille Thränen* (Silent Tears) is in the same style, but a more elaborate song. *Alte Laute* (Bygone Tones) again shows remarkable melodic invention in a small compass, this time with a countermelody in the accompaniment. (The same music was used by Schumann for another set of words, *Wer machte dich so krank?*)

A simple melodic pattern, used with rare taste, makes a lilting, folk-like song of *An den Sonnenschein* (To the Sunshine), and the contrasting *Mondnacht* (Moon Night) offers another of those ineffable slow melodies that only genius can create. *Frühlingsnacht* (Spring Night) set a standard of emotional expression that was clearly a model for Strauss many years later, as also the light and fast-moving *Aufträge* (Messages).

Dein Angesicht (Thy Countenance) is another lovely slow melody, with a religious significance, and there is much charm in the *Volksliedchen* (Little Folk-song), beginning *Wenn ich früh in den Garten geh'* (When I go into the garden early), as well as the familiar *Marienwürmchen* (Ladybug), from *A Song Album for the Young.*

The best known dramatic song of Schumann is probably *The Two Grenadiers* (*Die beiden Grenadiere*), with its echo of the *Marseillaise* near the close. It has stood the test of time and overwork admirably.

SCHUMANN'S SONG CYCLES

Frauenliebe und Leben (Woman's Life and Love) has been called an astonishing interpretation of the feminine point of view, but it would never do for the modern female. The poems (by Adelbert von Chamisso) are almost abject in their adoration of the human male, and Schumann's translation of this complete surrender into musical terms is almost embarrassing to admirers of independent womanhood. Yet if the sacrificial mood can be accepted, the combination of text and music cannot fail to make a deep and lasting impression on every hearer.

Dichterliebe (The Poet's Love) is a longer cycle, although some of the individual songs are very short. Its text is by Schumann's favorite poet, Heine. The opening song is the popular *Im wunderschönen Monat Mai* (In the lovely month of May), a delicate and tender song of Nature, similar to the equally popular *Nussbaum,* with the effect of both voice and piano trailing off into space, without any real ending. The modulation at the close forces the singer to go right on into the second song, *Aus meinen Thränen spriessen* (Where'er my tears are falling), again with the effect of an "unfinished symphony," although this time the piano echoes and completes each cadence.

Die Rose, die Lilie, die Taube, die Sonne (The rose, the lily, the dove, the sun) dashes away at top speed, to give the cycle its most cheerful tone, and this tiny song is one of the best tests in music of a singer's command of phrasing. The ecstatic spirit is again typically Schumannesque. *Wenn ich in deine Augen seh'* (When I look into your eyes) goes back to slow time and the tenderly sentimental spirit, with the accompaniment echoing the voice in snatches of counter-melody, a splendid example of Schumann's musicianship as applied in even the simplest song.

Of the remaining numbers in the *Dichterliebe* cycle, the most important are *Ich grolle nicht* (I'll not complain), which has become so hackneyed as to hide something of its real dramatic power; *Ich hab' im Traum geweinet* (In dreams my tears were falling), something of a parallel to the final song of *Frauenliebe und Leben*, but with the novel effect of letting the voice remain unaccompanied, except for brief interludes, up to the last page of the music; and *Die alten, bösen Lieder* (The old, bad songs), which is marked by a rugged strength of words and music (as the poet buries his love and his sorrows in the world's biggest coffin), and by a long and beautifully modulated postlude for the piano.

THE SONGS OF BRAHMS

Johannes Brahms was the logical successor to Schumann in the world of song, and he carried still further forward the principles of individual melody, rich and musicianly accompaniment, beauty of style and technical finish, and fidelity to the mood and form of the text. Schumann himself helped him considerably in his career, and Clara Schumann, after her husband's death, added constantly to the reputation of Brahms by playing his works in public.

Brahms, however, had within him something of the classic spirit of Bach and Beethoven, which Schumann did not possess, and in this rare combination of the romantic and the classic he was perhaps superior to all the musicians that had preceded him. In his wonderfully musical *Lieder*, not always fully appreciated at a first hearing, this fact becomes most apparent.

Even in his very early song, *Liebestreu* (Faithful Love), written at the age of twenty-one, Brahms shows his power to produce his effects with limited materials, using in this case a basic pattern of only three tones. The sudden change from minor to major in this song has been described as "a triumphant flash of sunrise." Such folk-like songs as his *Sandmännchen* (Little Sandman), written for the Schumann children, and the immortal *Wiegenlied* (Lullaby) show a simplicity and purity of musical inspiration equaled only by Schubert at his best.

Emotion and sentiment of the highest order are found in the *Minnelied* (Love Song), the two *Nightingale* songs, *Von ewiger Liebe* (Eternal Love) and *Die Mainacht*, and it would be difficult to find any songs in the whole literature of the *Lied* to surpass these masterpieces of lyric expression. *Feldeinsamkeit* (In Summer Fields) shows greatness in its repose and in its unerring reflection of one of the subtlest moods of Nature.

Meine Liebe ist grün (My love is green) has the ecstasy of a Schumann, but a finer conception of the possibilities of an accompaniment. For calm serenity, *Wie Melodien* (Like Melodies) and *Meine Lieder* (My Songs) may be recommended. *O wüsst' ich doch den Weg zurück* (Ah, if I but knew the way) again has the emotional quality and an unutterable feeling for home ties. *Wie bist du, meine Königin* (My Queen) is tenderly sentimental, with a beauty of melody that permits one to forgive a bad accent at the end of the first phrase. *Verrath* (Treachery) is one of the most elaborate of the Brahms songs, in ballad style, with dialogue, dramatically carried out to its tragic ending.

By contrast there is the delightful humor of *Vergebliches Ständchen* (The Vain Serenade) and the charm of the *Serenade* itself, a realistic echo of all the sentimentality of German student life. For a beautiful, straightforward melody, without a trace of artificiality, listen to *Erinnerung* (Remembrance), a song that is not nearly so well known as it should be. Simplicity, in a lighter vein, marks *An ein Veilchen* (To a Violet), and the Schumannesque command of sustained melodic line, plus a highly developed accompaniment, appears again in *O kühler Wald* (O thou cool forest), as well as in the familiar *Sapphic Ode*, with its baffling harmonies and piano syncopations.

The lighter touch of Brahms is revealed once more in *Auf dem Schiffe* (On Shipboard), suggesting the flight of a bird in the accompaniment, and also in the popular song of the blacksmith's sweetheart (*Der Schmied*), in which the clang of the anvil creates a rhythm of pure joyousness. The quietly tender *Therese* belongs to the same high class in its flawless command of pure sentiment.

Wild life and passion are to be found in the *Gypsy Songs*, of which the seventh, *Kommt dir manchmal in den Sinn* (Do you often call to mind?), possesses a great potential popularity, especially in its irresistible refrain. Another passionately emotional song is *Immer leiser wird mein Schlummer* (Ever softer grows my slumber), with characteristically Brahmsian touches in both melody and accompaniment. Any of these songs will serve as an introduction to Brahms, and all of them are worth hearing over and over again. The old accusation of academic pedantry, so often made against Brahms, falls to pieces in the light of his great *Lieder*. Quite aside from his symphonic and chamber music, he would deserve a high place among the masters for his contributions to art-song alone.

OTHER SONG WRITERS

Robert Franz stands, as it were, between Schumann and Brahms, a composer of the diligent, meticulous type, who made a close study of the *Lied*, but chose to express himself mostly in those simple forms that often result from "the infinite capacity for taking pains." It is as a melodist that he is chiefly remembered today, and most of his songs are so direct in their appeal that almost anyone can sing them with considerable pleasure. He was careful to choose only such lyrics as were admirably adapted to musical interpretation, and his greatest success was with short, comparatively obscure poems.

In a number of cases Franz set to music the same texts used by Schumann, and the comparison between the two is always interesting. *Die Lotosblume* (known as The Water Lily) and *Im wunderschönen Monat Mai* (In the lovely month of May) are good examples for a comparison of styles. Franz produced over three hundred songs, among which special mention is demanded by the charming *Widmung* (Dedication), *Es hat die Rose sich beklagt* (The rose complained), *Er ist gekommen* (He has come), *Aufbruch* (Departure),

Aus meinen Grossen Schmerzen (Out of my soul's great sorrows), *Mädchen mit den roten Mündchen* (Maiden with the mouth so red) and *Für Musik* (To Music).

Mendelssohn wrote some delightful songs, but generally without the depth of feeling shown by the other romantic composers of the *Lied*, and with less attention to the importance of the accompaniment. His *Auf Flügeln des Gesanges* (On Wings of Song) has been popularized by radio and in various instrumental transcriptions, exhibiting a beautiful melody of the simple, unaffected type, over a smoothly flowing but conventional accompaniment.

Hugo Wolf went further than any of his predecessors in the determination to make the *Lied* a really important art-form, and his songs too often give the impression of a studied, rather labored style as a result. His melodic inspirations in general do not compare with those of Schubert, Schumann, Franz or Brahms, but occasionally he showed flashes of genius that compel his recognition in that same select company.

The songs of Hugo Wolf are mostly very difficult, for the singer, the accompanist and the listener. But they are worth careful study, for they show how far an extraordinary intelligence can go within the restricted limits of the *Lied*. The melodies are seldom obvious in their appeal, the harmonies almost never, and the subject matter is often abstruse and psychologically complex. Yet once a real understanding is established, a Hugo Wolf song will show wearing qualities that are most gratifying.

The easiest introduction to this composer is by way of his *Verborgenheit* (Secrecy), whose "profound pathos" is expressed in a clear and beautiful melody, unhampered by too elaborate an accompaniment, although some of the modulations are highly original. The *Gesang Weylas* (Weyla's Song) is dignified and impressive in its broadly sustained tones, over a slow, harplike accompaniment, rising to an overpowering climax on the word *Könige* (kings). *Das verlassene Mägdelein* (The Forsaken Maiden) presents an exquisite series of harmonies, blending perfectly, but never obviously, with the voice.

These three songs will quickly create an enthusiasm for Hugo Wolf. An early example of his art, *Zur Ruh'* (To Rest) is full of depths worth exploring, but its beauties require an interpreter of the highest type to do them justice.

Two collections, the Spanish and Italian Songbooks, contain some of Wolf's finest work. (He was severely self-critical, and at one time remained inactive for several years because he believed that inspiration had left him.) Among other individual songs worth mentioning are the humorous *In dem Schatten meiner Locken* (In the shadow of my locks) and *Storchenbotschaft* (Stork's Message), the playful *Elfenlied* (Song of the Elf), *Der Tambour* (The Drummer), *Der Soldat* (The Soldier), the graceful *Er ist's* ('Tis he), the religiously fervent *Gebet* (Prayer) and *Fussreise* (Travel on Foot), the pathetic *Heimweh* (Homesickness), the simple *Auch kleine Dinge* (E'en little things), *Lieber Alles* (Rather Everything), *Der Musikant* (The Musician), *Der Jäger* (The Huntsman), *Der Scholar* (The Scholar), *Seemann's Abschied* (Sailor's Farewell), *In der Frühe* (Early Morning) with its theme of only five notes, *Denk' es, O Seele* (Think, O Soul) with a single rhythmic pattern variously used, and *Auf einer Wanderung* (On a Journey), a richly harmonized and bitterly pathetic song.

Richard Strauss is still too close to our practical experience to be given the recognition that a dead man secures automatically, but it is already obvious that quite aside from his orchestral tone poems and his operas he will be remembered permanently as a great song writer. Certainly his melodic inspiration has reached its highest level in some of his *Lieder*.

Strauss has carried on the tradition of Hugo Wolf and Brahms, with the addition of a truly Wagnerian independence of structure and harmony. He is particularly fond of the bold, sweeping type of song, with arpeggiated accompaniment (covering the whole keyboard with broken chords) and great emotional climaxes. Such songs are the *Heimliche Aufforderung* (Secret Tryst), *Cäcilie* (Cecily) and *Wie sollten wir geheim sie halten?* (How should we keep our love a secret?), all overwhelming in their effect, and popular with concert singers for the close of any group of *Lieder. Allerseelen* (All Souls' Day), an early song of Strauss, has a similar quality, but is quieter in mood and more definite in its melodic line, as is the familiar *Zueignung* (Devotion), with its fine climax just before and on the final *habe Dank* (thanks to thee).

Lightness and grace are in the popular *Ständchen* (Serenade) again with a cruelly difficult accompaniment of the sort that Strauss did not hesitate to write, and there is a disarming simplicity in *Du meines Herzens Krönelein* (Thou, my heart's little crown) and *Ich trage meine Minne* (I bear my love), both of the inevitable type of melodic beauty. *Traum durch die Dämmerung* (Dream in the Twilight) is another melody of utter loveliness, atmospherically sustained by a perfect accompaniment, and its steadily growing popularity is shared by the ineffable *Morgen* (Tomorrow, not Morning, as so many writers translate it), a song whose real melody is in the piano part, given completely before the voice even begins, and then repeated under a free recitative of countermelody by the singer, with a final shortened version as postlude, altogether one of the most original creations of art-song. Mention should be made also of *Die Nacht* (The Night), a hauntingly beautiful interpretation of a highly imaginative poem, *Breit über mein Haupt dein schwarzes Haar* (Spread thy black hair above my head), *Nachtgang* (Night Errand), *Das Schloss am Meer* (The Castle by the Sea), *Ach, Lieb! ich muss nun scheiden* (Ah, love, I must away), *Heimkehr* (The Journey Home), and *Das Geheimnis* (The Secret).

Other German composers who have produced excellent specimens of the *Lied* are Gustav Mahler (as elaborate as any in technique, but not always inspired), Max Reger (whose *Mariae Wiegenlied* has attained real popularity), Peter Cornelius (famous chiefly for his *Ein Ton,* or *Monotone,* a song which gives only one repeated note to the voice, with both melody and harmony in the accompaniment), Georg Henschel (whose *Morning Hymn* is now a favorite with choruses as well as solo voices) and Alexander von Fielitz, best known for his *Eliland* cycle. Richard Wagner wrote several fine songs, including a setting of *The Two Grenadiers* which makes even more use of the *Marseillaise* than did Schumann, *Schmerzen* (Sorrows), *Im Treibhaus* (In the Greenhouse), and the lovely *Träume* (Dreams), which contains the material of the love music that later appeared in the opera *Tristan und Isolde.*

ART-SONG IN OTHER COUNTRIES

By this time it should not be difficult to detect the finer qualities of art-song and to analyze in some detail almost any example of the *Lied.*

The form has been well developed in many countries outside of Germany, often with some national individualities of style.

Franz Liszt was a Hungarian by birth, but wrote his *Lieder* mostly to German words and in the manner of his song-writing contemporaries. It is interesting to compare his setting of *Du bist wie eine Blume* with those of Schumann and Rubinstein, and he has to his credit plenty of other good songs, including an elaborate *Loreley* (to which most people would prefer the simple melody of Silcher), *Die drei Zigeuner* (The Three Gypsies), *Mignon's Song, The Fisher Boy*, and several with texts in French. The Bohemian Dvorak is popular in America through his *Songs My Mother Taught Me*, which is only one of several good ones.

Anton Rubinstein, a Russian, really belongs also to the German school, and his *Lieder* show no particularly national characteristics. *Der Asra* (The Asra) remains a popular piece of dramatic declamation, partly because it is easy to sing it effectively.

Tschaikowsky is another Russian whose song writing closely follows the German tradition. His *Nur wer die Sehnsucht kennt* (None but the longing heart) has already been mentioned in comparison with Schubert's setting of the same words (from Goethe's *Wilhelm Meister*). Tschaikowsky's is frankly sentimental, perhaps too much so, yet highly effective for the average interpreter because of its very obviousness. *The Pilgrim, At the Ball* and *When on the Piazetta* are deservedly popular, but one of his finest songs (though little known) is *Er liebte mich so sehr* (He loved me so much), a despairing lament that makes its message absolutely convincing. Another beautiful but comparatively unknown piece of Tschaikowsky's vocal music is the Romeo and Juliet duet, whose melody appears in his orchestral Fantasy Overture of the same name.

For truly Russian characteristics, however, one must turn to Moussorgsky and his followers of the national group. Chaliapin and other singers have made *The Flea* a familiar bit of sardonic drama (the words are originally those of Mephisto in *Faust*, describing the plight of a court whose king made a pet of the household insect), and there are other songs by Moussorgsky of a similar effectiveness, such as *The Ram, The Seminar*, a *Cradle Song of the Poor* and the lively *Hopak*. Moussorgsky is the natural leader of the Russian school, brutally sincere and direct in his expression, steeped in the atmosphere of folk-music, often uncouth in his details of expression and almost painfully bold in his harmonies and rhythms, but as original and convincing as any song writer in history. His limited output includes a dramatic set of *Songs and Dances of Death,* as well as a splendid cycle, *Without Sunlight.*

Rimsky-Korsakoff, pupil and musical administrator of Moussorgsky, with a strong feeling for the Oriental atmosphere in all his work, has attained immense popularity with his familiar *Song of India* (really part of the opera *Sadko*) and has made other important contributions to art-song. Borodin, Balakirew and César Cui all have good songs to their credit, and the modern Rachmaninoff showed a special gift in that direction. His charming *Lilacs, Floods of Spring* and *In Silent Night* are all found frequently on concert programs. Gretchaninoff's children's songs, *Snowflakes,* and *The Steppe,* a bleakly realistic musical description, well deserve their popularity. In recent years Stravinsky has produced some startling songs in a rather extreme idiom of the modern dissonant type. But the real treasures of Russian song are still to be found in the folk-music of that country.

Scandinavia also enjoys a heritage of folk-song and can claim some unusually fine creators of art-song who have been fittingly influenced by this background. The Norwegian Edvard Grieg belongs at the top of this group, and is generally considered among the leading song writers of the world. Much of his work was distinctly in the German style (due to his musical education at the Leipsic Conservatory), but eventually he asserted his nationality quite clearly, and it is not difficult to recognize his characteristic idiom. His most obvious songs are still the most popular, such as the familiar *Ich liebe dich* (I love you), and *Solveig's Song* from *Peer Gynt,* but there is no denying the appeal of these melodies. A deeper dramatic significance is found in the *Swan* (also increasingly popular) and *A Dream,* and the lover of fine songs inevitably discovers in time such gems as *Im Kahne* (In a Boat), *Lauf der Welt* (The Way of the World), *Es schrie ein Vogel* (A Bird Cried Out), *The First Primrose, The Old Mother, Fair Vision, The First Thing, My Goal, False Friendship, Another Spring,* and the *Minstrel's Song.*

Other significant song writers of Scandinavian origin are Nils Gade, Kjerulf, Svendsen, Sjogren, Jensen and Sinding, while Finland has to its credit some fine songs by its leading composer, Jean Sibelius, as well

Chopin plays a song to remember

To MUSICAL PARIS OF THE 1830's came a young Polish genius, brilliant as both pianist and composer. His name was Frédéric François Chopin, and the ladies swooned over his playing, especially of his own music.

Chopin fascinated his hearers, not only because he played beautifully, but also by his personality and the fact that he was a perpetual invalid. Berlioz said of him, "He is something you have never seen—and someone you will never forget."

His best friend and patroness was Mme. Aurore Dudevant, better known by her pen name of George Sand. They met at her country place near Paris and later spent much time together on the island of Majorca, where Chopin wrote some of his most charming music, even though his health steadily declined.

According to the film, *A Song to Remember*, George Sand influenced Chopin to compose light salon pieces in preference to the larger works he might have undertaken. In that case the world may be her debtor, for it is by his Waltzes, Preludes, Mazurkas, Nocturnes, and Etudes that he is best known today. It was at the home of Mme. Sand that he wrote the popular *Minute Waltz*, often called "the waltz of the little dog chasing his tail."

Chopin's melodies have been turned into popular songs, and his *Funeral March* is known all over the world. No other composer has equaled his command of tonal effects at the piano. In a sense he was the founder of the whole modern school of creative music. The screen, records, and radio have combined to make Chopin the idol of millions.

as Jaernefelt and Selim Palmgren. The Polish Chopin, best known for his piano compositions, wrote seventeen songs, of which the mazurka, *The Maiden's Wish*, is the most popular.

ITALIAN ART-SONG

Italy is of course the natural home of song, and since the beginnings of civilized music there have always been Italian singers and song writers. (An explanation of the remarkable vocal ability of the Italians has been made on the ground that because of their warm climate they find it easier to keep their mouths open than do their northern neighbors.)

Some of the finest early art-song came out of Italy, and most of the Italian operas are primarily songs with instrumental interludes and passages of recitative. The Italian style of singing, known as *bel canto*, smooth and lyric rather than dramatic, and generally making the text secondary to the melody, lends itself to long-sustained phrases, with "legato" tones (literally "tied together"), and demands a beauty of quality as well as a high technical skill. (There are no "talking singers" in Italy except the patter artists of low comedy.)

Solo singing, as such, really began with a group in Florence, which included the father of the astronomer Galileo, and some of the most important developments in music were due to the work of Claudio Monteverde, beginning about the close of the sixteenth century. He was the first to introduce dissonances into harmony, for dramatic effect, and there is a fine example of this in his *Lament of Ariadne* (*Lasciatemi morir'*, Let me die).

Such names as Caccini, Carissimi, Alessandro Scarlatti, Rossi and Caldara are prominent in early Italian art-song (closely associated with opera), and even modern concert programs are often adorned by their songs. There are few melodies in music lovelier than the *Amarilli* of Caccini, Pergolesi's *Se tu m'ami* (If you love me) or the *Caro mio ben* (Thou, all my bliss) of Giordani. There is a sturdy vigor in Carissimi's *Vittoria* (Victory) and Scarlatti's description of sunrise on the Ganges (*Gia il sole dal Gange*).

The Italian composers concentrated so much on opera and had so little of the necessary lyric poetry in their own country that art-song did not develop among them as elsewhere, in spite of the national love of singing. But Rossini and other composers wrote some excellent songs, while Italian words were effectively set to music by Gluck, Mozart and Beethoven. In modern times, Wolf-Ferrari, with his *Rispetti* and other songs, Sgambati, Zandonai and Mascagni have contributed significantly to the literature of art-song, and the popular melodies of F. Paolo Tosti (such as the well known *Good-bye*, *Mattinata*, etc.) seem likely to maintain their wide appeal. There is real charm also in the so-called folk-songs of the Neapolitan type, actually written by individual composers, often in prize competitions (*Santa Lucia*, *Funiculi-Funicula*, *O Sole Mio*, *Spagnola*, *Maria Mari*, etc.)

THE FRENCH SCHOOL

France, with a splendid background of folk-music also, succeeded in bringing the art-song to a high level of delicate refinement, almost too precious in attention to detail, yet decidedly individual in style, with extreme freedom of harmony and the closest possible fidelity to the text. The French art-song is largely impressionistic, a natural result of the poetry of Paul Verlaine and others, and the leader in this modernistic movement was Claude Debussy, one of the unquestionably great song writers of the world, as well as a significant composer of orchestral and piano music and of the unique music-drama, *Pelléas and Mélisande*.

Debussy wrote his songs with a subtlety of expression that no other composer has equaled, and his style is completely removed from the straightforward melodiousness of the German *Lied*. Shimmering harmonies, of a pleasantly dissonant type, with new effects of color in both the voice and the piano accompaniment, are characteristic of the Debussy songs. There is seldom a definite rhythmic or melodic pattern; everything is vague, ethereal, disembodied, hauntingly elusive.

It is not always easy to enjoy a Debussy song at a first hearing, but there is a growing fascination in listening to this music, and for most people his compositions are a splendid introduction to modernism. To ears long accustomed to the most extravagant distortions of musical conventions, Debussy no longer sounds heretical or revolutionary. His technique has been accepted as the basis of all modern music, and his ideas now seem entirely logical.

Beau Soir (Lovely Evening) is a good song to hear as an introduction to Debussy, and the sparkling lightness of his *Mandoline*, to words by Verlaine, must capture every listener. His *Romance, Fantoches, Les Cloches, Harmonies du Soir* and *La Chevelure* are all worth some effort of attention, and there are thrilling rewards for those who will follow him through his *Ariettes Oubliées* (containing the atmospheric *C'est l'extase langoureuse* and the two *Aquarelles*) and the *Chansons de Bilitis*, with words by Pierre Louys.

Quite different from Debussy in style, but held in the highest regard by his fellow countrymen and popular the world over is Gabriel Fauré, often wrongly credited in America with the setting of *The Palms*. He is primarily a melodist, and his most familiar songs are only slightly affected by modern harmonic tendencies. There is a fine, sustained beauty in *Après un Rêve* (After a Dream), and *Les Berceux* (The Cradles), while simpler in its melody, is equally effective and far easier to sing. A more elaborate song is *Les Roses d'Ispahan* (The Roses of Ispahan) and there are others in the Fauré list well worth hearing.

César Franck, the classicist among modern French composers, wrote some impressive art songs, of which the best known are *La Procession* and *Le Mariage des Roses*. Chausson's *Papillons* (Butterflies) is a popular concert song because of its combination of delicacy and brilliance, and Duparc has an honored place in French song-literature through his *Chanson Triste, L'Invitation au Voyage* (after the painting by Watteau) and other compositions.

Reynaldo Hahn is among the most popular of the French song writers, through the familiar *L'Heure Exquise* (also established by radio) and other songs, and the *Psyché* of Paladilhe is an effective example of the combination of two melodies, one in the accompaniment and one for the voice. Among the older French composers, Gounod maintains his standing as a song writer, chiefly through his *Ave Maria* (written over the accompaniment of a Bach prelude for the piano) and the rather cloying *Sing, Smile, Slumber*, with Bizet contributing such excellent numbers as his *Agnus Dei*, and Delibes some lighter material, like *Les Filles de Cadiz*, popular with coloratura sopranos. Massenet's *Élégie* and *Ouvre tes yeux bleus* (Open your blue eyes) have been sadly overworked, but stand up well under the strain, as do the *Chère Nuit* of Bachelet, Godard's *Chanson de Florian*, Leroux's *Le Nil* and Lalo's *L'Esclave*.

Spain and other European countries do not figure prominently in art-song, although they possess a wealth of folk-music, but crossing the channel into England one finds plenty of material of both kinds. The folk-music of England, Scotland and Ireland is as fine and as varied as any in the world, and the madrigal period (sixteenth century) placed English song for a time at the head of all contemporary composition.

ENGLAND AND AMERICA

Early English music contains such fine tunes as the *Carman's Whistle, The Bailiff's Daughter of Islington, Green Sleeves, The Friar of Orders Grey*, the *Willow Song, Drink to me only with thine eyes*, the *British Grenadiers, The hunt is up, Lord Rendall, Barbara Allen* and *Lilliburlero*, besides a host of other ballads; and the songs of Shakespeare were set to beautiful music both in his own time and later. Henry Purcell reached perhaps the highest level of English art-song toward the close of the seventeenth century. He established a definite style, which unfortunately was discarded by later English composers, who preferred to imitate Handel. But Purcell still figures prominently on concert programs with such songs as *Full Fathom Five, Come unto these yellow sands, I attempt from love's sickness to fly, I'll sail upon the Dog Star, From Rosy Bowers* and *Dido's Lament*.

The famous *Beggar's Opera* contains some interesting examples of English song writing, and music-lovers still honor the names of Thomas Arne (composer of *Rule, Britannia* and other patriotic melodies), Dibdin, Sir Henry Bishop (best known for his *Home, Sweet Home* tune and that war horse of trilling Amazons, *Lo here the gentle lark*) and Sir Arthur Sullivan (by no means limited to the popular operas that he produced with Gilbert, or even to *The Lost Chord*).

Modern English song writers have developed no distinctive style, but added some excellent material to the literature of the concert stage, besides arranging and preserving the best of their folk-music. Sir Edward Elgar, Goring Thomas, Hubert Parry, Charles Villiers Stanford, Sterndale Bennett and Frederick Cowen are all respected names in art-song. Vaughan Williams and Granville Bantock show a fine feeling for folk-idioms, and a deserved popularity has been won by John Ireland's *Sea Fever* (to Masefield's words), Cyril Scott's *Lullaby* and other modern songs, with some rather advanced specimens from the pens of Arnold Bax, Gustav Holst, Frederick Delius and Eugene Goossens.

America is also contributing its full share to art-song today, although again there is no evidence of any particular distinction of style, and popular taste continues to respond chiefly to the ephemeral fox-trots, waltzes and ballads. There is historical interest in the surviving songs of Francis Hopkinson, a signer of the Declaration of Independence and friend of Washington, and the permanence of the Foster songs is well established, along with other folk-like material such as Bland's *Carry me back to old Virginny*, Henry Work's *Kingdom Coming* (a great tune), Malloy's *Love's Old Sweet Song*, etc.

John K. Paine first gave real scholarship to American art-song and was worthily followed by his pupil, Arthur Foote, and those outstanding New Englanders, Horatio Parker and G. W. Chadwick. Ethelbert Nevin has attained a popularity close to that of Foster himself with such appealing melodies as *The Rosary* and *Mighty Lak a Rose*, and Reginald De Koven is remembered for his straightforward songs as well as his light operas.

Edward MacDowell, still considered America's leading composer of serious music, although primarily Celtic in his characteristics, holds a high place among the world's masters of art-song. *Thy Beaming Eyes* and *The Sea* are perhaps his two most popular songs, but there are many others worth hearing, such as the Nature studies, *From an old Garden, The Robin Sings in the Apple Tree, The Wind Croons in the Cedars, Is It the Shrewd October Wind?* and his songs to poems by William Dean Howells. In many cases MacDowell wrote both the words and the music of his songs, as in *Constancy*, *Sunrise*, *Fragrant Love*, *Fair Spring-time*, and *To the Goldenrod*.

In recent years American song writers have been increasingly prolific, and it has become a difficult matter to separate the obviously popular and perhaps transient material from that which may prove to have a permanent value. The late Mrs. H. H. A. Beach is recognized for her musical setting of Browning's *Ah, love but a day*, and the effective recital climax, *The year's at the spring*. Charles Martin Loeffler (with *To Helen* and other songs), John Alden Carpenter (with his lovely music to the Tagore poems) and the late Charles T. Griffes belong to the same high class, and there is much to be said for the songs of Edgar Stillman-Kelley, Margaret Ruthven Lang, Mary Turner Salter, A. Walter Kramer, Howard Brockway, Frank La Forge, Henry Hadley, Wintter Watts, Ernst Bacon, Charles Ives, Granville English, Sydney King Russell, John Tasker Howard, Virgil Thomson, Richard Hageman, Mortimer Browning and others. Deems Taylor immortalized the old English *May-day Carol* in his beautiful arrangement, and adds a stirring ballad of his own, *Cap'n Stratton's Fancy*. Walter Damrosch did justice to Kipling's *Danny Deever*, and Oley Speaks performed the same service for *The Road to Mandalay*, winning equal popularity with the smoothly melodious *Sylvia* and other songs. Charles Wakefield Cadman, a fine musician, is almost resentful of the popular success of his *At Dawning* and *The Land of the Sky-blue Water*, as compared with his more serious work, but there is no evidence of similar irritation on the part of James H. Rogers, Carrie Jacobs Bond, Jessie Gaynor, Gena Branscombe, Thurlow Lieurance, Geoffrey O'Hara, Haydn Wood, or any other of the dozens of Americans turning out honest melodies, unburdened by too great subtlety or an overabundance of technique, but still far ahead of the average popular song.

If even a few of the great songs of the world are heard as often as possible, it will be a simple matter to apply similar tests of beauty to others. Many of them are available today on records made by the world's leading singers.

Ask yourself these questions: Are the words worth setting to music? Does the music express their meaning? Does it interfere with their natural accents? Does it have a melodic beauty of its own, regardless of the words? Is it carried out in a logical and satisfying form? Does the accompaniment enhance and enrich the melody, or is it a mere background or even a disturbing element? The art song that passes these tests is likely to be a good one.

CHAPTER XII THE CHURCH'S CONTRIBUTION

THE ART-MUSIC of the modern world (as opposed to folk-music) began in the church, and its ecclesiastical significance has been maintained to the present day. While minstrels, troubadours and jongleurs roamed over Europe, instinctively creating songs which often showed vitality and qualities of permanence, the monks in the monasteries were working out a laborious science of music, and it is upon their efforts that most of the later technique of music is based.

Although the early Church encouraged music, and almost literally created its theory and the rules of notation, composition, harmony and counterpoint, it was very jealous of what it considered its property, and frowned upon all the "natural" music of the secular type. To the religionists of the Middle Ages music was intended for the glorification of sacred subjects and nothing else. Whatever music was made outside of the church was inherently evil. (This intolerant attitude has been characteristic of some musical scholars in every period of the art's development, and the most inspired composers have generally been the ones who were quickest to recognize the merits of folk-music and popular song.)

Sacred music is almost necessarily choral to a great extent, for solo singing, up to quite recent times, had no place in church except for conventional responses, while instrumental music was almost entirely limited to that of the organ. The effect of religion on song, therefore, has been to create hymns, chants and chorales, in which a whole congregation could join, to develop anthems, cantatas and elaborate pieces of polyphonic vocal music for performance by trained choirs, and finally to combine solos and choral singing, with orchestral accompaniment, in the impressive art-form known as oratorio. (The name is derived from the fact that this type of music was originally sung in an actual oratory.)

The oldest Latin hymns were in the style of "plain-song," following the ancient modes, but without definite rhythm, and within a limited range of melody. They were sung by a single voice or by a choir in unison, amounting to little more than a chant or recitative.

CONGREGATIONAL SINGING

One of the revolutionary ideas of the Reformation was that the congregation should take a more active part in church singing, and this was the basis of hymnology as we know it today. Martin Luther insisted on using good tunes for congregational singing, and in characteristically practical fashion adapted the best German folk-tunes to sacred words in the vernacular (instead of the traditional Latin of the priests).

It is interesting and sometimes amusing to compare the words of the Lutheran chorales (later arranged by Bach) with those of the folk-music which supplied the melodies. For instance, *Innsbruck, ich muss dich lassen* (Innsbruck, I must leave you) became *O Welt, ich muss dich lassen* (O world, I must leave thee). *Mein G'müth ist mir verwirrt* (My spirit is distracted), a love song originally, developed into one of the noblest of the Lenten hymns, *O Haupt voll Blut und Wunden* (O Sacred Head now wounded). Another love ditty of the lighter sort, *Ich hört' ein Fräulein klagen* (I heard a young lady complain) was neatly turned into *Hilf' Gott, wem soll ich klagen?* (God help me, to whom shall I complain?). Perhaps the two most striking examples of this adaptation of folk-song to ecclesiastical needs were the chorales *O lieber Gott, das dein Gebot* (O dear God, this Thy command) and *Auf meinen lieben Gott* of which the first was originally *O lieber Hans, versorg' dein' Gans* (O dear Hans, take care of your goose) and the second *Venus, du und dein Kind* (Venus, you and your child).

When Luther failed to find a folk-tune to suit his purpose, he composed one himself, playing it on the flute, according to tradition, while a musical friend put down the notes. The best and most popular example of the Reformer's creative work is of course *Ein' feste Burg ist unser Gott* (A mighty fortress is our God), which has been sung by all the Protestant congregations of the world.

In France the Psalms were early put into metrical verse for congregational singing, also using the popular tunes of the day, and a psalter of this type was published by Calvin in Geneva in 1542. (Luther's first hymnbook had appeared in 1524.) England took naturally to hymn singing, as a result of the vogue of the madrigal in the sixteenth century, and collections were soon published in four-part harmony, the most important of which, Ravenscroft's Psalter, came out in 1621.

Wesley and his followers had a significant influence on the development of sacred song, and in America the early attempts at music were all of a religious character. The name of William Billings, often called "America's first composer," is worth remembering. He published *The American Psalm Singer* in 1770. Among later composers of sacred music (outside of oratorio), Thomas Hastings and Lowell Mason (still recognized as one of our finest musicians) were prominent. The liturgical music of Russia has a strongly racial quality, and some wonderfully impressive settings of sacred words have been made by the old and new composers of that country.

Before sacred music finally found the elaborate form of oratorio, which has become its most popular and dramatic expression, it experimented with a great variety of technical devices that permitted increasing freedom, without interfering too much with ecclesiastical routine. Among the most successful of these experiments were the motet, the Mass and the cantata.

FORMS OF SACRED MUSIC

The motet was originally a sacred song, based upon some Biblical text, to be performed during High Mass, in the manner of an offertory. Its melodies were either secular or a combination of chants, and often secular words also crept in. As the motet developed in polyphonic harmony, it became customary to let each voice sing a different set of words, which must have been confusing to the listeners but fun for the singers. In due time the motets in all European countries were sung in the vernacular instead of church Latin, and thus became an important feature of the whole madrigal movement. (The modern successor to the motet is the anthem, as sung in most Protestant churches.)

Like so much other sacred music, the motet reached its highest point of art in the work of Palestrina. He wrote over three hundred pieces of this type, for various combinations of voices numbering from four to twelve. The Flemish Orlando di Lasso, one of the greatest composers of part-song and perhaps the most prolific musician of all time, is credited with over one thousand motets, in addition to other examples of sacred and secular music reaching a total of nearly twenty-five hundred separate works. His *Penitential Psalms* constitute a masterpiece worthy of Palestrina himself.

In England the motet form was successfully used by practically all the composers of the madrigal period, using both sacred and secular texts. Italian composers after Palestrina, such as Alessandro Scarlatti, Durante and Pergolesi, developed a new style of motet, often with instrumental accompaniment, and after the revolutionary treatment of harmony by Monteverde, much of the traditional formula was abandoned. The great Bach, however, wrote beautiful motets, in the purest style, and there were some fine examples also, though less known, in the work of Handel.

The Mass, next to oratorio the most elaborate form of sacred music, reached its highest point in the creative genius of Bach. Originally a mere succession of plain-song melodies, without rhythm or harmony, intoned by a single priest or by a choir in unison, as a regular part of the church service, the Mass became through the development of polyphony a most important vehicle for choral music, which today has a definite place in the concert hall as well as in the church.

There are six principal parts in the traditional Mass, a Kyrie, a Gloria, a Credo, a Sanctus, a Benedictus and an Agnus Dei, all of which were and still are important features in the Roman service, as well as in many Protestant churches. Originally a single plain-song (*canto fermo*) served as a basis for all of these movements and gave its name to the entire Mass, and sometimes this basic tune was of secular character. (A number of Masses were written on the tune of an old French love song, *L'Homme armé*, including one by Palestrina.)

The Kyrie ("Lord, have mercy upon us") gave an opportunity for elaborate counterpoint on a comparatively limited text. The Gloria

("Glory to God in the highest") usually had less of the contrapuntal architecture and more of melodic breadth, due to the greater amount of text available. It was generally in two parts, the second beginning at *qui tollis.* The Credo (Creed) was also in at least two parts, the second starting at *et incarnatus est* or *crucifixus* and sometimes a third at *et in Spiritum Sanctum.* The Sanctus was similar in design to the Kyrie, although often more elaborate, with the Hosanna almost always treated as a separate part. The Benedictus was generally sung by a small group of solo voices, followed by a choral Hosanna. Finally the Agnus Dei (generally in two parts) permitted the greatest exhibition of musical skill on the part of the composer, ending often in a fugue and demanding more choral parts than any other section of the Mass.

MUSIC OF THE MASS

The name of Palestrina again looms mightily among great composers of the Mass. The abuses in church music had become so great (chiefly along the lines of secular interference and triviality of theme and treatment) that a commission of eight cardinals appointed by Pope Pius IV almost forbade the further use of polyphonic music for ecclesiastical purposes, but agreed to wait until it could be proved that such music could be written in a dignified and fitting style, with beauty as well as technical skill. Palestrina, then choirmaster in the Church of Santa Maria Maggiore, was challenged to produce a Mass that fulfilled these requirements. His answer consisted of not one but three Masses, one of which, the famous *Missa Papae Marcelli* (named for the Pope Marcellus, who had died ten years earlier) was accepted as the perfect model for that kind of music, and has continued to be so regarded ever since. It was entirely original in its melodic material, written for six vocal parts, and its apparent simplicity consistently hides an amazing command of all the technique of polyphonic composition. The style is solemn and devotional, but full of life and imagination. Palestrina wrote many more Masses, of the highest quality, but none that quite equaled his masterpiece.

After the Golden Age of the Mass, in which Orlando di Lasso and other composers also played a prominent part, there was a period of decadence, similar to that which affected the motet, with the rebellion against harmonic formulas partly to blame. Musicians became more and more interested in the instrumental accompaniment to singing and in instrumental music as such. But one gigantic masterpiece was yet to be produced, combining the dignity and solemnity of the old school with an individual invention and technical skill far in advance of anything that had gone before. This climax in the whole history of sacred music was Johann Sebastian Bach's *Mass in B minor*.

It would not be fair to compare the Bach Mass with any earlier examples of the form, for it could hardly have been intended for actual performance as part of a church service. Its extent and elaborateness of design clearly fit it for the concert hall, or at least for special presentation such as it has received so often and so satisfactorily in the Bach festivals at Bethlehem, Pennsylvania. If any comparisons are to be made, they should be with the oratorio form itself, to which the *B minor Mass* virtually belongs.

There are important solo parts in this Mass (soprano, contralto, tenor and bass) as well as choral passages of far greater extent than the practical church form would warrant. The mastery of contrapuntal writing, the beauty and grace of the solos and duets, the dignity and grandeur of the choruses, and the richness of instrumental coloring (achieved with the simplest of materials) combine to place this great work among the most sublime of all expressions of musical genius. If any passages were to be picked out for special comment, they would include the opening of the Credo, an astonishingly modern harmonic treatment of a typical *canto fermo*, with a complex orchestral accompaniment, the convincing expression of grief in the *Crucifixus* of the same section, the exquisite polyphony of the *Qui tollis*, after the Gloria, and the seraphic chanting of the Sanctus, "in affirmation of the deathlessness of beauty and the holiness of those immortals who are pure in heart."

LATER DEVELOPMENTS

After Bach, the Mass tended more and more toward dramatic expression and the devices of secular music, maintaining its close relation to oratorio and becoming practically a sacred cantata. Haydn's Masses are similar to his oratorios (to be discussed later in this chapter), and those of Mozart show the same grace and beauty that one finds in his operas. (The so-called *Coronation Mass* contains the actual music of *Cosi fan tutte.*) Cherubini composed three great Masses, one of which was written for the coronation of Charles X, all quite individual and strongly dramatic, and these qualities are even more evident in the *Missa solemnis* of Beethoven, as when he introduces a martial passage for drums and trumpets for a realistic contrast to the phrase *dona nobis pacem* (Give us peace). There are passages in this Mass that bear comparison with Bach himself, although some of the writing is unnecessarily difficult for the singers. Particularly notable is the beauty of the Benedictus, with a highly original use of a solo violin, over a subdued chorus and accompaniment.

Weber, Schubert, Rossini, Gounod and many other composers wrote Masses, some of which exhibit both beauty and distinction, and with a remarkable consistency in adhering to the letter, if not the spirit, of the original ecclesiastical form, at least so far as the text is concerned.

The church cantata, in its finest form, was almost the exclusive property of Bach, whose work as organist and choirmaster compelled him to create one such composition for every Sunday and holiday of the ecclesiastical year. He wrote nearly three hundred such cantatas, of which about two hundred are available in twenty volumes published by the Bach Gesellschaft. While they represented merely his routine activity, written very much as a minister would write his weekly sermon, and always interrupting work on some composition in the larger forms, they contain a tremendous amount of truly lofty musical invention and show an astonishing versatility as well.

The Bach cantatas vary in length from about twenty minutes to a full hour and are written regularly in several movements, for chorus and solo voices, with accompaniment of the organ and often additional instruments. The Lutheran chorales figure prominently in these cantatas, one of which is written entirely on the music and words of *Ein' feste Burg,* with the final chorus sung unaccompanied.

Chorales are also an important part of the Passion Music of Bach. He is known to have composed five such works, although only three of them are in existence, named for the Apostles Matthew, Luke and John. Of these the *Passion according to St. Matthew* is by far the greatest, and it stands close to the sublimity of the *B minor Mass* in its conception and musical expression. It is in this work that the chorale, *O Haupt voll Blut und Wunden* (O Sacred Head now wounded) receives its most memorable choral treatment.

Handel, Haydn and other composers wrote excellent Passion Music, and the cantata itself had a long and varied life in every country of the world. In its earliest form it was merely a recitative by a single singer, accompanied by one instrument. Various experiments developed it into an important type of sacred music, showing all the diversities of style characteristic of the motet and the Mass.

While no other composer approached the greatness of Bach in the field of the cantata, much interesting work was done in this line by the early Italians, particularly Carissimi and Alessandro Scarlatti, and with the definite leaning toward dramatic realism which gradually affected all church music, the later cantatas were practically small oratorios, and should be considered logically in that category.

CANTATA AND ORATORIO

It was only natural that sacred music should struggle more and more against the restrictions of the ecclesiastical formula, as well as the limited text material of the Mass, the Passion, the Psalms and the hymns. The early Miracle Plays and Moralities whetted the appetite of the public for more and more realistic presentations of the Biblical stories, and the music that went with these plays unquestionably had its influence on both oratorio and opera.

In the course of the past four centuries a great deal of music has been composed that did not properly belong in the church at all, although it dealt primarily with religious subjects, and those examples of it that have survived are heard today almost entirely in the concert hall. It is fair to class such music as oratorio in its larger forms, and to apply the rather loose name of cantata to the more modest combinations of solos and vocal and instrumental ensembles, each dealing with a definite theme, of a religious or semireligious character.

The church cantatas of Bach might themselves be called small oratorios, and his three Passions as well as the *Mass in B minor* are today rightly included among the great oratorios of musical literature. There is also a *Christmas Oratorio* by Bach, really a combination of several cantatas, but of independent significance. Aside from Bach, the most important composer in the field of oratorio is the Anglicized German, Georg Friedrich Handel.

The cantatas of Handel are mostly on secular subjects, and do not compare in significance with his great sacred works. There is a charming *Acis and Galatea*, taking its material from mythology, a setting of Milton's familiar poems *L'Allegro* and *Il Penseroso* (to which a profane librettist added *Il Moderato*, with sage advice on the propriety of steering a middle course), and a dramatically effective *Alexander's Feast*, to Dryden's words, containing some of Handel's finest choral music.

Handel's early oratorios, such as *Esther*, *Deborah* and *Athaliah*, are little more than cantatas, with an emphasis on the solo parts and only faint indications of the choral magnificence that he was later to achieve. It was in this remarkable development of the chorus, added to an almost unique beauty of melodic line, that Handel made his greatest contributions to oratorio.

Saul and *Israel in Egypt* were the first works to display this larger style, the former containing the famous *Dead March*, which is still played at public funerals, while the latter, with its twenty-eight double choruses, represents perhaps the most massive piece of choral writing in all music. The climax of Handel's creations in the oratorio form appeared in the *Messiah*, now a regular part of the observance of Christmas in most countries of the world.

HANDEL'S "MESSIAH"

There is no need of discussing this great work in detail, for it can be heard frequently and lends itself to complete or partial performance by almost any good amateur chorus. The *Messiah* is in three parts, the first using for its text the prophecies of the coming of Christ and the story of the Nativity, the second dealing with the life, suffering and death of the Savior, and the third expressing religious faith in the manner of a Credo.

The first part contains a beautiful opening recitative by the tenor soloist, *Comfort ye, my people*, and an ornate aria, *Every valley shall be exalted*. The bass recitative, *Thus saith the Lord*, and the aria, *But who may abide?* likewise make heavy demands upon the flexibility of the solo voice. Similar flexibility is demanded from the chorus in the fugal passage, *And He shall purify*, which is followed by a beautiful contralto aria, *O thou that tellest good tidings to Zion*, also chorally developed.

One of the finest choruses of the *Messiah*, *For unto us a Child is born*, precedes a lovely *Pastoral Symphony*, played by the orchestra, one of the most perfect musical expressions of the spirit of Christmas Eve. The contralto solo, *He shall feed His flock*, is one of the great melodies of all time, although much of it, as so often with Handel, consists of quite simple scale progressions. There is deathless beauty also in the soprano aria, *Come unto Him, all ye that labor*, and the first part closes with another fugal chorus, *His yoke is easy*.

The opening chorus of the second part, *Behold the Lamb of God*, reaches a true nobility of utterance, and is followed by still another expressive aria for the contralto soloist, *He was despised*. There are several more dramatically effective choruses in this part, reaching their climax in the familiar *Hallelujah*, to whose majesty every audience still rises spontaneously, a tradition established by King George II of England.

The third part is short, but includes the marvelously beautiful soprano solo, *I know that my Redeemer lives*, and two great choruses, *Worthy the Lamb* and the final *Amen*, built up into a tremendous fugue. While oratorio no longer enjoys the vogue in America that it once did, there is little likelihood that such music as this of the *Messiah* will ever be forgotten. In England, which claims Handel as its own, the popular masterpiece has become almost a religion in itself.

Several other oratorios by Handel are worthy of attention. *Judas Maccabaeus*, in three parts, with splendid choral writing and effective solos, contains the familiar melody *See the conquering hero comes* (originally written for another oratorio, *Joshua*). *Samson*, also in three parts, still competes with *Judas Maccabaeus* and the *Messiah* in popularity, and is so dramatic in its music that it might well be played as an opera.[1] Samson's lament, *Total eclipse*, is one of the truly touching songs of the world, with a particular significance in the fact that Handel himself suffered blindness in his later years. There is a fine funeral march in the last part, to which Handel afterward added the

[1]The operatic version of the same story by Saint-Saëns, conversely, has often been presented as oratorio.

Dead March from *Saul.* Handel's final oratorio was *Jephthah*, during whose composition his eyesight failed him.

Haydn heard a performance of the *Messiah* in Westminster Abbey on his first visit to England, in 1791, and was so impressed by it that he determined to try his hand at the same style of music. The result was the *Creation*, now generally considered Haydn's greatest work. Its text is based upon Milton's *Paradise Lost*, as well as parts of the book of Genesis, first translated into German and then back again into English (not always happily).

Like its great model, the *Creation* is in three parts (the conventional oratorio form), but with emphasis on the solo voices rather than the chorus. The overture contains a dramatic idea, rather naïvely carried out, first attempting to depict chaos and then gradually establishing harmony through the voices of various instruments. The first vocal solo is a recitative by the archangel Raphael (bass) to the words "In the beginning." A fine effect is achieved when the chorus bursts into the words "And there was light." The first part also contains the beautiful soprano solo, *With verdure clad*, and the magnificent final chorus, *The Heavens are telling*.

The second part of the *Creation* describes the beginnings of animal life on earth, affording the composer a wonderful opportunity to write descriptive music, touched with a definite sense of humor. There is no mistaking the musical representation of various birds, the roaring lions (double bassoons), "flexible tigers" (rapid passages in the strings), the neighing of the horse or the buzzing of the insects. Man's creation is celebrated in the fine tenor aria, *In native worth*, and there is a superb final chorus in the form of a fugue, *Achieved is the glorious work*. The third part includes a dialogue between Adam and Eve, and ends in another great fugal chorus, *Jehovah's praise forever shall endure*.

Haydn wrote one more significant oratorio, *The Seasons*, based upon Thomson's poem of the same name. It is not so elaborate or impressive a work as the *Creation*, but full of individual beauties. Of particular interest, once more, is the descriptive music dealing with Nature in its gentler and also its stormy aspects, a foretaste of what Beethoven later accomplished even more realistically in his *Pastoral Symphony*.

Only one actual oratorio is credited to Beethoven himself, generally known as *The Mount of Olives* (*Christus am Ölberge*). It suffers from a poor libretto, and is musically in the style of Haydn and Mozart. Ludwig Spohr, a minor composer, but popular in his own day, wrote three oratorios, of which *The Last Judgment* is still performed.

MENDELSSOHN'S "ELIJAH"

But the one musician who can really be compared with Handel in the field of oratorio is Mendelssohn. His first work of this type, *St. Paul*, was clearly superior to Haydn's *Creation*, particularly in his fine command of choral writing. Mendelssohn's *Elijah*, written ten years after *St. Paul*, marks a second climax in the history of oratorio, and has proved itself a work of as great importance as the *Messiah* itself.

Certainly the *Elijah* goes as far as it seems humanly possible in the direction of dramatic realism, without actually resorting to costumes, scenery and stage action. (It has, incidentally, been given in that way, with considerable success.) While the life of Christ might be called as dramatic a story as could well be imagined, the career of the prophet Elijah admittedly contains qualities and incidents of everyday human interest that make it easier for the average listener to visualize.

Mendelssohn himself was largely responsible for the libretto of the *Elijah*, and at the very outset he introduced a highly original device in having his hero sing a short recitative (bass) before the overture. This recitative is a prophecy of the drought, which is then musically described in the orchestral overture itself, leading right into the opening chorus, *Help, Lord*, voicing the anguish and terror of a famine-stricken people.

After another chorus, *Lord, bow Thine ear to our prayer*, the beautiful tenor aria, *If with all your hearts*, is heard. The story develops through the calling of Elijah to the waters of Cherith and the raising of the widow's son from the dead. Then comes the most dramatic scene of the whole oratorio, the challenge to the priests of Baal and the trial by fire. The chorus of the priests, *Baal, we cry to thee*, interrupted by Elijah's taunts, "Call him louder," the dignified prayer of the prophet, *Lord, God of Abraham*, the simple chorale, *Cast thy burden on the Lord*, with the exciting chorus, *The fire descends from heaven*, and Elijah's brilliant and difficult aria, *Is not*

His word like a fire?—all this represents a gradual ascent toward the climax of the whole work, when the rain finally descends (realistically suggested in the orchestra) and the chorus breaks into a paean of thanksgiving, *Thanks be to God.*

The second part opens with the fine soprano solo, *Hear ye, Israel,* followed by a majestic chorus, *Be not afraid.* Elijah, condemned by King Ahab and the wicked Jezebel, is forced to flee into the wilderness, and there utters the plaintive *It is enough,* whose beautiful melody is also played by a solo cello in the orchestra. As Elijah sleeps, the angels sing to him in that loveliest of all trios for women's voices, *Lift thine eyes.* (It was originally written as a duet, but changed after Mendelssohn realized its harmonic possibilities.) Elijah utters further complaints, and an angel (contralto) sings the aria, impressive in its calmness, *Oh, rest in the Lord.* Another powerful chorus, *He shall endure to the end,* brings this part of the oratorio to a close.

The final scene represents the ascent of the prophet to Heaven in the fiery chariot. There is much choral preparation for this last climax, with more realistic effects by the orchestra, suggesting both storm and fire. After the dramatic end of the prophet's life on earth, a tenor aria and a quartet, *Oh, come, every one that thirsteth,* lead to the great closing fugue on the words "Lord, our Creator."

OTHER ORATORIOS

Beyond the *Messiah,* the *Elijah* and the *Creation,* few oratorios require extended comment. Liszt's *Legend of Saint Elizabeth,* once produced as an opera by the Metropolitan Company in New York, has charm and the brilliant technique always associated with its composer. His *Christus* is deeply religious, with effective use of old church themes, closing with an overwhelming choral and orchestral arrangement of the Latin hymn, *Stabat Mater.*

In England, the land of greatest devotion to oratorio, excellent works in this form were written by such composers as Sterndale Bennett, Charles Villiers Stanford, Arthur Sullivan (*The Prodigal Son* and *The Light of the World*) and Edward Elgar (*The Dream of Gerontius, The Apostles,* etc.). France produced *The Childhood of Christ,* by Hector Berlioz (an enlargement of an earlier cantata, *The Flight into Egypt*), Gounod's *Redemption,* which retains its popularity, in spite of a rather obvious sentimentality, several fine and scholarly works by César Franck, of which *The Beatitudes* is generally considered his masterpiece, a *Christmas Oratorio* and *The Deluge*, by Saint-Saëns, *The Seven Last Words of Christ*, by Dubois, popular chiefly because it is easy to perform, several minor works of Massenet, Debussy's *Prodigal Son* (*L'Enfant prodigue*), which first brought him fame and won the Prix de Rome, and his later *Martyrdom of Saint Sebastian*, a far more elaborate composition, the charming *Children's Crusade* of Pierné, and some of the less familiar creations of Reynaldo Hahn, Florent Schmitt and Vincent d'Indy.

Italy's contribution to this type of music, aside from the early cantatas, includes a popular but cheaply operatic *Stabat Mater* by Rossini (not to be compared with the later version of Dvorak), the fine *Manzoni Requiem* of Verdi, too seldom heard, and the modern *Vita Nuova* (New Life) by Wolf-Ferrari, which commands increasing respect with each performance. Horatio Parker, with his *Hora Novissima*, and G. W. Chadwick, with *Judith* and *Noel*, worthily represent America in this field.

A number of other works might be mentioned, chiefly of the secular type and of the dimensions of the cantata rather than the oratorio. Beethoven's music to the *Ruins of Athens* belongs in this class, as does the *Damnation of Faust* by Berlioz, Schumann's *Paradise and the Peri*, and some of the work of Weber and Schubert. Wagner wrote a cantata, *The Love Feast of the Apostles* (*Das Liebesmahl der Apostel*), and Liszt added several more to his own versatile catalogue. The Brahms *Song of Triumph* and *Song of Destiny* belong among the great choral works of music, as does his *German Requiem*, written on the death of his mother. The last, unfinished work of Mozart was a *Requiem*, and there are fine examples by Berlioz and Cherubini.

Dvorak is remembered not only for his *Stabat Mater* and *Requiem*, but for a realistic piece of musical horror, *The Spectre's Bride* and an impressive *Saint Ludmila*. Sullivan's *Golden Legend*, Cowen's *Rose Maiden*, Coleridge-Taylor's *Hiawatha*, and the cantatas of Elgar have added to England's reputation for good choral writing. Modern German music includes interesting choral works by Richard Strauss and Georg Schumann, and Arnold Schönberg at one time created something of a sensation with his *Gurrelieder* and *Pierrot Lunaire*. Other composers in the cantata style are the English Bantock, Parry and

Holbrooke, the American Hadley and Converse, the Russian Moussorgsky and Ippolitoff-Ivanoff, and the Norwegian Grieg.

It is a mistake to attach too much importance to such music merely because it demands large forces for its performance, or because it deals with sacred subjects. The choral Finale of Beethoven's *Ninth Symphony*, which annually draws huge crowds to the New York City College Stadium, chiefly because of the impressive combination of soloists, chorus and orchestra, is perhaps the weakest part of that great work, ungrateful for the singers and generally less effective than the preceding instrumental portions.

There have been amazing expressions of genius in the choral forms created by the church, but these stand out sharply from the mass of ecclesiastical music in general, and the opportunities for hearing them are by no means rare, through records or public performances, although it must be admitted that the interest in choral singing has steadily declined in the United States. The chief reason for this is the unwillingness of the average amateur to take the necessary time for rehearsals. A local choral society used to be considered one of the necessary labels of civilization, but in too many communities that tradition has given way to automobiles, bridge and the movies. Choral singing is likely to be more fun for the participants than the listeners, and the way to get the most out of the world's great choral music is to take an actual part in it.

CHAPTER XIII GRAND OPERA

It was inevitable that music should sooner or later try to combine its own natural elements with the popular trappings of not only words but action, costumes and scenery, in that heterogeneous form of art known as opera. While it is becoming more and more apparent that America is not outstandingly an opera-minded country, the form has flourished to some extent by reason of its very magnificence, appealing to the inherent megalomania of the average listener, and profiting also by its obvious social possibilities. In recent years, however, with the help of radio and records, a real opera audience of sincere enthusiasm has been developed in this country.

Opera represents the extreme of program music, giving the listener as well as the composer every possible aid, even to the translation of the libretto where necessary. Whether all this artificial support actually aids in creating significant works of art is still an open question. If it is assumed that the most obvious art is not necessarily the greatest, then opera will have a hard time claiming any position of honor, as compared with absolute music in general. It may well be argued that there is more significance in the ability to create a mood or transfer an emotion through pure instrumental music than when words, costumes, scenery and action make the intention perfectly evident. Even within the field of vocal music, there may be more art in a song which has to tell its story without the help of even dramatic gestures than in an elaborate succession of arias and recitatives, acted out in every detail.

Opera is eternally confronted with the problem of how far the music may legitimately be sacrificed to dramatic realism and vice versa. If rhythm, melody, tone color and form are practically ignored in the insistence on projecting a piece of stage realism, the musical results cannot be considered particularly happy. On the other hand, if an opera sacrifices all claim to a convincing stage presentation by its insistence on purely musical values, nothing has really been accomplished that could not have been equally well done by the music alone.

The greatest handicap to opera in America has been the insistently practical attitude of the listener. He is continually aware of the fact that the characters are actually singing when they are supposedly talking, and this immediately creates a feeling of artificiality that is hard to overcome. If the lines are in an everyday English (corresponding to the average text in a foreign language), the whole thing is likely to sound prosaic and silly, while the use of a "poetic" English, substituting "locks" for "hair," "raiment" for "clothes," etc., may give the impression of being even more artificial and unnatural.

The Latin temperament seems able to adapt itself far more easily to such absurdities than the Anglo-Saxon, and this is one reason why opera has always been, and always will be, more popular in Italy and France than in any of the Germanic countries. The matter-of-fact Anglo-Saxon finds it difficult to adjust his practical viewpoint to the incongruities that he is asked to accept, and even when an opera contains admittedly great music, the descent from the sublime to the ridiculous is all too constant a menace.

The question of the language of opera cannot be discussed here beyond the suggestion that it is idle to claim that a translation can have exactly the same effect as the original, particularly when the one is a Latin and the other a Germanic language. It has never been proved that a familiar language made the words of opera intelligible in any case, for this depends largely on the quality and volume of the orchestral accompaniment. Furthermore it may be argued that most operatic librettos are better off if they are not too clearly understood. Their stories and lines are often either downright revolting or too absurd to be taken seriously, according to accepted literary standards.

In answer to the continued cry for "opera in English," it may be pointed out that there is plenty of such material constantly available, but mostly in the lighter forms (with the works of Gilbert and Sullivan as shining examples) to which the English language seems best adapted. This is particularly true of operas or operettas dealing with modern scenes and characters. The composers of "grand opera" were generally careful to take their material from either the dim and distant past or from legend and mythology, so that the unreality of the whole thing would be accepted as a matter of course. (Wagner did this most successfully, and his music-dramas should not be included in any discussion of opera as such.)

THE BEGINNINGS OF OPERA

It is a curious fact that the founders of opera, a little group of serious reformers in Renaissance Italy, thought that they were restoring the Greek drama, when actually they were creating a new combination of words and music. While it is probable that the ancient Greeks chanted their lines and sang their choruses, the effect must have been something quite different from that of the early Italian opera, aside from all distinctions of the musical structure itself. Strangely enough, also, the insistent demands for realism uttered by practically all the composers of opera from the very outset have in most cases resulted only in the most flagrant of artificialities. But this was the nature of the thing itself, and only an occasional genius has been able to overcome the fundamental handicap of the whole operatic form.

The first real opera (resulting from the efforts of the group that also produced the secular cantata) was the *Euridice* of Jacopo Peri, performed in Florence in the year 1600. It is a work of more than merely historical interest, for it shows an abundant command of melody in its purest forms, and one of its beautiful arias, the *Invocation of Orpheus*, is still sung with great effect.

Claudio Monteverde took a step forward dramatically in his *Arianna* (containing the famous Lament, with its revolutionary dissonance), and must be considered one of the most important of the early composers of opera, as well as an outstanding figure in music as a whole. But these primitive specimens were naturally little more than an alternation of recitative and arias (recitative being the musical equivalent for spoken words, following the accents of the text, but with little of melodic line or rhythmic measure).

Alessandro Scarlatti, another great figure in music, improved opera, as he did everything else that he touched, particularly in the development of the musical and dramatic possibilities of recitative and its accompaniment. In France the first important operatic compositions were those of Giovanni Battista Lully (Lulli), an Italian by birth, but imported early in life to the French court. They were followed by the equally significant operas of Rameau. In England the great Purcell wrote the first works that could be properly called operas. The German-English Handel wrote a tremendous number of operas, all of which have been completely forgotten, except for some individual numbers such as the famous *Largo*, originally an aria in *Xerxes.*

It was not until 1762 that any serious attempt was made to correct the faults of the old recitative-aria style of operatic writing. The reformer was Christoph Willibald von Gluck, whose name remains an honored one among the pioneers of music. Gluck's operas sound almost as artificial as their predecessors to modern ears, but in their day they were completely revolutionary, and they unquestionably made possible the later technique of Weber, Wagner and Richard Strauss.

THE REFORMS OF GLUCK

Gluck knew quite well what he wanted, even though he was not always able to accomplish it musically. He rebelled against the artificiality of the formal technique of Italian opera, which had concentrated more and more on the display of vocal powers at the expense of realism, and he insisted on at least attempting to suggest some fidelity to actual life on the stage. His *Orfeo* was the first successful demonstration of his theories, and it still lives in the operatic repertoire, a noble work, in the classic style, full of rich melody, yet extraordinarily dramatic in spots, especially considering the period of its composition. (The story of Orpheus and Eurydice was immensely popular with early operatic composers, obviously because of the musical qualities of its hero, which made it natural for him to sing his way through the plot, and because of its combination of mythological background and human interest.) *Che faro senza Euridice?* (What shall I do without Eurydice?) is the finest individual number in Gluck's *Orfeo,* and still deservedly popular.

Other important operas by Gluck were *Alceste*, *Iphigenia in Aulis*, and *Iphigenia in Tauris.* The first of the two Iphigenia operas, both of which were produced in Paris, made use of an overture, which was really the first of its kind as we know it today. (The overtures of opera are so often more important than the operas themselves that they deserve special treatment in a chapter of their own.) Gluck himself described the overture as intended "to prepare the audience for the action of the piece, and serve as a kind of argument to it." Naturally it was entirely instrumental.

That great musical genius, Mozart, did more for opera than any composer before him. His greatest operatic works were all in the Italian style, and to Italian texts, but with a new conception of dramatic expression, without any sacrifice of melodic values, and with an extraordinary development of the orchestra in its relation to the singers. Mozart's *Marriage of Figaro* and *Don Giovanni* are recognized as masterpieces of the highest order, and they are closely followed in rank by his *Cosi fan tutte* (Thus do all women), *Die Entführung aus dem Serail* (The Abduction from the Seraglio) and *The Magic Flute*. The last two were written to German texts, and that of *The Magic Flute* has been criticized because of its unintelligible allusions to Freemasonry. But they all contain beautiful melodies and impressively dramatic moments. To appreciate the operatic style of Mozart it is necessary only to listen to one of the following numbers (or to any of the overtures): *Voi che sapete* (Ye who know), from the *Marriage of Figaro, Deh vieni alla finestra, La ci darem la mano* and *Batti, Batti,* from *Don Giovanni*, and the Invocation, *Isis und Osiris, In diesen heil' gen Hallen,* and the coloratura aria of the Queen of the Night from *The Magic Flute.*

Beethoven's only opera, *Fidelio*, is remarkable chiefly for its four overtures and for the fact that it contains spoken lines, making it technically *opéra comique* (which has nothing to do with comedy, although *Fidelio* ends happily). Much of its music is impressive, but dramatically it means little. The soprano aria, *Abscheulicher* (Thou frightful one) is often heard as a concert number, and there is an effective chorus of prisoners, blinded by the sunlight, which had to be repeated at early performances of the work. But the heroic music has to make up for too many dramatic deficiencies, and *Fidelio* lives today chiefly in the overture known as *Leonore No. 3.*

The Romantic period of opera begins with Carl Maria von Weber, the real forerunner of Wagner and the music-drama. His operas dealt largely with the supernatural, and he was well aware of the advantage of using unfamiliar characters and settings. Weber's operas, *Der Freischütz* (The Freeshooter), *Oberon* and *Euryanthe*, are still played, and their overtures are among the most popular of orchestral pieces. Dramatically they are not of great importance, except insofar as they foreshadow Wagner in their attempts at a continuously moving melodic line, with uninterrupted accompaniment, in place of the stilted set numbers formerly in vogue.

LESSER LIGHTS OF OPERA

The names of Spontini, Cherubini, Cimarosa, Grétry and Méhul were important in their day, but their works are now practically forgotten, although all of them exerted a real influence on the development of opera. Rossini, however, still lives on the operatic stage through his great comedy, *The Barber of Seville*, and such serious works as *William Tell* and *Semiramide*. His style was brilliant, and he loved vocal display, but there was no great depth to his melodies, and he was at his best in the sparkling superficialities of the coloratura manner. *The Barber of Seville* is technically *opera buffa* (literally full of buffoonery), and it is interesting to compare Rossini's treatment of the popular story of the barber Figaro with that of Mozart, who handled it rather more seriously, although with plenty of humor. There is much charming music in the *Barber*, and the *Largo al factotum* (Make way for the Factotum) is one of the pet display pieces of baritones. *Una voce poco fa* is equally popular with coloratura sopranos. Both *Semiramide* and *William Tell* are remembered chiefly for their overtures, although the latter also contains some effective ballet music.

Rossini's immediate successors were Donizetti and Bellini, both of whom have retained their popularity up to the present time. Donizetti's *Lucia di Lammermoor* (founded on Sir Walter Scott's story of the Bride of Lammermoor) is still a war horse for florid singers, and contains not only the coloratura *Mad Scene* but the remarkable *Sextet*. Donizetti also composed several examples of *opera buffa*, worthy of comparison with Rossini. *L'Elisir d'Amore* (The Elixir of Love) contains that favorite aria of lyric tenors, *Una furtiva lagrima* (A furtive tear), while the *Daughter of the Regiment* and *Don Pasquale* are full of delightful music. Another more serious opera, *La Favorita*, includes the aria, *Spirito gentil*, also popular with tenors.

Bellini wrote in a larger dramatic style, and his *Norma* is still considered one of the greatest of all tests for operatic sopranos, as it requires both flexibility and the volume and quality worthy of its leading character. *Norma* goes back to the days of the Druids for its plot, and *I Puritani*, as its title indicates, has to do with the Puritans. *La Sonnambula* (The Sleepwalker) is a vehicle for coloratura singing, but otherwise unimportant.

Giacomo Meyerbeer, a Jewish German of Italian training, did most of his composing in Paris and made of opera a spectacular affair, immensely popular with the French public. His first great success, *Robert le Diable*, was followed by such historical works as *Les Huguenots*, *Le Prophète* and *L'Africaine*, in which fiction mingled freely with fact. To these he added *Dinorah*, another display piece for coloratura sopranos, whose *Shadow Dance* is still popular. *L'Africaine*, dealing with exploits of the explorer, Vasco da Gama, contains a fine tenor aria, *O Paradiso*, and *Le Prophète*, best known today by its *Coronation March*, also supplies contraltos with one of their showpieces in the aria, *Ah, mon fils*. *Les Huguenots* contains more good music than any of the others, including the quotation of Luther's *Reformation Hymn*.

Other operatic composers of the French school are Halévy (with *La Juive*, a real rival to Meyerbeer's spectacular productions), Herold, whose *Zampa* is remembered only by its overture, Auber, with *Fra Diavolo* and *Masaniello*, and Felicien David, whose *Pearl of Brazil* contains a still popular coloratura piece, *Charmant oiseau*. Berlioz wrote some unimportant operas, but achieved greater dramatic force in his *Damnation of Faust*, which is really a cantata. Its instrumental music is more remarkable than its vocal, particularly the charming *Dance of the Sylphs* and *Will-o-the-wisps* and the exciting *Rakoczy March*.

VERDI'S GREATNESS IS RECOGNIZED

The greatest name in opera, excluding the music-dramas of Wagner, is Giuseppe Verdi. In his long life, covering most of the nineteenth century, he produced a number of important works, in several styles. His early operas (*I Lombardi* and *Ernani*) were simple and melodic, but with *Rigoletto*, *Il Trovatore* and *La Traviata*, he already showed a dramatic power combined with musical invention that no previous composer in the Italian manner had achieved. All three of these popular operas contain melodies that are constantly heard today. One need mention only the *Caro nome* (another coloratura favorite), *La donna e mobile* and *Questa o quella* (for tenors) and the famous *Quartet* in *Rigoletto*, the *Miserere* and *Anvil Chorus* from *Il Trovatore*, and *Ah, fors e lui*, from *La Traviata*, all deservedly popular, and excellent illustrations of an effective balance of the musical and the dramatic.

After adding such works as *The Masked Ball*, *The Force of Destiny* and *Don Carlos* to his list, Verdi went far beyond all these when he composed *Aida*, for the opening of the grand opera house at Cairo. This is one of the few ideal combinations of drama and music in all opera, with an excellent, melodramatic plot and a constant succession of highly effective numbers for the soloists and chorus alike. The influence of Wagner is apparent in Verdi's use of the orchestra in *Aida*, and there is a convincingly Oriental atmosphere in much of the music. There should be special mention of the opening tenor aria, *Celeste Aida*, the two soprano arias, *Ritorna vincitor* and *O patria mia*, the various duets, including the final scene in the living tomb to which the hero and heroine are consigned, and the stirring *Triumphal March and Chorus*, not to speak of the modest but convincing off-stage melody given to a priestess, with harp accompaniment, or the excellent ballet music.

Late in life, Verdi wrote *Otello* and *Falstaff*, still more Wagnerian in style, and musically his finest works, although less obviously popular than some of those that had preceded them. *Otello* is a worthy treatment of the Shakespearean tragedy, with a great baritone aria in the familiar *Credo*, and a lovely prayer, sung by Desdemona. *Falstaff* sparkles throughout with an effervescent music that gets away as far as possible from the older Italian formula of set numbers and vocal display. Its comic hero is a baritone, and it was in the minor baritone rôle of Ford that Lawrence Tibbett made his first great success at the Metropolitan Opera in New York.

In addition to Verdi, we find Boito, primarily a librettist, composing one impressive opera in *Mefistofele*, a favorite with the basso

Chaliapin, making the devil the real hero of the Faust story, Ponchielli scoring with *La Gioconda,* which contains the overplayed *Dance of the Hours,* and then a succession of Italian composers of the modern realistic school who treated opera in various ways. Of these, Leoncavallo rests his reputation almost entirely on the popular *Pagliacci,* usually paired with the *Cavalleria Rusticana* of Mascagni. The first is an opera of the "play within the play," proving that actors are people after all, and that a clown may suffer enough to commit a double murder, to the complete satisfaction of his audience. It is hardly necessary to remind anyone today of the baritone *Prologue* or the tenor *Vesti la giubba,* with its agonized "Ridi, Pagliaccio," or the *Bird Song* of the soprano, or the *Serenade of Harlequin,* or the various effective choruses. This is tabloid opera in its most effective form. Similarly the Mascagni masterpiece (musically equaled by his later and less popular *Iris*) offers the melodious *Intermezzo* as a bit of instrumental sugar, the off-stage *Siciliano,* the dramatic *Voi lo sapete* of the heroine, Santuzza, a rousing *Brindisi,* or drinking-song, and a really fine chorus, sung outside the church.

Franchetti's *Germania,* Giordano's *Andrea Chenier, Fedora, Mme. Sans Gêne* and *La Cena della beffe* (known to America as *The Jest*), and Zandonai's *Conchita* and *Francesca da Rimini* all attracted attention in the modern Italian field of opera, and Wolf-Ferrari holds his own with the startling melodrama of *The Jewels of the Madonna* (with a charming *Intermezzo*) and the light comedy of *Le Donne curiose* and the *Secret of Suzanne.* Montemezzi may be called a one-opera composer, but his *L'Amore dei tre re* (Love of the Three Kings) is unquestionably one of the finest things since Wagner, and worthy to be called music-drama, in spite of its limited scope. It profits by a beautiful libretto, by Sem Benelli, who also wrote *The Jest,* and its music has a vitality that does not depend at all upon the performance of an individual star.

FROM VERDI TO PUCCINI

But the most popular modern composer of Italian opera is of course Giacomo Puccini. He had the advantages of the melodic background of Verdi, the dramatic and orchestral technique of Wagner, and the ultra-realism of his Italian contemporaries, and by a careful choice of subjects he succeeded in creating several works that may be destined to immortality. Verdi himself picked Puccini as his successor, and he seems to have been right in his estimate.

The opera public wavers between *Madame Butterfly* and *La Bohême* as its first choice, and both of these charming works have much to commend them. In his musical story of the Parisian Bohemia, Puccini managed to maintain a consistent atmosphere and a convincing realism, at the same time writing a succession of beautiful melodies, among which the dialogue of Mimi and Rodolfo, the song of Musetta and various ensembles stand out.

Madame Butterfly, based on the familiar story of John Luther Long, first staged by David Belasco, successfully achieves pathos and a surprising amount of conviction in its Italian interpretation of Japanese and American characters. The aria, *Un bel di* (One fine day) has become its most popular quotation, but there is far finer music in some of the ensembles, the duet at the close of the first act, the "flower duet," and the "waiting scene."

But the feeling is growing that Puccini's best opera from all angles is *La Tosca*, a condensation of the Sardou drama. Certainly this work has the most powerful moments of real tragedy. Its plot is unusual and on the whole convincing, and the music always accomplishes its purpose. The most obviously popular numbers in *La Tosca* are the interpolations, *Vissi d'arte* (Visions of Art) by the soprano, and *E lucevan le stelle* (The stars shone) by the tenor, but there are better wearing qualities in the choral scene of the first act, the utterances of the villain Scarpia, the torture scene and the music preceding the execution of the hero.

Puccini composed a workmanlike version of the Manon story (more charmingly handled by Massenet) with the title *Manon Lescaut*, but his *Girl of the Golden West* was too much of a caricature to be taken seriously, and his three short works, *Il Tabarro*, *Suor Angelica* and *Gianni Schicchi*, are little more than charming potboilers. *Turandot*, produced after Puccini's death, added nothing to his reputation, in spite of its spectacular stage effects.

In France the conventional opera of the nineteenth century offered Gounod's popular version of *Faust*, full of sugary melodies, and completely missing all but the obviously sentimental significance of the Goethe drama, and an equally sentimental but musically more significant setting of *Romeo and Juliet* by the same composer. Ambroise Thomas is represented by a fairly popular *Mignon* (with a familiar coloratura aria, the popular *Connais-tu,* and a charming gavotte) and a grandiose *Hamlet,* now almost forgotten (except for one of those inevitable drinking-songs).

Jacques Offenbach, writing mostly in lighter vein, produced the piquant and quite original *Tales of Hoffmann,* containing the much abused *Barcarolle;* Benjamin Godard's *Jocelyn* is remembered only by the similarly exploited *Berceuse;* Lalo composed an opera *Le Roi d'Ys,* whose overture is still played; and Delibes added to his delightful ballets, *Sylvia* and *Coppelia,* a colorful and atmospheric *Lakmé,* which is operatically effective and gives another prized opportunity to coloratura sopranos, particularly in the well-known *Bell Song.*

THE MIRACLE OF "CARMEN"

Among all these French composers of opera, Georges Bizet stands out like a giant with his one great work, *Carmen.* It ranks with Verdi's *Aida* as the ideal combination of music and theater, from the conventional operatic standpoint, and its exciting story receives a musical treatment that is at once colorful, melodious and realistic. *Carmen* is the best possible introduction to opera in general, and if the literature held more such works, the whole artificial form might easily hold its own in competition with the more convincing types of music and drama. The *Toreador Song* is perhaps a little too obvious, as is the interpolated sweetness of Micaela, but Carmen's own *Habanera* and *Seguidilla,* with true Spanish flavor, the card scene, the various dances and ensembles, the charming intermezzi and the final music outside the bull ring are all of real importance. Bizet also wrote an Oriental opera, *The Pearl Fishers,* and some excellent incidental music to Daudet's *L'Arlesienne,* but his reputation rests chiefly on *Carmen.*

The Wagnerian influence is found in the operas of Massenet, mixed with the melodic charm and sentimentality of the typical French school. His *Herodiade,* dramatizing the Biblical story of Salome and her wicked mother, contains some fine music, of which the baritone aria, *Vision fugitif,* and the soprano *Il est doux* have won the greatest popularity. Massenet's setting of *Werther* is musically perhaps his best work, but too dull for the public. *Thaïs* has spectacular qualities (and the inevitable *Méditation*, as a violin solo), and there are musical and dramatic virtues in *Don Quixote*. But the two most effective works of Massenet are *Manon* and *Le Jongleur de Notre Dame*, both full of charm, grace and delicacy of treatment, and musically close to inspiration at times. The *Dream*, the *Farewell to the Table*, *Ah, fuyez* and the *Gavotte* from *Manon* are all worth hearing as individual numbers.

Charpentier's *Louise* is another charming French opera in the style of Massenet, which won great success in America, with the help of Mary Garden's interpretation of the heroine. Its most familiar number is the soprano aria, *Depuis le jour*. Saint-Saëns, in his *Samson and Delilah*, wrote what is practically an oratorio in costume, but the music has recognizable merits, and the aria *My heart at thy sweet voice* has become widely popular as a vehicle for contraltos.

Beyond this, it is sufficient to mention the names of Fevrier's *Monna Vanna*, Ravel's sardonic little *L'Heure Espagnole*, Erlanger's spectacular *Aphrodite*, and Rabaud's *Marouf*, all successfully produced in America, as was the *Goyescas* of the Spanish composer Granados. Debussy's *Pelléas and Mélisande*, as well as the modern operas of Richard Strauss and others, should properly be considered under the head of music-drama. America's own most important contributions to operatic literature have been Deems Taylor's *Peter Ibbetson* and *The King's Henchman*, Gruenberg's *Emperor Jones*, George Gershwin's *Porgy and Bess*, Howard Hanson's *Merry Mount*, Virgil Thomson's *Four Saints in Three Acts*, Douglas Moore's *The Devil and Daniel Webster*, Cadman's *Shanewis*, Victor Herbert's *Natoma*, Harling's *Light from St. Agnes*, Hadley's *Azora*, Parker's *Mona*, and *The Pipe of Desire*, by Frederick Converse, both prize winners at the Metropolitan.

Amid all this operatic activity, Russia alone, with the possible exception of the Bohemian Smetana's *Bartered Bride*, has presented a truly national school of composition, employing its own folk-music to good purpose. The outstanding monument of this Russian school is Moussorgsky's *Boris Godounoff*, which ranks with the great operas of all time, in spite of its manifest crudities of style and lack of stage technique. Its virtues lie in the direct and overwhelmingly sincere treatment of its dramatic materials, free from all artificiality, its consistent use of folk-like themes, and its magnificent choral numbers. The rôle of Boris himself is the greatest ever written for a basso.

With this masterpiece one may fairly compare the lesser works of Rimsky-Korsakoff (*The Snow Maiden*, *Sadko*, *Tsar Saltan*, *Coq d'Or*), Borodin (*Prince Igor*, containing the popular *Polovetsian Dances*), Glinka (*A Life for the Czar*, *Russlan and Ludmilla*) and Moussorgsky's own *Khovantchina*. Tschaikowsky leans more to the Italian style in his *Eugen Onegin* and *Pique Dame*, and Rubinstein's *Demon*, still popular abroad, is not particularly national in flavor.

In Germany, Humperdinck succeeded in putting something of the folk spirit into his *Hänsel und Gretel*, which remains a delightful opera for adults as well as children, and his *Königskinder* also contains some beautiful music. D'Albert's *Tiefland* (Marta of the Lowlands), Kienzl's *Kuhreigen*, and operatic works of Goldmark, Cornelius and Goetz retain some life, and in the lighter field mention should be made of Nicolai's *Merry Wives of Windsor* (another overture to the general public), and the operettas of Suppé, Johann Strauss, Lortzing, Millocker, and such moderns as Lehar, Herbert, Oscar Straus, Friml, Romberg, Kern, Kalman, Rodgers, Weill and Gershwin. A special place in the affections of the public seems reserved for Flotow's *Martha*, perhaps chiefly because it contains the popular Irish tune, *The Last Rose of Summer*. England can rest her laurels on the satirical masterpieces of Gilbert and Sullivan (far more important than any of her grand operas) and that old-time collection of ballads known as *The Beggar's Opera*.

But the chief significance of the whole operatic trend in music is that it produced the unique art-form known as music-drama, and a consideration of this phenomenon requires detailed concentration on the work of one composer, the greatest genius that dramatic music has known, Richard Wagner.

THE CLIMAX OF MUSIC-DRAMA

Wagner stands supreme in dramatic music, just as the "three B's"—Bach, Beethoven and Brahms—are supreme in absolute music. His greatest compositions for the musical stage are so far beyond everything else that goes by the name of opera that they have been unanimously given his own title of "music-drama."

Even a few hearings of Wagner's music will make it clear to almost any listener that it represents an entirely new technique, something quite distinct from the conventional conception of opera. Many other composers had dreamed of such a thing, and even stated their belief in words; but Wagner was the first and almost the only one to realize the ideal.

Briefly stated, the individuality of Wagnerian music-drama consists in the complete blending of text, action, and vocal and instrumental music, the elimination of set numbers and all suggestion of the old-fashioned recitative and aria, substituting a continuous flow of polyphonic music in which the orchestra and the voices are equally important, and finally the perfection of the *Leitmotif* (leading or guiding motive), whereby the characters, episodes and even inanimate objects or abstractions figuring in the drama are definitely labeled with short melody-patterns which appear throughout the score, clarifying its meaning and literally dramatizing the music itself. Beyond all these innovations, Wagner must be credited with a melodic invention that consistently shows the inevitability of true genius, and a technique of harmony and instrumentation that is unsurpassed.[1]

Wagner did not reach these unique heights immediately. His early works are operas, much like those that had gone before, although almost from the outset of his career he showed signs of originality in his conceptions. *Rienzi*, his first work of importance, is a spectacular historical drama in the manner of Meyerbeer, whom Wagner knew first as a friendly patron and later as a jealous enemy.

The *Flying Dutchman* already showed a long step forward, although it is still an opera of the romantic type, owing much to the influence of Weber. But in addition to its set numbers, the *Flying Dutchman* shows distinct signs of the *Leitmotif* in its simpler form, and the dramatic atmosphere is supplied by the orchestra quite as much as by the singers. It is also characteristic of Wagner's leaning toward the supernatural in his search for plots.

Tannhäuser, which today seems the most obviously melodious of any of the Wagnerian scores, was considered revolutionary in its

[1]Exception might be made in favor of some of the modern harmonists and such masters of the orchestra as Richard Strauss, Debussy and Stravinsky. But not one of them shows the melodic invention of a Wagner, and it has yet to be proved that a mere continuation in the direction of dissonance and complexity of instrumentation adds any real value to music.

Out of the storm—a ghost opera

RICHARD WAGNER and his actress wife, Minna, decided to leave Riga when his debts threatened to land him in jail. They sailed away over the rough Baltic Sea, accompanied by their Newfoundland dog, to seek a new life in Paris, then the musical center of the world.

The passage was a stormy one, but sitting up with the steersman, Wagner evolved the music of an opera, a story of sailors and the sea. It was *The Flying Dutchman*, dealing with the ghost ship of the legendary Hollander, Vanderdecken, who defied even Satan in his attempt to round the Cape of Good Hope. For his bold challenge the Dutchman was condemned to sail the seas without rest until a loving woman sacrificed her life for his sake. Heinrich Heine had told the tale in prose, but Wagner developed it into the first of the music-dramas that brought him fame.

The premiere of *The Flying Dutchman*, in Dresden, was a failure, even with the great soprano, Schroeder-Devrient, in the role of the heroine, Senta. The public was not yet ready for anything beyond the obvious spectacles of Meyerbeer, which Wagner himself had imitated in *Rienzi*. Today his early operas are known chiefly by their overtures, which are still popular on concert programs, records, and the radio.

But the ghost opera inspired by that stormy sea voyage led to *Tannhäuser*, then *Lohengrin*, and finally the immortal cycle of the *Ring of the Nibelung*, *Tristan and Isolde*, *The Mastersingers* and *Parsifal*. The greater Wagner, creator of music-drama rather than mere opera, was born in battle with the elements and fought his way to recognition through storms of criticism and disapproval, until the people themselves, as always, placed the seal of greatness on his music.

THET

time (1845), and the musical public accepted it with the greatest reluctance. In Paris, Wagner had to add a ballet to satisfy the orthodox listeners, and his fellow Germans suggested that the opera should have ended happily, with the marriage of Tannhäuser and Elisabeth! The story is built around the contests of the Minnesingers at the historic Wartburg, the hero falling under the spell of a very real Venus, but eventually repenting and undertaking a pilgrimage to Rome, only to find the beautiful Elisabeth dead on his return. Everybody knows the *Pilgrims' Chorus*, the *March*, and the *Song to the Evening Star* (sung by the baritone, Wolfram von Eschenbach), and Elisabeth's greeting to the hall of the Minnesingers (*Dich, theure Halle*) is a popular concert number with dramatic sopranos. (Naturally, Wagner never wrote a coloratura rôle, although his demands upon vocal technique are severe.)

WAGNER'S LOGICAL DEVELOPMENT

Lohengrin, first produced by Liszt (Wagner's father-in-law) at Weimar in 1850, was the real turning-point in Wagner's career, and may properly be called his first music-drama, although it still has many of the old operatic qualities. But while such numbers as Elsa's *Dream*, Lohengrin's *Narrative*, King Henry's *Prayer*, the familiar *Wedding March* and other choruses have a certain independence, and are often heard individually, the score as a whole shows a new unity, with a beautiful use of the *Leitmotif*, particularly in its suggestion of the Holy Grail, to whose service the mystic knight is dedicated.

Music-drama reaches its climax in the tremendous cycle known as *The Ring of the Nibelung*. (It should be realized that the word "ring" does not refer to the cycle itself, but to an actual ring, first worn by the Nibelung, Alberich, made from the treasure known as the Rheingold, and fated by a terrible curse to bring tragedy to all those who possess it.) Generally called a trilogy, the cycle actually contains four music-dramas, a Prologue, (*Das Rheingold*), *Die Walküre, Siegfried* and *Götterdämmerung* (Twilight or Dusk of the Gods).

Wagner wrote all his librettos himself, using for the Nibelungen-cycle an alliterative form of poetry, modeled after the songs of the *Edda*, basis of the *Nibelungenlied* and *Volsungasaga*, from which he derived his materials. He wrote most of the text of *Götterdämmerung* first (calling it *Siegfried's Death*) and then worked backward, gradually creating a complete story. In its final form this does not agree with any of the original legends, but it makes a logical plot, following the course of the fateful treasure from the time that it is stolen from the Rhine maidens until the ring is finally thrown back into the river, and Valhalla itself, the abode of the gods, is overwhelmed in the general destruction.

OTHER WAGNERIAN OPERAS

The four music-dramas of the *Ring* occupied a large part of Wagner's life, and the cycle was not completed until 1876. Meanwhile he also composed two works of contrasting character, each supreme in its field, *Tristan und Isolde* and *Die Meistersinger*. The first is considered by many the finest of his masterpieces, and the second is unquestionably the world's greatest musical comedy.

Tristan und Isolde is again an adaptation of old materials, based on the story of the immortal lovers as told by Gottfried von Strassburg. It is a Celtic legend, known all over Europe, and, as in the *Ring* dramas, Wagner has succeeded in making an effective libretto for his own purposes without slavishly following any single version of the tale.

In *Die Meistersinger* Wagner temporarily deserted his technique of music-drama and deliberately returned to a conventional operatic form, but carried it out on such a magnificent scale as to throw every other comic opera into the shade. There are set numbers, with some particularly effective choruses, and the *Prize Song* itself is of course the most popular of the solos. Hans Sachs has a fine baritone solo in *Wahn, Wahn,* and the scene of the contest is excellent comedy, both in the music and in the action. Wagner utilized this satirical opera to poke fun at all the pedants of music, caricaturing the attempts of the Mastersingers to compose music by rule and formula, and glorifying the natural, spontaneous expression of talent, as represented by Walther's *Prize Song* (although admitting the need of a technique to give form to such inspiration). The famous *March* of the Mastersingers (which appears also in the popular *Prelude*) is based upon an actual theme of these medieval musicians, known as the *Long Tone*.

Wagner's final work was *Parsifal*, a religious music-drama built around the Knights of the Grail, and long considered sacred to Bayreuth, where it was first performed in 1882, only a year before the composer's death. While it is generally ranked below its immediate predecessors, *Parsifal* contains deeply impressive music, with a sustained atmosphere of mysticism which no other composer has achieved in a stage work.

The ritual of this music-drama need not be taken too literally, and from the mere standpoint of the musical theater it has wonderfully effective moments, such as the *Entrance of the Knights of the Grail*, with its monotonous tolling of bells, the sensuous flower music, and the miraculous calm of the *Good Friday Spell.*

To a modern listener there are undeniably dull spots in all the Wagnerian music-dramas. Great genius that he was, Wagner never quite grasped the vital need of condensation. He was able to reduce his plot materials to a compact and convincing story, but allowed his musical imagination to run away with him and was perhaps too wrapped up in his personal interpretations and symbolism to give free play to his undeniable command of stage technique.

Yet the true Wagner enthusiast would not willingly allow one note of any of his great scores to be cut out. Even when he is thoroughly familiar with every obvious or implied significance, he listens with rapture to the endless rise and fall of this illimitable sea of inspired music. Wagner was one of the few creative artists who could conceive a thing in big terms and then carry it out on the scale of its conception. He is the one and only master of the sublime in dramatic music, and in this respect Bach, Beethoven and Brahms are his only rivals in the entire literature of the art.

LATER EXAMPLES OF MUSIC-DRAMA

Since Wagner there have been only a few operas that could be honored with the name of music-drama. Perhaps the title can most fairly be applied to the unique *Pelléas and Mélisande* of Debussy. This strange, almost incomprehensible work is the ultimate in combining words and music so closely that one is scarcely aware that the text is being sung. Debussy's technique is that of a continuous recitative, but always completely fused with the orchestration, so that no effect of artificiality is produced. There is no suggestion of regular melody, as conventionally recognized, although the music has definite patterns and a continuous form. Debussy's vague, unresolved harmonies and delicacy of orchestration are marvelously fitted to the elusive, symbolical text of Maeterlinck, and even to those who may confess themselves ignorant of what it is all about, the charm and intuitive rightness of the music must eventually prove appealing.

A far more robust style is that of Richard Strauss, who has written several operas that may well claim kinship with Wagner's. His *Rosenkavalier* is a masterpiece of sardonic humor, full of modern sophistication and an intimate knowledge of Viennese court life, as it was in the past. The music alternates between extreme dissonance and a Mozartian charm, with some waltzes that would have done credit to the Viennese Johann himself. The plot is an absurd hodge-podge from the pen of Hugo von Hofmannsthal, but the satire is well sustained and can be very funny, once the difficulties of performance are surmounted. In spite of its light character, it is quite possible that *Der Rosenkavalier* will eventually be regarded as Strauss's finest dramatic work.

His treatment of classic tragedy is displayed in *Elektra*, a most impressive musical version of the ancient Greek story of the daughter of Clytemnestra and her vengeance after the murder of her father Agamemnon, aided by her brother Orestes. Strauss has given this gruesome drama of a female Hamlet a setting of inspired directness and simplicity, even though the musical technique is of the most modern type, with elaborate orchestration and cruel dissonances. When first produced in America it was considered rather shocking in its brutality, but today it is recognized as a great work of art.

Salome, the music-drama of the daughter of Herodiade who danced for the head of John the Baptist, was similarly criticized at its first presentation, but has come to be considered a rather mild oratorio in costume. (Oscar Hammerstein made the gesture of a true impresario when he once gave both *Salome* and *Elektra* in one day, at popular prices.) The notorious *Dance of the Seven Veils* is often played as a concert number, and while interesting musically, it fails to take advantage of the possibilities of its Oriental background.

The operas of Humperdinck are far simpler musically, but possess something of the Wagnerian quality, with frequent melodic inspiration. Montemezzi's *Love of the Three Kings* is also close to this standard, with actual echoes of the style of *Tristan und Isolde*. Moussorgsky's *Boris Godounoff* might also be called a music-drama, written far ahead of its time, but with an instinctive grasp of the possibilities of such a nationalistic art.

Ultramodern composers have gone beyond any of these works in cacophony and the maltreatment of the human voice (with Alban Berg's *Wozzek* a conspicuous example), as well as in advanced conceptions of realism and atmosphere, but it is impossible to give their creations a fair appraisal until they have had some chance to prove their wearing qualities.

SOME POPULAR OPERA PLOTS

Here are the capsule stories of the operas most likely to be heard on the air and also most generally recorded. The English titles are given first, followed by the original versions, with credit for the librettos and dates and places of first performances.

ORPHEUS AND EURYDICE
(Orfeo ed Euridice)

CHRISTOPH WILLIBALD VON GLUCK

Libretto by Calzabigi.

First produced in Vienna, 1762.

Orpheus, the fabulous musician of Greek mythology, mourns the death of his beloved Eurydice and is permitted by the gods to rescue her from the Lower World, provided he does not look upon her face until she is free. He finds her in the Elysian Fields, but before they reach the earth, she innocently makes him break his promise, so that he loses her again. But the god of love finally takes pity on them and they are eventually reunited in his temple.

THE MARRIAGE OF FIGARO
(Le Nozze di Figaro)

WOLFGANG AMADEUS MOZART

Libretto by Lorenzo da Ponte.

First produced in Vienna, 1786.

Figaro, the Barber of Seville (hero of Rossini's opera of that name and of the original play by Beaumarchais), is valet to Count Almaviva, now married to Rosina. But the philandering Count flirts with Susanna, the maid, although she and Figaro are actually engaged to be married. A comic plot of mistaken identity is built from this farcical situation. The Countess, learning of her husband's plan to meet Susanna in the garden, dresses her page boy, Cherubino, in the maid's clothes and sends him to keep the rendezvous. Figaro also goes out to spy on his sweetheart, and when the real Susanna makes love to the barber, the Count believes her to be his own wife. All misunderstandings are finally cleared up, and the opera ends with the wedding of Susanna and Figaro.

DON GIOVANNI

WOLFGANG AMADEUS MOZART

Libretto by Lorenzo da Ponte.

First produced in Prague, 1787. The traditional great lover, Don Giovanni, tries to force his attentions on the beautiful Donna Anna, without revealing his identity. She drives him from the house, and when challenged by her father, the commandant of Seville, Don Giovanni kills him and escapes without being recognized. Don Ottavio, her suitor, joins Donna Anna in swearing vengeance. They receive cooperation from Donna Elvira, a discarded sweetheart of Don Giovanni, who becomes involved with a peasant girl, Zerlina, whose lover, Massetto, also joins in the man hunt. But it is the statue of the commandant that eventually puts an end to the Don's licentious career. With his servant, Leporello, he mockingly invites the stone image of his victim to have supper with him, and the invitation is weirdly accepted. At the height of the feast, portentous knocks are heard, and the statue stalks into the room. Don Giovanni refuses to repent, and the statue causes the earth to open and swallow up the libertine in eternal fire. At the close Leporello and the virtuous characters point the moral to the audience.

THE MAGIC FLUTE

(*Die Zauberflöte*)

WOLFGANG AMADEUS MOZART

Libretto by Emanuel Schikaneder.

First produced in Vienna, 1791. The plot of this final opera by Mozart, which mingles spoken dialogue with musical numbers, is founded upon the mysteries of Freemasonry and is largely allegorical. Tamino, saved by three maidens from the attack of a giant serpent, acquires the protection of the magic flute and undertakes the rescue of Pamina, daughter of the Queen of the Night, from the high priest Sarastro. His companion is the bird catcher, Papageno, who plays upon a Pan pipe and supplies a comic counterplot in his courting of Papagena. Tamino himself becomes a disciple of Sarastro and, after passing various tests of his courage, eventually wins Pamina as his bride.

FIDELIO

LUDWIG VAN BEETHOVEN

Libretto by Joseph Sonnleithner.

First produced in Vienna, 1805. Beethoven's only opera tells the story of the faithful Leonora, who disguises herself as a man (Fidelio), in an effort to save her husband, Florestan, from the prison of the cruel Spaniard, Don Pizzaro. The jailer, Rocco, whose daughter Marzelline has fallen in love with the handsome Fidelio, orders Leonora to help him dig Florestan's grave. When Pizzaro enters the dungeon, with the intention of killing Florestan, Leonora threatens the villain with a pistol. The sound of a trumpet off stage announces the timely arrival of the Minister of Justice, Don Fernando, who releases Florestan and the rest of the prisoners and sends Pizzaro to a well-merited punishment.

THE BARBER OF SEVILLE
(*Il Barbiere di Siviglia*)

GIOACCHINO ROSSINI

Libretto by Cesare Sterbini.

First produced in Rome, 1816.

Count Almaviva is in love with Rosina, the ward of Dr. Bartolo, who himself intends to marry her for her money. With the aid of the versatile barber, Figaro, the Count manages to see Rosina, first pretending to be a drunken soldier and then taking the place of her singing-teacher, Don Basilio. The lovers plan an elopement, and Bartolo's attempts to make Rosina suspicious are unavailing. But when her guardian realizes that the Count is willing to renounce her dowry, he gladly consents to their marriage.

NORMA

VINCENZO BELLINI

Libretto by Giuseppe Felice Romani.

First produced in Milan, 1831.

Norma is a high priestess of the Gallic Druids, who has broken her vows by secretly marrying the Roman proconsul, Pollione. After they have had two children, he falls in love with another priestess, Adalgisa, who innocently asks Norma for advice. They both denounce the treachery of the Roman, and Norma demands that he give up Adalgisa or die. When he chooses death, Norma declares herself to be the guilty one and is joined on the Druidic funeral pyre by Pollione, whose love has been revived by her nobility.

THE ELIXIR OF LOVE
(*L'Elisir d'Amore*)

GAETANO DONIZETTI

Libretto by Giuseppe Felice Romani.

First produced in Milan, 1832.

Nemorino is in love with Adina, who seems to favor a soldier, Sergeant Belcore. Dr. Dulcamara sells Nemorino a supposed love potion, actually strong wine, with which the lover gains confidence. But when he wishes to buy more of the elixir, he can earn the money only by joining the army. This impresses Adina, and she capitulates when she sees Nemorino surrounded by other girls, who have heard of the death of his rich uncle. All ends

The stormy beginning of a great concerto

YOUNG PETER TSCHAIKOWSKY owed much to the Rubinstein brothers. Anton, the spectacular pianist, had taken him as a pupil in his conservatory at St. Petersburg, and after his graduation the other Rubinstein, Nicholas, gave him a chance to earn thirty dollars a month teaching harmony in Moscow.

It was a shock, therefore, when the aspiring Tschaikowsky played his first Piano Concerto for the friend and patron whose opinion he valued so highly. Nicholas Rubinstein listened to the whole piece in silence. Then the storm broke. As Tschaikowsky himself later described the scene, "by degrees his passion rose, and finally he resembled Zeus' thunderbolts. It appeared that my Concerto was worthless and absolutely unplayable . . . clumsy . . . bad . . . trivial . . . commonplace. . . . In short, an unbiased spectator of the scene could only have thought that I was a stupid, untalented, and conceited spoiler of music paper who had had the impertinence to show his rubbish to a celebrated man."

The youthful composer had the courage to stick to his guns, in spite of this cruel criticism. Without making any changes, he showed the Concerto to Hans von Bülow, one of the leading pianists of his day, who praised it highly and gave it the first public performance, in Boston, in 1875. The Concerto became a favorite with music-lovers, but the general public was practically unaware of its existence until Freddy Martin, in 1941, played and recorded a fox-trot version under the title *Tonight We Love*. Simultaneously there appeared another popular treatment called *Concerto for Two,* and since then that stirring theme has numbered its admirers in the millions.

First impressions are not always correct, but public taste eventually discovers the good things in music if given half a chance.

happily when Adina secures Nemorino's release from service and dismisses the Sergeant, who philosophically looks for a substitute.

LUCIA DI LAMMERMOOR

GAETANO DONIZETTI

Libretto by Salvatore Cammarano.

First produced in Naples, 1835. Sir Walter Scott's novel, *The Bride of Lammermoor*, is in its operatic form one of the most popular vehicles for the coloratura-soprano voice, besides containing the famous Sextet. Henry Ashton, for financial reasons, arranges to have his sister Lucy marry Lord Arthur Bucklaw. But she is in love with Edgar Ravenswood, who is absent in France. Her brother intercepts letters from Ravenswood and finally commits a forgery to prove to her that her lover is unfaithful. In desperation she consents to marry Bucklaw, only to have Edgar return too late, to denounce her and the whole house of Lammermoor. Lucy kills her husband on their wedding night and goes insane (as dramatized in the famous Mad Scene). Edgar learns of her death and fidelity and kills himself in the graveyard of his ancestors.

THE AFRICAN GIRL
(*L'Africaine*)

GIACOMO MEYERBEER

Libretto by Eugene Scribe.

First produced in Paris, 1865. Meyerbeer's last and greatest opera was not produced until a year after his death. It represents the pre-Wagnerian type of musical spectacle at its best. The Spanish explorer, Vasco da Gama, brings back from an African voyage two slaves, Selika, who had been a queen in India, and her servant, Nelusko. Inez, daughter of the Admiral Don Diego, is in love with Vasco, but her father insists that she marry the cruel but powerful Don Pedro. The latter succeeds in having Vasco thrown into prison and himself goes to find the mysterious land, taking Selika and Nelusko along as guides. Vasco follows in another ship, to warn Don Pedro that Nelusko means to betray him. His warning is ignored, and when Don Pedro and his men are all captured or killed by the Africans, Selika, who has fallen in love with Vasco, takes him to her own country, which inspires the great aria, *O Paradiso*. Vasco, however, finds that Inez is still alive, although she had paid for his release by marrying Don Pedro. Hearing the beloved voice in the distance, he leaves Selika, who ends her life by poison as the ship sails away with Vasco and Inez on board.

MARTHA

FRIEDRICH VON FLOTOW

Libretto by W. Friedrich.

First produced in Vienna, 1847. This is really a comic opera, best known through its two popular melodies, *The Last Rose of Summer* (borrowed by Flotow from Thomas Moore and the old Irish tune, *The Groves of Blarney*) and *M'Appari*, which became a Tin Pan Alley hit as *Marta.* Two English ladies of Queen Anne's court, Harriet and Nancy, disguise themselves as servants and go to Richmond Fair, where they are engaged by the country gentlemen, Lionel and Plunkett. Mutual love develops, with complications when the ladies leave their employers and return to court. Lionel fortunately turns out to be the son of the deceased Earl of Derby, and his wealth and position make it possible for him to marry Lady Harriet (Martha), while Plunkett weds her friend Nancy.

TANNHÄUSER

RICHARD WAGNER

Text by the composer.

First produced in Dresden, 1845. Although preceded by *Rienzi* and *The Flying Dutchman*, *Tannhäuser* is the earliest Wagnerian opera to be heard regularly today. Its hero, Tannhäuser (Heinrich von Ofterdingen), is a Minnesinger or troubadour, in love with Elisabeth, daughter of the Landgrave of Thuringia. But Tannhäuser falls under the spell of Venus, taking part in the wild orgies of the near-by Venusberg. In a singing contest held at the historic Wartburg, with Elisabeth's hand as the prize, Tannhäuser disgraces himself by offering a glorification of sensual love and is forced to do penance by making a pilgrimage to Rome, where the Pope tells him that his pardon will be assured only when his pilgrim staff sprouts leaves. Tannhäuser eventually returns (to the music of the *Pilgrims' Chorus*), only to find that Elisabeth is dead. When he himself dies beside her lifeless body, a miracle occurs as the pilgrim's staff breaks into leaves, assuring pardon for the penitent Minnesinger.

LOHENGRIN

RICHARD WAGNER

Text by the composer.

First produced at Weimar, 1850. Elsa of Brabant is falsely accused of the murder of her brother Gottfried by her wicked uncle, Frederick Telramund, and his evil wife, Ortrud. She is permitted to select a champion to defend her, and calls upon a mystic knight whom she knows only in her dreams. To the astonishment of all, the knight appears in a boat drawn by a swan. He easily defeats Telramund in combat and marries Elsa, but with the condition that she shall never ask his name or whence he came. The familiar *Wedding March* introduces the ceremony, preceded by the lively music of a torchlight procession (*Prelude to Act III*). Ortrud, however, arouses the curiosity of Elsa, until she asks the fatal question. As Telramund rushes in, he is killed. The mystic knight then gives a public account of himself. His name is Lohengrin, the son of Parsifal, and he is in the service of the Holy Grail, to which he must now return. The swan boat reappears, and Elsa falls lifeless as Lohengrin departs, first turning the swan into her brother Gottfried, who had been thus bewitched by the sorceress, Ortrud.

TRISTAN UND ISOLDE

RICHARD WAGNER

Text by the composer.

First produced in Munich, 1865. This may be considered Wagner's first real music-drama, as compared with the more conventional operas before it, and it is perhaps his greatest work. Cornwall's King Mark sends his nephew, Tristan, to bring back his affianced bride, Isolde, an Irish Princess. But Tristan and Isolde had met before, when she nursed him back to life after he had killed her lover in battle. During the voyage to Cornwall, they become aware of their love and decide to end their lives with poison. But Isolde's maid, Brangäne, substitutes a love potion for the fatal drink, and the situation is now hopeless. They meet at night in the castle garden and are caught by King Mark and his men. Tristan is severely wounded by Melot and taken back to his old home in Brittany by his faithful servitor, Kurwenal. There Isolde joins him as he is dying, and herself reaches the climactic "love death" just as the sorrowing King Mark arrives to forgive the innocent lovers.

THE MASTERSINGERS

(*Die Meistersinger*)

RICHARD WAGNER

Text by the composer.

First produced in Munich, 1868. Wagner's only musical comedy (generally considered the greatest of all time) tells the story of Hans Sachs, the shoemaker poet of Nürnberg, and his fellow guildsmen, the Mastersingers, with the love of Eva, the goldsmith's daughter, and young Walter von Stolzing. The conflict is created by the absurd Beckmesser, who also aspires to the hand of the wealthy girl. Hans Sachs unselfishly instructs Walter in the art of mastersong, after Beckmesser had judged against him in the preliminary contest. The clumsy rival is himself eliminated in the final competition, and Walter wins Eva with his famous *Prize Song*.

THE RING OF THE NIBELUNG

(*Der Ring des Nibelungen*)

RICHARD WAGNER

Text by the composer.

First produced in Munich, 1869.

(a) THE RHINEGOLD

(*Das Rheingold*)

This cycle of three music-dramas and a Prologue, actually four complete operas of gigantic dimensions, constitutes the most colossal

How a great love song was born

"EDVARD GRIEG is a nobody," said her mother. "He has nothing, and he writes music that nobody cares to listen to." After all, only two copies of his first printed song had been sold.

Barred from the house of his beloved, young Edvard Grieg found solace in his art and composed one of the most popular of all the world's love songs. The Norwegian title was *Jeg Elsker Dig*, but Europe came to know it as *Ich Liebe Dich*, and today it is in plain English, *I Love You*, as Lauritz Melchior sings it on the screen, on the air, and on the concert stage.

Grieg eventually married the girl of his choice, the inspiration of *I Love You* and many other great songs. His story, with some embellishments, has been turned into a Broadway musical hit, *Song of Norway*, with a score arranged from his own most popular melodies.

Grieg has other fine songs to his credit, such as *A Swan*, *A Dream*, and the lilting *Boat Song* (*Im Kahne*). His *Peer Gynt* Suites are universally loved, and his *Piano Concerto* is known both in its original form (as played by Iturbi in the film, *Music for Millions*) and also in various jazz versions. Three violin sonatas and a string quartet are included in the Grieg music that the general public is just beginning to discover.

The old rule of the survival of the fittest still works. Critics and scholars may select a composition for immortality, but it is the vast audience of the people themselves who place upon it the stamp of permanence. That distinction has been amply won by Edvard Grieg.

achievement in the entire history of music. The four works tell a continuous story, founded on a combination of the *Edda*, the *Volsungasaga* and the German *Nibelungenlied*. In the Prologue, Alberich, the Nibelung, a dwarf, steals the golden treasure, guarded by the Rhine maidens, from the bottom of the river. With it he acquires a magic ring and a helmet which permits the wearer to assume any form he desires. The gods employ the giants to build a celestial palace for them, called Valhalla, where heroes will be brought after their death on the battlefield. To pay for this, the gods take the Rhinegold away from Alberich, who curses the ring. The giants demand that the treasure cover the entire person of Freia, goddess of love, and this is achieved only by the addition of the fatal ring. One giant immediately kills the other, thus carrying out the curse, and the gods enter Valhalla over a bridge formed by a rainbow from earth to heaven.

(b) THE VALKYRIE
(*Die Walküre*)

First produced at Munich, 1870. Wotan, king of the gods, has founded the super-race of the Volsungs with the twins, Siegmund and Sieglinde, who, however, are separated in childhood and grow up as strangers. Siegmund staggers exhausted into the hut of Hunding, husband of Sieglinde, and innocently falls in love with his sister. They flee together, and Siegmund meets Hunding in mortal combat. Fricka, goddess of the hearth and home, has persuaded her husband, Wotan, that Siegmund must die, but Brünnhilde, the Valkyrie, one of the nine daughters of Wotan, disobeys orders and tries to help Siegmund to win. Wotan intervenes, and, with both fighters dead, sentences his daughter to sleep on a fire-ringed mountain, where she can be awakened only by a hero brave enough to pass the flames. Meanwhile Brünnhilde has hidden Sieglinde in the forest, where she can bear a child of destiny, Siegfried.

(c) SIEGFRIED

First produced at Bayreuth, 1876. Siegfried, whose mother, Sieglinde, died at his birth, is brought up in the forest by the dwarf, Mime, a silversmith. Near by is the dragon, Fafner, transformed from the giant-killer, and guarding the Rhinegold with its fatal ring. Siegfried, arrived at manhood, forges the sword, Notung, from the fragments that his mother had saved and goes out to slay the dragon. The blood of the monster gives him an understanding of the language of animals, and he hears the forest bird warn him against Mime, whom he quickly kills. Siegfried is guided by the bird song to the fiery mountain, where he fights his way past Wotan and the magic flames and wakens Brünnhilde from her long sleep.

(d) TWILIGHT OF THE GODS
(*Götterdämmerung*)

First produced at Bayreuth, 1876. After a Prologue by the Fates (Norns), Siegfried is seen bidding farewell to his beloved Brünnhilde, giving her the ring of the Nibelung as he departs on a journey of exploration down the Rhine. He visits the Gibichungs, where the evil Hagen robs him of his memory by a magic potion. Hagen persuades Siegfried to bring Brünnhilde as a bride for Gunther, while the hero himself is to marry Gunther's sister Gutrune. Brünnhilde, not realizing the trick, thinks she has been betrayed and plots with Hagen to end Siegfried's life. On a hunting-trip Hagen drives his spear into Siegfried's back, finding the one vulnerable spot. The dead hero is carried back to the hall of the Gibichungs on his shield, to the music of a great funeral march. Brünnhilde, realizing her folly, rides her horse, Grane, into the funeral pyre. The river Rhine rises as she throws in the ring, and Valhalla is engulfed in a final immolation scene.

PARSIFAL

RICHARD WAGNER

Text by the composer.

First produced at Bayreuth, 1882. This religious drama was Wagner's last work. Its hero (already mentioned as the father of Lohengrin) joins the Knights of the Holy Grail, guardians of the cup used at the Last Supper and the spear which pierced the side of Christ on the cross. But the spear was stolen from Amfortas by the wicked magician Klingsor, through the lure of his Flower Maidens, and Amfortas now lies wounded, with no hope of recovery until the spear shall again touch his body. Parsifal, "the pure fool," resists the wiles of Kundry and her maidens, recovers the spear, demolishing Klingsor's castle, and heals Amfortas.

RIGOLETTO

GIUSEPPE VERDI

Book by Francesco Maria Piave.

First produced in Venice, 1851. The Duke of Mantua's hunchbacked jester, Rigoletto, helps his master in his notorious love affairs. As a joke the courtiers blindfold the jester and use his co-operation in abducting his own daughter Gilda. Rigoletto swears vengeance and hires the assassin Sparafucile to kill the Duke at an appointed rendezvous. But, in place of the Duke, Gilda herself enters the fatal doorway, disguised as a young man, and is stabbed by the assassin and placed in a sack. Rigoletto discovers the tragic error too late and dies beside the dead body of his daughter.

THE TROUBADOUR
(*Il Trovatore*)

GIUSEPPE VERDI

Book by Salvatore Cammarano.

First produced in Rome, 1853. Manrico, a troubadour, is in love with Leonora, but has a rival in the Count di Luna. They meet in combat, and Manrico is the victor, but spares the life of the Count. Manrico, wounded in battle, is nursed by his foster mother, the gypsy Azucena, who seeks vengeance against the house of Di Luna because the Count's father had her mother burned at the stake. Manrico rescues Leonora from the Count, but hears that Azucena has been captured and tries to save her also. Defeated and imprisoned, he is visited by Leonora, who has promised herself to Di Luna for her lover's release, meanwhile taking poison. Assuming that Manrico is actually Azucena's son, Count di Luna orders his death by fire, to avenge her supposed killing of his own brother. But too late she reveals that it was her own child she had mistakenly killed, and that Di Luna has now put his brother to a horrible death.

THE ONE WHO STRAYED
(*La Traviata*)

GIUSEPPE VERDI

Book by Francesco Piave.

First produced in Venice, 1853. Based upon the famous *Camille* of Dumas, *La Traviata* tells the story of the carefree Violetta, who falls in love with Alfred Germont. His father succeeds in persuading her to give up her lover for his own good. Unaware of her self-sacrifice, Alfred publicly denounces her, and realizes his mistake too late as she dies in his arms.

AIDA

GIUSEPPE VERDI

Book by Antonio Ghislanzoni.

First produced in Cairo, 1871. An Ethiopian Princess, Aida, daughter of King Amonasro, has become the slave of the Egyptian Princess Amneris, who loves the hero Rhadames. But Rhadames is in love with Aida, and complications arise when he defeats the Ethiopians in battle, capturing her father. Amonasro tries to make a traitor of Rhadames through his daughter, but fails. Nevertheless the hero is arrested and condemned to be buried alive. Amneris tries in vain to save him, and Aida joins him in a living tomb.

FAUST

CHARLES GOUNOD

Book by Barbier and Carré.

First produced in Paris, 1859. The world-famous story of *Faust*, dramatized by Goethe, Marlowe and others, receives a largely sentimental operatic treatment from Gounod. The aged scholar, Faust, renews his youth by making a pact with Mephistopheles. He wins the love of Marguerite, kills her brother Valentine in a duel and eventually abandons her. Imprisoned for the murder of her child, Marguerite spurns Faust and is wafted to heaven by angels, while her lover carries out his contract and gives his soul to the devil.

CARMEN

GEORGES BIZET

Book by Henri Meilhac and Ludovic Halévy. First produced in Paris, 1875.

Prosper Mérimée's unique character, the Spanish cigarette girl, Carmen, is the heroine of perhaps the most popular of all operas, abounding in melody and exciting drama. Carmen, arrested after a fight with another girl, uses her seductive wiles on the soldier, Don José, to make her escape. Spurning his own true love, Micaela, the soldier joins Carmen in a smugglers' camp, only to see her newly infatuated with the toreador, Escamillo. Micaela persuades Don José to go home to his dying mother, but he returns on the day of the bullfight and stabs Carmen to death outside the ring.

BORIS GODOUNOFF

MODEST MOUSSORGSKY

Book by the composer, after Pushkin. First produced in St. Petersburg, 1874.

The Russian Czar, Boris Godounoff, having attained the throne by the murder of the infant Dimitri, is tortured by remorse. A young monk impersonates the dead Czarevitch and tries to seize the throne, first visiting Poland and wooing the beautiful Princess Marina. Boris defeats the pretender and presents his own son as the future Czar before dying in the throne room of the Kremlin.

MANON

JULES MASSENET

Book by Henri Meilhac and Philippe Gille. First produced in Paris, 1884.

On her way to a convent, Manon Lescaut meets and elopes with the handsome Chevalier des Grieux. His father breaks up the match by abducting his son, and Manon consoles herself with other men. But when the Chevalier is about to take religious orders, she dissuades him and they are reunited. Des Grieux is accused of cheating at cards, and while his father saves him from disgrace, Manon is condemned to be deported to America. The Chevalier finds her on the road to Havre, and she dies in his arms.

RUSTIC CHIVALRY
(*Cavalleria Rusticana*)

PIETRO MASCAGNI

Book by Targioni-Tozzetti and Menasci. First produced in Rome, 1890.

Santuzza, a Sicilian girl, is spurned by her lover, Turiddu, who flirts with Lola, the wife of Alfio. Seeking vengeance, Santuzza tells Alfio of his wife's infidelity, and he kills Turiddu in a duel.

THE CLOWNS
(*I Pagliacci*)

RUGGIERO LEONCAVALLO

Book by the composer.

First produced in Milan, 1892.

This tragedy is enacted by a group of strolling players, after a Prologue, sung by Tonio, who tries to make love to Nedda, the wife of Canio. Spurned by her in favor of the villager, Silvio, he rouses the suspicions of the husband. Canio tries during the course of their play to find out Nedda's lover. Finally he stabs her. Silvio rushes to the stage from the audience, and Canio kills him also. The curtain falls as he sings, "The comedy is finished."

BOHEMIA
(*La Bohême*)

GIACOMO PUCCINI

Book by Luigi Illica and Giuseppe Giacosa. First produced in Turin, 1896.

Rodolfo, a poet, Marcello, a painter, Colline, a philosopher, and Schaunard, a musician, live a Bohemian life in a Paris attic. Mimi, a seamstress, meets Rodolfo and they fall in love. Marcello and Musetta are also in love, punctuated with quarrels. Mimi and Rodolfo are separated by a misunderstanding, but meet again when she comes to the Bohemian attic to die.

MADAME BUTTERFLY

GIACOMO PUCCINI

Book by Illica and Giacosa.

First produced in Milan, 1900.

This popular opera is based on the play by David Belasco and John Luther Long. Lieutenant Pinkerton, of the U. S. Navy, goes through a Japanese marriage with the geisha girl, Cio-Cio San, known as Madame Butterfly. He leaves her, and returns eventually with an American wife, to find that Cio-Cio San has borne him a child. She solves the problem by committing hara-kiri.

LA TOSCA

GIACOMO PUCCINI

Book by Illica and Giacosa.

First produced in Rome, 1900.

This opera, the most powerful of Puccini's works, comes from Sardou's play of the same name. Tosca is a singer, in love with the painter Cavaradossi, but desired also by the cruel Baron Scarpia, Rome's Chief of Police. The escape of a political prisoner, Angelotti, who hides in Cavaradossi's garden, gives Scarpia his opportunity. He tortures the painter in Tosca's presence until she reveals the truth. She then bargains for her lover's release by promising herself to Scarpia, who signs an order. But when the Baron claims her, she stabs him to death, surrounding his body with candles. The lovers believe that Cavaradossi's execution is to be a mere pretense. But the bullets are real, and as Tosca realizes the treachery of Scarpia, she eludes the advancing soldiers and leaps from the parapet of the prison tower to her death.

CHAPTER XIV OVERTURES AND OTHER PIECES

In many cases it may fairly be said that the overture to an opera is more worth listening to than the opera itself. Certainly this form of instrumental music has achieved an independent popularity and significance, perhaps because of its great convenience for the average concert program. It is always wise to start a concert with an overture, not merely because it has the effect of an introduction but because of its practical aid in allowing latecomers to find their seats without interrupting a symphony or a concerto.

The overture has the unique distinction of belonging rightly to both absolute and program music. To anyone who knows the opera which it introduces, it is of course program music pure and simple. But the successful overtures have been those which could stand on their own musical feet, regardless of any acquaintance with their story, and in this respect all great operatic music has its absolute qualities. Excerpts from the music-dramas of Wagner are played on the concert stage (with or without singers) quite as effectively as in the pit of the opera house, and for those to whom opera is merely an elaborate succession of solos and ensembles, it hardly seems worth the trouble to give a complete stage presentation.

There is no better way of becoming interested in opera and orchestral music in general than through a constant hearing of the best overtures. Fortunately such opportunities are plentiful nowadays. They have all been recorded by the finest symphony orchestras, they are played frequently on radio programs, and they form an important part of the concert repertoire. Best of all, it will be found that many beautiful overtures are not difficult music for amateurs, and can be performed effectively even by small groups of instruments, when a symphony orchestra is not available.

The overture is literally an introduction to an opera (and sometimes a play, with incidental music), and in its most obvious form it consists of nothing more than a medley of the best tunes in the opera. (This is the way it is also used regularly for musical comedies and operettas, as well as the typical Broadway revue.) Under any circumstances it should act as a guide to the spirit and atmosphere of the work that it precedes, but in its highest forms the overture exhibits an independent musical beauty, often including such an elaborate structure as the sonata form, and is fully worthy of performance for itself alone. (Whether it is called by some other name, such as Prelude or *Vorspiel*, makes little difference. Technically, an overture comes to a full stop before the opera begins, whereas a prelude does not.)

Following the course of operatic development once more, it appears that the great reformer, Gluck, wrote the first real overtures, and it is significant that they are still played in the concert hall. There had been so-called overtures before Gluck, but they had little or nothing to do with the operas that they preceded. Often they amounted to little more than an instrumental flourish, to secure the attention of the audience.

The earliest overtures in Italian opera were called *Sinfonia* or *Toccata*, and it was only through such composers as Lully, Alessandro Scarlatti and Handel that they assumed any real significance. Gluck made the overture a real "argument" for what was to follow, at the same time preserving an independent musical structure. His overtures to *Alceste* and *Iphigenia in Tauris* run right into the music of the operas themselves, and in the latter he definitely announced in advance the storm of the opening scene. The overture to *Iphigenia in Aulis* is complete in itself, and perhaps the finest specimen of a dramatic orchestral composition of its period.

Mozart's overtures are as popular today as they ever were. They sparkle with life, and unerringly reflect the spirit of the dramatic action which they foretell. His earliest overture, to the opera *Idomeneo*, shows a nobility of style in keeping with the character of the whole work, although there is no definite musical connection with what is to follow. For the comedy of the *Seraglio*, Mozart wrote a charming overture, containing one direct quotation of a later aria, in slow time and minor key.

The overture to the *Marriage of Figaro* is an independent creation, far in advance of any such music up to that time. While it does not directly quote any of the melodies of the opera, it reproduces its entire atmosphere with an amazing lightness and graceful delicacy. For *Don Giovanni*, Mozart introduced into his overture some of the actual music used later in the weird scene of the statue's coming to life. The *Magic Flute* overture opens with solemn chords by the trombones, indicative of the opera's ritualistic significance, and later a fugal passage, in faster tempo, creates a similar effect. This is generally considered the masterpiece among the Mozart overtures.

Beethoven's four overtures to *Fidelio* have been mentioned, and it is customary to play at least two of them in the course of a performance. The most popular with concert audiences is No. 3, and this is a veritable music-drama in itself. The whole story of the opera is told in advance by this overture, not only in literal quotation from the later scenes but in the dramatic treatment of the instrumental music itself. Most surprising of all is the fact that the whole overture follows a definite sonata form, with exposition, development and recapitulation, in spite of the wealth of thematic material and the realistic nature of the musical narrative.

The opening notes, descending the scale, may be said to represent the heroine, coming down the steps of the dungeon where the hero, Florestan, is confined as a political prisoner. The chief themes that follow are the slow melody from Florestan's own *scena* in the dungeon, and the heroic Allegro which typifies the spirit of the heroine, Leonora, from whom the overture takes its name. (Only one of the overtures bears the name of Fidelio, which was assumed by Leonora in her male character, to rescue her husband.) The most dramatic moment in the entire overture comes with the off-stage trumpet call, announcing that help is at hand. This actually occurs in the opera at the moment when all seems lost, and Florestan is about to be murdered and buried in the grave which Leonora herself helped to dig. The overture repeats the call shortly, somewhat louder, thus making the action entirely clear, and everything ends happily in a repetition of the syncopated theme representing Leonora herself. An unusual touch of instrumentation is the rapid passage for the double-basses near the close.

Beethoven's second Leonora overture used still more of the actual material of the opera, including one of Florestan's themes even in the coda. But this great composer is equally remembered for several overtures that had nothing to do with operas, but are as alive today as they ever were. One of the most popular is the *Coriolanus,* written as a prelude to a play by Von Collin, and full of beautiful melodies. The overture to Goethe's *Egmont* is equally effective, and in both cases the Beethoven overtures have kept the names of their heroes alive long after the plays themselves had been shelved. There is also an early overture to the ballet of *Prometheus.*

FROM WEBER TO MENDELSSOHN

Weber's overtures are the most popular of all on the modern concert stage, and rightly. They may lack the majesty of Beethoven's music, but their romantic qualities are more appealing and their local color is more convincing. There is a Spanish flavor to the *Preciosa* overture, an atmosphere of the wild forest in that of *Der Freischütz;* the spirit of chivalry enters into the *Euryanthe* overture, and the *Oberon* delicately suggests the supernatural and an Oriental color. While melodies from the operas themselves are constantly quoted by Weber, there is never any effect of patchwork or a mere potpourri. Instances of beautiful instrumentation are numerous, such as the horn quartet in the *Freischütz* overture, the unaccompanied horn call of *Oberon,* and the gay passages for full orchestra coming invariably at the close. The Weber overtures are not only "grateful" from the standpoint of the listener, but distinctly playable by any orchestra of average ability.

Among the more conventional operatic overtures, those of Rossini stand out because of their melodic qualities, although their structure is often careless and one easily tires of their rather obvious strains. But the overture to the *Barber of Seville* has a sparkle and a grace that make one forget that it was actually written for an entirely different purpose. *Semiramide* enjoys a popular overture, which will probably outlive the opera itself, and the themes of the *William Tell* overture were long ago made familiar to aspiring young pianists in duet form.

(It is interesting to note that Schubert wrote an *Overture in the Italian Style,* which was intended as a parody of Rossini.)

Berlioz supplied his opera *Benvenuto Cellini* with two overtures, one of which used the hero's name, while the other was called *Carnaval Romaine.* Both are still popular as concert pieces, full of bold instrumentation and bizarre effects. Schumann's overtures are not particularly important except for the one called *Manfred,* written as an introduction to the incidental music for Byron's tragedy. Here the composer has reached a high level of dramatic composition.

Mendelssohn's overture to *A Midsummer Night's Dream* is not only one of the world's greatest pieces of program music, but in the same class with Schubert's *Erlking* and Mozart's early works as an example of youthful precocity, composed, as it was, when Mendelssohn was but seventeen. Originally intended as an independent piece, it eventually became the foundation for a whole set, as incidental music to Shakespeare's play, including the familiar *Wedding March* (exit), and a *Scherzo* that is almost as effective as the overture itself. There is a realistic daintiness in this fairy music, with dramatic touches in the suggestion of royal festivities and the theatrical performance of Nick Bottom and his companions (including authentic brays).

The same composer in his maturer years created some of his finest orchestral work in the *Hebrides* or *Fingal's Cave* overture, *Calm Sea and Prosperous Voyage,* and the *Beautiful Melusine.* All are program music of the highest type, with particular realism in the musical motion of waves in the cave of the Hebrides. Mendelssohn's overtures to his oratorios, *St. Paul* and the *Elijah,* are also notable, the latter coming after a short recitative by the prophet.

Most of the minor operatic composers wrote effective overtures from time to time, and in some cases, as with Herold's *Zampa* and the *Raymond* of Thomas, the overture has definitely outlived the opera. Verdi was not inclined toward special overtures, however, and usually contented himself with a short introduction leading right into the action. (In *Aida* this prelude is built upon two themes of the opera.) It was Wagner who turned the operatic overture into a new art-form, and made of every prelude or *Vorspiel* a vital and significant part of the music-drama.

WAGNER'S OVERTURES

The overtures to *Rienzi* and the *Flying Dutchman* are still played, even though the operas themselves are seldom heard, and the *Tannhäuser* overture is a legitimate successor to Weber and Beethoven, with qualities that carry it beyond the work of even these great composers. The *Tannhäuser* music is so well known that it scarcely requires description. But the form is most interesting, using the familiar *Pilgrims' Chorus* as an opening theme and again for a brilliant recapitulation at the close, with decorations by the violins over the brass. As contrasting material there is the Venusberg music (introduced by the violas) and the defiant song of Tannhäuser, in revolt against the Wartburg ritual. It is all developed in a most elaborate and musical fashion, rising to a tremendous climax at the end. The *Tannhäuser* overture is one of the safest of all pieces for the finish of a concert.

Very different in character is the prelude to *Lohengrin,* which concentrates on creating the ethereal atmosphere associated with the Grail, using the high register of the violins for this purpose, very softly. This one theme suffices for the whole prelude, giving the effect of a celestial being descending to earth, as the music grows louder and more radiant, and then gradually fading again into the distance and finally dying away as softly as it first appeared. There is a special prelude to Act III of *Lohengrin,* representing a torchlight procession, with a resounding brass theme that has often been imitated in popular music, and this also is frequently played as a concert piece.

More satisfying than the preliminary music of either *Tannhäuser* or *Lohengrin* is the matchless prelude to the *Meistersinger*, another example of a complete music-drama within the space of an overture. It opens with the glorious theme of the Mastersingers themselves, leading into their stately march, and immediately establishing the complete atmosphere of old Nuremberg. Contrast comes first in the luscious melody of the *Prize Song*, and later in a variety of development. The Mastersinger theme is heard in an impudent quick time, with bassoon tone color, as though mocking at the pedantry of a Beckmesser, and an amazing feat of counterpoint near the close brings out no less than five themes simultaneously, with the Mastersinger melody emphasized in the bass, the march in the middle, and the *Prize Song* at the top.

The orchestral introduction to *Tristan und Isolde* has been called the world's most perfect summary of sensuous love, and again it proves that a whole drama can be compressed into a single instrumental composition. The opening tones of the cellos are full of tender yearning, answered by a "bitter-sweet discord" in the wood-winds, dissolving chromatically into a sigh, and already indicating that the course of true love will be far from smooth. This elusive phrase is developed throughout the prelude with a passionate insistence that leaves no doubt as to the significance of the subsequent drama. It is the tragedy of love in its most convincing terms, and there is nothing else quite like it in all music. A somber variation of this same theme introduces the last act, and there is a definite reference to it by Hans Sachs in the *Meistersinger*.

The prelude to *Das Rheingold* is the realistic suggestion of the river itself, already mentioned, and leads directly into the action, as do the orchestral introductions to each of the later dramas of the cycle. In every case the intention is merely to supply the proper mood and atmosphere, and the copious employment of the *Leitmotif* naturally eliminates any necessity for a conventional overture.

Parsifal, however, has a real *Vorspiel*, quite simply constructed on three themes. The first represents the Love Feast of the Knights, and is played four times, twice in major and twice in minor. The second is the Grail motif itself, known also as the *Dresden Amen*, and the third, announced by the trombone, and then developed considerably, is the theme of Faith. The music of the Love Feast returns just before the rise of the curtain.

Wagner composed one concert overture, which he called *Faust*, an early work, but full of rich music and a clear indication of the orchestral mastery that was to come.

LATER COMPOSERS

Most of the modern operatic composers followed the example of Verdi in limiting themselves to short orchestral preludes, leading directly into their dramas. Puccini has been particularly successful in this. But the ever popular *Carmen* has a real overture, first giving the atmosphere of the bull ring, to the music which occurs again in the last act, and then introducing a note of sinister foreboding, only to finish on a cheerful note as the curtain rises.

The short prelude to Gounod's *Faust* is musically as fine as anything in the opera, with a slow fugal treatment of melodies that suggest the mystery of life. Richard Strauss produced an overwhelming effect in modern times by introducing *Elektra* with one dissonant chord, like a thunderclap, and then immediately raising the curtain on his tragedy.

The Russian composers have shown a liking for the full-sized overture, and those written by Glinka for *A Life for the Czar* and *Russlan and Ludmilla* are still played. Rimsky-Korsakoff composed what is essentially a concert overture in his colorful *Russian Easter.*

Debussy called his *Afternoon of a Faun* a prelude, but rather in reference to Mallarmé's poem than in the technical sense. By any name it would be an utterly fascinating piece of music, with an exotic, languorous atmosphere that no other composer has achieved.

Brahms wrote two splendid concert overtures, the *Tragic* and the *Academic Festival,* of which the second is built largely on German student songs, including the familiar *Was kommt dort von der Höh?* (known to us as *The Farmer in the Dell*) and *Gaudeamus Igitur.* Tschaikowsky put some of his most eloquent music into the Fantasy Overture known as *Romeo and Juliet,* which he evidently intended to develop into a complete opera. A lovely duet exists for the balcony scene, whose melodies appear also in the overture. His *Francesca da Rimini* is a piece of similar merit, but less popular. For the general listener, however, Tschaikowsky's *1812 Overture* is the most effective of them all, strongly national in character, and closing with the triumphant strains of the *Russian Hymn.*

Smetana's overture to the *Bartered Bride* is the best thing in the opera, and Dvorak wrote some excellent concert overtures, of which the *Carnaval* is best known.

In the lighter field there is a fine bit of writing by Nicolai in his popular *Merry Wives of Windsor* overture, and such numbers as Von Suppé's *Poet and Peasant* and *Light Cavalry*, the Strauss *Fledermaus* overture, etc.

Leoncavallo performed a clever trick in substituting a vocal prologue for the overture to *Pagliacci,* letting the baritone, who plays Tonio in the opera, explain to the public the meaning of the drama that is to come. It generally stops the show before the curtain is allowed to rise.

Humperdinck's overture to *Hänsel und Gretel* should have special mention because of its effective use of the beautiful melody that represents the prayer of the children in the forest. There are some excellent American overtures, including Sessions' *Black Maskers*, Hadley's *In Bohemia*, Mason's *Chanticleer*, Roy Harris' *When Johnny Comes Marching Home*, William Schuman's *American Festival* and Copland's *Outdoor Overture*.

The overture in general is a versatile and flexible form of music. Whether it actually introduces an opera or merely serves as an independent concert piece, it makes an admirable link between program music and absolute music and is therefore worthy of careful attention, regardless of its theatrical connections.

MARCH, DANCE AND BALLET

It must have become fairly evident by this time that the best way to develop the enjoyment of music is by the simple process of listening to it. If a piece of music appeals to you the first time you hear it, then hear it again at the first opportunity, or get a record and keep on playing it. Listen to it as often as possible, and see how well it stands the test of repetition. (This is where most popular music falls down.)

Conversely, if a piece of music fails to make a good impression at a first hearing, don't give it up on that account, particularly if it happens to be something that other good judges have declared excellent. Give it another chance. Hear it played under other circumstances, perhaps by other performers. The fact is well established that very few of the recognized masterpieces of the world are so overwhelming as to make an immediate impression on every listener. Most of them were coldly received in their own day and had to make their value felt gradually and with the help of a few fanatical enthusiasts who were willing to stake everything on their opinions.

The preceding chapters have mentioned the names of a great many pieces of music, all of which are worth hearing, but many of which are not likely to become a part of the average experience unless they are definitely sought out. While nobody could be expected to listen to all of this music unless practically unlimited time and enthusiasm were available, a fair proportion can certainly be included in any schedule, and it should be an easy matter to make a selection that will prove both pleasing and profitable.

In the pursuit of such "creative listening," it will be well always to keep in mind the definition of music given earlier in this book: Music is the Organization of Sound toward Beauty. Every individual composition should be heard from the standpoint of all five of the organizing factors: Rhythm, Melody, Harmony, Tone Color and Form. They may not always be of equal importance, but they all play a part in every composition in the established literature of music.

Listen for patterns, for they always occur, with varying degrees of clearness. It is perhaps significant that Wagner, the greatest of all composers of dramatic or program music, should have been the most definite in his use of melodic patterns. His *Leitmotifs* are actually dramatizations of absolute music, and even to those who do not know their meaning, in relation to the characters and episodes of the music-dramas, their orchestral development will provide intensely interesting, even exciting, material.

Patterns of harmony are not so evident to the average ear, although any variation from the conventional is generally noticeable. Patterns of tone color are more easily detected when the instruments are visible than by the ear alone, and patterns of form are perhaps the most difficult of all to recognize. With the possible exception of melody, the most obvious patterns are those of rhythm, and it is for that reason that the simplest rhythmic and melodic music is the easiest to comprehend. (This of course is the best explanation of popular music in general.)

In discussing the subject of program music, it is necessary to include some types of composition that are far more obvious than some of those previously discussed, particularly in their rhythmic patterns. This includes marches, social dance music and the ballet. Such music, however, affords a pleasant recess and relaxation before the more difficult approach to absolute music is renewed. All these definitely rhythmical compositions are program music by their very form, and when actual dancing or marching is added, they take on an extra pictorial and perhaps dramatic quality that makes them almost as intelligible as vocal music or opera itself.

The very beginnings of music imply a march, a dance or some rhythmical accompaniment to manual labor. Therefore it is only natural that marching and dancing music should have maintained a strong hold upon the people of every country. The rhythm of a

He conquered the world—with waltzes

First his native Vienna, then all Europe, fell under the sway of the lighthearted, lilting waltzes of Johann Strauss, Jr. In 1872 he added the conquest of America, conducting a huge orchestra and chorus through the flowing rhythms of the *Beautiful Blue Danube* at the Boston music festival. Here, as abroad, his magnetic personality and striking appearance—a slim figure, untamed black hair, fierce mustaches, and "gypsy eyes"—captivated the public.

The younger Johann Strauss was one of three brothers, all musical. But their father, who also wrote waltzes, wanted no competition in that line and did his best to prevent their study of composition. Nevertheless Johann, Jr., persevered, and in time the title of "waltz king" was bestowed upon him by spontaneous acclaim.

The popular *Blue Danube Waltz* was originally written with words for a male chorus, but is now heard mostly as an instrumental piece, often with elaborate variations. *Tales from the Vienna Woods*, *Artist's Life*, *Voices of Spring*, *Wine, Women and Song*, and the great *Emperor Waltz* are almost equally well known. There is also the enchanting music of *The Bat* (*Die Fledermaus*), with its *Laughing Song*, and still more waltzes, delightfully combined in the *Overture*.

The name of Strauss belongs to several famous composers, including the serious but unrelated Richard, who himself put excellent waltzes into his *Rosenkavalier*. But Johann Strauss, Jr., remains "the waltz king," and it is to him that the millions of melody lovers have instinctively flung their bouquets of approbation.

march has a definite appeal, regardless of melody, harmony or form. The beat of the drum alone is sufficient music for men on the march. Whatever is added to this basic rhythm tends to give a march its particular character. It may be a military march, or a wedding march, or a funeral march. The underlying rhythm is always the same; but the other organizing factors combine to determine its final effect.

MARCHING IS INSTINCTIVE

Practically all primitive music includes marches of some sort, and much folk-music and even church music are in a distinct march time. One of the oldest marches in use today is the Welsh *March of the Men of Harlech*, a great melody, said to have been composed in 1468, at the time of the siege of Harlech.

Gluck's *Alceste* contains a fine march, later used as a *Tantum Ergo* in the church. Mozart has a good one in the *Magic Flute*. Wagner's marches have already been mentioned, but there cannot be too many repetitions of his great *March of the Mastersingers*, or the one used by the Minnesingers in *Tannhäuser*, or the more solemn measures given to the Knights of the Grail in *Parsifal*.

Siegfried's Funeral March in *Götterdämmerung* is considered the greatest of its kind, but it has close rivals in Beethoven's *Funeral March* from the *Eroica Symphony*, Chopin's from his piano sonata in B-flat minor, and Handel's *Dead March* from *Saul*. (The last-named has the distinction of being in C major instead of the customary minor key.) Beethoven also has an impressive funeral march in his piano sonata, op. 26. Gounod's *Funeral March of a Marionette* is a charmingly satirical piece, caricaturing the more serious examples of this style.

The tradition of weddings is still to play the Wagnerian march from *Lohengrin* at the entrance of the bride, and Mendelssohn's wedding music from the *Midsummer Night's Dream* at the conclusion of the ceremony. Grieg wrote a characteristic march which he called *Norwegian Bridal Procession* and some other wedding music of equal charm.

On the religious side there is the *Priests' March* from Mendelssohn's *Athalia*, and the well-known *Coronation March* from Meyerbeer's *Prophet*. But the great majority of marches, after all, are military or national in character. Bulgaria has two effective marches, the *Pirotski*, regarded as the national air, and the *Stambouloff*. Italy's *Garibaldi Hymn* is really a march, as are Germany's *Watch on the Rhine*, France's *Marseillaise*, and both the *British Grenadiers* and *Rule, Britannia*. Scotland has a fine march in the bagpipe tune, *Wi' a hundred pipers an' a'*, and Ireland contributes not only the *Wearing o' the Green* (whose words are generally forgotten in delight over the tune) and the very old minstrel melody of *The Girl I Left Behind*, which remains one of the greatest of all fife tunes. The old English *Rogues' March* is better known by name than by its music, but Elgar's *Pomp and Circumstance* (one of several marches of the same name) has become almost a national anthem, with the words "Land of Hope and Glory" set to the trio section.

In America the marches of John Philip Sousa rule supreme, and rightly. No other composer in the history of music showed such an individual talent for creating practical and satisfying marches of the military type. The *Stars and Stripes Forever* is now generally included in the list of America's national music, and it has become almost necessary to give such a march official recognition, since both the *Star-Spangled Banner* and *America* are in triple time. *Dixie* is a splendid marching tune, and so is *Yankee Doodle*, our oldest march, of unknown origin. Other marching tunes that have shown vitality are *Tramp, tramp, tramp, the boys are marching*, *Columbia, the Gem of the Ocean*, *Marching thro' Georgia*, *When Johnny comes marching home*, and *Hail, Columbia*, originally known as the *President's March*, and possibly written for the inauguration of George Washington. Victor Herbert's *March of the Toys* and Gershwin's *Strike Up the Band* are among the best of the newer American marches.

Canada has a splendid march in the *Soldiers of the King* (originally Queen), now used by Haverford College as its Alma Mater song. France not only gave us the *Marseillaise* and the still older *Malbrouck* (*We won't go home until morning*), but added a number of fine military marches, such as *Sambre et Meuse*, the beautiful *Marche Lorraine* (containing the old folk-tune, *Avec mes sabots*), *Partant pour la Syrie*, etc.

The Hungarian *Rakoczy March*, immortalized by Berlioz in his *Damnation of Faust*, is perhaps the most exciting of all national marches, and it is easy to believe the stories of its driving listeners into a frenzy of patriotism. It was composed by Michael Barna, a gypsy violinist, court musician to Prince Franz Rakoczy, and later revised by another gypsy violinist, Ruzsitka.

Tschaikowsky's *Marche Slave* is also strongly national, with its main melody built on the Oriental pattern that appears also in César Cui's *Orientale* (in triple time) and curiously enough in the Negro *Water Boy*, the Jewish *Mazzultoff*, the *St. James Infirmary Blues*, one of Liszt's *Hungarian Rhapsodies* and an American Indian melody. Tschaikowsky again introduces the Russian Czarist hymn, somewhat as he did in his *1812 Overture*.

Rimsky-Korsakoff has a beautifully satiric military march in *Coq d'Or*, and Richard Strauss accomplished even more sardonic effects in his *Heldenleben* and the march to the gallows in *Till Eulenspiegel*. The third movement of Tschaikowsky's *Pathétique Symphony* is really a triumphal march, as is the Finale of Beethoven's fifth. Saint-Saëns has a French *Military March* in his *Suite Algérienne*, and there is a *Marche Caractéristique* in Tschaikowsky's *Nutcracker Suite*.

Schubert's *Marche Militaire* remains one of the classics of its kind, no matter what form its instrumentation may take. (Originally it was one of a set for four hands at the piano.) Beethoven wrote several four-handed marches, and his dainty *Turkish March*, from the incidental music to the *Ruins of Athens*, will always be a popular example of exceedingly simple melodic patterns.

The *Triumphal March* in *Aida* holds its own with any of the operatic examples, but the quiet effectiveness of the *Smugglers' March* in *Carmen* should not be overlooked. The *Soldiers' Chorus* in *Faust* is an excellent military march, which has built up additional popularity through a ribald version, whose chorus starts with the word "Glorious." Similarly the *Pirates' Chorus* from the Gilbert and Sullivan *Pirates of Penzance* has become notorious as *Hail, hail, the gang's all here*. (It may have been meant as a burlesque of that other rousing march-time, the *Anvil Chorus* from Verdi's *Il Trovatore*). Grieg's *March of the Dwarfs* and a *Comedians' March* from Smetana's *Bartered Bride* are worth including among the more picturesque of the species, and Schumann's *March of the Davidsbündler against the Philistines* is full of personal as well as musical interest. Prokofieff's *March* from *The Love of Three Oranges* is a good example of modern technique in this form.

COMMON FORMS OF THE DANCE

It is only a step from the march to an actual dance, and the best of the world's marches have often served this purpose with no more change than a possible quickening of the time. All dances in duple time, whether it be written as 2-4 or 4-4, or even the compound 6-8, are actually built on march rhythms, and their variations are chiefly those of melodic accent and speed. The two-step, fox trot and one-step, staples of the ballroom, are literally marches, and frequently their dancers seem all too well aware of the fact. Even the tango, rumba, samba and conga represent variants of march time.

The polonaise is the nearest thing to a march in triple time, and while it is considered a dance, its actual character is that of a stately procession. Chopin's knowledge of the Polish character makes him the supreme master of the polonaise form, and he has to his credit the two most popular examples, the so-called *Military Polonaise*, and the one in A-flat. The American MacDowell wrote an excellent polonaise, and there is a beautiful specimen in Moussorgsky's *Boris Godounoff*, made all the more effective by the action on the stage.

The most popular dance in triple time is of course the waltz, with its close relatives, the minuet and the mazurka. The German *Ländler* is the ancestor of the waltz, which also shows Polish influences.

Today the most famous waltzes in the world are those of Vienna, characterized by a particular swing which is secured by a slight accent on the second beat of each measure. No less than six composers bearing the name of Strauss have written Viennese waltzes. The eldest of them was Johann Strauss, father of three sons, and the eldest of these, also named Johann, has been given the title of Waltz King. All the world knows and loves his *Blue Danube*, *Artist's Life*, *Tales from the Vienna Woods*, etc. His two brothers, Joseph and Eduard, also won considerable reputation as composers. Richard Strauss, unrelated to this family, nevertheless proved himself worthy of the name with the charming waltzes that he included in his opera, *Der Rosenkavalier*. Finally Oscar Straus (dropping one s) produced such popular operettas as the *Chocolate Soldier*, with *My Hero*, and other favorites. Franz Lehar, Emmerich Kalman, Victor Herbert and Rudolph Friml have all followed the Viennese tradition and written highly successful waltzes.

Of the classical composers, the first to write real waltzes was Schubert. He created a number of exquisite themes, one of which is preserved as the second half of Romberg's *Song of Love,* in *Blossom Time.* (The first half is from the *Unfinished Symphony.*) The waltzes of Chopin are magnificent piano works, but hardly practical for dancing. Brahms contributed a number of remarkable waltzes, and his *Liebeslieder,* for quartet and piano (four hands) are all in waltz time, but again are intended chiefly for concert performance. Liszt's *Mephisto Waltz* is not so diabolic as its title would suggest, but the *Valse Chromatique* of Godard fully carries out its promise, as does the *Valse Triste* of Sibelius (borrowed for the start of a popular *Moon Song*). Debussy has a beautiful slow waltz, and Ravel wrote an elaborate orchestral composition, *La Valse,* of real musical value.

The main melody of the Saint-Saëns *Danse Macabre* is a gruesome waltz, to which the dainty *Waltzing Doll* (*Poupée valsante*) of Poldini and the brilliant waltz in Gounod's *Romeo and Juliet* offer cheerful contrasts. The *España Rhapsody* of Chabrier is a set of Spanish waltzes (built partly on a melody by Waldteufel, another popular composer of the Viennese type), and such real Spanish composers as Albeniz and De Falla have done much with these characteristic national dances. (The tango, generally considered a Spanish dance, is really of African origin. It came to Spain by way of the Moors, and was carried to Cuba by Negro slaves. W. C. Handy, a Negro, composed his *St. Louis Blues* partly in a tango rhythm.)

One of the greatest of all contributions to dance music was Weber's *Invitation to the Dance,* a whole set of beautiful waltzes, often used as a ballet, and a fitting introduction to that larger form of dance music. While the word "ballet" was not always in good musical standing, it has an honorable record in the literature of composition. Beethoven himself wrote a ballet, *Prometheus,* and the ballet music from Schubert's *Rosamunde* is the most charming part of that score.

BALLET BECOMES SIGNIFICANT

The operatic tradition produced many ballets of dubious worth, but some of the best are quite worthy of independent performance, aside from their dancing significance. Wagner's much-discussed ballet in *Tannhäuser* turned out to be a striking piece of music, now often played on concert programs. The ballets in *Carmen, Aida* and other operas, including the famous *Faust* waltzes, are well worth hearing apart from their pictorial background.

Delibes wrote lovely ballet music in his *Coppelia, Sylvia* and *Naila* (whose waltz has been effectively transcribed for piano by Dohnanyi). *Giselle*, originally created by Heinrich Heine, Théophile Gautier and Adolphe Adam, is one of the most popular of all ballets, and deservedly famous. Tschaikowsky's charming *Nutcracker Suite* was written as a ballet, but survives as a piece of sure-fire orchestral music, particularly the *Flower Waltz*. (The waltzes from Tschaikowsky's opera, *Eugen Onegin*, are also very popular.)

The ballet music from Gluck's *Alceste* has been turned into a splendid piano piece by Saint-Saëns, and the Elysian Fields music from *Orfeo* includes one of the loveliest of all slow melodies, most effective as a flute solo, but often heard on the violin as well.

The Russian ballet, particularly under the direction of Diaghileff, and with the inspiration of such geniuses as Nijinsky, Pavlowa, Karsavina and others, long ago established a special reputation for colorful, imaginative and highly dramatic performances, which have been imitated all over the world. Much music was composed especially for these dancers, and for further material they adapted various stories to works already in existence, under the leadership of such choreographers as Fokine, Bolm and Massine. *Scheherazade* made a splendid ballet of this type, as did the exotic *Afternoon of a Faun* of Debussy.

Stravinsky has contributed the most important compositions to the actual ballet form. His *Petrouschka* has become widely popular, perhaps because it contains some good Russian folk-tunes, as much as for its fascinating story of a puppet that developed a soul. *The Fire Bird* (*L'Oiseau de Feu*) is now almost equally popular, and was given a beautiful stage presentation by the Diaghileff dancers. But the most important work of Stravinsky in this form seems to be the *Sacre du Printemps* (Rites of Spring), created as a ballet, but heard in America mostly as an orchestral composition. This masterpiece is a veritable dramatization of rhythm, utterly sensuous in its effect and overwhelming in its realism.

Ravel's *Bolero* is a similar but far more direct treatment of rhythm, with its effect depending entirely on the instrumentation. It has been staged in various ways, and its popularity has been sensational from the start. Casella's *La Giara* (The Jar) is a modern Italian ballet which was presented in the Metropolitan Opera House. Richard Strauss has written two successful ballets, *Joseph* and *Schlagobers* (Whipped Cream). His *Salome* has been performed as a ballet as well as an opera, and a choreographic treatment has been applied even to the *Heldenleben.*

It was that strange but sincere genius, Isadora Duncan, who went furthest in the practice of creating dances to fit music of the classical type. She often danced to entire symphonies, and, with her talented pupils, made beautiful stage pictures out of the absolute music of Beethoven, Gluck, Schubert, Brahms and Tschaikowsky. Her unique performances indicated that a program can be added to practically any piece of absolute music (as also proved by the experiments of the modern motion-picture theater), and that even intentional program music does not necessarily mean the same thing to every listener.

American ballet music has included two interesting works by John Alden Carpenter in the jazz style, *Skyscrapers* and *Krazy Kat* (based upon the familiar comic strip). Henry Gilbert wrote a *Dance in the Place Congo*, which, like *Skyscrapers*, was produced at the Metropolitan Opera House.

In recent years the ballet has become enormously popular in America, largely through the efforts of that determined impresario, S. Hurok, with outstanding new works like Anthony Tudor's *Pillar of Fire*, to the music of Schoenberg's *Verklärte Nacht.* Agnes de Mille's highly individual choreography came into its own with *Rodeo* (to a Copland score) and reached a climax in *Oklahoma!*, *One Touch of Venus* and *Carousel.* Jerome Robbins and Leonard Bernstein collaborated in the successful *Fancy Free* (later expanded into the musical comedy, *On the Town*), and there was typical Americanism in Copland's *Billy the Kid* and *Appalachian Spring*, Virgil Thomson's *Filling Station*, Paul Bowles' *Yankee Clipper*, Alec Wilder's *Juke Box* and the Jerome Moross-Ruth Page *Frankie and Johnny*. Ballet is today very much of a living art in the United States.

CHAPTER XV MUSIC ON A SMALLER SCALE

ABSOLUTE MUSIC can best be studied in the various forms of chamber music, so called because it demands only a limited number of instruments or voices, and can therefore be performed most effectively in a small room, as compared with the large auditorium needed for a symphony orchestra, a chorus or an opera. Many sincere lovers of music find its most perfect, though not its most exciting, expression in the instrumental forms of chamber music, particularly the string quartet.

Here is the combination of instruments that permits a fascinating use of rhythmic and melodic patterns, of four-part harmony and well-defined tonal coloring, and of an exquisite refinement of form, including a sufficiently complicated polyphony. It is perhaps significant that only the greatest composers have written successful string quartets. The form is so clear, so mercilessly honest, that any slipshod workmanship is easily detected, and it is so completely an expression of absolute music that only the most genial melodic invention will pass muster with the intelligent listener.

It is perhaps unfortunate that chamber music has developed the reputation of appealing to such rarely refined tastes, for as a result of this a great many people have pretended to like chamber music when it really bored them to tears. On the other hand, the sincere lovers of chamber music have always been plentiful, and too often the elect performers of such music have been unduly modest, and unnecessarily fearful of presenting it to the general public. (Chamber music is also a fascinating game for amateurs, but they should be warned to pursue it mostly for their own pleasure.)

The term "chamber music" is an old one, and the smaller instrumental combinations were popular long before the symphony orchestra reached its perfection. Strictly speaking, vocal music by small groups or individual singers should also be classed as chamber music, but since such music is nowadays performed mostly in large concert halls, it is more practical to limit the term "chamber music" to the instrumental side.

Louis XIV maintained a "master of chamber music," and such early Italian composers as Peri and Caccini produced *cantate da camera,* using one voice and one instrument. There were so-called "sonatas" (but without sonata form) written both for the clavier and for string combinations. Purcell's *Golden Sonata* was for two violins and bass. Bach composed trios (using both flute and violin), but no quartets. His "concertos," however, contained sections written for small groups of solo instruments that might well be classed as chamber music, and even the complete orchestra of Bach does not require the wide-open spaces of a concert hall.

Handel's trios and sonatas show something of the later sonata form. But it is Haydn who should be considered the real father of chamber music, and particularly of the string quartet. The first actual string quartets were written by Franz Richter, and the most prolific composer of chamber music was Boccherini, who wrote ninety-three quartets and 125 quintets (and is remembered today for one little minuet).

EARLY STRING QUARTETS

Haydn composed eighty-three string quartets, but his importance lies in his development of the form rather than in the mere number of his creations. His earliest experiments in this style were little more than violin solos, with accompaniments by a second violin, viola and cello. But he soon discovered the importance of a more equal balance among the four parts, and this principle was carried on to its logical climax by Mozart and Beethoven.

One of Haydn's quartets (op. 33, no. 3) is known as the *Bird Quartet.* Its first movement definitely suggests the twittering of birds (as in the *Creation*) and there are similar suggestions in the trio of the second movement, while the Finale introduces the cuckoo call and other bird songs. The *Kaiser Quartet* (op. 76, no. 3) has a slow movement consisting of variations on the familiar Austrian hymn, known as *Gott erhalte Franz den Kaiser* long before it became *Deutschland, Deutschland über Alles*.

The Mozart quartets are full of his characteristic charm, and show several different styles, of which the earliest is decidedly Italian. The later quartets have real individuality, distinct independence of the four parts, and a deeply musical flow of ideas. Six of Mozart's finest quartets were dedicated to Haydn, who outlived the young genius and greatly admired his work. (Haydn was twenty-five years older than Mozart, but there was a warm friendship between them, a relationship almost like that of father and son.) Of these six quartets, the last, in C major, is perhaps the greatest, profound and impassioned in feeling, bold in its harmonies, and with a tender, slow melody that is Mozart at his very best.

Mozart wrote twenty-six quartets altogether, of which the last three were dedicated to the King of Prussia, who was an excellent amateur cellist. As a result, the cello part in these quartets rather overbalances the others, with considerable solo work. Two of Mozart's quartets are for piano and a string trio, and one is scored for oboe, violin, viola and cello.

The outstanding master of the string quartet (with only Brahms as a real rival) was Beethoven. His very first quartet (op. 18, no. 1) shows a new equality of the four parts, with one phrase distributed impartially among all the players. Later, Beethoven developed the quartet form into something ethereal, unearthly, hinting at musical conceptions which could not be expressed by any mere instrumental ensemble.

There were six quartets in Beethoven's earliest set. Eight years later he published a set of three (op. 59) dedicated to Count Rasumowsky, and still called by his name. (Rasumowsky was the Russian ambassador to the court at Vienna.) An extraordinary development of style is shown in this second group, a broadening of technique to almost symphonic proportions. The quartets are all bold and vigorous in their treatment of highly individual melodic material, and the four instruments are used in a thoroughly polyphonic manner.

Two isolated quartets (op. 74 and op. 95) stand between these three and the final great series, in which Beethoven clearly foretold the whole tendency of modern music. The first, in E-flat, dedicated to Prince Lobkowitz, is similar to the Rasumowsky quartets. The second was inscribed by the composer *serioso*, but has a very lively Finale, suggesting horn calls and galloping huntsmen.

With op. 127 Beethoven began the final series of quartets, which have baffled most of their hearers and yet convinced the musical world that in the closing years of his life the deaf, unhappy composer had just begun to realize what music might be made to express.

LATER QUARTET MUSIC

After Beethoven there are no string quartets of equal significance until Brahms. Spohr and Cherubini both wrote quartets, the former as many as thirty-five, but they are commonplace and without distinction. Schubert's quartets, written with less technical skill, are nevertheless far more interesting.

The best known of the Schubert quartets is that in D minor, whose slow movement is a set of variations on the beautiful melody of the song, *Death and the Maiden*. But his greatest quartet is probably the one in G major, written near the end of his short life. It is not polyphonic, in the manner of Beethoven's quartets, for Schubert did not lean toward this type of composition. But it has a warmth and a fullness of harmony, a rich glow of spontaneity, such as one inevitably associates with Schubert alone.

Mendelssohn wrote six quartets, all elegant in form, correct in every detail, but in no sense inspired. Schumann accomplished more interesting things with the quartet form, although obviously working through a strange medium. He wrote three, dedicating them to Mendelssohn, and the last, in A, is worthy of his best creative style. They all have touches of originality and an individuality of both melody and harmony, but musically they are affected by their composer's absorption in the piano, which he knew far better than any other instrument. Yet it is easy to feel that Schumann, like Beethoven, selected the quartet form for thoughts that were too subtle for clear expression in musical terms.

Brahms, in his three quartets and other chamber music, suggests once more a combination of the best features of Schumann and Beethoven, although he does not seem to strive for the expression of "unfathomable mysteries" such as are found in the last of the Beethoven quartets. But there is the same breadth of style that characterizes the Rasumowsky quartets, the same ability to put symphonic material into smaller and more intimate forms, and a melodic invention which, if not completely original, is at least always individual. To the classic qualities of Beethoven, Brahms adds the lyric romanticism of Schumann, and the combination is highly satisfying. He has in common with the great song writer also a command of tricky rhythms, which provide endless fascination in all his works.

BELGIAN AND FRENCH

One of the recognized masterpieces of chamber music is the great quartet in D minor by César Franck. It is a mature composition, written after a careful study of the earlier quartet writers, but, like so much of his work, built upon the polyphonic ideas of Bach, with whom Franck was in close sympathy, because of their common interest in the organ. The later composer, however, shows a freedom of harmonizing characteristic of most French music, with a leaning toward chromatic progressions, and his detailed treatment of short melodic phrases is a clear mark of his individual style. In the introduction to the last movement he sums up melodic materials that have already appeared, a habit which also appears elsewhere in his work.

There are two fine quartets by Vincent d'Indy, a pupil of Franck, but the outstanding examples of the modern French school of chamber music are the quartets of Debussy and Ravel. Both have in common the ability to accomplish much with an extreme economy of material, and both are harmonically in advance of even César Franck. Debussy develops all four movements of his quartet on a single phrase, consisting of two motifs. There are no clear outlines of melody, and no easily recognizable form, of the classic type, yet everything is orderly in the highest sense, and the close-knit quality of the instrumental fabric becomes more and more apparent, even to the inexperienced listener.

The second movement begins with pizzicato chords, followed by a variant of the fundamental phrase by the viola. There is a strange network of seemingly unrelated sounds, cross-rhythms, broken phrases, all at a lively tempo, and finally the pizzicato effect of the opening measures returns. The third and fourth movements disguise the melodic material still more, but it is finally heard quite clearly, played by the first violin in octaves, and transformed once more in the closing coda. The quartet as a whole is not polyphonic, for one instrument is almost always in the position of a soloist, with the others accompanying. But with all its disregard of traditions, the Debussy quartet has created something new and vital, and is recognized today as an important milestone in the history of chamber music.

Ravel's quartet is a bit more conventional, but perhaps on that account easier for the listener. It shows Debussy's tendency toward economy of materials, with fairly clear references to its opening melody in the later movements, but it also comes close to the polyphonic style of the classical composers. In its harmonies the Ravel quartet is continually interesting, but not too heretical. Altogether, it is one of the most appealing examples of modern music, which is growing steadily in the affections of the public.

Modernism gets a real hearing in the D minor quartet (op. 7) of Arnold Schoenberg, played without a break between movements, and lasting nearly an hour. Its discords were once considered quite terrific, but the human ear has accustomed itself to far more extreme cacophonies since then. The opening theme is really a broad and attractive melody, although far from conventional in its unexpected leaps through two octaves. The treatment of this and other material is primarily intellectual, but often musically effective. There is a Scherzo section whose syncopated chords create a lively theme that is full of interest and excitement. Actually, this entire quartet represents one huge movement, in what is no more than an elaboration of the old sonata form. With its heretical ideas of harmony, and its inexhaustible command of technique, it affords a fine mental exercise for anyone who likes to absorb music through the brain rather than the heart.

There have been interesting quartets by Bela Bartok, Kodaly, Shostakovitch and other ultramodern composers, but it is well to become thoroughly acquainted with the established literature of chamber music before attempting too many experiments. For preliminary experience there are plenty of quartets of a far more obvious appeal than the best of the classic works, and some of these have a solid musical value in addition to their immediate attractiveness.

Notable among these pieces of chamber music is Tschaikowsky's quartet in D (op. 11) which contains the familiar *Andante Cantabile*, often played by itself on concert programs, and transcribed for other instrumental combinations. (It is now known also as *On the Isle of May.*) The same composer wrote two other quartets, all in the classical style, yet with a distinct flavor of romanticism, and full of the endearing sentimentalities that one encounters in so much of his music.

Another Russian composer, Borodin, wrote two excellent quartets, and there is one quartet, dedicated to the publisher Belaieff, to which four composers, Rimsky-Korsakoff, Liadoff, Borodin and Glazounoff, each contributed a movement. Other Russian quartet writers are Glière, Taneieff and Gretchaninoff, of whom the second is most significant.

The Norwegian Grieg wrote a most charming quartet, although without much relationship to the accepted forms. One movement, a *Romanze*, consists of a characteristically appealing melody and, like the Tschaikowsky *Andante Cantabile*, is often played as a separate piece.

Smetana put some of the nationalism of Bohemia into his autobiographical quartet, *Aus meinem Leben* (From my life), and this ranks with the finer things of chamber music. Dvorak produced several splendid quartets, of which the most interesting is the one in F (op. 96), generally called *American*, and written in this country in 1893. It is closely related to his *New World Symphony* in manner and materials, using themes which were unquestionably influenced by the Negro spirituals, if not actually borrowed from that source.

There are fine American string quartets by Quincy Porter, Walter Piston, Harold Morris, Roy Harris, William Schuman, Henry Hadley, Leroy Robertson, M. Wood-Hill, Daniel Gregory Mason and others.

Outside of the string quartet, chamber music contains other four-part combinations, as well as trios, quintets, sextets, and even an occasional septet or octet. Beyond this limit, any instrumental combination may be regarded as a miniature orchestra, and the "Little Symphonies," Chamber Music Societies and other small ensembles are becoming increasingly popular in concert halls of modest size.

Mozart's two piano quartets (with strings) have already been mentioned. Beethoven wrote one quartet for the same combination, Mendelssohn three, Schumann one, and Brahms three, uttering once more what may be considered the last word in this form. Dvorak, however, contributed two splendid piano quartets, and there are good ones by other composers.

The conventional trio is a combination of piano, violin and cello, with the emphasis usually on the piano. The Bach sonatas for flute, violin and bass, or two violins and bass are really trios, and contain some beautiful music. Handel wrote excellent trios for strings, as well as one for oboe, violin and viola. Haydn's string trios are rather thin, but he wrote one for the interesting combination of two flutes and a cello.

Beethoven's op. 3, op. 8 and op. 9 are all string trios, and later he wrote a trio for flute, violin and viola, as well as one for two oboes and English horn. (This was rescored for two violins and viola, appearing as op. 87.) In modern times, Max Reger composed an interesting trio for strings alone.

VIOLIN, CELLO AND PIANO

The early piano trios are little more than piano solos, with the violin doubling the melody and the cello supporting the bass. It was in this style that Haydn wrote most of his trios, and they have little significance as chamber music, although the form and melodic content are interesting. The popular *Gypsy Rondo* has been mentioned as a clear example of that form, but it is curious that even in this rapid movement Haydn forced the violin and piano to play the melody in unison.

Mozart's eight piano trios are far better balanced, and full of characteristic grace and charm. Although musically not particularly important, they represent a real advance toward the later established trio style. Beethoven also wrote eight trios of the conventional type, three of which appeared as op. 1, showing no advance over the work of Mozart. But three others, published as op. 70 (two trios) and op. 97, are a very different story, fully worthy of the mature Beethoven at his best. In fact, the B-flat trio (op. 97) is considered one of the

A white man discovers Negro folk-music

STEPHEN FOSTER'S FAMILY did not want him to become a musician, even though he had shown extraordinary talent as a child. Respectable Pennsylvania folks, they sent the boy to his brother in Cincinnati to learn to be a bookkeeper.

But Stephen had been listening to the blackface minstrels that visited Pittsburgh, and on the Mississippi waterfront he found the real thing. Tunes and words formed in his mind, inspired by the rhythm of the banjo and the clapping of black hands to rich voices.

When scarcely of age, Stephen Foster had already written *Oh! Susanna* and *Old Uncle Ned*, the first of which became the theme song of the Forty-niners and all other pioneers, while the second revealed a new and sympathetic understanding of the Negro character. The young man foolishly gave away these early works to a Cincinnati publisher, whose ultimate profits ran into the thousands.

His masterpiece, *Old Folks at Home*, also known as *Swanee River*, was for years credited to the minstrel, E. P. Christy, who had paid Foster a pittance for the privilege of having his own name printed as the composer. Even though Foster drew royalties on this and other hits that flowed from his pen, he never made a commercial success of his chosen work. His marriage turned out badly, and he spent his later years alone in New York, generally in debt and lacking the bare necessities of life. He died penniless at the age of thirty-seven in Bellevue Hospital, after falling in a faint at his cheap lodgings in the Bowery.

Stephen Foster wrote no symphonies or operas, but his songs are immortal, representing in simple terms the true spirit of America.

masterpieces of this great composer, with a quality that is almost symphonic.

Schubert's two trios are full of melodic inspiration, but do not add anything significant to the form as a whole. Nor can the charming trios of Mendelssohn be considered particularly important, except insofar as they provide attractive and readily playable material for amateurs. Spohr and Schumann also contributed trios to the literature of chamber music, the latter displaying the romantic and poetic qualities usually to be found in his work.

Once more, however, it is Brahms who supplies the final touch of genius to an established form of chamber music, and his three trios (op. 8, op. 87 and op. 101) are the recognized masterpieces of their kind. More than any other composer he has succeeded in giving equal importance to all three parts, paying particular attention to the hitherto neglected cello, whose low tones are admirably adapted to the instinctive melodic line of Brahms, which leans toward somber effects. Nobility and dignity of style are to be found in all of these trios, and in addition to the value of their musical content they represent the perfection of form, so far as the combination of piano, violin and cello is concerned. Brahms also wrote a trio for the French horn, violin and piano, and one for clarinet, cello and piano, in both of which the high level of his chamber music is sustained.

Among the rest, it is necessary to mention only a few of the Russian trios, of which those of Rubinstein are primarily displays of piano virtuosity, as might have been expected. Tschaikowsky's one trio is a passionately romantic piece of music, almost orchestral in effect, and emotionally powerful in spite of its disregard of the conventions. Arensky's in D minor is one of the most popular trios in the entire literature, and deservedly so, in view of its melodic charm and facile workmanship.

Dvorak again takes a high place in chamber music with three trios, of which the so-called *Dumky* (named for a Bohemian dance) is the most popular. César Franck's first compositions were three trios, of no particular importance, and later Saint-Saëns produced several such works, of which the opening one (op. 18) is the best, with a particularly brilliant piano part. Ravel's trio, in the modern style, has been recognized as an important composition, with a fascinating use of cross-rhythms and unusual devices of harmony and form. American composers have produced effective trios in recent years, including an orthodox but appealing work by Arthur Foote and more modern compositions by Cadman, Harold Morris, Hadley, Copland and others. The Scandinavian school is well represented by Nils Gade, whose trios have the virtue of melodic intelligibility and are practical material for amateurs.

FOR FIVE INSTRUMENTS

The quintet has become a popular form of chamber music, either with or without piano. There are three quintets, written for the regular string quartet and piano, that stand out beyond all other music in that form. Their composers are Schumann, César Franck and Brahms. The first is perhaps the most lucid and therefore the most immediately attractive; the second is the most original in its harmonic treatment (although it often suggests the same composer's violin sonata); the third is the most vigorous and the most solidly musical. All three are tremendously worth hearing, not once but many times. Dvorak also has to his credit a splendid piano quintet, with effective use of Bohemian dance forms, and there is a good one of more modern date by Dohnanyi.

Schubert's *Forellen* quintet is famous because he used the novel theme of his song, *The Trout* (*Die Forelle*) for a set of variations. The instrumentation adds a bass-viol to the piano, violin, viola and cello. Beethoven appears again with a quintet for piano and wind instruments, and Brahms adds another fine work to his list in the quintet for clarinet and strings. There are interesting American piano quintets by Roy Harris, Harold Morris, Leroy Robertson, Edgar Stillman-Kelley, Henry Hadley, Paolo Gallico and others.

The best of the sextets are again by Brahms, op. 18 in B-flat, and op. 36 in G, with interesting specimens also by Dvorak and Raff, all written for two violins, two violas and two cellos. Haydn wrote an *Echo Sextet* for four violins and two cellos, and Beethoven one for strings and two horns and another for wind instruments. The finest modern sextet is the *Verklärte Nacht* (Transfigured Night) of Schoenberg, which represents this heretical composer in his most orthodox and appealing style.

Among the septets is one by Beethoven for strings and wind instruments and also one by Saint-Saëns for piano, strings and trumpet. The great octet is that of Schubert, for string quartet, bass-viol, clarinet, horn and bassoon. But Beethoven also wrote a *Grand Octuor* (op. 103), for two oboes, two clarinets, two horns and two bassoons, which was actually a revision of his early string quartet, op. 4. Mendelssohn, Gade and Svendsen are all represented by octets for strings, but one soon realizes that in such large groups it is almost impossible to maintain instrumental individuality, and the music might as well have been written for a small orchestra.

In listening to chamber music, keep in mind the following principles: There should be as much independence as possible among the instruments concerned, with a natural polyphony arising from their related parts; the form should be clear in its general outlines, but with sufficient elaboration of detail to avoid monotony; the melodic invention should be definitely appealing, with enough character and individuality to make up for lack of volume or versatile instrumental coloring. The greatest chamber music consistently lives up to these simple standards of excellence.

AT THE KEYBOARD

The music of the pianoforte (conveniently shortened to piano in modern usage) could fairly be included with chamber music, for even the highly developed instruments of today, with their almost orchestral effects of tone, are heard most effectively in comparatively small concert halls. The grouping of the organ with the piano is, however, quite artificial, for they have in common only the identity of the keyboard. The organ is a wind instrument, heard mostly in churches and motion-picture theaters, and capable of real concert effects. The piano is an instrument of percussion, with a unique position as the practical basis for composition, the study of notes and harmony, and as an accompaniment for other instruments, in addition to its own important place as a soloist. It is universally recognized as the most practical of all musical instruments, and the best possible medium for the study of music from any angle.

Actually the organ is a much older instrument than the piano or its immediate ancestors, although some forms of stringed percussion instruments were known in very ancient times. The principle of striking upon strings with hammers goes all the way back to the Biblical dulcimer; and the lyre and harp, played originally by plucking the strings with the fingers, became the basis of the string arrangement of the modern piano. In fact, if you look into the top of any grand piano, you will immediately receive the impression of a harp lying on its side.

The direct parents of the modern piano were the clavichord and harpsichord, and the distinction between these instruments is a very simple one. The tones of the clavichord were produced by having a wood or metal tangent, attached to each key lever, spring upward against a wire string, causing it to vibrate, and at the same time stopping it at a definite point and thus controlling the pitch of the resulting tone. The harpsichord, on the other hand, used quills instead of hammers or tangents, and therefore literally plucked the strings instead of striking them, being thus closer to the actual harp from which it got its name. The clavichord was much smaller than the harpsichord, generally without legs, looking like an oblong box, and played either on a table or lying across the lap. The tone was very small, but clear and pleasing, with possibilities of a *vibrato*, similar to that of a violin. The harpsichord looked somewhat like a grand piano, but was very lightly built and with a tone similar to that of a zither. Neither instrument was able to produce a really sustained tone, and therefore demanded music of the rather brilliant, staccato type.

The small harpsichords of England were called "virginals," possibly in honor of Queen Elizabeth, but more probably because their range corresponded to that of a young woman's voice. The term "spinet" was loosely applied to various instruments of the harpsichord family, originating perhaps with a Venetian maker of musical instruments whose name was Spineta.

The music written for these ancestors of the piano was given various names, such as sonata, toccata, fugue, prelude, and the dance forms eventually comprising the conventional suite. It should be remembered, however, that the word sonata originally meant merely an instrumental piece, as contrasted with a cantata, or singing piece. Toccata was at first the technical name for any keyboard composition requiring touch, but later applied only to the brilliant examples of the staccato style.

Some of the earliest harpsichord (or virginal) music is found in

English collections, such as the *Parthenia* of 1611, and it is clear that John Bull, William Byrd, Orlando Gibbons and other English composers wrote much good material for these instruments. But the harpsichord did not realize its full possibilities until the time of the Scarlattis (father and son) and their contemporaries. The virtuosity of Domenico Scarlatti, and the refined style of the French composers, Couperin, Daquin and Rameau, led directly to the masterpieces of Bach, who actually composed all of his so-called piano music for the harpsichord or clavichord. (Much of his organ music has also been transcribed for the modern piano.)

The harpsichord compositions of these precursors of Bach are still played (generally on the piano), and they possess far more than a mere historical interest. Listen, if possible, to a few samples, such as the charming *Pastorale* of Domenico Scarlatti, Daquin's *Cuckoo*, Rameau's *La Poule*, *Tambourin* and *Gavotte* in A minor, and Couperin's little pieces of program music, including his delightful musical portraits of court ladies.

BACH TEMPERS THE SCALE

But the most important set of compositions in the history of the piano is unquestionably Bach's *Well-tempered Clavichord*, a set of forty-eight preludes and fugues covering all the keys, both major and minor. This unique work not only established the "tempered" tuning of the scale as we know it today, but contributed a wealth of beautiful music to the literature of the piano. (The very first prelude, in C, is the one which has become most familiar as the accompaniment to Gounod's *Ave Maria*, but should really be heard by itself, as a piece of pure music.)

Bach's *Inventions*, in two and three parts, supplement the music of the *Well-Tempered Clavichord*, in a simpler polyphonic style, and some of these little pieces afford the best possible introduction to Bach, besides being adapted to the abilities of amateur pianists. (The most familiar of the *Inventions* is probably the one in F, in canon style, and this is as good as any for the listener as well as the performer.)

The Bach fugues are far more elaborate than the *Inventions*, and some of his greatest were written for the organ. In all of them there is a form that is more than merely polyphonic, an application of the principle of statement, contrast and reminder, common to the simple song and the complex sonata form. For Bach builds his fugues in such a way that the ear may clearly perceive first an exposition of themes, then a development of the material, sometimes almost beyond recognition, and finally a recapitulation that brings back the main melodic ideas to the basic key.

The Bach *Suites,* written for the harpsichord, represent the finest music of that type in the entire literature. There are three sets, known as the *French,* the *English* and the *Partitas,* which might be called the German.

There is a wealth of other keyboard music from the prolific pen of Bach, toccatas, fantasias, concertos, sonatas, chaconnes, passacaglias and variations. Of the last-named the most famous are the *Goldberg Variations,* written on order for a gentleman who suffered from insomnia. Far from being in any sense a soporific, these thirty variations on an original theme are among the most vivacious, charming and altogether brilliant pieces in all music. They are the final answer to the absurd statement so frequently made that Bach is a purely intellectual musician, for they bubble with life and personal warmth and human qualities that are universally recognizable. It is these factors, combined with a consistent emotional power, a rare dramatic sense, and an unflagging melodic inspiration, that give to Bach's music a place all its own, quite aside from its amazing perfection of technique.

FROM HANDEL TO MOZART

Handel composed much music for both harpsichord and organ, but it was far less significant than that of his matchless contemporary. One of his suites contains the famous set of variations known as the *Harmonious Blacksmith,* still popular with pianists today.

Haydn and Mozart developed the sonata (for the primitive, light-toned piano) to a point where it was ready for the genius of Beethoven, but both of the earlier composers had individuality of style and contributed much of personal significance to keyboard music. Haydn leaned toward simple melodies, in the manner of folk-song, while Mozart reflected his brilliance as a performer in the compositions that he wrote for the piano as well as the harpsichord. Today they seem comparatively simple music, but only the finest concert pianists can play them properly. Mozart's sonata in A minor and one in A major, containing a beautiful theme with variations as well as the familiar *Rondo alla Turca* (Turkish Rondo) are excellent introductions to his style at the keyboard, and there is a heavier sonata in C minor and a great *Fantasia* in the same key, both of which are decidedly worth hearing many times.

Mozart was not only an important creator of sonatas, in the modern sense, but the real father of the piano concerto as we know it today. He fixed the form of the three movements, the first in sonata style, the second a slow movement in song form, and the third a rondo. He also made the pianist a real soloist, instead of merely a part of the orchestra, and his cadenzas (brilliant interludes by the solo piano) are said to have been miracles of improvisation.

A Florentine named Cristofori had built the first real piano as early as 1711, using hammers whose force could be controlled by the keys (which was impossible in either the clavichord or the harpsichord). By the time of Beethoven, the piano had already undergone great improvement. (The name "pianoforte" was used, obviously, because the instrument could be made to play either soft or loud.) Meanwhile, Clementi and other composers had been developing a new virtuosity of piano technique, based upon the possibilities of the improved instruments. (Clementi's *Gradus ad Parnassum* is still recognized as a sound foundation for piano-playing.)

THE IDEALS OF BEETHOVEN

Beethoven's genius made such demands upon the piano that the manufacturers vied with each other in trying to build instruments to suit him. He must have heard his music on a larger scale than any piano of his day could actually reproduce. It is the first music to abandon completely the tinkling delicacy of the harpsichord and clavichord, and it paves the way definitely for Schumann, Chopin, Liszt and Brahms.

As with Bach, one finds in Beethoven a passionate, emotional nature, expressing itself through a technique of astonishing complexity. Both composers represent, though in quite different styles, the ideal creative artist, combining greatness of conception and overwhelming inspiration with a masterly command of the forms and instruments at their disposal.

The Beethoven piano sonatas are all worth hearing, and a few of them have become so familiar that they require no description. The so-called *Moonlight* sonata (which has nothing to do with moonlight or any love story) is perhaps the most popular, and the *Appassionata*, the *Pathétique* and the *Waldstein* are now almost as well known. They should be studied carefully both for their form and for their content.

Beethoven not only brought the sonata to perfection (as he did also the symphony), but he added much to the importance of the concerto. Of the five that he wrote for the piano and orchestra, two have won a high rank in musical literature, the fourth in G and the fifth, known as the *Emperor*, in E-flat. The slow movements of both these concertos are among the most beautiful things in all music. There are plenty of smaller piano works by Beethoven, including dances of various kinds, some of them quite easy to play; but while they give attractive glimpses of the composer in his lighter moments, they are insignificant by comparison with his concertos and sonatas.

Weber and Schubert, contemporaries of Beethoven but much younger men, contributed definitely to the literature of the piano, although not significantly in the larger forms. They both represent Romanticism in its early manifestations, and their sonatas and other examples of absolute music no longer seem particularly significant. Weber's *Invitation to the Dance* is his most popular composition, and a *Concertstück* in F minor is also famous. Schubert's sonatas are not nearly so effective as some of his short pieces for the piano, such as the *Musical Moments* (one of which is a war horse for classic dancers) and the charming *Impromptus* and *Waltzes*. The *Wanderer Fantasy* (built upon the song of the same name) is an impressive piece of larger size, and the *Military March*, written for four hands at the piano, remains one of the favorites in the whole melodious Schubert list.

ROMANTIC PIANO MUSIC

With the development of Romanticism, piano music becomes less and less formal and more and more personal. The program music of

Schumann has already been mentioned. He brought from the keyboard new sounds, less orchestral than those of Beethoven, but more thoroughly pianistic. He was original, often fantastic in his conceptions, and even in such absolute music as his great *Symphonic Variations* he succeeds in firing the imagination of the listener. With the exception of Chopin and possibly Debussy, Schumann is the most consistently interesting composer for the piano as such. The world will never tire of his *Carnaval* or his *Papillons*, and his *Concerto in A minor* is one of the permanently popular masterpieces in that form. Schumann also has to his credit a magnificent *Fantasy* in C and two sonatas, of which the one in G minor is best known. His smaller piano compositions (*Fantasy Pieces*, *Album for the Young* and *Scenes from Childhood*) are all gems, including the overplayed but charmingly melodious *Träumerei*.

Mendelssohn's piano music is today remembered chiefly through the familiar *Songs without Words* (including the *Spring Song*, *Consolation* and the *Spinning Song*) and a *Rondo Capriccioso* in E. His larger works for the piano include a *Prelude and Fugue* and a set of "serious variations." Charm and melodious grace are to be found in all this music, but no great depth or originality.

Brahms, as a composer for the piano, is a logical successor to Schumann, and owes much to his style. His shorter pieces, particularly the waltzes, intermezzi and capriccios, are delightful, and his ballades, rhapsodies and sonatas suggest a modernized Beethoven. This is even more true of his two great concertos, which belong with the gigantic creations of orchestral as well as piano music. Here one finds again the nobility of utterance that is shared only by Bach, Beethoven and Wagner in the literature of music.

But the composer who knew the piano better than any other, and who created its most individual and best loved music, was of course Chopin. His unique ability to create effects of the inevitable type, through the medium of the keyboard, may have obscured the fact that, quite aside from his pianistic supremacy, Chopin possessed outstanding creative genius, with an originality of workmanship that entitles him to be considered a pioneer of modern music. Chopin turned to the piano as his natural medium of expression, and his devotion to this one instrument is perhaps the only thing that keeps him from recognition as one of the supreme masters of music in general.

CHOPIN AND LISZT

Chopin's Polish nationality comes out strongly in his mazurkas and polonaises, but aside from these dance forms his music is geographically unlimited. His waltzes are not really dances at all, but amazing concert pieces in triple time. His *Nocturnes* contain some of the most beautiful melodies in all music, and in his ballades, scherzos, sonatas and particularly the wonderful *Fantasie in F minor*, there is an emotional power that transcends any physical weakness or seeming effeminacy in the man himself.

The *Preludes* and *Etudes* are among the finest and most popular of Chopin's compositions, although mostly of comparatively small size. It is hardly necessary to refer again to the popularity of the *Funeral March*, which occurs in the sonata in B-flat minor, possibly Chopin's greatest work as a whole. His two concertos are interesting, but hardly equal to the sonatas, perhaps because of his unfamiliarity with orchestral writing. There is a lovely *Barcarolle*, a favorite with concert pianists, and a *Polonaise-Fantasie* that expresses his most profound feeling for the tragedy of his native land. The originality of Chopin's harmonization, the universal appeal of his melodies, and the remarkable command of tonal coloring that he showed within the limitations of the piano, all combine to make him a composer of unique significance, baffling in his subtleties of expression, yet the deathless idol of his fanatical worshipers. As long as pianos are played, his name will lead all the rest.

The piano inevitably brings up one other name, the greatest among its interpreters and of real significance also among the creators of its music—Franz Liszt. It is generally agreed that nobody ever played the piano with more spectacular and overwhelming effect than did Liszt. This was partly a matter of personality and partly the result of technical and physical resources that have never been equaled.

As a composer, however, Liszt holds an uncertain position. His brilliance is readily granted, as is his scholarly command of the materials of music. He was able to bring orchestral and operatic works as well as songs and organ music within the limits of the piano, transcribing them in sensational, often ultra-theatrical fashion. But his own melodic invention was generally cheap and commonplace, and he continually sacrificed beauty and nobility of style in order to create his claptrap bravura effects, for easy applause. In his devotion to fast and loud music he set a precedent for that curious megalomania which still persists as a menace to the standards of art.

It would be unfair to belittle the musicianship of Liszt, and his tremendous popularity during the nineteenth century was undoubtedly deserved. But in going through his piano works (and even his orchestral creations) one finds surprisingly little that can be given unqualified praise. His *Etudes* are valuable as expositions of the ultimate in piano technique, and frequently they are real program music, as his own titles indicated (*Un soupir*, *Mazeppa*, *Harmonies du soir*, *Feux-follets*). In fact Liszt wrote very little absolute music in the best sense. His imagination was always full of pictures and dramatic scenes, and he was willing to translate almost anything into music, sometimes all too obviously.

The two Legends, *St. Francis Walking on the Waves* and *St. Francis Preaching to the Birds*, are excellent descriptive music, however, and there is plenty of realism in the suggested twittering and the surge of the waters. The familiar *Waldesrauschen* (Murmuring Woods) and *Gnomenreigen* (Dance of the Gnomes) make their subject matter unmistakable, and there is honest sentimentality in the melodious *Liebestraum* (Dream of Love), one of a set of three *Nocturnes*. The *Mephisto Waltz* has been mentioned, and there is also a charming *Loreley*, with pieces descriptive of Lake Wallenstedt, the chapel of William Tell, various fountains, springs and even tears.

Almost as though aware of his limitations as an inventor of melody, Liszt constantly arranged and transcribed the works of other composers, including all the nine symphonies of Beethoven, songs of Schubert and operas of Mozart and Verdi. (His *Rigoletto Fantasie* is one of his popular pieces.) He did all this in a spirit of deep appreciation, although the results were often not particularly happy. But one set of melodies was provided for him by his native Hungary, and these he glorified and made immortal in the astonishing series of nineteen *Hungarian Rhapsodies*, known and loved all over the world.

Liszt wrote two piano concertos, of which the one in E-flat is musically the finer, although both have been popular with concert pianists. His sonata in B minor is an elaborate composition of great length, full of original experiments, yet lacking in true inspiration. Brilliant, spectacular, sensational, successful—all these adjectives can rightly be applied to Franz Liszt, but for piano music as such the listener inevitably turns back to Chopin, to Schumann, to Beethoven and to Bach.

RUSSIA AND FRANCE

Rubinstein was the only piano virtuoso whose brilliance could be compared with that of Liszt, but as a composer his significance is comparatively slight. He wrote five concertos, of which the one in D minor (no. 14) seems to be the best. But the public remembers Rubinstein today as the composer of the sugary *Melody in F* and *Kammenoi-Ostrow*, a respectable bit of program music, but certainly not a cosmic work.

Of the other Russians, Tschaikowsky achieves importance through his great piano concerto in B-flat minor, whose popularity in the concert hall is well deserved. Some of his smaller pieces, such as the *Troika, Song without Words* and *The Seasons* (containing the popular *June Barcarolle*), are quite charming. Balakirew wrote an Oriental Fantasy, *Islamey*, which is considered one of the most difficult of all compositions for the piano, and the modern Russians, Scriabin, Stravinsky, Shostakovitch and Prokofieff, have all contributed interesting material to the keyboard. The late Rachmaninoff is perhaps of the greatest current importance, with several fine concertos to his credit, and some excellent smaller pieces, including the famous *Preludes.*

Grieg managed to express a Scandinavian nationalism in his piano music (some of his short pieces have become immensely popular) and also produced one of the few great piano concertos, a wonderfully effective work, full of typically Norwegian rhythms and harmonies. Sinding is another popular nationalist, best loved for such little pieces as the *Frühlingsrauschen* (Rustle of Spring) and the *Marche Grotesque.*

France has added much to the world's piano music, creating a new idiom of the impressionistic type, which had been foretold by Chopin but never completely realized until the advent of Debussy. Before him, César Franck had asserted his nobility of spirit through the piano, as also the organ and the orchestra, and his *Symphonic Variations* and the great *Prelude, Chorale and Fugue* belong among the masterpieces of all musical literature. Saint-Saëns wrote several splendid piano concertos, and there are attractive smaller works by such composers as D'Indy, Fauré, Chaminade and Godard.

But it is Debussy who has given real individuality to French piano music, and his novel effects of tonal coloring, suggesting gray, nebulous backgrounds and blurred outlines, like the landscapes of Corot, or the impressionistic painting of Monet, represent something unique in music, thus far defying imitation by any other composer. Debussy is primarily a composer of program music, and most of his pieces have descriptive titles, such as *Gardens in the Rain*, *Goldfish*, *Reflections in the Water*, *The Submerged Cathedral*, *The Joyous Island*, *Pagodas*, *The Girl with the Flaxen Hair*, *Evening in Granada*, *Moonlight* (*Clair de lune*). But there are some fine *Preludes*, which must be called absolute music, as well as a *Danse* and other music whose program is only faintly suggested. The most popular and obviously picturesque material in the Debussy repertoire is the famous *Children's Corner*, containing the *Golliwogg's Cakewalk* and other amusing bits.

Ravel's piano music suggests that of Debussy, yet with an individuality of its own and a tendency toward more directness of style. Two sets of pieces, *Miroirs* and *Gaspard de la nuit*, contain interesting material, and there is an elaborate series of *Valses nobles et sentimentales*. Of his smaller works, the *Pavane for a Dead Infanta* is of a rare loveliness, and *Jeux d'eau* (The Fountain) remains a favorite because of the brilliancy of its flashing colors. A satirical style has been successfully developed by Eric Satie, Poulenc and others.

The modern Spaniards, Albeniz, Granados, Grovlez and De Falla, have written remarkable piano music, full of a real national spirit, with the *Iberia* of Albeniz a particularly colorful work. England has also produced some piano music of real value in modern times through Percy Grainger, Cyril Scott, Frederick Delius and other composers, and Poland has contributed Paderewski (eminent as a creator as well as an interpreter, and not to be judged merely by his popular *Minuet*) and more recently the heretical Szymanowski. MacDowell is America's most important composer of piano music, with three sonatas, two concertos, and numerous little pieces (*Woodland Sketches*, *Witches' Dance*, *Uncle Remus*, *Sea Pieces*) and attractive material has also been created by Ethelbert Nevin, Daniel Gregory Mason, Arthur Foote, John Powell, Mrs. Beach, John Alden Carpenter, Leo Sowerby, Harold Morris, Eastwood Lane and others. George Gershwin's piano concerto in F and his epoch-making *Rhapsody in Blue* have already won recognition as significant music of a definitely American type, while Charles Ives, Aaron Copland, Henry Cowell and others have produced important examples of modernism at the keyboard.

While the piano and the organ have nothing in common except the arrangement of the keyboard (and even here the organ has an advantage of at least three to one), they are worth bracketing if only because the early popularity of the organ led directly to the more practical keyboard instruments of percussion.

The organ, however, is too detached from everyday music to be of vital interest to the average listener. He is no longer likely to hear great organ playing in any church, and the performances in theaters and over the radio are cheapened by spectacular tricks, abuse of the tremolo stop, and mere experiments in freakish tone colors.

The piano, on the other hand, remains the household instrument (although sadly neglected by amateurs in recent years), the most practical and useful of all purveyors of music, with unlimited possibilities for concert use, as well as endless opportunities to help the composer, the interpreter, the teacher and the student in whatever branch of music may be preferred.

OTHER SOLO INSTRUMENTS

Outside of the piano and the organ, the instrument most heard as a soloist is the violin, generally requiring some accompaniment, however, such as that of the piano. Much beautiful music has been written for the combination of violin and piano, largely in the form of the sonata, and the violin concertos, with orchestral accompaniment, are as significant and certainly as popular as any of the similar compositions for piano.

The structure of the violin has already been described in some detail. It is impossible to tell how early the idea of playing on strings with a bow may have been carried out. Certainly this method of producing musical tones was soon differentiated from the plucking or hammering of strings, and with new and significant effects of tonal coloring. Any bowed instrument has a great advantage over a strict percussion instrument in the fact that a tone can not only be sustained at will, but also made to swell and diminish without any break in its continuity. The tone of a piano or any plucked instrument necessarily begins to die the moment it actually sounds, and this is a distinct handicap to expression. But the passage of a bow across a string can always be affected by varying pressure, and in this respect the bowed instruments are similar to wind instruments, including the organ and the human voice. The percussion instruments make up for their handicap, however, by the ability to sound many notes at one time, thus creating a compound tonal coloring that may prove exceedingly effective, as indicated by the piano music of Chopin and Debussy.

The violin itself had reached perfection as early as the sixteenth century, and the work of the great school of violin makers of Cremona (including Stradivarius, Amati and Guarnerius) has never been improved upon. The instrument was actually in advance of its composers and interpreters, but the seventeenth century saw the rise of such giants as Vitali, Corelli and Vivaldi, and they were followed by Veracini, Tartini, Nardini, Pugnani, Viotti and others, maintaining an unbroken line of Italian violin composers and virtuosi right up to the time of the spectacular Paganini himself.

The works of these early composers are still played on the concert stage, and they laid the foundation for all modern violin technique. Corelli's variations on an old melody known as *La Folia* (also treated by Vivaldi) give a good idea of his style and technical resources. Vivaldi's concertos were carefully studied by Bach, and unquestionably influenced him considerably. Tartini is best remembered by his famous *Devil's Trill* sonata, while Pugnani and others have been kept alive by the attractive arrangements of their smaller pieces by Fritz Kreisler (now admitted to be mostly his own creations).

But some of the finest violin music has been written by men who were not primarily violinists. Handel, Bach, Haydn and Mozart all contributed masterpieces to the literature of the instrument, although Mozart alone was distinguished as a performer on the violin, and even his abilities were overshadowed by his virtuosity at the harpsichord. Handel's violin sonatas are of a broad melodic beauty, but less brilliant than those of the Italian composers. Bach wrote six unaccompanied sonatas for the violin, reminding one of his organ style, yet very effective even for modern performers. Three of them could more properly be called suites, for they consist of dance movements, and one

Gilbert and Sullivan attack the pirates

THE ENTIRE ENGLISH-SPEAKING WORLD surrendered to *H.M.S. Pinafore*, that fascinating combination of words and music put together by the incomparable team of William Gilbert and Arthur Sullivan. In 1879 an American newspaper reported that "at present there are forty-two companies playing *Pinafore* about the country. Companies formed after 6 P.M. yesterday are not included."

But this great American success brought not one penny of profit to the author or the composer of that eternally popular operetta. There was no international copyright law in those days, and anyone could "pirate" words and music, even to the extent of publication.

Gilbert and Sullivan solved the problem by coming to the United States and staging an "authorized version" of *H.M.S. Pinafore*. Gilbert acted as stage director, and Sullivan conducted the orchestra. The New York performance was a revelation and scored a sensational success.

While here, the English team finished their work on *The Pirates of Penzance*, on which they were thus able to get an American copyright, and it also proved a hit. Our familiar *Hail, Hail, the Gang's All Here* is a ribald version of the Pirates' Chorus from that opera.

The list of Gilbert and Sullivan works is a fabulous hit parade. Starting with *Trial by Jury*, in 1875, they successively and successfully presented *The Sorcerer*, *Pinafore*, the *Pirates*, *Patience*, *Iolanthe*, *Princess Ida*, *The Mikado*, *Ruddigore*, *The Yeomen of the Guard*, and *The Gondoliers*. Then came a break in their friendship, and eventually the ideal collaboration of author and composer died a natural death, with *The Grand Duke* as its tombstone. But the words and music of these gifted creators will go on forever, as will Sullivan's immortal melodies, *The Lost Chord* and *Onward, Christian Soldiers*.

of them includes the famous *Chaconne*, Bach's most popular piece of violin music and unquestionably one of his great inspirations. (It has been transcribed for piano, and conversely much of Bach's other music may be found today in transcriptions for the violin, like the popular *Air on the G String.*) Bach's violin concertos are also essentially polyphonic music of the organ style, and on the whole less significant than the unaccompanied sonatas.

Haydn's violin sonatas are of no great importance, except as they aided in the development of what is now known as the sonata form. Mozart did much more with the violin sonata, and his works in this form are admirable material for any amateur possessing musical sense and an average technique. The Mozart concertos are even more important, and still hold their own on the concert stage.

BEETHOVEN'S VIOLIN SONATAS

Once more the name of Beethoven looms large in the making of musical history. His violin sonatas are far greater even than those of Mozart, and for the first time the piano is given an importance equal to that of the solo instrument. Like the later sonatas of César Franck and Brahms, these works are not really solos at all, but a high type of ensemble music. The sonata in A, op. 47, originally written for the English violinist, Bridgetower, was later dedicated to Rodolphe Kreutzer, a leading virtuoso of his day, and has been known ever since as the *Kreutzer Sonata.* Its first movement contains emotional power (but little of the sensuous significance read into it by Tolstoy and others). The second is a lovely slow theme, followed by quite orthodox and conventional variations. The Finale is brilliant, with a skipping melody in the folk-tune style.

Many of the other violin sonatas of Beethoven are well worth hearing, and most of them are not beyond the ability of good amateur performers. Possibly the finest, from a purely musical standpoint, is the one in G, op. 96, written for the French violinist, Pierre Rode. Two *Romances*, op. 40 and 50, for violin and orchestra, still popular with concert players, foreshadowed the great *Concerto in D,* op. 61, which ranks among the masterpieces of Beethoven and close to the highest place in the violin music of the world. (The Brahms concerto is its only real rival.) Here, as in his sonatas, Beethoven does not treat the violin as a mere soloist, but rather as an individual balance to the orchestra. Nor is he concerned with virtuosity as such. He aims only to express great musical thoughts, for which the violin and the orchestra happen to be the medium at the moment. Even the opening movement contains broad melodic lines, adapted to sensuous beauty rather than brilliance, with the orchestra furnishing a long introduction out of which the violin part grows only gradually. The slow movement again emphasizes melodic beauty, and the Finale has a definite folk-theme, of Russian origin, lively and attractive in its vigorous tunefulness.

Schubert wrote a concerto, a sonata and three sonatinas for the violin, but they are of no great importance. Schumann's two sonatas have a greater significance, both for the violin and for the piano, and their musical content is up to his usual high standard. Mendelssohn takes an honored place among composers for the violin solely because of his *Concerto in E minor*, written for one of the greatest of violinists, Ferdinand David, and unquestionably influenced by his technical knowledge of the instrument. The Mendelssohn concerto is the most grateful of all the larger works for the violin, and it is likely that listeners and performers alike will never tire of its appealingly melodious measures. Emotional power is not conspicuous, but the first movement has its dramatic moments, particularly in the immediate announcement of a broadly exultant theme; the slow melody is of an ethereal loveliness, and the brilliant Finale has technical and musical qualities that make it absolutely sure-fire.

VIOLIN MUSIC BY BRAHMS

Brahms contributed three of the finest sonatas to the literature of the violin, as well as perhaps the greatest of all the concertos. All of the Brahms sonatas are worth hearing, the most popular being the second, op. 100, which opens with a melody rather startlingly reminiscent of the Prize Song in *Die Meistersinger*. The concerto is in the same key as Beethoven's, D major, and has proved itself at least the peer of that masterpiece. It was dedicated to the great Joachim, and its technical difficulties are of a type that represented the personal specialties of that virtuoso, particularly the complicated double-stopping. Melodically, the Brahms violin concerto stands among the supreme musical inspirations of the world. Its opening theme, immediately announced by the orchestra, enjoys a great variety of treatment, and is contrasted with vigorous chords by the violin and a soaring melody whose original intervals produce inevitable shivers of ecstasy. The second movement has a slow theme of "linkèd sweetness long drawn out," and the Finale brings a rush of brilliant double-stops that are breath-taking.

Among other violin concertos, a high place must be given to that of Tschaikowsky, also in D major, op. 35, dedicated originally to Leopold Auer, the most famous of modern teachers, and containing not only extreme difficulties of the technical sort, but a wealth of romantic melody and dramatic effects. The slow movement is a simple and plaintive song, in minor key, not at all hard to play, so far as the notes are concerned, but requiring great beauty of tone for its proper interpretation. In the riotous Finale there is a distinct flavor of Russian folk-music.

There are two concertos and a *Scottish Fantasy* by Max Bruch, all well established in the violin repertoire. The concertos are melodious and orthodox, safe material for any audience not too sophisticated, and the Scotch piece disguises its folk-themes so well that the Scotch people themselves did not recognize them. Saint-Saëns is represented by three violin concertos, all dedicated to the brilliant Sarasate, and all excellent music. In addition to these, the French composer produced a colorful *Havanaise*, an *Introduction and Rondo Capriccioso*, a *Romance* and a *Concert Piece*, all for violin and orchestra, and two sonatas for violin and piano.

The so-called *Spanish Symphony* of Lalo is really an elaborate violin concerto, in five movements, some of which are generally omitted in performance. It is full of striking melodic effects, and uses in its Finale a Spanish folk-tune known as *The Silversmith*. Lalo also composed an earlier concerto in F minor, a *Romance-Serenade*, a *Norwegian Fantasia* and a *Concerto Russe*, all for violin and orchestra.

Ludwig Spohr wrote no less than seventeen violin concertos, most of which are now forgotten. This is also true of the once popular works of the Belgian de Beriot, which included seven concertos. But another Belgian, Henri Vieuxtemps, a famous virtuoso and composer for the violin, still lives in the concert hall through his five brilliant concertos, as well as a *Ballade and Polonaise* and a *Fantasie-caprice*.

Henri Wieniawski was another virtuoso whose compositions showed vitality, and his two concertos, a *Légende* and a rather cheaply showy *Fantasia* on airs from *Faust* are still heard occasionally. Joachim also wrote three concertos, of which the most popular had the title *Hungarian.* Other violin concertos worth mentioning are those of Glazounoff, Sibelius, Carl Goldmark (with a very effective slow melody), Sinding, Reger, Sinigaglia, Dvorak, Emanuel Moor and the modern Prokofieff.

The spectacular Paganini did little composing in the larger forms, but his twenty-four caprices, unaccompanied, became very popular, and several of them were transcribed for other instruments, as in Liszt's treatment of *La Campanella.* (The Brahms piano variations on a Paganini theme are famous.) He is credited with two concertos, and wrote variations on the well-known melody of the *Carnival of Venice*, as well as a *Witches' Dance.* Sarasate, another great virtuoso, also wrote brilliant violin solos, including spectacular arrangements of Russian and gypsy airs.

The one violin sonata that stands out as a highly original work, quite different from its conventional companions, is that of César Franck. It shows all its composer's best characteristics of style, particularly the ingenious use of short phrases as thematic material, polyphonically developed, the bold harmonies, and the subtle atmosphere of mysticism. The balance between piano and violin is admirable throughout, and the piano is actually the more difficult of the two parts. The opening movement shows how a beautiful melody may be constructed from a succession of two-tone patterns. In the second the piano takes the lead, developing a passionately romantic theme in minor key, with a wild accompaniment of broken chords, covering the entire keyboard, and continuing in dramatic dialogue with the violin. Next comes an Intermezzo, consisting mostly of recitative passages for the violin, in response to suggestions of earlier thematic material by the piano. The Finale is a perfect canon, with the two instruments overlapping in their presentation of a singing melody, in exact duplication, an amazingly effective movement throughout.

Grieg's three violin sonatas have made a permanent place for themselves in the repertoire, showing individuality of material and a fine sense of form. Fauré, D'Indy, Richard Strauss, Rubinstein, Juon, Ornstein and others have also produced violin sonatas of merit. On the whole, the instrument is well supplied with material, both on the side of pyrotechnics and along the classic lines of purely musical value.

SOLO MUSIC FOR THE CELLO

As compared with the literature of the violin, that of the violoncello, or cello, is almost infinitesimal. In spite of the frequent exclamations of rapture over the "human voice" of the cello, it is not really a popular concert instrument. There is too little flexibility in its tones, and the rich baritone or bass quality, easily exaggerated in an oversentimental fashion, becomes monotonous when deprived of contrasting colors. People like to hear the cello as a soloist in short pieces, like the *Swan* of Saint-Saëns, or in transcriptions from other instruments, but they are seldom willing to sit through any of the larger works. In the string quartet and trio the cello has assumed an important place, and its position in the orchestra is one of great responsibility, with frequent opportunities for the announcement of broad themes, and even individual solos. As a member of any ensemble, the cello has a tremendous value, but in the field of the sonata and the concerto it will never threaten the supremacy of the violin.

One of the most effective cello concertos is that of Haydn, a favorite with that master interpreter, Pablo Casals, containing many passages in the higher registers that have the lightness and grace of violin music. Schumann and Dvorak both wrote excellent cello concertos, and the double concerto of Brahms, for violin, cello and orchestra, is one of the great works of musical literature. By letting both solo instruments play frequently in double-stops, Brahms creates the effect of a string quartet, and thereby imitates the form of the old Bach concertos, in which a group of solo instruments was heard in contrast with the full orchestra.

Beethoven's five sonatas for cello and piano are classics of their kind, full of good music, but not calculated to display the possibilities of the instrument to modern ears. He also wrote three sets of variations for the cello, of no great importance. A triple concerto for violin, cello and piano with orchestra is historically interesting, and also shows something of the Bach concerto style.

Schumann wrote five short pieces for the cello, under the title *Im Volkston* (In the Folk Style). Mendelssohn was responsible for two sonatas and some variations, but the best modern cello sonata is probably that of Grieg, which contains typically sturdy melodies and incisive rhythms, in the Norwegian idiom. The César Franck violin sonata can also be played on the cello, quite effectively, and there is a respectable but not too exciting sonata by Richard Strauss. Saint-Saëns, Ropartz, Moor and Reger are other composers of cello sonatas. Show pieces for the cello have been written in quantity by Popper, Goltermann and other virtuoso composers, and there is a rather spectacular set of *Variations on a Rococo Theme*, by Tschaikowsky.

Solo music for the viola is even more limited than that for the cello, although it is often given important leading parts in the string quartet and the orchestra. (One of the most effective solo passages for the viola occurs in the *Caucasian Sketch* of Ippolitoff-Ivanoff, *In the Village*.) Schumann wrote some *Märchenbilder* for viola and piano, which are important chiefly as a musical curiosity, and there are sonatas by York Bowen and a few short pieces by other composers, including a *Concertino* by David and some *Hebrew Melodies and Variations* by Joachim. A prize-winning *Suite* by Ernest Bloch is outstanding among modern works for the viola. Paul Hindemith, himself a virtuoso of the viola, has also written effective solos for that instrument.

WOOD-WIND AND BRASS

Wind instruments have had a number of solo opportunities, in the orchestra and various chamber-music combinations, as well as individually, with piano accompaniment. The flute has been a popular solo instrument, and always will be, when played by such a master as the late Georges Barrère, for example. Bach's sonatas and trios for the flute (with violin added in the latter) are fine music, still heard in the concert hall. But much of the later flute music consists of transcriptions, largely of operatic excerpts, and variations on rather obvious tunes. There are some French compositions in the modern style, written for the flute, and a *Poem*, for flute and orchestra, is one of the outstanding works of the American, Charles Griffes (introduced by Barrère shortly before the untimely death of its composer).

The clarinet enjoyed some special attention from a number of great composers. Mozart wrote a charming quintet, featuring the clarinet, and Brahms did the same thing on a much larger scale, inspired by the playing of Mühlfeld. Brahms also composed a clarinet trio (for the same player) and two fine sonatas for clarinet and piano. Weber and Spohr both wrote clarinet concertos, Reger contributed a sonata and Debussy a rhapsody.

The French horn is the leading instrument in a trio by Brahms, and Richard Strauss wrote a concerto for the horn (op. 11). The oboe enjoys a modest solo repertoire, and the French-American Loeffler produced some of his most delicate and subtle work in two rhapsodies for oboe, viola and piano.

The trumpet, cornet and trombone were formerly heard as soloists mostly in transcriptions of the world's worst music. Today they have become exciting individuals in the brilliant variations, often improvised, which contribute the greatest fascination to our popular "swing" music, sharing this distinction with the clarinet, the saxophone, the piano and occasionally the violin. Such jazz virtuosos as Louis Armstrong, Benny Goodman, Harry James and the Dorsey brothers have developed the technique of wind instruments to an astonishing degree, producing many new and legitimately musical effects.

CHAPTER XVI SYMPHONIC SUPREMACY

THE FURTHER ONE ADVANCES on the road to music, the more one is likely to be convinced that it finds its highest levels in the symphonic form. No other type of music offers the opportunities for sublimity of invention, perfection of workmanship, and the direct transference of abstract moods and emotions that are to be found in the symphony.

Bach composed his music before the symphonic form had been developed, but he instinctively followed its basic principles of statement, contrast and reminder in his greatest contributions to absolute music. Wagner, Verdi and other operatic composers wrote very little absolute music as such, and therefore did not arrive at symphonic composition, although they balanced this shortcoming by their dramatic works. Chopin's unique devotion to the piano precluded any symphonic composition on his part, but he used the sonata form with complete success, and a symphony, it should be remembered, is after all a sonata for orchestra. Debussy's art also was too highly specialized for symphonic expression, but some of his orchestral works have a formal significance equal to that of a symphonic movement. Except for these few composers, every really important creator of music since the middle of the eighteenth century has written something in the symphonic form; and it is by their symphonies that the final standing of most great composers is estimated.

Just by way of reminder, remember that a symphony is an elaborate composition, generally in four movements, written for the full-sized orchestra (which should have from eighty to one hundred players for a proper performance), and that at least one of the movements (regularly the first) must be in sonata form. Some analysis has already been made of three great symphonies, the *Unfinished* by Schubert, Mozart's in G minor, and the fifth of Beethoven, in C minor. All of these three masterpieces should be heard again in the course of this general survey of the symphonic music of the world.

While some symphonies were written before Haydn, notably those of K. P. E. Bach (son of the great Johann Sebastian), it is fair to bestow upon Haydn the title of "father of the symphony." He not only perfected the sonata form, a most important feature of every symphony, but his experiments with the orchestra made it possible for him to work out an instrumentation that is the basis of all modern orchestral music. His simple, naïve, human qualities gave to his symphonies a sincere straightforwardness, and his close association with the Croatian folk-music unquestionably aided in the directness and beauty of his own melodic inspirations.

Haydn has been credited with about 125 symphonies, although the exact number is not known. Many of them still appear regularly on concert programs, and their freshness of style and sterling musicianship are as impressive as ever. Some of the Haydn symphonies have titles that indicate a definite program in the mind of their composer, although they should all be considered primarily as absolute music. An amusing example is the *Farewell Symphony*, in whose last movement the parts drop out one by one (each player originally blowing out his candle as he departed), leaving at the end only two violinists. This was Haydn's way of hinting to his patron, Prince Esterhazy, that the orchestra men were entitled to a vacation.

The *Surprise Symphony* contains much of interest in addition to the slow theme with variations, whose crashing interruption gave the symphony its name. It is one of the so-called Salomon set, written for performance in England at a series of concerts managed by J. P. Salomon. These Salomon symphonies include the greatest of Haydn's works in this form. In addition to the *Surprise*, there is one in E-flat, known as the symphony "with the drum roll" (a feature of the introduction to the first movement), one called *Military* (because of certain percussion effects in the second movement), one in B-flat and another in E-flat, a *Clock* symphony (with bassoons and strings supplying the tick-tock), two symphonies in D and a familiar one in C minor, and finally another in B-flat and one in C major. An earlier set, known as the *Paris Symphonies*, includes the *Oxford* and several others with descriptive titles, which, however, were not the composer's own.

Haydn wrote his first symphony when Mozart was three years old. But by the time Mozart was eight, he himself had already composed a symphony, and before he died at the tragically early age of thirty-five, the younger composer had given his old friend and preceptor many ideas for the improvement of the symphonic form, which are apparent in Haydn's own masterpieces. Haydn was first the model but eventually the follower of the young genius whom he outlived.

MOZART'S TRIO OF MASTERPIECES

Among over forty symphonies written by Mozart, three stand out prominently, demanding recognition among the supreme creations of musical art. They are the last three symphonies of his career, and were all composed within the incredibly short space of about six weeks. The first is in E-flat; the second is the masterpiece in G minor, already described; and the third is the famous *Jupiter Symphony*.

The E-flat symphony is of great melodic beauty. Its most popular movement is the Minuet, which starts in a rugged style, quite different from the conventionally dainty music associated with this dance, but goes into a trio of real charm and sweetness, melodically related to the slow theme of the *Jupiter* and to the Finale of Beethoven's *Fifth Symphony*.

The G minor symphony is perfect music from start to finish, and better known today than either of the others. But the *Jupiter*, in C major, goes beyond it in classic dignity and grandeur. Its themes are simple, but they are treated with a musical mastery that give the whole symphony a truly Olympian splendor. The Minuet contains a melody that is reminiscent of the second theme in the opening movement of the G minor symphony, and the Finale is built largely on a four-tone pattern appearing at the start, which is polyphonically treated and finally inverted for the subject of a brilliant fugue that brings the symphony to a close.

The giant Beethoven picked up the symphony where Haydn and Mozart had left it, near the close of the eighteenth century, and his first works in this form might have been credited to either of these predecessors. But it was not long before his original genius began to assert itself. Beethoven's first and second symphonies are conventional, but pleasing. (The second contains a beautiful slow movement whose opening theme is embodied in the hymn-tune, *Berlin*, and incidentally presents a melodic pattern that has become far too familiar.)

BEETHOVEN'S GREAT SYMPHONIES

The third symphony of Beethoven is the stupendous *Eroica*, perhaps the greatest of the nine that he composed. Originally inspired by Napoleon, but later dedicated merely "to the memory of a hero," there is a majesty of style all through this symphony that makes it truly representative of the noblest creative work of its composer, and worthy to stand beside any of the other inspirations of musical literature. The first theme is announced immediately by the cellos, starting on the familiar pattern of the major triad. The second theme is of the chromatic type, tenderly sung by wood-winds and strings in alternation. The development is bold, even going so far as to introduce new thematic material, against all previous rules of symphonic writing.

The second movement of the *Eroica* is a sublime funeral march, one of the greatest of them all, rivaled only by that of Siegfried, in Wagner's *Götterdämmerung*, and the familiar masterpiece of Chopin. The third movement is a Scherzo in fast triple time, with a middle section that suggests horn calls on the notes of the major triad once more. The Finale has a brilliant introduction of scale passages and chords, after which a simple theme, played by pizzicato strings, leads to a series of remarkable variations. The third variation develops what is essentially a new melody, serving as a second theme for the movement, with the first theme as a bass. It is this second theme, played in both a lively and a somber style, that gives the closing pages of the symphony some of their most appealing moments.[1] The first theme is finally made the subject of a fugal passage, and the symphony ends brilliantly, with a new motif added to the complex treatment of the other melodic material.

[1]The tune must have been a favorite with Beethoven, for he also used it in a *Country Dance*, in the *Prometheus* ballet and as the basis of a set of variations.

The *Fourth Symphony* of Beethoven, in B-flat (op. 60), goes back to the style of Mozart, and seems rather simple, almost naïve, after the emotional depth of the Eroica. It contains charming melodies and a sparkling gaiety which make it a fitting interlude between the dramatic third and fifth symphonies. (The latter has already been analyzed.)

The sixth symphony is known as the *Pastoral* (in F, op. 68) and was introduced on the same program with the fifth. It is quite definitely program music, and Beethoven himself supplied such descriptive titles as "Awakening of joyful feelings on arrival in the country," "By the brook," "Village Festival," "Thunder Storm," "Shepherd's Song," "Thanksgiving of the peasants after the storm." Much of the music contains imitations and suggestions of the sounds of Nature. At the close of the second movement, three bird songs are heard simultaneously, the flute representing the nightingale, the oboe the quail (the song of the German bird is quite different from our own bobwhite), and the clarinet playing the cuckoo call in major thirds. There is a realistic country dance, and the musical description of the storm is quite convincing, finally dying away in muttered trills of the double-basses. The major triad supplies the chief melodic material for the last movement, first sounded by the clarinet in pastoral fashion, then answered by the horns, and finally creating a typical Beethoven tune, which permits a variety of treatment. (This melody has been successfully adapted to the "Come hither" of *Under the Greenwood Tree* in Shakespeare's *As You Like It.*)

The *Seventh Symphony* is in A major (op. 92), and belongs among Beethoven's greatest, although its tone is light and cheerful rather than dramatic or emotional. Wagner's description of it as "the apotheosis of the dance" has been generally accepted, but its rhythms do not by any means represent actual dance forms. The first movement has a very long introduction, leading eventually to a Presto section in which a short theme in 6-8 time provides most of the material for the movement. The second movement (Allegretto) has a fairly slow theme which begins on a monotone, getting its character entirely from the harmony. This harmony soon develops into an actual countermelody, distributed among various members of the string group. A contrasting theme, in major key, turns the rather somber character of the movement into a lyric mood, and the materials of both these themes are interestingly developed to the close of the movement. Then comes a Scherzo of the liveliest character, in triple time, with a trio which quotes an Austrian folk-song. The Finale has a strongly Celtic flavor, and its first theme is practically the same as the Irish tune, *Kitty Coleramie*. Beethoven had previously used this tune in his accompaniment to another Irish song, *Nora Creina*, and at the time of the composition of the seventh symphony he seems to have been deeply interested in Irish folk-music. Actually, this final movement is an Irish reel, in 2-4 time, but carried out on a gigantic scale. It is in this Finale and the preceding Scherzo that the symphony rightly earns its dance title.

The *Eighth Symphony*, in F, again suggests Haydn and Mozart, particularly in the opening movement and the Minuet. There are beautiful melodies, and some original touches in the workmanship, with a final Rondo of unusual length. But the significance of this symphony today is chiefly that of an interesting contrast, leading to the monumental ninth and last of the series, which came eleven years later.

BEETHOVEN'S NINTH

While there is a tendency to exaggerate the importance of the *Ninth Symphony*, merely because of its size and the novel use of a chorus and soloists in the last movement, it holds its own musically with the *Eroica* and the fifth, and goes beyond both of these masterpieces in its effects of originality. The first movement has a mysterious introduction, hinting at the first theme, which is finally announced in unison, fortissimo. The second theme is more melodious, and there is much development of these and other materials. Next comes an ingratiating Scherzo, introduced by several announcements of its chief rhythmic and melodic pattern, one of which is by the drums alone. A contrasting middle section changes the triple to common time, with a more dignified scale melody. The Adagio has a beautiful slow theme, and its mood is of calmness and repose. But the opening notes of the Finale indicate strife and struggle. The argument is definitely shown to be over the proper climax for the symphony, with the cellos and double-basses first stating the case in a rugged recitative. The themes of each of the preceding three movements are suggested in turn, but all are rejected, with the recitatives seeming to utter increasingly angry protests. The repeated efforts of the Scherzo theme to make itself heard are rudely interrupted by the kettledrums, and find no favor whatever. At last the wood-winds hint at the melody that is to become the choral theme, and the bass strings immediately take it up with complete approval, playing the entire theme in octaves but with the effect of a unison. Its development begins at once, first with the addition of a simple bass, then with a countermelody in the strings, and finally in a full wood-wind harmony. (At one point in the Finale, this choral theme is given a distinctly jazzy treatment, with the melody broken up in syncopations and a strange instrumental color of trumpets, wood-wind, triangle and drums.) A brilliant coda brings the instrumental portion of the Finale to a close. The noise of battle is heard again (this time in a dissonant chord which actually contains every one of the seven notes of the diatonic scale), and a baritone soloist takes up the recitative formerly left to the cellos and basses. His invitation to the chorus meets an immediate response in the words "Joy! Joy!" and the entire theme is soon heard in full choral harmony. From here to the close the music is mostly vocal, with one vigorous syncopated passage announced in unison by the male voices, in contrast with the smoothness of the principal theme, and another section, both beautiful and difficult, allotted to the solo quartet, with each singer given some measures of flexible legato that constitute a real test of breath control. There are cruel difficulties for the chorus also, particularly in the sustained high pitch demanded of the sopranos. The music rises to one impressive climax after another, until the triumphant mood of universal joy overrides all difficulties, leaving the final purpose of the symphony convincingly realized.

In summing up the nine symphonies of Beethoven, it may be noted that three of them, the *Eroica*, the fifth and the ninth, are great masterpieces of original thought and dramatic power; three others, the first, second and fourth, are little more than echoes of Haydn and Mozart; and the remaining three, the sixth (*Pastoral*), seventh and eighth, fall between the two extremes, showing individual touches of Beethoven's characteristic style, but by no means throwing off the shackles of tradition. With the possible exception of Brahms, no other composer made so significant a contribution to symphonic music.

TWO MASTERPIECES BY SCHUBERT

Of Schubert's ten symphonies, only two are commonly heard today. The *Unfinished Symphony* has already been analyzed in part. The seventh symphony, in C major, "of heavenly length," according to Schumann, marks the end of the classical period and the beginning of the romantic. It is essentially a transition symphony, and appeals equally to lovers of pure melody, in correct form, and to those who like their music with a dash of drama or emotional appeal. The second theme of the first movement has an almost Oriental flavor, and melodically foretells the corresponding theme of the second symphony of Brahms. The leading melody of the second movement, in minor key, has a lilt and a nonchalant loveliness that could only be Schubert's. There is an entrancing Scherzo, in a fast waltz time, with suggestions of actual Viennese dances, particularly in the trio. The Finale is full of sparkling vivacity, with the atmosphere of the dance still predominant. Its vigorous, straightforward second theme has something of the spirit of the popular *Marche Militaire*. This C major symphony is quite as well worth hearing as the more familiar *Unfinished*, and musically of perhaps greater importance.

Mendelssohn wrote his first symphony when he was only fifteen years old. While this has little more than historical interest, three of his later works in the symphonic form, known as the *Scotch*, *Italian* and *Reformation* symphonies, are fully deserving of attention. They are program music in name only, for although their composer intended to justify his titles, their influence was evidently of the most general sort, and he ended by writing what was practically absolute music. The *Scotch Symphony*, supposedly inspired by a visit to Scotland, shows a trace of the Scottish folk-dance in the second movement, a lively Scherzo, but the rest is mainly conventional German composition. The *Italian* also shows little of local color until the last movement, which is a Neapolitan Saltarello, in a typically furious rhythm. But the *Reformation Symphony* uses both the *Dresden Amen* (later immortalized in Wagner's *Parsifal*) and Luther's *Ein' feste Burg*, in direct quotation, and the program of this work is altogether the clearest of the three.

SCHUMANN AND BERLIOZ

The four symphonies of Schumann are significant in their musical ideas, but suffer from an inadequate command of the orchestra. The first, in B-flat (op. 38), is generally given the title of *Spring*, the composer's own idea. It contains some lovely melodies, particularly the second theme of the first movement and the first of the Scherzo, which is anticipated in the coda of the preceding slow movement. The Finale uses a syncopated scale for an introduction, and then goes into a charmingly graceful pattern for the violins, really not symphonic in character, but thoroughly pleasing to the ear.

The second symphony, in C major (op. 61), is considered superior to the first, and perhaps the best of the four. Its introduction presents a trumpetlike theme which provides a melodic basis for the whole symphony, thereby producing an unusual unity of design and mood. The second movement is a lively Scherzo, originally written for strings alone, with wind instruments added later. The Adagio contains a beautiful slow melody, and the Finale brings back material from the earlier movements, added to new themes, in a well-wrought musical texture.

The third of Schumann's symphonies is known as the *Rhenish* (E-flat, op. 97) because of the composer's own statement that it records impressions received during a trip down the Rhine to Cologne. There are passages representing the feelings created by a religious ceremony in the famous cathedral, but the greater part of the symphony leans toward lightness and gaiety.

The so-called fourth symphony was really the second written by Schumann, and its original title was *Symphonic Fantasia*, indicating some unconventionalities of form. The movements are played without a pause, and there is an interchange of thematic material throughout, as in the second symphony. The second melody of the first movement is one of those soaring flights of fancy that one associates naturally with the work of Schumann, and there is a similar example of inspired tunefulness in the Scherzo. The Romanze, or slow movement, has an expressive minor melody, sung by the oboe, which unquestionably influenced the slow movement of the César Franck symphony and the third section in the F major symphony of Brahms, many years later.

The program type of symphony reached its extreme in the compositions of Hector Berlioz, who evidently found it almost impossible to write absolute music. His *Fantastic Symphony* has the subtitle "An Episode in the Life of an Artist" and an introductory note which explains that the music represents the dream of a young musician, drugged by opium, with his beloved represented by a definite melody, appearing as a "fixed idea" all through the symphony. The first movement concerns itself largely with this leading theme. The second describes a ballroom scene, the third is pastoral (Scenes in the Country), and the fourth is a gruesome March to the Gallows, in which the love theme is interrupted by the stroke of the executioner. The Finale is called Dreams of a Witch's Sabbath, attaining an atmosphere of frenzied horror such as music seldom has attempted, and perhaps never with such success. A burlesque version of the *Dies Irae* is introduced, as an interruption to the witch's dance, and at the close the dance takes the form of a fugue, whose climax again introduces the sinister theme of the *Dies Irae.*

The next symphony of Berlioz has the title *Harold in Italy*, and is based upon the Byronic character of Childe Harold. Again the composer uses the "fixed idea," this time in a theme representing the hero, played by the viola, which has a prominent part throughout the entire work. Every movement has its own title, ending with an "Orgy of Brigands," which is sufficiently terrifying.

Berlioz produced his symphonic masterpiece in the *Romeo and Juliet* symphony, which consists of eight parts, mostly definite scenes from the Shakespearean play. The Introduction represents the strife of the Montagues and the Capulets, expressed in fugal style. Then comes a Prologue, in which a solo voice and three-part chorus are used to give a synopsis of the drama. Outstanding among the later movements is the Queen Mab Scherzo, which not only follows the Shakespearean lines with considerable fidelity, but creates a convincing atmosphere of Fairyland. The funeral of Juliet is not interpreted by a conventional march, but in a fugue, with monotone comment by the chorus. There are dramatic scenes at the grave, with the double tragedy and the final reconciliation of the warring families.

Franz Liszt also wrote program symphonies, one called *Dante* and the other *Faust.* The latter is similar to the Berlioz *Romeo and Juliet*, but attempts to suggest the psychology of the characters in the Faust story, instead of describing definite scenes. The *Dante* symphony has only two movements, Inferno and Purgatorio, and is more descriptive in character. In both cases, however, the conception was somewhat greater than the realization.

Liszt's finest orchestral writing is to be found in his *Symphonic Poems*, which are really miniature symphonies, with strongly marked characteristics of program music. The first of these is sometimes called *Mountain Symphony*, and is based on a descriptive poem by Victor Hugo. The second is far more dramatic, representing the lament and triumph of the poet Tasso. The third is the popular *Les Préludes*, whose inspiration came from a line of Lamartine, "What is one's life but a series of preludes to that unknown song of which death shall intone the first solemn note?" (The chromatic theme in this poem has been much imitated in modern popular songs.) *Orpheus*, *Prometheus*, *Mazeppa* and *Hamlet* are among the other subjects treated by Liszt in his symphonic poems.

Two minor symphonies of programmatic character are the *Leonore* and *Im Walde* (In the Forest) of Raff, the former containing a famous march melody, once featured in a musical novel called *The First Violin*. There is also a *Rustic Wedding Symphony* of Carl Goldmark, with charming melodies and a sufficiently convincing atmosphere. But all of these program symphonies pale into insignificance when compared with some of the absolute symphonic music written late in the nineteenth century.

BRAHMS AS SYMPHONIST

Beethoven seemed to have carried the classic symphony as far as it could go when he wrote his ninth, with the choral Finale. Berlioz and Liszt approached the limits of program music in symphonic form in their dramatically realistic compositions. But suddenly a symphonic composer appeared who calmly went back to the pure classic style of absolute music, and by a combination of nobility of ideas and perfection of workmanship turned out four symphonies that are fully equal to the finest work of Beethoven and possibly superior to everything else in the symphonic literature. That composer was Johannes Brahms.

Strongly influenced by Schumann, and a thorough Romanticist at heart, Brahms nevertheless found it possible to adhere to classic ideals and standards, and to make his appeal through music alone, without any trappings of program or title, and without striving for effects of originality, bizarre tonal coloring or perversions of form. He was able to accomplish more with conventional materials than even Beethoven, chiefly because the whole technique of music had advanced considerably by that time, but he did not depend on the modern harmony and instrumentation that were at his disposal to make his symphonies sound different from those that had gone before. Greatness of invention and greatness of musicianship were enough to make the Brahms symphonies stand out above all their contemporaries with a truly heroic stature.

The first symphony of Brahms, in C minor (op. 68), appeared in 1877, after ten years of preparation. He approached the form with the greatest reverence, and did not allow himself to attempt a symphony until he felt ready and fully equipped for the task. By way of practice in scoring for the orchestra he had composed two *Serenades* as early as 1860, both in the manner of the classic composers and with modest instrumentation. In 1874 he had orchestrated his *Variations on a Theme by Haydn*, originally written for two pianos, showing a great advance in instrumentation, as well as a remarkable command of formal technique.

When the first symphony of Brahms finally appeared, it was hailed by Von Bülow as "the tenth," implying immediate equality with Beethoven. Actually, it stands repeated hearing better than any of the older master's works, and the testimony of orchestral players and conductors who perform all the symphonies over and over again is to the effect that Brahms in general is the least likely of all composers to become tiresome.

Certainly the C minor symphony is a monumental work in every way. The opening chords, thrilling in their broad dignity, with portentous beats of the kettledrum in a slow 6-8 time, prepare the mind for music of the highest quality, and this standard is never relaxed for a moment. The entire first movement is built on closely knit thematic materials, baffling in their originality, yet always logical in structure.

The slow movement is far more orthodox, starting with a broad theme of clear melodic outline, yet quickly developing unexpected harmonic changes. The latter part of this melody, introduced as an oboe solo, brings out some pungent discords in the accompaniment, yet maintains a spirit of tender sweetness to the very end. The rhythmic decorations given to this leading theme are of amazing variety, and much of the movement thus has the effect of variations. There is another oboe solo, over a curiously syncopated accompaniment, whose development points forward to the opening melody of the third movement, and the coda is a remarkable interweaving of thematic fragments, in which, however, the mood of tenderness and calm is never lost.

Instead of a Scherzo there follows a lilting Allegretto, with its main melody first sounded by the clarinet, which also introduces a new theme in minor mood, followed by a second section of unearthly mystery, in which there are strange echoes of the triplets that made up Beethoven's Fate motif. These triplets persist until the close of the movement, which recaptures a mood of sunny good humor, in spite of all hints of a deeper emotional content.

The Finale has a strange introduction of chords combining the chromatic harmonies of the first movement with a suggestion of the broad final melody yet to come. Then comes a pizzicato passage in which the strings seem to compete with each other, rushing to a sudden climax and then starting all over again. There is a slow theme, announced by the horn, that has been identified with the downward notes of the Westminster Chime (but actually representing an Alpine horn) and an answering brief chorale, to be heard later in a sublime climax. But at the moment all this is merely an introduction to the sweeping melody that has so often been compared with the choral theme of Beethoven's *Ninth Symphony*.

This broad, folk-like tune in C major is developed in ways that suggest the style of the opening movement, and after a brief reminder of the horn motif, a new theme enters with an animation that seems to point toward a quick finish. But Brahms manages to sustain the triumphant spirit of his Finale through further incredible development of his materials, and eventually lets the broad march melody be heard once more all the way through, followed by still further development, and finally a return of the horn motif, now imitated in canon style at different levels, leading once more into the animated closing theme. The coda still holds some surprises in reserve, for after two crashing "Amens" a rapid rush of notes suddenly "opens the heavens" to a final overwhelming announcement of the chorale by the brass, an effect that is nowhere surpassed in symphonic music. From there to the end there is little more than the determination to get into the key of C major and stay there, forcibly and unmistakably, somewhat as Beethoven did it at the end of his *Fifth Symphony*, but with far more originality and real excitement. It is a great finish to a great symphony.

The *Second Symphony* of Brahms, in D (op. 73), is the most obviously melodious of the four, and the most easily comprehended at a first hearing. Its mood is pastoral, where the first might be called heroic. A pattern of three tones, heard in the very first measure from cellos and basses, forms the basis of much of the melodic material of the symphony, with almost the effect of a "motto." The first theme follows it immediately, built on the tones of the major chord, like so many of the fine Brahms melodies. (Compare it with the opening theme of the *Violin Concerto*, in the same key, and also that of the *Sapphic Ode.*) A secondary theme, constructed from the notes of the motto, is added to the first, but the real contrast comes in a singing melody, with the violins and cellos harmonizing in thirds, which has the indescribable quality of the noblest Brahms inspirations.

The second movement has a mysterious mood, with its thematic material built upon a descending scale, with much individual harmonizing. It leads directly into the Allegretto, which announces a gracefully tripping tune, sung by the wood-winds over a pizzicato accompaniment of the cellos. This is soon repeated in very fast time, duple instead of triple, creating an entirely new effect. A further variation introduces striking syncopations, and finally the melody returns in its original form, with one poignant octave near the end of the coda to remind the hearer once more of the genius of the composer.

The Finale begins with a flowing theme, constructed from the motto, and later introduces a broader melody, syncopated in typical Brahms fashion. The themes as well as the workmanship show a directness and a buoyancy that make one think of a modernized Haydn, and the sunny charm of the music is maintained to the end.

THE GREATEST SYMPHONY?

Musicians are beginning to think that the *Third Symphony* (in F, op. 90) is the finest of all the Brahms works, and possibly the finest in all musical literature. Certainly it is the most consistently interesting, with a combination of melodic beauty and nobility of mood seldom equaled and never surpassed. A motto again stands at the opening, this time consisting of two chords whose harmonies are a basis for much of the later material. The first theme follows immediately, sweeping down over intervals clearly suggested by the preceding chords and creating an irresistible impression of bold and rugged strength. The second theme is a romantic dialogue between the clarinet and the bassoon, over a drone-bass, giving a charmingly rustic effect. This is developed in the wood-winds through a series of entrancing harmonies, and later appears in a minor version in the strings. The recapitulation brings back the opening theme in a variety of treatment, and with frequent reminders of the motto chords a coda is finally reached, transforming the original sweeping intervals into a quiet tranquillity, like that of a sunset after the blazing heat of a summer day.

A pastoral theme of intimate beauty and great simplicity opens the second movement, and this melody is developed in an amazingly subtle fashion, with harmonies seeming to spring again and again out of a clear sky and leading logically to new and surprising effects. The whole movement is one whose thematic material might have been invented by any of the classic composers but could not possibly have been treated by any of them in the unique fashion employed by Brahms.

The Allegretto has a plaintive, romantic theme that unquestionably stems from Schumann, but again with an originality of treatment that only Brahms commands. It is played first by the cellos, with the other strings weaving arpeggio decorations around it, and then repeated by the violins and the wood-winds, with increasing ornamentation. The contrasting material is also Schumannesque, leading into a series of modulations of unearthly beauty, which eventually bring back the opening theme in as lovely a passage as music has ever known.

In the Finale there is first a portentous whispering of the strings, *sotto voce*, and then a suggestion of strife and struggle in which a reminiscence of the Beethoven Fate motif again makes itself heard. But a melody of victorious joy is eventually reached by the cellos, with a curious cross-rhythm that is endlessly fascinating.

The fourth and last symphony of Brahms is the most austere, the most somber, and in some respects the most difficult for the listener. It is only after several hearings that its beauty becomes manifest, and the scholarly technique of its structure becomes less forbidding. It may never become so popular as the other three, but it will always maintain its fascination for the lover of pure musicianship. This symphony is in E minor, op. 98, and is dated 1885.

The opening theme is built on two-tone patterns, apparently simple in construction, but full of surprises. The second is a sturdier melody for the wood-winds, of almost martial character, followed by a broadly sustained song of the cellos. The slow movement has a beautiful theme in 6-8 time, remarkably harmonized, with contrasting material presented by the strings in broad melodic lines. The third movement is a real Scherzo, full of impetuous vivacity, and fairly obvious in its tunes. Brahms builds his Finale on a scale theme in E minor, used as a bass or harmonic background for a set of variations in the style of a passacaglia. The theme itself is first given out by the brass and then treated in a great variety of ways, ending in another impressive announcement by the entire orchestra.

CÉSAR FRANCK'S SYMPHONY

One modern symphony that can be safely ranked with those of Brahms is that of César Franck in D minor, which has become so popular that it now appears on orchestral request programs. It is in three movements, of the "cyclic" style, with its earlier themes reappearing in the Finale. The chromatic mood predominates, and there is much of Franck's characteristic musicianship in the interweaving of short phrases. The opening pattern of three tones, in minor key, becomes the actual first theme, for which there is a contrasting melody, following the scale, with some chromatic intervals. A third theme is strongly syncopated, and of a very popular type, running again into chromatic progressions. There is a free and interesting treatment of all this material, and the coda brings back the slow introduction once more.

The second movement has a plaintive melody, first sung by the English horn and then by the clarinet, over a sharply accented accompaniment of chords by the harp and pizzicato strings. (This effect may also have been influenced by Schumann.) The contrasting melody is of the smoothly flowing type, again with chromatic touches. The Finale begins with a joyous melody which is practically ragtime in its persistent syncopation, and contrasted with a still more triumphant theme given out by the brass. The cyclic structure of the symphony becomes evident in this last movement, when all the important earlier melodies are heard again in various forms. In this way the symphony acquires an unusual unity, and seems even stronger at the close than at the beginning.

Tschaikowsky composed six symphonies, of which only the last three are commonly heard. They all have a certain programmatic character.

TSCHAIKOWSKY'S THREE FAVORITES

The *Fourth Symphony* opens with a motto, intoned by the horns in the manner of a call to battle, or perhaps again a Fate motif. It is followed by a highly original theme, with syncopation and chromatic intervals, which leads to another melody in the wood-winds, started by the clarinet, in which the chromatic scale appears literally at different levels of pitch. The second movement begins with a tenderly haunting strain, in minor key, which is contrasted with a vigorous chord progression in the strings. The slow theme is repeated by the bassoon near the close. The Scherzo is unique in its long section for pizzicato strings, played at a very rapid tempo, and followed by contrasting material from the brass and wood-wind choirs, each treated independently and all finally combined in clever fashion. The movement is supposed to represent the crowds at a country fair. In the Finale, a noisy introduction, coming right down the diatonic scale (as in the hymn, *Joy to the World*) leads to the direct quotation of a Russian folk-song known as *The Birch Tree.* This material is variously treated, with occasional echoes of the opening motto, and the symphony comes to a brilliant close.

The fifth is longer and more elaborate. Again there is a motto, first stated in a lugubrious minor key, but later to reappear triumphantly in major. The main theme of the first movement is also in minor key, with a contrasting melody that goes up the scale in a literal spirit of aspiration. The slow movement has a long, sustained melody (once used in the play, *The Song of Songs,* and frequently supplied with words, as in the popular song, *Moon Love*), perhaps overly sentimental, but unquestionably appealing, with a second strain that breathes optimism, even though the mutterings of the motto are heard ominously from time to time. A beautiful waltz follows, one of the rare uses of this common dance form in symphonic surroundings, and again the mutter of the opening motto theme is heard. In the Finale this motto serves both as introduction and as coda, but in major key and unmistakably triumphant spirit. Between the two there is much evidence of a final struggle, with the thematic material first tearing its way through the minor scale and then soaring confidently above the short, vicious beats of the accompaniment. The final statement of the major motto is preceded by a pause and two measures of a rhythmic figure which continues right through the triumphant melody, with the effect of three beats against one. At the finish the triple rhythm is emphasized, with a reminder of the first theme of the opening movement, now in major key, closing the symphony in noisy exultation.

The *Pathétique Symphony* was for a time so popular that there was danger of its being played to death. It has survived this ordeal, and remains today an established masterpiece, the most dramatic music in the modern symphonic literature. While its effects are sometimes obvious, there is no denying the genius of its creator in achieving the results he desires, with a combination of well-conceived melodies and brilliant orchestration.

Tschaikowsky himself never divulged the program of this final symphony, but he admitted that it had a definite meaning, and his title of *Pathétique* is sufficiently illuminating. It might be said that all three of his great symphonies deal with man's struggle against Fate, as already popularized by Beethoven. But while the fourth and fifth symphonies end happily, with distinct indications of the triumph of the individual, the *Pathétique* closes in a spirit of impenetrable gloom and deepest melancholy. This is all the more emphatic by contrast with the next to the last movement, which is a triumphal march, quite as exultant as Beethoven's C major Finale in his *Fifth Symphony*.

The *Pathétique* opens with a mournful theme, in minor key, uttered by the bassoon over double-bass harmonies, but soon translated to a higher key and a sprightly spirit in the strings, with increasing decoration. The second theme is a lovely melody, introduced by the strings and given a great variety of treatment, both in the exposition and in the recapitulation. The development starts with a crashing, dissonant chord, after a lulling pianissimo by the clarinet, and proceeds to work on the opening theme at great length and with continued agitation. A mood of hopeless resignation finally settles over the music, relieved only in the coda by a new theme which suggests that all is not lost, as the pizzicato strings plod through the descending scale over and over again.

The second movement is famous for its graceful melody in 5-4 time, one of the few instances of the successful use of this irregular beat over a considerable stretch of music. The middle section continues in the same time, but changes from a piquant melodiousness to tragic minor strains. Next comes the triumphal march, which is built up in a highly original fashion, with snatches of the melody first heard through whirring figures in the strings, until the complete statement of the inspiring tune can no longer be postponed. From this cheerful movement to the pessimistic Finale is a long step, but the intentions of the composer are convincingly carried out. There is nothing more despairing in all music than the opening measures of that *Adagio lamentoso*. A contrasting melody of great beauty, played over syncopated triplets, seems to offer a ray of hope, but even this theme eventually goes into the minor key of dull despair, and the symphony ends in an abyss of complete dejection.

DVORAK'S "NEW WORLD SYMPHONY"

The only modern symphony that shares today the popularity of the three by Tschaikowsky, César Franck's and the four by Brahms is the Dvorak favorite, *From the New World*. Its vogue in America may have been helped by the fact that it was written in this country, with direct quotations or at least suggestions of Negro themes, but it would probably have proved successful in any case, for it is a vividly dramatic work, of continued interest in its thematic material, grateful for the orchestra, and with an undeniable solidity of workmanship as well.

After a rather mysterious introduction, a minor theme of decided syncopation introduces the unmistakable Negro spirit. This is considerably developed and followed by another minor melody of quite different character, this time Bohemian rather than Negro in its folk-background, particularly in the use of a drone-bass. The real second theme of the movement is generally associated with the Negro spiritual, *Swing Low, Sweet Chariot*, which it undoubtedly resembles. But there is also an old slave song, still closer to Dvorak's melody, which may have been the source of both the spiritual and the symphonic theme.

The famous Largo has a melody that cries out for words—and gets them, plentifully. It does not particularly suggest Negro music, but since it has been given the text of *Goin' Home* by William Arms Fisher, it has been practically accepted as an authentic spiritual, even Negro singers claiming both words and music as their own. In its symphonic form, the melody is a beautiful medium for the voice of the English horn. There is a more agitated middle section, also far removed from the Negro spirit or spiritual.

The Scherzo harks back to the corresponding movement of Beethoven's *Ninth Symphony*, with suggestions also of the joyous part of Tschaikowsky's *Pathétique* in the manner in which scraps of theme are pieced together. The trio has a melody which represents a cheerful version of the Largo, with more than a hint of rustic dancing. There is still another theme, built on the major triad, in the style of a trumpet call, and the coda quotes portions of the syncopated opening theme of the first movement.

The Finale of the *New World Symphony* soon announces a broadly dramatic theme in E minor (possibly adapted from the American folk-song, *Peter Gray*), and this is furnished with a contrast of skipping triplets in the violins. The development introduces material from the first and second movements, and at one time there is a remarkable suggestion of the tune of *Yankee Doodle*, rising from a treatment of the chief theme of the Finale in major key. (This may have been entirely accidental, but there is a possibility that Dvorak had it in mind when he created the theme.) The final measures of the symphony are a struggle between major and minor key, with the major finally winning in a triumphant finish.

BRUCKNER AND MAHLER

Two symphonic writers who have thus far failed to appeal to the public, yet are greatly admired by musicians, are Gustav Mahler and

Anton Bruckner. Each of them composed nine symphonies (perhaps hoping that the magic number would automatically turn them into Beethovens) and each had a command of orchestral technique that would have gone far with any inspired material. But neither succeeded in carrying out his great conceptions to the full satisfaction of the listener.

Felix Weingartner, a great conductor, wrote three symphonies which are almost never heard. An *Alpine Symphony* by Richard Strauss has been given some attention, but has proved far less popular than the much discussed *Domestic Symphony*, a piece of outright program music, in which realism goes so far as to include a musical description of the baby's bath.

France has contributed much to symphonic literature in addition to the masterpiece of César Franck. Vincent d'Indy wrote a *Wallenstein Trilogy*, which is program music of symphonic scope, and his *Istar Variations* are really a symphonic poem, with the theme saved until the close, instead of following the conventional style. There is also an important D'Indy symphony in B-flat. Debussy's *La Mer* was called by its composer "three symphonic sketches," and may be considered his orchestral masterpiece. It is rich in instrumental color and of great originality throughout. Bizet's *L'Arlesienne Suites* are of almost symphonic proportions, although written with his familiar lightness of touch. Saint-Saëns wrote three symphonies, of which the last includes the piano and organ in its instrumentation, and also won success with a series of picturesque symphonic poems (*Le Rouet d'Omphale, Phaëton, Danse Macabre*, etc.).

The Finnish Sibelius has made for himself an almost unique place in modern symphonic music, writing in a highly original style, but with a power that indicates true inspiration. His symphonic poem, *Finlandia*, is among the most popular of modern orchestral works, and all seven of his symphonies are now recognized as masterpieces, with the first perhaps still the favorite.

Among the Russians, Glazounoff and Borodin have written excellent symphonies, while the *Scheherazade* of Rimsky-Korsakoff frequently appears on concert programs as a symphonic work. It is full of orchestral color and Oriental atmosphere, a most effective piece of program music, and well worth hearing aside from its picturesque background of the *Arabian Nights*. Other symphonic poems by this gifted composer are *Sadko, Antar*, a *Capriccio Espagnol* and the *Russian Easter.*

Rachmaninoff proved his genius in two splendid symphonies, as well as a symphonic poem based upon Böcklin's picture, *The Island of the Dead*. Scriabin is represented by several important orchestral works, including the *Prometheus* (with color-organ), a *Divine Poem*, and a *Poem of Ecstasy*. Stravinsky has also written symphonies, and the *Classical Symphony* of Prokofieff, imitating Mozart in modern style, has become one of the hits of radio and the records. The prodigious Shostakovitch made a deep impression with his first symphony, increased it with a fifth, perhaps his best, and created wartime sensations with his seventh and eighth, composed during Russia's successful resistance of German aggression. The English Elgar has composed two symphonies, and there is an Irish symphony by Villiers Stanford. Ottorino Respighi's orchestral works are Italy's most important contributions to the modern symphonic literature.

American symphonies have been successfully written by Henry Hadley and others, including a work by Ernest Bloch (Swiss by birth) which has the title *America*. MacDowell's *Indian Suite* is symphonic music of high quality, and there are solid orchestral works also to the credit of John K. Paine, Edgar Stillman-Kelley, Henry F. Gilbert, George W. Chadwick, Horatio Parker, Frederick S. Converse, Charles Martin Loeffler, Mrs. H. H. A. Beach, Rubin Goldmark, Charles T. Griffes and Ernest Schelling. A later school of symphonic composition is represented by Daniel Gregory Mason, John Alden Carpenter, Howard Hanson, Charles Wakefield Cadman, John Powell, Edward Burlingame Hill, David Stanley Smith, Albert Stoessel, Randall Thompson, Douglas Moore, Deems Taylor, Charles Haubiel and Samuel Barber. Definitely in modern vein are the symphonic works of Roy Harris, Aaron Copland, Roger Sessions, Charles Ives, William Schuman, Lazare Saminsky, Walter Piston, Henry Cowell, Virgil Thomson, Paul Creston, Harold Morris, David Diamond, Nicolai Berezowsky, Harl McDonald, Leo Sowerby, William Grant Still and Emerson Whithorne. The lighter style of George Gershwin has been successfully carried on by Robert Russell Bennett, Ferde Grofé, Robert McBride, Morton Gould and Meredith Willson.

CHAPTER XVII MODERNISM AND JAZZ

IN A BROAD SENSE, modernism and jazz amount to the same thing. Both may be most simply defined as the distortion of the conventional in music.

It is human nature to fly off at a tangent from time to time, and the modern tendency has been to deny the value of all traditions and to upset all formulas. Carried to an extreme, this is a mere absurdity, for conventions, traditions and formulas do not exist without good reason. Yet every great creative artist has expressed something of heresy against the established beliefs of his time, and some of the greatest composers of music were considered the most revolutionary in their own day.

Every musician who has destroyed a tradition, as did Monteverde and Beethoven and Mozart and Chopin and Wagner and many others, was in spirit a modernist; and in most of these cases the heresies of one generation became the accepted formulas of another. Even Debussy, who was considered an apostle of dissonance only a few years ago, has come to be accepted as a thoroughly respectable, law-abiding composer, although his original genius is unquestioned. It is quite possible that most of the ultramodernists who have risen since Debussy will in time be considered equally normal, but it is illogical and rather dangerous to contend that because revolutionists of the past turned out to be correct prophets, therefore any revolutionary doctrine must be accepted as equally right. There is also no way of proving that music can be distorted without limit, and that every established formula of melody, harmony and rhythm may be disregarded indefinitely. Somewhere a point must be reached (and seems already to have been reached) when music becomes a mere scientific process, of interest to the intellect, but totally deprived of its human and emotional qualities and hence of the universality of its appeal.

The same thing has happened in the other arts, and here also there seems to be a limit beyond which scientific experiment cannot go without a definite sacrifice of beauty. The futuristic and cubist schools of painting are now generally discredited, although many of the offshoots of impressionism continue to command attention and respect. The absurdities of modernistic furniture, sculpture and architecture are no longer taken very seriously, and the silly, formless puerilities that have masqueraded as literature are gradually finding the oblivion that they deserved.

But it would be foolish and shortsighted to condemn all modernistic art as mere absurdity, and while there has been much charlatanism in all its phases, it must be admitted that a great many artists of the modern school are thoroughly sincere and worthy of recognition as pioneers in a new technique. The difficulty today is that we are so close to the whole subject that a fair perspective is almost impossible; and with so much insincerity, prejudice and ballyhoo rampant in every field of art, nobody can be blamed for feeling a bit suspicious of anything that departs too violently from the accepted paths of truth and beauty.

DISTORTING THE CONVENTIONAL

If modernism and jazz are bracketed under the general definition of the distortion of the conventional, an analysis of the situation becomes fairly easy, and each individual can then be left to draw his own conclusions and follow his own tastes. Unquestionably the hypocrisy which once pretended a love of the classics that was not really felt is just as prevalent and just as irritating today in the form of an affected enthusiasm for anything "different," but unquestionably also there are plenty of people who honestly enjoy hearing the rather horrible sounds and seeing the rather horrible pictures of modern art. Most modernistic music is of the programmatic type, and this is almost a necessity, since the idiom could not possibly be sufficiently comprehensible to assure the direct transfer of moods and emotions in the manner of absolute music. When the program is definitely stated in advance, there is no great difficulty in winning the interest and holding the attention of even inexperienced listeners. In fact, children have been found particularly susceptible to the idiom of modern music, but always from the standpoint of listening to a musical story or looking at a musical picture. A fountain is just as convincing when its waters are scattered in dissonant showers as when it plays with respectable tonic and dominant harmonies, and certain phases of ugliness (which must be conceded a place in art, whether in contrast to beauty or because of their own undeniable truth) are more easily expressed in modern terms of cacophony (literally "bad sounding") than in any of the conventional formulas of the past.

Jazz distorts the conventions of popular music just as modernism in general distorts those of the serious, classic type. A reminder of the general definition of music as the Organization of Sound toward Beauty will simplify the analysis of possible distortions. Since rhythm, melody, harmony, tone color and form are the five organizing factors in music, their distortion, individually or collectively, creates the idiom of modernism and jazz. Rhythm is distorted chiefly by syncopation, but may also be robbed of all regularity (which is nothing more than a reversion to the unrhythmic plain-song of the Middle Ages). Melody is distorted by a refusal to follow the logical patterns offered by the scales and the conventional harmonic combinations, deliberately seeking intervals that are as unexpected as possible. (It is difficult to decide on the dividing line between the reminiscent familiarity of universal patterns, maintaining an honest popularity, and the hackneyed combinations of mere routine. Similarly, there is often a rather fine distinction between inspired originality and the mere dogged determination to be different at all costs.) Harmony may be distorted by any departure from the recognized concords (as it was originally by Monteverde), or by definitely unconventional, dissonant chords like those of Debussy, or by a complete disregard of technical relationships or pleasing sounds, resulting in the Schoenberg theory that anything may be made to harmonize with anything. (One of the common tricks of modernism, easily burlesqued, is that of playing in two keys at the same time, preferably only half a tone apart, creating the most hideous discords possible.) Tone color is easily distorted by giving to individual instruments the opportunity for abnormal sounds (as in the muting of brass, or playing on the wrong side of the bridge of a violin), and by combining them in unaccustomed ways, to create new effects. (The whole instrumentation of a jazz band is different from the conventional orchestral combinations.) Finally, there are plenty of ways to distort form, from the free rhapsodic style to all kinds of caprices, fantasies and musical whims. So far as form is concerned, distortion is far easier than conventional correctness of technique.

The serious modern music and jazz alike will supply a great quantity of all these distortions, sometimes with excellent effect and sometimes for no apparent reason beyond the love of distortion as such. There is certainly a fascination in syncopated rhythms, whimsical melodies, acrid harmonies and novel tone colors, and freedom from the restraints of form may be interesting up to a certain point, even though it eliminates one of the most absorbing phases of music for the analytical listener. In the long run every music-lover must decide for himself which kind of music he prefers, and it is quite possible to enjoy every kind, formal classicism, sentimental romanticism, exaggerated modernism and unbridled jazz, with equal sincerity and a fair distribution of physical, mental and spiritual profit. Novel music and popular music cannot be ignored, and it is just as silly to lift holy hands in horror over these "brutalities" as to scorn the orthodoxy of those who still find enough satisfaction in the well-established masterpieces of recognized composers.

It is impossible even to mention by name all the possibly significant composers who have contributed to ultramodern music and jazz. In many cases their reputation depends largely upon commercialized publicity or the propaganda of influential friends, and the mere fact that a composer is comparatively unknown is in no sense a reflection on his ability. Conversely, it would be a mistake to ascribe merit to a composition simply because it succeeded in getting a public performance.

For example, that greatest of all conductors, Toscanini, has deliberately and effectively made propaganda for the works of modern Italian composers. Some of them were unquestionably worth performing, not only once but many times, and of course all of them sounded well under his inspired baton. But it would be absurd to contend that all these works are equal or superior to others that might have been presented if the conductor's personal interest had happened to be aroused. Similarly that other genius among conductors, Leopold Stokowski, has occasionally presented novelties in which it is hard to believe that he himself found much merit, but whose ability to create spectacular publicity paid tribute to his well-known talent for showmanship.

Among the Italians who have had the benefit of current exploitation, a high place must be given to Ottorino Respighi, whose orchestral tone poems, describing the *Festivals*, the *Pines* and the *Fountains of Rome* are all immensely effective as program music of the greatest virtuosity. The climax of the *Pines of Rome* builds up an orchestral volume such as no other piece of music has been known to surpass, and this, to many listeners, is a virtue in itself. Respighi leans also toward the use of older forms and archaic modes, as illustrated by his *Gregorian Concerto* for violin and the triptych, *Maria Egiziaca.*

Other modernists of Italy are G. Francesco Malipiero, a very gifted creator of unusual effects, Alfredo Casella, leaning toward the satirical (but credited with some important music in serious vein, including the ballet, *La Giara,* performed at the Metropolitan, a *Serenata* for small orchestra, two symphonies, a violin concerto and one for organ, strings and tympani), Ildebrando Pizzetti, with two great violin sonatas and some important orchestra music, and his pupil, Mario Castelnuovo-Tedesco, also inclined toward satire, but represented by a fine violin concerto and some delightful piano music.

FRENCH IMPRESSIONISM AND MODERNISM

France, which may claim in Debussy the founder of the whole modern school of composition, has another worthy representative in Maurice Ravel, who has written music in a wide variety of styles, with great and well-deserved success. His chamber music is of the highest quality, and his satirical little opera, *L'Heure Espagnole* made a favorable impression at the Metropolitan. His piano music is perhaps most appealing of all (his *Sonatine* has become almost as popular as the familiar *Pavane*), and all through his work there runs a thoroughly individual style, reminiscent at times of Debussy, yet quite different in its essential make-up. The spectacular *Bolero,* a really extraordinary study in rhythmic monotony and instrumental variety, has penetrated the movie theaters as well as the concert halls, and such orchestral compositions as *Daphnis et Chloë*, *La Valse* and *Mother Goose* are frequently performed.

A more advanced modernism has appeared in the compositions of the so-called "six," a group comprising Darius Milhaud, Arthur Honegger, Germaine Taillefer, François Poulenc, Durey and Georges Auric. Their inspiration was Eric Satie, whose *Gnossienne* and other piano music has become popular, and they have been aided by the teachings of Nadia Boulanger, whose sister Lili had made a real impression as a composer before her untimely death. The best known work by any of the six is Honegger's orchestral description of a locomotive, *Pacific 231*, which, he says, is not intended "to imitate the noises of a locomotive but to translate into music a visual impression and a physical sensation." (In any case, it sounds like a locomotive.)

Russia has contributed some important examples of modern music through the work of Alexander Scriabin, Igor Stravinsky, Serge Prokofieff and Dmitri Shostakovitch. Scriabin is the direct descendant of Chopin, and similarly gifted in his instinct for the piano. Like Chopin, he wrote preludes, mazurkas, études, nocturnes and waltzes, with a fastidious perfection of detail and a courtly grace of style. In many cases his harmonic experiments did not go much beyond Chopin himself. Particularly in his ninth sonata does he show a classic command of form. But in his orchestral tone poems, the *Prometheus*, the *Divine Poem* and the *Poem of Ecstasy*, he creates a musical language that is all his own, a method of harmony based on "mystic chords," a freedom of rhythm and tonal coloring (aided in *Prometheus* by an actual "color-organ") that marks him as possibly the most advanced craftsman of his day, with real inspiration and emotional depth besides.

Stravinsky's ballet music is extraordinary, but with the possible exception of *Le Sacre du Printemps*, it needs the stage pictures to be completely effective. This musical interpretation of the Rites of Spring is an overwhelming orchestral *tour de force*, with a barbaric insistence of rhythm that produces definite physical reactions in the listener. *Petrouschka*, thus far his most popular work, is by comparison a mild combination of sound-effects and folk-music. It gives a vivid picture of the noisy bustle of a country fair, and it makes effective use of the Russian folk-tune, *Down St. Peter's Road*, but there is little real depth or absolute value to its music. *L'Oiseau de feu* (The

Falling in love with someone

VICTOR HERBERT came to America because he had fallen in love with an opera singer. From his native Dublin he had arrived in Stuttgart in pursuit of his musical studies, playing the cello and learning the art of composition. There he met the charming soprano of the opera, Therese Förster.

When the Metropolitan Opera Company sent its scouts to Europe in search of talent in 1886, a contract was offered to the Stuttgart soprano. Miss Förster was willing to accept, on one condition. It must include her intended husband, the Irish Mr. Herbert. If her singing was good enough for New York, so was his cello-playing. Thus America acquired not only an adequate voice but a great conductor and composer.

Mr. and Mrs. Victor Herbert sailed into New York Harbor, past the newly built Statue of Liberty, with high hopes for the future. Therese Förster made a fair success at her debut, but was soon content to be known as the wife of one of our most popular musicians.

From the modest position of solo cellist at the Metropolitan Opera, Victor Herbert went on to the conductorship of the Pittsburgh Symphony Orchestra and finally emerged as Broadway's favorite creator of light operas. His *Naughty Marietta, Mlle. Modiste, Babes in Toyland*, and *The Red Mill* made history, and America is still singing *Kiss Me Again, For I'm Falling in Love with Someone, Ah, Sweet Mystery of Life*, and *I Can't Do this Sum*. Added to such popular tunes are light classics of the type of *Babillage, Al Fresco, Pan-Americana*, and a *Suite of Serenades*, with the grand opera, *Natoma*, and a cello concerto among the more serious of the Herbert works. As usual, it was the great "unmusical" public that made the final decision.

Firebird) is similar, with great charm and flashing color, but significant chiefly as an interpretation of its story. A piano concerto, supposedly containing a jazz movement, has thus far failed to create much interest, and an orchestral piece named *Ragtime* fell far short of America's understanding of that term. In his opera, *Le Rossignol* (The Nightingale), Stravinsky shows his feeling for Orientalism and at the same time expresses an interest in the modern machine, which much of his music reflects.

A Soviet composer who has arrived at real popularity in America is Dmitri Shostakovitch, whose theory of composition rests upon the "negation of thematic development." Instead of inventing a theme and then working out its materials in a variety of ways, he tries to make every measure of his music different from the rest. He is an apostle of atonality, adhering to no definite key, and it can be imagined that his music is not easily followed by the average listener. Yet his "Leningrad" symphony made a deep impression, with the help of international propaganda, and the clever little *Polka* from *The Golden Age* has become honestly popular.

Serge Prokofieff, once considered an extreme cacophonist, seems to have modified his style somewhat, and to be content with merely stirring up enough excitement to make people want to hear his compositions. He is best known today by his *Classical Symphony* and the delightful fairy tale, *Peter and the Wolf*. His opera, *The Love of the Three Oranges,* is satirical, but dramatically of doubtful importance. A violin concerto has won considerable attention, and some of his smaller compositions for the piano, such as the attractive *March*, enjoy a real popularity, especially in his own interpretations at the keyboard. A new Prokofieff opera, based on Tolstoy's *War and Peace*, was recently announced.

Schoenberg is still a leading modernist, but much of his work now seems almost conventional. His *Gurrelieder* and *Pierrot Lunaire* are mild echoes of Wagnerian Romanticism, and his lovely sextet, *Verklärte Nacht*, definitely suggests the idiom of *Tristan und Isolde*. The *String Quartet* in D minor is an important piece of chamber music, however, and in his *Five Orchestral Pieces* and some of his piano music he goes to the limit of a purely intellectual treatment of music, regardless of the resulting sounds. More and more the public is beginning to suspect that the early Schoenberg was a deliverer of portentous platitudes, while his later self has produced only brain problems, with no relation to human life and emotions.

Other modernists of the Teutonic type are Hans Pfitzner, Franz Schreker, Egon Wellesz, Webern, Hanns Eisler, Alois Haba and Paul Hindemith, of whom the last-named wrote an opera called *Neues vom Tage* (News of the Day) whose overture has been performed in New York. It seems to be a jazzy piece of work, deliberately intended for sensational effects. The Viennese Ernst Krenek also attracted attention by a so-called jazz opera, *Johny Spielt Auf*, very successful in Europe but a failure in America. He has been described as "devoid of sentimentality, greedy for fame, fond of sensation, anarchist in his aesthetic views, and without the least respect for tradition." His music is polyphonic in a discordant way, and atonal (without definite tonality). Krenek has composed five symphonies in addition to his opera and other works.

An even greater European success has fallen to the opera *Schwanda the Bagpiper*, by Jaromir Weinberger, which has had more performances abroad than any other modern work. It is really a *Volksoper*, deriving its character from a background of folk-music and popular legend, and quite melodious and simple as compared with most modern music. Weinberger has also written incidental music for several Shakespearean plays.

Alban Berg's *Wozzeck* is another opera that has caused much discussion in America. Written to a strange libretto by Georg Büchner, psychoanalyzing a pitiful human being, it presents perhaps the theatrical extreme of atonal music. The characters on the stage do not really sing at all, yet they are not permitted the realism of actual speech. A curious whim of the composer is to use the forms of absolute music throughout his opera, so that the score is found to contain a passacaglia with twenty-one variations, fugues, examples of sonata form, etc. But so completely unmelodious is this music that it is literally impossible to follow these intellectual accomplishments by ear. *Wozzeck* has been called a masterpiece, but if so it belongs to an entirely new art, for neither as music nor as drama does it suggest reality or give any true satisfaction.

MODERNISM IN ENGLAND AND AMERICA

England has dipped lightly into the modern idiom, with the charming, Debussyan pieces of Cyril Scott, the more serious experiments of Delius, Arnold Bax and Gustav Holst, and the satires of Lord Berners and Arthur Bliss. Finland, however, has a real modernist in Sibelius, whose fourth symphony placed him definitely among the unconventionals, but with every evidence of a significant inspiration behind the novel technique. The Hungarians, Kodaly and Bela Bartok, also have given indications of having something to say of permanent interest, and their use of folk-themes has been highly effective, even in extremely modern terms.

America has adopted the English Eugene Goossens, the Swiss Ernest Bloch, the Russian Godowsky and the Alsatian Charles Martin Loeffler, among others, and they all have added significantly to the literature of modern music. Goossens has composed a *Sinfonietta* with a motto theme which he heard whistled in the streets of London. His early *Variations on a Chinese Theme*, later symphonic poems and a concerto for oboe are all interesting.

Bloch is a specialist in the Hebrew idiom, and his rhapsody for cello and orchestra, *Schelomo* (Solomon), must be considered one of the masterpieces of modern music. He has also made highly significant settings of some of the Psalms, in a definitely Hebraic style, composed several symphonies, including the prize-winning *America*, and contributed one of the outstanding pieces of pure modernism in absolute music with a suite for viola, which also won a prize. Godowsky's *Triakontameron* is a beautiful set of piano pieces in triple rhythm, and his brilliant paraphrases of the Strauss waltzes are famous.

Loeffler has written some splendid orchestral music, mostly in the form of symphonic poems (*The Death of Tintagiles*, *A Pagan Poem*), and his style is mildly modernistic, with an evident fear of putting on paper anything that might be considered similar to the traditional compositions of the past.

Charles T. Griffes might have become one of the greatest American modernists if he had lived longer, and even the few compositions of his short life showed a fine musical sense and a definitely modern style. But the man who actually discovered modernism for himself in America is Charles Ives. Brought up in a small New England town, his ear became accustomed to the slightly off-pitch singing of the village choir, and the uncertainty of both melody and rhythm shown by the village band, or, worse still, the several bands competing in a holiday parade. He made these slight inaccuracies of pitch and rhythm the basis of an actual musical technique, and was dealing in quarter-tones, off-beat accents and other eccentricities of modernism long before the term had become well known. Ives has written two important violin sonatas, a *New England Symphony*, a *Concord Sonata* for piano, and some program music depicting American life in rural communities.

Leo Ornstein is another pioneer of modernism in America, but unfortunately seems to have stopped composing in recent years. Sonatas for violin and cello and some highly interesting piano music have been among his contributions, and he was really the first composer to bring modernism into the limelight in this country and focus public attention on its characteristics.

George Antheil, once an *enfant terrible*, has developed into a solid composer, with four operas to his credit, and much other music that shows great talent, perhaps even genius. Unfortunately, he is still judged largely by his *Ballet Mécanique*, written for player-pianos and a strange percussion orchestra, and produced chiefly as a bid for spectacular publicity. Of late he has worked mostly in Hollywood.

Henry Cowell also has made some interesting contributions to modern music with his theory of "tone clusters," literally substituting dissonant combinations for individual tones, and securing them from the piano by playing with the flat of the hand and even the whole forearm. The effect is often strangely harmonious, with the top tone of a cluster governing the pitch. Recently Cowell has gone far beyond these experiments and is now a truly significant composer.

Carl Ruggles, also developing his modernism independently, should be mentioned for his orchestral tone poem, *Men and Mountains*, and there are some arresting compositions by the Negro, William Grant Still.

Louis Gruenberg has also been much in the limelight, particularly since the production of his opera, *The Emperor Jones*, a musical background of the atmospheric type for the immensely successful drama of Eugene O'Neill. Gruenberg is also known by his *Daniel Jazz*, to a poem by Vachel Lindsay, a *Jazz Suite*, a symphonic poem,

The Enchanted Isle, and *The Hill of Dreams*, which won the New York Symphony Orchestra prize in 1919. But Gruenberg's real significance today is as a composer of motion-picture scores, among which *The Fight for Life* and *An American Romance* are outstanding.

Other American modernists of real significance are Aaron Copland, who likewise has done some of his most effective work for motion pictures; Roger Sessions, formerly associated with Copland in concerts, and now teaching at Princeton, with *Black Maskers* and other important compositions to his credit; William Schuman, an impressive creator of symphonic and choral works, recently succeeding Ernest Hutcheson as head of the Juilliard School of Music; Paul Creston, several times a prize winner, consistently producing music that is both impressive and appealing; Roy Harris, a rugged individualist, with his own way of composing and promoting symphonies and other major works and reaching an ever growing public; Lazare Saminsky, with a leaning toward the Hebrew idiom, supported by an unusually solid scholarship; David Diamond, whose work is greatly admired by his own colleagues and gradually winning general recognition; Edgar Varese, originally imported from Switzerland, but long a leader in the modern American school; Norman Dello Joio, who recently scored with a choral symphony to words by Stephen Vincent Benet; Harold Morris, Charles Haubiel, Jerome Morross, Randall Thompson, Virgil Thomson, Bernard Herrmann, Douglas Moore, Marion Bauer, Quincy Porter, Walter Piston, Otto Luening, Abram Chasins, Arthur Kreutz, Leonard Bernstein, Lukas Foss, etc. They are developing a creative activity that still includes such substantial musicians, of less extreme idiom, as Daniel Gregory Mason, John Alden Carpenter, Howard Hanson, Leo Sowerby, Philip James, etc., with Morton Gould and a few others making interesting contributions on the lighter side.

AN UNSUSPECTED RELATIONSHIP

It should be fairly obvious by this time that the dividing line between modern music in general and jazz in particular is a very faint one. The modern idiom, whether in a popular or a serious vein, is merely a new treatment of old materials, not actually a new music. In the field of jazz, the distortions of the conventional are more easily recognized than in the so-called concert music, which too often sounds like a frightful and meaningless jumble.

Jazz rhythms have become so familiar that many people still think this is the whole material of jazz, whereas it is only one phase, although an important one. Syncopation, which is the basic distortion of rhythm, consists in either anticipating or delaying the strongest beat, thus creating an artificial accent which is decidedly provocative. Jazz-lovers unquestionably like syncopation because in order to keep time they have to exert their natural sense of rhythm to the utmost. There is a resulting sense of triumph and satisfaction similar to that which was felt after completing a crossword or jigsaw puzzle.

Syncopation is of course nothing new in music. All the great composers have made use of it, and with Brahms and Schumann it is a favorite device. With the beginnings of ragtime, syncopation became more and more emphasized, until in the modern jazz it has reached the extreme of off-beat accentuation. The Negroes seem to have a racial feeling for syncopation and for the slow, dragging "blue" rhythms, and the technique of jazz owes much to their improvisations.

Distortion of melody in jazz may be largely rhythmic (as in ragtime), or it may consist of variations and "breaks," in which the melody line is often completely concealed. (Even the classic type of variation is in a sense a distortion.) Such treatment is noticeable in the elaborate and often highly musical "arrangements" for the modern jazz bands.

Distortions of harmony are much the same in popular music as in the serious type, except that jazz does not go to the extremes affected by some composers of the concert hall. Usually the jazz harmonizations are satisfied with Debussyan chords of the ninth and the milder dissonances of Ravel. A pet distortion, however, is the notorious "blue chord," which is generally no more than the introduction of a minor seventh into the tonic major chord. There is an undeniably mournful effect in this harmony, which is sufficient explanation of the term "blue," and when it stands at the close of a piece, as it often does, the listener has a sense of being left in the air.

Distortion of tone color is one of the most obvious and at the same time interesting phases of jazz. The muting of the brass has created many new individual effects (and these have been much imitated by serious composers), while the emphasis on percussion (with extra drums, two pianos, banjo, guitar and the pizzicato double-bass) has entirely changed the orchestral balance. Realistic imitations of decidedly unmusical noises, such as the plaintive "wa-wa trumpet" and the trombone's "hyena laugh," have added still more to the distortion of tone color in a jazz band, but it is worth noting that such conductors as Paul Whiteman have insisted on pleasing musical effects also, using strings and harmonizing saxophones with great success.

Jazz composers have done comparatively little in the direction of distorting form, for the simple reason that much of their music is written for the practical purpose of accompanying ballroom dancing, and therefore must maintain quite definite outlines. Most popular songs of the day stick to a conventional A-A-B-A form in their choruses, with a routine length of thirty-two measures. But when such choruses are "arranged" for the more elaborate dance orchestras, certain distortions are allowed to creep in, by way of "breaks," interludes and codas. The traditional forms of the sonata, the rondo and the ancient dances have been practically ignored by jazz, but subjected to plenty of distortion by the more serious modern composers; and since form is the most artificial and didactic phase of the organization of sound toward beauty, its distortion, being so easily accomplished, has little significance beside the distortions of established patterns of rhythm, melody, harmony and tone color.

Ragtime was prevalent as early as the gay nineties, with Harry von Tilzer one of its best exponents. Irving Berlin's famous song, *Alexander's Ragtime Band*, is really not ragtime at all, but a very simple march melody. Berlin's most popular music has been of the ballad type, usually in waltz time, and he is definitely a throw-back to the nineties themselves, with all their dripping sentimentalities. But Berlin has the great talent of combining a few words and a few tones in musical slogans that everyone remembers, at least for a time, which accounts for his undisputed popularity.

Jerome Kern also is essentially a melodist, as was Victor Herbert before him, but his musicianship enables him to create elaborate effects of counterpoint and complex instrumental and vocal ensembles which give his operettas a real musical value, although they are in no sense modernistic. From a purely practical standpoint, *Showboat* is one of the best operas yet written by an American.

The creative giant in the field of popular music, by general con-

How music entered George Gershwin's life

THE MAN WHO is recognized today as perhaps the leading American-born composer, George Gershwin, was not considered by his parents a musical boy. He liked baseball and roller-skates, and when the Gershwin family bought a piano, it was intended for his older brother, Ira.

But George had been listening to the violin of his friend, Max Rosen, and also visiting the penny arcade, where there was a player-piano. There he stood fascinated by the strains of *Rubinstein's Melody in F,* a tune which he never forgot. When the new piano was hoisted into the Gershwin apartment, little George sat down and played the Rubinstein piece by ear. From then on he became the family musician, much to Ira's relief.

Later George Gershwin found his best lyric-writer in the talented older brother, and a good singer in his younger sister, Frankie. He had his first song published when he was only eighteen; at twenty he had a smash hit in *Swanee,* introduced by Al Jolson.

But George Gershwin's ambition was to write serious music. He wisely followed the advice of friends who told him first to make a living in the popular field. By 1924 he was established as the top hit writer of Tin Pan Alley. It was then that Paul Whiteman persuaded him to compose a larger work in the jazz idiom. The result was the epoch-making *Rhapsody in Blue,* now immortalized in a motion picture of the same name. A *Piano Concerto,* the tone poem, *An American in Paris,* and the opera *Porgy and Bess* more than carried out the promise of the *Rhapsody.* George Gershwin is now known to millions through these significant compositions as well as his unique popular songs.

DROP ONE CENT IN

sent, was George Gershwin, whose work has been recognized in Europe as well as America for its individual qualities. His popular songs, such as *The Man I Love*, still stand out prominently in the ceaseless output of Tin Pan Alley, and his satirical operetta, *Of Thee I Sing*, which was honored with a Pulitzer Prize, achieved perhaps the best results in this field since Gilbert and Sullivan, whose style it frankly represents in modern terms. Gershwin wrote three serious works which succeeded in putting jazz on the concert stage. His *Rhapsody in Blue* (built largely on the famous blue chord, but full of melodic inspiration and interesting workmanship) is already a classic of its kind, and the *Piano Concerto in F* seems an even finer composition, destined to a longer life. *An American in Paris* is frankly program music, in which both the French and the American strains are sufficiently convincing, and it is worthy of a place beside the two more elaborate pieces.

Ferde Grofé, who was responsible for the instrumentation of the *Rhapsody in Blue* and for much of the tone coloring of jazz in general, has emerged as a composer in his own right, with an effective *Mississippi Suite*, containing some fine melodies, a series of *Grand Canyon Sketches*, also melodically attractive, and a realistic musical description of the modern newspaper called *Tabloid*. With Russell Bennett and a few others, Grofé has contributed much to modern ideas of orchestration, quite aside from actual creative ability.

SWING AND BOOGIE WOOGIE

The fanatics of jazz, whose number is still considerable, are inclined to speak contemptuously of those who fail to appreciate the subtleties of their favorite music or to make the nicer distinctions of detail that to them are apparently obvious. Actually there is a snobbery among jitterbugs and hepcats very similar to that which once handicapped the serious music of the world, and anyone so ignorant as to lump all popular music in one general category is automatically condemned to outer darkness.

The devotees of swing and hot jazz (between which they frequently make a distinction) are so contradictory in their sage pronouncements and so vague when it comes to definitions that their insistent belligerence cannot be taken very seriously. In general they are content to shout that if you don't feel it, you don't feel it, and there is no health in you. They may argue that hot jazz was all improvised, whereas true swing is carefully arranged and written out, and they are unquestionably right in preferring the small groups of the New Orleans type to the overloaded commercial bands, whose chief object often seems to be mere noise.

But a few facts should be clear even to the novice or the confirmed outsider. Jazz has already been defined as a distortion of the conventional in music. Hot jazz emphasized improvisation, sharing with swing the common feature of technically brilliant variations on almost any melodic material. It may be true that swing is more deliberately manufactured, but essentially the effects are similar. Boogie woogie is a type of jazz that concentrates on a continuous figure in the bass (what the classicists called *basso ostinato* or sustained bass), over which variations are improvised, generally by the right hand on the piano. "Blues" have a definite form, founded in folk-music, and regularly follow a twelve-measure sequence of rhythm and harmony, over which the melody again has an improvisational character. The arrangers and interpreters of jazz are actually more important than the composers.

It is easy to argue that none of the music composed recently will live, particularly that which shows the characteristics of jazz. Much of it seems only a caricature of true art, yet it must be remembered that a caricature often has more truth in it than a portrait. Whatever else may be said about ultramodern music and jazz, they are certainly representative of their time. It is a jazz age, an era of rebellion and the smashing of traditions, a period of wild, often absurd and futile experiments. Out of it may come some things of permanent beauty, but it is too early to risk any predictions.

The spirit of the day is perhaps also too mechanical, with life in general geared at too high a rate of speed to permit the leisure that produces great art. The forces of ballyhoo are continually at work, and the greatest popular successes are not necessarily the best creations. Some will even go so far as to say that the days of great art are over and that only imitation or artificial sensationalism will exist in the future. But that sort of thing has been said many times before, yet artists continue to be born and made. Music has reached a stage where originality seems difficult without an abandonment of principles that have been in force for a very long time. Yet there is music in some parts of the world, particularly in the Orient, which has never been affected by those principles, as we know them. Such music may sound terrible to conventional ears, just as do the distortions of modernism and jazz, but it seems right and important to its followers, and who is to be the final judge of permanent standards?

The best advice that can be given to the listener bent on acquiring the art of enjoying music is to become as familiar as possible with compositions whose merits have been well established, to try to find out for himself why so many people liked them, and then to listen to more novel experiments with an open mind, unswayed by prejudice or the ravings of hysterical enthusiasts and self-appointed press-agents, scorning to agree with an opinion merely because it seems to be the fashion of the moment, yet ready to admit that there may be significant musical values which are still beyond the comprehension of one who has become thoroughly saturated with the classics.

How George M. Cohan found music in the American flag

THE GRIZZLED VETERAN raised his eyes as the breeze picked up the folds of Old Glory and spread them over the little ceremony. "She's a grand old flag," he murmured.

Standing at his elbow, hat in hand, young George M. Cohan heard the saluting veteran's words. In his mind he already had a martial tune that would make that phrase vocal all over the United States. "Born on the Fourth of July," as quoted in his *Yankee Doodle Boy*, George M. Cohan instinctively expressed patriotism in his songs. He did not wave the flag for mere effect, but deeply believed in its power and its permanent significance. When we needed a stirring song for the first World War, this composer of words and music came through with *Over There*, and since then there has evidently been no one to fill the prescription again.

Cohan was a typical song-and-dance man, immersed in the atmosphere of the sidewalks of New York. When he wrote *Give my Regards to Broadway*, he meant it, and our boys in uniform sang that one too over there. *Mary*, *Harrigan*, and other popular Cohan hits dealt with simple, everyday people, and they appealed to the same type of listener, a type that is still in the majority.

George M. Cohan did not have to experiment with serious art of any kind, although he was a skilled playwright and an actor of unquestioned authority. He sought no artificial glamour, but contented himself with putting his own United States into characteristic words and music, sincerely and honestly. To that extent he belongs to our folklore, like Stephen Foster himself.

SMITHS BLOCK
STORE

CHAPTER XVIII A DASH OF MUSICAL HISTORY

DURING THE DISCUSSIONS of various pieces of music throughout this book, the names of a number of composers have come up with perhaps a surprising frequency, and little or no effort has been made to place these composers historically, or to give any biographical background to their work. After all, a composer becomes personally interesting to a listener only after his music has caught and held the attention, and it often happens that a too great insistence on biographical and historical detail keeps the music itself from its possible effect.

Nobody is expected to take an interest in a famous boxer or baseball player unless he is first of all interested in boxing or baseball, and in the same way an interest in the personality of a composer should grow naturally out of an interest in his music. There are many sources of information concerning the great composers, and for the convenience of readers or students of this book a biographical glossary is appended which at least places them in the right time and country, with a list of their important compositions. But before concluding this guide for those at home with music, it may be helpful to present a bird's-eye view of musical history (nowadays it would be called an airplane picture), showing as quickly as possible where the important composers belong and how they were affected by the spirit of their times.

It is not necessary to go deeply into primitive music or even the early efforts of the Church. Nor can folk-music as such occupy much space; it has always existed, even among uncivilized peoples, and it probably always will. The popular songs of America today are in a sense folk-music, presenting the unique phenomenon of being created in highly civilized surroundings, often in a thoroughly sophisticated spirit, yet showing all the traits of primitive folk-music, the monotony of rhythm, the simplicity of melody, the vivid tonal coloring and the atmosphere of improvisation. Some musicians have always created and interpreted by instinct, playing and singing "by ear," and composing tunes that they were unable even to write down in notes. There will always be such musicians, in contrast to the well-taught scholars of the art, and it is quite possible that the work of some of these "natural" musicians will at least temporarily find a larger audience than the more serious and studied efforts of their trained colleagues. Folk-music and popular music in general will always have a quick and easy appeal, and there is no more art in enjoying it than ordinarily enters into its creation. When it has proved its permanence, as is often the case, it may usually be found in other than its most primitive forms.

So far as the art-music of the world is concerned, it lends itself fairly easily to a division by periods, generally known as the classic, romantic and modern, and it should not be difficult to identify music belonging to any of these periods. It must be remembered that vocal music in general preceded instrumental music, that melody existed long before harmony, which began merely as combinations of melodies. Out of this habit of combining melodies grew the whole polyphonic school of composition, which spread all over Europe long before the development of the homophonic and instrumental forms.

The earliest known piece of polyphonic music is the English round, *Sumer is icumen in*, which dates back to the first half of the thirteenth century. It is not merely a historical curiosity, but an excellent piece of music, having four voices in strict canon, singing over a two-part bass. Arrangements of this famous round are available for modern singers, and it is well worth performing.

But the first polyphonic composers of eminence were Netherlanders, with whom even the native English John Dunstable is generally grouped. William Dufay, Johannes Okeghem and Josquin des Près are the names that stand out in the early period. The last was a pupil of Okeghem, and highly praised by Martin Luther for his ability to put human emotion and sentiment into music. These men carried polyphonic music forward into the sixteenth century, when another

Netherlander, Adrian Willaert, sometimes called "the father of the madrigal," became organist at St. Mark's in Venice, while Dufay, des Près and later Jacob Arcadelt all became associated with the Papal Chapel in Rome.

MASTERS OF POLYPHONY

The two greatest names of the sixteenth century are Palestrina and Orlando di Lasso, both of whom died in the same year, 1594. Meanwhile, the madrigal school reached its height in England under Queen Elizabeth, producing such fine composers as Thomas Tallis, Weelkes, Wilbye, William Byrd, John Dowland, Thomas Morley, Orlando Gibbons and the organist John Bull. England's greatest musician, Henry Purcell, came nearly half a century later, his comparatively short life ending in 1695. By that time Bach and Handel were already ten years old, and with Italy's interest in opera and the development of the various forms of clavier to add to the organ, the polyphonic monopoly had practically ended.

Peri, Caccini and their fellows had made homophonic (single-voiced) music popular in Italy at the very start of the seventeenth century, and their experiments were carried on by Lully in France and later by Rameau. Meanwhile, Claudio Monteverde had laid the foundations of modern harmony by his revolutionary innovations. The early masters of violin music, Corelli, Vivaldi, and their followers, also advanced the cause of individual melody, while Couperin in France and Alessandro Scarlatti in Italy brought clavier music up to a very high level. (The younger Scarlatti, Domenico, was also born in the Bach-Handel year, 1685, and became perhaps the greatest keyboard virtuoso of his day, the spiritual ancestor of all modern pianists.)

The classic period of music begins with Bach and Handel (even though they both wrote much in the polyphonic style), and everything before them, excepting perhaps the unique ecclesiastical glories of Palestrina, may be considered as mere preparation for their genius and that which was to follow. Johann Sebastian Bach was only one of a large musical family, but by far the greatest. His ancestors had composed music for nearly two centuries before his birth, so he came by his genius naturally. Left an orphan at the age of ten, he lived with an elder brother, an organist, who discouraged his enthusiasm for music by confiscating the manuscripts that the boy had copied by moonlight.

At fifteen the young Bach became a choirboy at Lüneburg, near Hamburg, where he had a chance both to hear and to learn good music. A little later he played the violin in the court orchestra at Weimar, and at eighteen he was organist at Arnstadt. Eventually he became court organist at Weimar, where he built his reputation as a performer and composer. For several years he was music director for the Prince at Cöthen, where he had an opportunity to compose for orchestra and the clavier. The last twenty-seven years of his life were spent in Leipzig, as cantor and director of church music, and there he wrote his greatest masterpieces, the *B minor Mass,* the *Passions* and many of the cantatas. It was not a very exciting life, but enormously productive, and of inestimable benefit to the whole art of music. Bach is equally significant in the field of organ and choral music. He established the tempered scale of the modern piano and thus laid the foundation of our whole system of harmony and modulation. He wrote splendid music for the orchestra and for such individual instruments as the violin, flute and clavier. He commanded both the polyphonic and the homophonic style of composition, and by his combination of matchless technique and instinctive emotional expression he set a standard for all subsequent music that only a few composers approached.

Although born in the same year (1685) at Halle, only eighty miles distant from Bach's native city of Eisenach, Georg Friedrich Handel never seems to have met his great contemporary. Their lives ended only nine years apart, both in blindness. (Handel outlived Bach, and was about a month older.) But in spite of all these coincidences, their careers were very different. Handel had no musical background, but was an inexplicable prodigy from boyhood. He composed many operas in the Italian style, now almost forgotten, but showing a fine melodic sense. Having been appointed chapelmaster to the Elector of Hanover, afterward George I of England, Handel eventually settled in London and became a naturalized British subject. It was here that he composed his great oratorios, and it is by this music, and particularly the popular *Messiah,* that he is remembered today. While he wrote great choral music in his oratorios, and was unquestionably a master of counterpoint, Handel must be considered essentially a melodist, with a particular gift for broad, smoothly flowing lines, such as are found in his familiar *Largo*.

Two of the sons of Johann Sebastian Bach became noted musicians in their own right. Karl Philipp Emanuel Bach was for many years court musician to Frederick the Great and had an important influence on the sonata form, which was to become so prominent before the end of the eighteenth century. A younger son, Johann Christian Bach, was for many years music master to the royal family in London, and before that he played the organ in the Milan Cathedral. As a composer he was less important than his older brother.

The great Bach wrote his music without any thought of fame or fortune, as a daily task. Handel was more dependent on the reactions of a fickle public, and less able to assert any individuality of style. But both were unique figures for their time, far in advance of all the musicians who had preceded them, and creators of an idiom that is still a model for composers and as popular as ever. After them the great composers were plentiful, and a golden age of music persisted right up to the close of the nineteenth century.

HAYDN AND MOZART

The two great composers of the latter half of the eighteenth century were Franz Josef Haydn and Wolfgang Amadeus Mozart, again with widely divergent careers but an intimate personal acquaintance and mutual sympathy that did not exist between Bach and Handel. Neglected as a child, Haydn made his way against all handicaps, working as an accompanist and general handy man for the popular singing teacher, Porpora, in Vienna, and finally winning the patronage of the wealthy Esterhazy family, whose support, over a period of thirty years, enabled him to devote nearly all of his time to composition. Late in life, Haydn visited England and was there inspired to write his oratorios, *The Creation* and *The Seasons*. Meanwhile, he had established the sonata form in a great number of symphonies and actual sonatas and laid the foundations of chamber music for all time. He was enormously prolific, doing most of his composing after he had passed the age of thirty, and continuing to be an active influence in music until his death in 1809.

Mozart was first of all the most extraordinary infant prodigy in history, playing the clavier at three, composing at four, and appearing as a public performer at six. Although acclaimed all over the world as a genius, his life was not a happy one. He left a court position in his home town of Salzburg to go to Paris, where success eluded him, and eventually, at the age of twenty-six, he arrived in Vienna. Here he lived the life of a Bohemian, scorning patronage, getting more and more heavily into debt, but composing the most entrancing music imaginable. He went far beyond Haydn in his development of the sonata form, and his symphonies and chamber music will forever be models of form and high lights of melodic inspiration. As an operatic composer he was also highly significant. Mozart died a pauper in 1791, at the tragically early age of thirty-five, perhaps the greatest natural genius that music will ever know.

CLIMACTIC BEETHOVEN

The work done by Haydn and Mozart in establishing the forms of chamber music and the symphony was completed by Ludwig van Beethoven, the third and greatest of the Viennese group. Born in Bonn, in 1770, of a musical family, he showed early abilities which were spurred to the utmost, in the hope of emulating the youthful Mozart, who himself showed a great interest in Beethoven when he first came to Vienna in 1787. Later, Beethoven studied with Haydn, but he soon broke away from all the conventions of his art and was regarded as an arch heretic, even by his friends and admirers. His vigorous, independent spirit, chafing under restraint of any kind, kept him continually in difficulties, and the latter half of his life was afflicted by the tragedy of deafness. Beethoven died in 1827, after producing some of the greatest symphonies, sonatas, string quartets and concertos the world has ever known, besides a heroic opera, *Fidelio,* some splendid choral music, and a wealth of smaller compositions. He may be considered the first romantic composer, for his individuality was striking and he refused to be bound by classic formulas. He made the sonata form much freer than it had been before, and injected an emotional power and dramatic intensity into his music that gave it an overwhelming effect. He died tragically, but with his genius already universally recognized.

Before the death of Beethoven, the movement generally known as Romanticism was well under way. The classic period, dominated by Haydn, had made much of form for its own sake. Mozart himself had proved the fallacy of this idea, and Beethoven definitely rebelled against it. Meanwhile, Christoph Willibald von Gluck had upset the traditions of Italian opera, in Paris, insisting that there must be dramatic realism in both the music and the action, and Carl Maria von Weber, composing during the latter part of Beethoven's life (up to 1826), had laid the foundations for Wagner with some truly romantic operas, in addition to absolute music of a high order.

With Franz Schubert, Romanticism became a reality, and his is the next great name in music after that of Beethoven, whom he knew personally and outlived by only a year, for Schubert died, also in poverty and neglect, at thirty-one. Schubert's natural and spontaneous musical genius, particularly in the ceaseless flow of melody, has been rivaled only by that of Mozart. He composed so rapidly and easily that he is often accused of carelessness in details, and he never mastered musical form in the sense that it was mastered by Beethoven and Mozart. Yet his symphonies, particularly the *Unfinished* and the seventh, in C major, are gems of technique as well as pure musical beauty, and he created some lovely chamber music that requires no apologies. But it is as a song writer that Schubert is chiefly remembered, and in this field he was a real pioneer, laying the foundations of the German *Lied*, and combining the melodic inspirations of folk-music with a highly imaginative and delicately personal art. By all standards he belongs among the elect of music.

Felix Mendelssohn (Bartholdy) and Robert Schumann were born only a year apart, the former in 1809 in Hamburg, and the latter in 1810 in Zwickau, a mining town. Both lived comparatively short lives. Mendelssohn was only thirty-eight when he died, and Schumann forty-six. But Mendelssohn's career was a happy and successful one, with all the advantages of wealth, culture and an admiring public, so rarely granted to musicians, while Schumann had to fight his way through troubles of all kinds, suffering a nervous breakdown and ending in an insane asylum.

Mendelssohn was another youthful prodigy (most musicians are, although the fact is not always known) and composed his astonishing overture to the *Midsummer Night's Dream* at the age of seventeen.

He was a brilliant pianist, and his charming compositions for that instrument have been deservedly popular. But his greatest creative work was in his later symphonies and overtures and in the oratorios, particularly the *Elijah*. Taste, refinement and elegance are characteristic of most of Mendelssohn's work, but the very fact that life was made easy for him has inclined critics to deal harshly with his creations. In fairness, Mendelssohn must be given a high place among the romantic composers, and while it was once the fashion to belittle him, there is no indication that his popularity is really on the decline.

SCHUMANN AND CHOPIN

Schumann is an arch rebel in music, and he devoted much of his life to critical writings on the art, surrounding himself with a group of friends and literally forming a society (the *Davidsbund*) against the Philistines. He was for a long time balked in his desire to become a musician, then robbed of the career of a concert pianist by an injury to a finger, then refused the hand of his beloved Clara Wieck (whom he eventually married, in spite of her father's objections), and finally irritated by an academic life that was not to his liking. Yet he composed some of the world's greatest piano music (particularly the *Concerto in A minor*, the *Symphonic Etudes* and *Carnaval*), produced a treasure of songs, largely under the influence of his romance with Clara (herself an extraordinary pianist, perhaps the greatest of her sex), and in later life wrote symphonies, chamber music and choral works, all of a high order. Like Schubert, Schumann was not essentially a formalist, but his music shows inspiration and an even greater originality, especially in his bold use of harmonies and cross-rhythms. The term "romantic" fits him perhaps better than any others of that school.

Frédéric Chopin, the outstanding genius of the piano, was an immediate contemporary of Mendelssohn and Schumann, born in 1810, near Warsaw, Poland, and meeting an untimely death from tuberculosis at the age of thirty-nine. He was also a prodigy, playing in public at the age of nine and publishing his first compositions at fifteen. He settled in Paris at the age of twenty-one and spent most of the rest of his life there, meeting with great success, and creating what was really a new technique of the keyboard, and the foundation of modern music. Because of his concentration on the piano, Chopin is not always given full credit for his remarkable melodic gift, nor for the individuality of his harmonies and his bold experiments in form. Pianists and lovers of piano music become so wrapped up in his mastery of that instrument that they overlook the great musical genius that breathes through all of his compositions.

BERLIOZ, LISZT, WAGNER

Hector Berlioz was born some years earlier than Schumann, Mendelssohn and Chopin, and Franz Liszt only a little later, but both of them outlived that trio of Romanticists by many years, Liszt living to the ripe age of seventy-five, and exercising an enormous influence on all the music of modern times. Both were composers of the spectacular type, with large ideas and conceptions, which unfortunately did not always live up to their promise. Berlioz is an extremist in program music, seeking to express the fantastic and the colossal, and succeeding superficially, without much evidence of the inspiration assumed by his intentions. Similarly, Liszt planned his music on a big scale, knew the technique of his art thoroughly, acquired the reputation of being perhaps the greatest piano virtuoso of all time, influenced Wagner and helped many other composers to recognition, yet never quite succeeded in convincing the modern world of his own creative genius, as compared with that of the real giants of music.

Richard Wagner was less than two years younger than Liszt (who became his father-in-law) but died three years earlier, in 1883. He represents the climax of the dramatic type of music and is the only operatic composer who can fairly be ranked with the greatest creators of absolute music. Before Wagner, opera had had a mixed career, starting with fine ideals in the old Italian days, but speedily degenerating into the lowest possible forms of artificiality, then profiting by the reforms of Gluck and the genius of Mozart, and definitely taking a step toward music-drama in the romantic works of Weber.

Paris early became the chief center of opera, with the tastes established by Lully and Rameau holding their own right up to the time of Luigi Cherubini (a Florentine by birth, but decidedly French in his music), developing through the work of Méhul, Grétry, Spontini and other composers, and finally reaching a popular climax in the spectacles of Halévy and Meyerbeer. Meanwhile, the tuneful Italian style of opera had received new life through the talents of Rossini, and to a lesser extent from Donizetti and Bellini, whose contributions to *bel canto* are still popular, merely as vocal art.

COMPOSERS OF OPERA

Giuseppe Verdi, whose life covered nearly the whole of the musical nineteenth century (1813—1901), brought Italian opera from the hurdy-gurdy type of melody and artificial recitative to a real dramatic significance, in which the example of Wagner eventually played its part. *Aida*, one of the most satisfying of all operas, is something quite different from the early Verdi works, and *Otello* and *Falstaff*, written in his old age, are definitely Wagnerian in their technique.

Bizet's *Carmen* ranks with *Aida* as a completely satisfying opera, and Gounod's *Faust* has achieved immense popularity because of the universality of its story and the immediate appeal of its sentimental tunes. French operatic composers of the late nineteenth and early twentieth century included Jules Massenet, the most successful of the sentimentalists, and Camille Saint-Säens, whose *Samson and Delilah* is less important than his large output of orchestral writing and chamber music in the absolute forms.

Wagner towers over all these composers, and remains not only one of the greatest revolutionists of music but one of the very few who possessed that compelling and overwhelming inspiration that carries the stamp of inevitability. His early operas were affected by the conventions of his predecessors and contemporaries, but starting with *Tannhäuser* (a failure in Paris) and *Lohengrin*, he came closer and closer to a musical realism on the stage, eventually creating a true music-drama in the great Nibelungen cycle, *Tristan und Isolde*, *Die Meistersinger* and *Parsifal*. Wagner was an exile from Germany during a large part of his life, for political reasons, but spent his last years at Bayreuth, which became a shrine for all lovers of music-drama. Liszt, who first produced *Lohengrin* and recognized the genius of its composer, remained a staunch supporter to the very end, and the patronage of King Ludwig II of Bavaria, extended at a critical time, unquestionably made it possible for Wagner to carry out the musical task that he had set himself.

BRAHMS THE GIANT

Running parallel to Wagner in the field of absolute music is the gigantic figure of Johannes Brahms, now recognized as belonging with Bach and Beethoven among the greatest musicians of all time. He wrote no operas, but proved himself supreme in every other branch of music, particularly the symphony, the concerto, the German *Lied* and chamber music, not to speak of several important choral works. Brahms is pre-eminently the musician's musician, but the general public seems at last to have discovered him and he is today in danger of becoming the most popular composer on concert programs. His life extended from 1833 to 1897, and was lived quietly, aided at first by the interest of the Schumanns and later of Joachim, but developing an unfortunate comparison with Wagner, not of his own choosing, which for a time turned the whole musical world into two rival camps, until it was suddenly discovered that there was nothing to argue about, as the two men were of entirely different types, each unsurpassed in his own line.

The art of song writing was carried on by most of the composers of the nineteenth century, but two men made it their specialty, Robert Franz and Hugo Wolf, the former possessing a fine melodic sense, while the latter concentrated on a realistic treatment of the voice and a polish of detail. Before them, Carl Loewe had specialized in ballads, showing considerable dramatic power, but without the melodic inspiration of a Schubert.

While Brahms was upholding absolute music in Germany, César Franck was doing the same thing for France, where the operatic tradition had become far more powerful. Born in Belgium, but spending most of his life in Paris, as organist and teacher, Franck quietly produced some music that may well be compared with the greatest. His one symphony, in D minor, is now among the most popular of them all, and his violin sonata, quintet, piano and organ compositions represent the highest standards. He derived his forms from Bach and Beethoven, but in his harmony and tonal coloring he pointed definitely forward to the modern school.

RUSSIAN NATIONALISM

Aside from such universal geniuses, the nineteenth century produced a number of composers of distinctly national characteristics. This was particularly true of Russia, where the group known as "the five" undertook to restore their folk-music to its rightful place and make Russian composition something more than a mere imitation of the conventional styles of other countries. The five men were Mili Balakirew, founder of the group, Alexander Borodin, César Cui, Modest Moussorgsky, and Nikolas Rimsky-Korsakoff. They found their inspiration in Michael Glinka, who had already begun the study of Russian folk-song and embodied it in his operas. Moussorgsky's *Boris Godounoff* is one of the monumental works of musical literature, and his use of the whole-tone scale and other bold devices of harmony makes him a most important forerunner of modernism.

Peter Ilitch Tschaikowsky remains the most popular of the Russian composers, and there are evidences of nationalism in his works, particularly the symphonies. But essentially he is a Teutonic composer, as was his countryman, Anton Rubinstein, before him, and later Serge Rachmaninoff.

A definitely national music was produced by Edvard Grieg in Norway, and his idiom is not only unmistakable but exceedingly attractive. His songs, his piano concerto and his chamber music are all of real importance. Finland has produced in Jean Sibelius a similarly important national figure, with a clear significance among the modernists.

Anton Dvorak, a Bohemian by birth, has endeared himself to America with his *New World Symphony*, in which he showed us how an American national music might be written. From the standpoint of his own nationalism, however, he was even more significant.

Edward MacDowell, on the other hand, generally considered America's leading composer, was in no sense a nationalist, but a fine workman in the traditional forms. Nor have the English composers of the nineteenth century, headed by Edward Elgar, produced anything of a distinctly national character.

THE MODERN SCHOOL

Of the composers of our own day, Richard Strauss is the closest follower of Wagner. His operas may well be called music-dramas, and his orchestral tone poems are marvels of program music, while his songs rank with those of the great masters of the German *Lied.* Bruckner and Mahler in their symphonies also showed a strong Wagnerian influence, whereas Max Reger adhered more to the classic style. The operas of Verdi led naturally to those of Puccini, Mascagni, Leoncavallo, Wolf-Ferrari and Montemezzi (to name only the best known), all somewhat affected by the Wagnerian style. Vincent d'Indy followed in the footsteps of his master, César Franck, who has influenced most of the modern French writers of absolute music.

Claude Debussy is the real founder of the modern school, and his highly original methods of harmonizing and creating tonal colors revolutionized the whole musical art. His *Pelléas and Mélisande* is unique among operas, his orchestral compositions speak a new and different language, and his piano pieces evoke from the keyboard something that only Chopin had suggested as a possibility. Debussy was worthily succeeded by Maurice Ravel, and since then there has been a constant stream of more and more unorthodox music, whose value, as previously indicated, cannot be properly estimated until the test of time has been applied.

CHAPTER XIX IN CONCLUSION

It would not be difficult to let a book like this run on indefinitely, for the subject of music is endless and the possibilities of enjoyment are infinite. But since its object is chiefly to stimulate the average listener to further personal discoveries through the simple process of listening, it is necessary to stop somewhere, and this is as good a place as any.

It is impossible to become literally at home with music simply by reading books about it. The one absolute necessity is to hear plenty of music of all kinds, and thus to get the habit of forming one's own opinions. If these opinions keep changing, so much the better. It probably means that a definite development of taste is taking place.

If a piece of music sounds dull and uninteresting at a first hearing, don't give it up on that account, particularly if it happens to be a piece in which thousands of others have found enjoyment. The fact that its beauties are not of the obvious kind is quite likely to be in its favor. Conversely, do not be carried away by a first favorable impression. Music that follows the line of least resistance may be temporarily popular, but is not necessarily good on that account. If your enthusiasm for a composition suddenly begins to wane, don't reproach yourself for being so easily satiated. The chances are that the music was not worth much more than passing attention in any case.

The one and only dependable test of greatness in music is the test of time. That is why it is so futile to spend a lot of energy in worrying over present and future standards. Nobody living is qualified to say either what is good or bad in the untried music of the moment, or what will be recognized as good or bad in the future. The more vehement the protestations of the enthusiasts or the attackers, the more likely they are to be founded on prejudice, personal bias (often by way of "inside information") or downright commercialism. If you happen to like the music of Ravel better than that of Schoenberg, that is your own affair, and no one can properly argue with you; and if your greatest enthusiasm is expended on Brahms, Wagner, Beethoven and Bach, don't worry about the jeers of the iconoclasts, for your taste is supported by millions of the best minds and ears of the past. America will never have a real taste for music until it is founded on sincerity and honesty. There has been far too much hypocrisy in our whole musical life, and it is still too easy to get on the band wagon, to ride with the crowd, and to utter opinions which are really not ours at all, but correspond with those that we slavishly respect, although their own foundation may be just as insincere and worthless.

If anyone could go through the process of not only reading this book but hearing every piece of music mentioned in it, it is likely that that person would end by having quite a good musical taste. But it would be possible to spend a lifetime in the process, if each piece were heard often enough to give it a fair chance of being enjoyed. Therefore, in every case an honest effort has been made to point out those things that are the most likely, in view of their past records, to create permanent enjoyment, and thus to make the listener's task of selection as easy as possible. If the potential music-lover concentrates on those compositions that seem to be recommended in advance (and there are many such mentioned in every chapter), he or she will acquire a fairly rapid acquaintance with the established masterpieces of permanent music. More detailed knowledge and experience are to be had by simply including more of the suggested material, and hearing each piece oftener. (The use of records is again recommended.)

In listening to music of any kind, try always to apply the definition of the Organization of Sound Toward Beauty. Listen from the standpoint of the five organizing factors, rhythm, melody, harmony, tone color and form. They will appear in varying degrees of importance, but they will inevitably be present in every significant composition.

TRIPLE APPEAL

The foot-listener, who merely responds to rhythm, is decidedly limited in his enjoyment of music, but the head-listener, who ap-

Rodgers and Hammerstein put Oklahoma on the musical map

After years of subservience to European music, even in its lighter forms, America suddenly discovered a musical background of its own. We found not only a vast treasure of folksongs and dances, including the Negro, the mountaineer or "hillbilly," the cowboy, the lumberjack, the riverman, and the Creole types, but also a native foundation of history and local custom that offered ideal material for the operatic stage.

Jerome Kern and Oscar Hammerstein II were pioneers in the field when they wrote the immensely successful *Showboat*, with its *Old Man River* and other truly American songs. George Gershwin put Charleston's Catfish Row into his Negro folk-opera, *Porgy and Bess*, besides satirizing American politics in the Pulitzer Prize-winning *Of Thee I Sing*.

The last word in such musical treatment of American life now seems to have been contributed by Richard Rodgers, with Hammerstein again as librettist. Their *Oklahoma!*, produced by the Theatre Guild, is unquestionably the most successful musical comedy of all time. Such songs as *People Will Say We're in Love*, *Oh, What a Beautiful Morning*, and *The Surrey with a Fringe on Top* are already in the permanent classification of "standard" popular hits. Oklahoma has taken a step forward comparable to its promotion to statehood and the discovery of oil.

The Rodgers-Hammerstein team again hit the bull's-eye with *Carousel*, an American version of Molnar's *Liliom*, set in New England. Their screen adaptation of *State Fair* glorifies Iowa in similar fashion. Through such talented creators of words and music America has become aware of its own resources and broken away from the old conventions of operetta. *Sing Out, Sweet Land*, *Bloomer Girl*, *Up in Central Park*, and *On the Town* carried on the delightful work of discovering America musically, with clearly unlimited possibilities for the future.

proaches the art with his intellect alone, is perhaps just as limited. Between the two are the heart-listeners, the emotionalists, to whom music is just a romantic and inexplicable stimulant. The great majority of haphazard listeners respond to music in this way. But anyone who makes an art of enjoying music approaches music from all three angles: physically, by way of the feet, emotionally, by way of the heart, and intellectually, by way of the head; and all the really great music of the world is written with this triple appeal.

It is impossible to say just why one rhythm or melody or harmony or tone color has more appeal than another. Unquestionably, it is partly a matter of habit and association; but unquestionably also there are certain patterns, at least of rhythm, melody and harmony, which rest upon universal laws and formulas, recognizable, consciously or unconsciously, by all human beings. The mere element of comfort may enter into these patterns, as in other arts. We like lines and colors which do not annoy or hurt the eye. Similarly, we like rhythms, melodies and harmonies that do not assault the ear with unexpected and illogical combinations. Such patterns as the 1-3-5 triad, appearing in both melody and harmony, rest upon a scientific foundation first of all, and then acquire a universality of appeal, if for no other reasons than custom and experience.

So it all comes back to the test of time. It may be that our ears will become accustomed to the most frightful noises in time, as they became accustomed to Debussy's chords of the ninth, which in their day seemed quite extreme. But there is no way of proving this except through the passage of time. The music that has become established as permanent, known by the convenient but much abused term "classical," arrived at its place partly through the efforts and propaganda of individual enthusiasts, men like Mendelssohn and Schumann and Liszt, who discovered genius in the past and in their own time and knew they were right, but even more through the direct, spontaneous reactions of millions of listeners all over the world, who were willing and able to say "This is beautiful," but were prepared to change their minds later if they chose. It is only thus that permanent beauty is found. If enough people over a sufficiently long period of time (which may be ten years or a century) respond in approximately the same way to any work of art, it rightly goes into the records as a classic, and eventually it may be taken for granted, which is a pity. There is a certain satisfaction even in discovering that a work of art is just as beautiful as you have always been told it was. But beware of getting into the habit of thinking a thing is beautiful merely because you have been told so.

THE ARTISTIC IDEAL

The ideal of every true artist is to express the abstract in concrete terms. In music, as in all other arts, the creative genius organizes his raw materials with all the means at his disposal, aiming to achieve a beauty which will be clear to any observer possessed of his five senses and a modicum of intelligence. Sometimes this public is not reached during the creator's lifetime. But if the work is really significant, the public is inevitably reached sooner or later.

It is not enough merely to transfer thoughts to other people. Anyone possessed of a medium of communication can accomplish that. But if the thought embodies an abstract mood or an emotion, its inevitable transfer to other human beings constitutes art in the highest sense. The miracle of music is that it can achieve this magic without the help of words or pictures or symbols of any kind. When a really great piece of absolute music is heard, there is no mistaking its mood or emotional content. That is why absolute music almost automatically ranks higher than program music, whereas the finest program music may be credited with an absolute value, quite apart from its descriptive or narrative interest. When words and music are combined, we really have two arts in one, and it is a difficult thing to decide how the credit for the final effect should be divided. It is only when different composers have set the same words to different music (a surprisingly frequent occurrence) that any comparisons can be made. Occasionally a text is so obviously unworthy that it drags down even the finest music into aesthetic futility.

Let it be clearly understood that a significant composer must have something more than the ability to write correctly in the established forms. Anyone can acquire such ability, just as anyone can learn to write the English language or any other. The mysterious thing called inspiration is a quality that cannot be explained, but in the long run it is inescapable. Inspiration has nothing to do with sudden flashes of complete creative power, or the ability to put these things down perfectly as they occur to the creator. Generally inspiration works slowly and painstakingly, with a knowledge of the ideal in view, but also a practical command of the means by which that ideal may be made a reality. Beethoven's notebooks, showing how slowly and carefully he developed the greatest of his melodic inspirations, are the best possible comment on this much misunderstood phase of art.

The direct pleasure that comes from the recognition of inspiration in a piece of music is something impossible to describe. Fritz Kreisler has given it the physical sensation of that tingling, shivering ecstasy commonly known as "goose-flesh," and he may be right when he says that only the music that produces that particular sensation is really worth while. Under any circumstances it is a compound emotion. Mere familiarity enters into it to some extent, the pleasure of being able to say to oneself (or perhaps to one's neighbor), "I know that," which also explains why people applaud in concert halls when they recognize the first measures of a familiar encore. But such harmless vanity is a necessary part of all aesthetic enjoyment. The fact that one responds again and again to the same musical stimulus in the same way makes each additional response all the more enjoyable.

The ability to experience this direct and perhaps wholly irresponsible pleasure and then to follow it up with the added pleasure of analysis, perhaps finding a logical reason for the earlier, instinctive response, marks the real music-lover of the highest type. If the approach is analytical from the start, much of the spontaneous enjoyment of music may be missed. But if the mere sensuous, emotional comfort of the listener is the whole sum and substance of his enjoyment, then even more is being missed, and there can be no possible claim to art on his or her part. A good music critic should get his impression of a performance directly, without letting too many intellectual processes interfere with his spontaneous enjoyment. After he has experienced the immediate thrills (or perhaps the opposite) he can analyze his response at leisure and put his analysis into words that the average listener or reader can understand.

But beyond this direct enjoyment and analysis of music there are unlimited possibilities of associating it with other interests, as well as other studies. If your mind is a mathematical one, you can find all sorts of opportunities to work out the mathematics of music. The relationship of vibrations to pitch is a mathematical one. (The 440 A is considered Standard Pitch, meaning that the sound of A above Middle C represents 440 vibrations per second.) Each interval of the scale has a mathematical relationship to the adjoining tones and all the others, although the "tempered" scale, which has been in use since the days of Bach, disregards this scientific scale for the convenience of the human ear, and rightly. The combinations of overtones are also mathematical, and the commonest effects of harmony can be worked out on a similar mathematical basis. All the details of time and rhythm are naturally mathematical in a very special sense, and the term "measure" really differentiates the modern, well-organized music from the haphazard "plain-song," which was not measured in terms of time.

If your interests are literary rather than mathematical, music offers an even larger field for enjoyment and aesthetic co-operation. Obviously the numerous musical settings of the world's great poems offer a real inspiration to the student of literature, and it is at least interesting, and often amusing, to observe how some of the composers have treated the authors of great literary masterpieces. In many cases it may almost be argued that the greater the text the less likely it is to receive great music, and vice versa. Shakespeare has not been very successfully set to music on the whole, although his songs all have been given attractive melodies, old and new. Verdi's *Otello* and *Falstaff* are the most important operatic treatments of Shakespeare, and Gounod's *Romeo and Juliet* is at least adequate. There are several *Macbeths* and *Hamlets*, none of great significance. Berlioz gave the *Romeo and Juliet* theme an impressive dramatic treatment in his symphony, and Tschaikowsky showed what he might have done with it in his fantasy overture and some fragments of an opera. The finest Shakespearean music is still the youthful overture to the *Midsummer Night's Dream*, by Mendelssohn.

Milton was set to music by his contemporary, Henry Lawes, and later by Handel, but the words were infinitely superior to the music in every case. Dante has been suggested in orchestral music, such as that of Liszt (who also put Petrarch into a piano piece), but there is no really significant setting of his actual poetry. Goethe, on the other hand, received his full due from the composers, and his shorter poems in particular have been most successfully set to music, with the *Erlking* as a shining example. The Faust story has had much musical attention, with varying success. Such miniaturists as Heine were a godsend to the song writers, and their purely lyric style offered the best possible material for musical settings.

The French poets have had an enormous influence on French music, and a large proportion of all program music owes its existence to such poetry. (Debussy's *Prelude to the Afternoon of a Faun* is a characteristic example, based on a poem by Mallarmé.) Narrative music is almost as common as descriptive, even when no words are actually used. Definitely pictorial music is also quite common, sometimes using a scene from Nature and sometimes an actual painting for its model, as in Rachmaninoff's tone poem, *The Island of the Dead,* inspired by the famous Böcklin picture.

Music has often been compared with language itself, and the comparison is quite legitimate. While it combines easily with actual language, it also speaks a language of its own, which it has become a platitude to call universal. To understand the significance of the organizing factors of rhythm, melody, harmony, tone color and form, the analogy of a familiar language is helpful. Music has its own alphabet, of only seven letters, as compared with the twenty-six of the English alphabet. Each of these letters represents a note, and just as certain letters are complete words in themselves, so certain notes may stand alone, with the force of a whole word. Generally, however, a note of music implies a certain harmony, and in most modern music the notes take the form of actual chords. So it may be said that a chord in music is analogous to a word in language. Several words form a phrase, and several phrases a complete sentence, and the same thing is true in music. Measured music corresponds to poetry, while the old unmeasured plain-song might be compared with prose. (The relationship of modern music to free verse at once becomes apparent, and impressionism, expressionism, cubism and futurism can all be found in music as well as the other arts.)

If you are interested in history or geography or both, the co-operation of music again becomes highly significant. There is no better way of studying nationalism than through the folk-music of individual countries, and wherever an art-music has been developed with strong national characteristics, these can be traced directly to the folk-music of that country. There is no mistaking the character of a Hungarian rhapsody, or an Irish jig, or a Russian hopak, or a Polish mazurka, or a Viennese waltz. The music of a country should always be an important part of the study of its geography and history.

Music has played a dramatic rôle on numerous historic occasions, such as the fall of the Bastille, when the *Marseillaise* was heard, the rise of Protestantism, inspired by Luther's hymn, *A Mighty Fortress*, even the surrender of Cornwallis at Yorktown, when *Yankee Doodle* turned from an army joke into a march of triumph.

Music is so closely knit with the other arts that one could not very well get along without the other. Ruskin called architecture "frozen music," and the whole technique of form is certainly an architectural matter. Painting, sculpture and literature all have their analogies in music, and the art of the dance could not exist without music, which is its heart and soul. It was also at one time a necessity to the drama, and even today incidental music is helpful to the stage, quite aside from definitely operatic productions. (If radio has become an art, its debt to music is of course unlimited.)

But the greatest significance of music is in its relation to life itself. It is unquestionably the most human of all the arts, and the one that enters most into everyday experience. It is unnecessary to repeat the hackneyed phrases that have been uttered so many times as to the necessity of music, the connotation of the mother's lullaby, or a favorite hymn, or a marching tune, or patriotic music of any kind, or the uplifting value of a really fine composition. The fact remains, in spite of all the platitudinous utterances on the subject, that music does have an ethical, an emotional, often actually a physical effect on human beings, and its importance cannot be ignored, even by those who would like to think of it merely as a luxury or an idle pastime. Religion has never been able to get along without music, and it is one of the greatest assets of the Church today. Patriotism, loyalty, love, courage, and all the other human virtues are not only expressed but stimulated by music.

If this book has given the impression that all music can be reduced to simple patterns, remember that all human beings offer the same possibility. Everyone is composed of the same raw materials, and everyone shows the same general patterns of form and feature. Yet there never were two human beings exactly alike. In the same way there have never been two pieces of music exactly alike. They may show similar arrangements of notes, in both their rhythmic and their melodic patterns; they may use the same harmonies over and over again, the same tonal coloring, and the same outlines of form. But the effect of the individual composition will always be different from that of any other, just as people having the same eyes, noses, mouths and other features will nevertheless be easily recognized as individuals.

No matter how similar two people might be in their externals, there would still be marked emotional, mental and spiritual differences. The same variations hold good in music, where a composer's mental, emotional and spiritual character will inevitably affect his use of even the most ordinary materials. Therefore, it is the least of all tributes to say that a composer is completely original. Rather is it a compliment to say that he has used the simplest and most universal materials in a manner that is distinctly and entirely his own. No great composer ever worried much about the originality of his themes. Many of the Wagnerian motifs are in themselves quite commonplace combinations of tones. His genius consisted in knowing how to use them to create the exact mood and atmosphere that he desired. The hearer recognizes melodic inspiration, even when it does not imply a completely original arrangement of tones, which is literally impossible today, unless all the logic of tradition is cast aside.

After hearing enough music of all kinds, it becomes possible for anyone to decide, either at a first hearing or later, that a piece has inspirational individuality, or that it is merely another correct composition of a certain type, not necessarily bad, but also clearly not of any particular merit. The same standards are being applied daily in the reading of books, magazines and newspapers. A piece of really fine writing does not escape the attention of the public any more than a really fine piece of music escapes the experienced listener.

SOME PRACTICAL SUGGESTIONS

Obviously the performance of music depends for its effect not only on the skill of the artists concerned, but also on the instruments themselves. A Kreisler or a Heifetz would probably be impressive even when heard on a mediocre violin, but with a Stradivarius or a Guarnerius or an Amati in their hands, the tonal results may well approach perfection. A Rubinstein or a Horowitz or an Iturbi will always insist on playing the finest type of concert grand piano and would be seriously handicapped by an inferior instrument. The astonishing feats of our popular masters of the trumpet, the trombone, the clarinet, and the saxophone are made possible not only by a highly developed individual technique but by a scientific improvement in the manufacture of these instruments that only a few years ago would have been considered impossible.

The position of the home radio and phonograph today may fairly be called analogous. The perfected combination of cabinet, tubes, motor, loud-speakers and turntable is no mere piece of furniture, nor should it be considered only the medium for mechanical transmission of a performance already established in complete detail. The modern radio-phonograph is in every sense a musical instrument, with a wide range of tonal quality and volume, definitely affecting the interpretations of great artists, and depending also to a considerable extent on proper care and handling by its fortunate owner.

While this magic box contains the mysterious power to bring into your home the performance of a great orchestra or chorus, or an entire opera, or the individual virtuosity of any outstanding singer or instrumentalist, it can do no more than its equipment permits. The human performers in the background are completely at its mercy, and if the listener fails to take advantage of its possibilities, he is guilty of artistic treason, an aesthetic injustice to himself as well as to the helpless creators and interpreters of the music.

In the earlier pages of this book there has been some discussion of musical tone resulting from air waves set in motion by the vibration of some surface. It was indicated that the quality of tone, sometimes called timbre or tone color, was due to the combination of "overtones" with the "fundamental," which determines the pitch of any given note. In the vocabulary of radio and the phonograph, the word "frequencies" is generally applied to the overtones, and these are called "high" or "low" in accordance with their actual position in the musical scale.

Every tone of music that is heard on an instrument, including that of the human voice, is actually a combination of many tones, of which most listeners are entirely unaware. All they know is that when some of the frequencies are missing, the tone loses its color and life. This is a common experience for those who twist the knobs on their radio dials, trying to find a certain station and failing to land squarely on the right number. When the desired "balance" is attained, the difference is obvious even to the uninitiated amateur.

Let it be admitted that no broadcasting or recording of sound is actually identical with its original. The limitations of air lanes and transmission do not permit the inclusion of the full range of potential frequencies. But it is equally true that human ears vary in their ability to detect these finer gradations of sound, and that too many of us are inclined to be satisfied with less than our musical due. We should at least demand an instrument whose tonal possibilities have been amply proved, and then see to it that this instrument lives up to its reputation.

GETTING THE BEST RESULTS

The ideal of any mechanical reproduction of music is of course the performance itself. It is not so important that the volume of tone be the same, but the quality must at all times be convincing. If this can be approximated even at lower dynamic levels, so much the better, for many of us do not like our music too loud, either on the air or on records.

With radio programs the best effects are secured through "frequency modulation," and today's top-notch receiving sets are all equipped for tuning in on the FM stations, whose number is steadily increasing. Frequency modulation not only eliminates the interference of "static," but takes care of most of the other unpleasant noises, like those caused by elevators, electric refrigerators, and other modern necessities of apartment life.

Of course it is entirely possible to become acquainted with great music through a machine of less than ideal equipment. A good lithograph gives an excellent impression of a great painting, even though it is far from the original, and any adequate reproduction of music has its educational and stimulating value, though it may fall short of the standards of complete aesthetic enjoyment. One can only urge the potential music-lover to secure the best instrument within his means, perhaps even at some sacrifice, and then to make the best possible use of it.

Aside from what may be considered the necessary features of satisfactory tonal reproduction, there are certain luxuries which most music-lovers will probably find desirable. For convenience and accuracy in picking up radio programs, the practical device of "push-button tuning" can be recommended; and an automatic record-changer is a help to the leisurely enjoyment of music in the larger forms. Recorded music can actually be heard at its best through a local radio station such as New York's famous WQXR (with its FM colleague, WQXQ). Here one gets not only the lightest pickup and the greatest fidelity to pitch and tonal quality, but also the advantage of two turntables, identically tuned, permitting the uninterrupted performance of a composition of any length whatever, by the simple process of dropping one needle at the moment that the other is lifted from the disc.

WQXR possesses a record library which might also serve as a model for the ambitious collector. Albums, transcriptions, and individual discs are placed in wooden cabinets, numerically arranged, while a carefully kept Cardex lists every record, alphabetically by composers, each card marked with the name of the piece, the interpreters, and the playing-time. Such a system is perhaps too elaborate for the average record-owner, but any home library of fifty albums or more should be properly housed and indexed if its purpose is to be served.

Closet space can generally be found for such a library, or special shelves can be built, preferably with sliding doors. Albums should be placed vertically, not too tightly pressed together, while single discs can be kept in stock cardboard envelopes, with wooden separators about a foot apart, to prevent possible breaking or warping of the records. When an album is being used one record at a time, it is well to stand it up vertically, half open, lifting the individual records out as needed.

It should hardly be necessary today to remind phonograph-owners that the ordinary steel or cactus needles should be changed frequently, and also handled very carefully to avoid scratching when placed upon a record. More or less permanent needles of the sapphire type are generally good.

A FINAL WORD

For those who are interested in acoustics and honestly anxious to get the best results from the instruments that make music in the home today, an Appendix of somewhat more technical character has been added to this book by a man who is an expert on the subject, with personal responsibility for many of the modern improvements in the reproduction of sound. If you are scientifically minded, and looking for practical results, by all means read this Appendix and apply its wisdom to your own selection and maintenance of a satisfactory radio-phonograph, an instrument which is now absolutely essential to the development of a real music-lover.

Those who form the habit of hearing good music in their homes inevitably find their greatest pleasure in the discovery of permanent beauty, regardless of whether the discovery has previously been made by others. Even if one's taste may later prove to have been wrong, the original enthusiasm was worth while, and it is far better to express a conviction sincerely than to play always the cautious rôle of making sure that one's opinion is conventionally correct.

The greater the experience in practical listening, the better will be the chances of arriving at unshakable conclusions, based upon deliberate analysis as well as instinctive reactions. When you have discovered for yourself something beautiful that proves to have passed the test of time, and to have stimulated millions of others as it stimulates you, then you have enjoyed an experience that is akin to that of the creative artist himself. Modern science, through radio and the phonograph, makes it possible for anyone to arrive at such discoveries, comfortably seated at the fireside, gaining constantly in understanding and enthusiasm, and becoming more and more, both literally and figuratively, "at home with music."

YOUR RADIO-PHONOGRAPH

by Frank Freimann

The miracle of science, through the modern radio and radio-phonograph, has brought the wealth of the world's great music from the concert hall to the home. The ever-growing popularity of good music in America has been greatly helped through this medium. It has not diminished the attendance at "live" concerts, but, on the contrary, has stimulated a new interest in millions of people who have never before been exposed to symphonic music. The concert hall is still the best place to hear the full beauty of good music superbly performed. However, a good modern radio-phonograph runs a close second and is, of course, far more easily accessible. The modern instrument has been developed to such a high stage of perfection that it can suffer only by a direct comparison with actual performance of the highest quality. It is capable of reproducing an excellent facsimile of the intricate and wide tonal range of an orchestration even though it is unable to reproduce the tremendous range of volume of a large orchestra, which, furthermore, would be impractical outside the concert hall for obvious reasons.

The purpose of this Appendix to Dr. Spaeth's stimulating book is to aid the reader in getting an appreciation of the possibilities and limitations of music-reproducing instruments. This information may serve as a guide to his future selection, from the numerous models usually available in every market, of one best suited to his needs.

Since the extensive development of radio broadcasting, placing powerful stations within reach of virtually every community, the fad of seeking distant stations has practically gone out of existence. Almost any radio receiver, regardless of price or size, will now serve to receive the programs of major importance. Most reasonably good sets are capable of discriminating between the dozens of stations serving the community and receiving the desired one without interference. The other principal elements of utility for consideration are convenience of operation—that is, dial tuning vs. the push-button tuning now embodied in even very low-priced sets—accessory control features, such as volume and tone controls, and, most important of all, tone quality. For those interested primarily in utility rather than novelty, a minimum of controls is desirable. A volume control is indispensable and the bass and treble control desirable—the latter being a misnomer, for it should serve only to control the upper range of the set sufficiently to suppress the surface noise of unusually noisy records, not to blanket out any portion of this important tone range. The bass control, which is less important on anything but large sets, is largely to compensate for acoustical conditions in various rooms and also to compensate for occasional deficiencies in the balance of a radio or recorded program. Although most radio sets incorporate an automatic volume control, this feature varies in effectiveness. On the larger sets it should be so efficient that when a program is switched from a weak to a more powerful station, the volume will remain approximately constant, eliminating the annoying burst of loudness.

Tone quality is a big subject and warrants some detailed treatment, as it is the element of greatest importance to the ultimate user and is the largest variable factor between instruments of various sizes and makes. A great deal of misinformation has been spread in terms of either vague or specific claims. The same superlatives have been applied to a set not much larger than a cigar box as to a sizable instrument capable of reproducing good music; this has left the average man in a general state of confusion, often of mistrusting his own ears.

As a rule the selection should be made with your own ears and your own musical feeling as the major authority and influence. If the music or speech to which you are listening lacks realism or doesn't "sound good" in your own judgment, it isn't the instrument to acquire and the salesman or manufacturer isn't a good authority, regardless of what he claims, because he doesn't live day in and day out with the instrument, as you will.

In defining tone quality, we should take a negative viewpoint and eliminate the most annoying forms of distortion first. If the reproduction is raspy and harsh, with tones actually breaking up into noises, the set doesn't warrant consideration—either as a radio or radio-phonograph combination. Reasonably good instruments are free from this type of distortion. Other forms of distortion not classified under that heading have to do with the tone range the instrument is capable of reproducing and the balance or uniform distribution of this range, which determines, among other things, clarity and definition.

Tone quality has become a generic term defining the capacity of a reproducing instrument. It must be remembered, however, that the ideal reproducer does not have a tone of its own, such as a violin, piano, or horn—instruments which actually generate tone. Reproducing instruments of poor quality usually do have an undesirable tone of their own, resulting from resonance in the cabinet, speaker, pickup, or combination of elements comprising the set.

The tone generated by a string instrument or horn is comprised of complex vibrations technically defined in frequencies. For example, the violin's tone range embodies frequencies from about 200 to 8000 cycles, bassoon from 60 through 7000 cycles, flute from approximately 250 to 9000 cycles; every note played on these instruments is comprised of dozens of vibrations of frequencies, starting with the fundamental frequency and including a multiplicity of harmonics and subharmonics, usually referred to as partials.

The music produced by a full orchestra embodies frequencies from approximately 40 to 15,000 cycles. Presumably to do full justice to the music, manufacturers occasionally claim this full reproducing range for their instrument.

It is currently not only impossible adequately to reproduce this wide range of frequencies under home conditions, but undesirable. The physiological as well as physical elements must be taken into consideration in the communication of music from the musician's instrument, via the radio or record, to the listener. There is a large percentage of people who do not hear frequencies above 10,000 cycles. Many people of apparently normal hearing cannot hear above 5000 cycles. Except in rare cases, the range of hearing of people under forty years of age does not extend beyond 16,000, the ears of children being the most sensitive in this respect. Although the tones of some instruments contain harmonics extending to 15,000, the claim that "half the music is lost" by reproducing only half of this range has no foundation in fact. The basic tone range of all instruments lies within approximately 45 to 4500 cycles. Most instruments are rich in overtones (partials) that extend to 8000 cycles; therefore richness of tone and definition is gained by extending the range from 4500 to approximately 8000 cycles. There is very little gain in extension beyond this figure. Furthermore, objectionable noises are introduced both by musicians' instruments and the media of transmission (records or radio) in doing so. Overtones in the range above 8000 cycles are so minute in in-

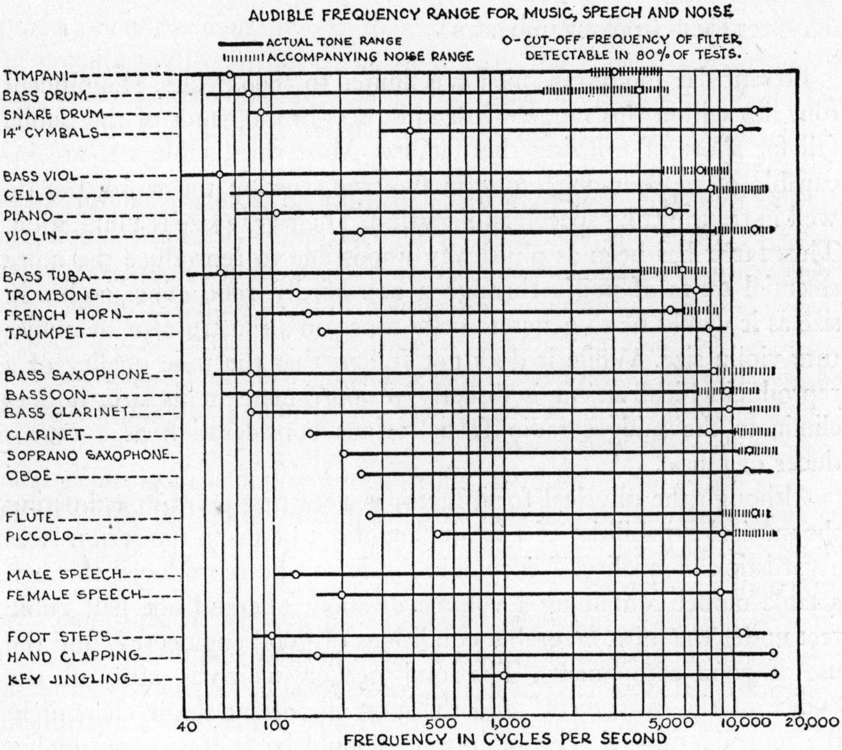

*Figure I**

*Redrawn from *Psychology of Music*, by Carl E. Seashore, by permission of McGraw-Hill Book Company, Inc., and the *Journal of the Acoustical Society of America*. Originally published in "Audible Frequency Ranges of Music, Speech and Noise," by W. B. Snow, *Journal of the Acoustical Society of America*, III, 1931, 151–66.

tensity and so directional that they have seldom reached the auditor in a large auditorium when listening to a "live" orchestra.

Figure I shows the audible frequency range for music, speech, and noise. Circles on the lines show the limit of effective listening range. The frequencies eliminated at either end of the two circles (low- and high-frequency range) do not make a perceptible listening difference.

The best motion-picture-theater sound-reproducing equipment does not extend beyond 8000 cycles. This practical reproducing range was arrived at after much research and is achieved with equipment that is beyond the home budget and space factor.

TABLE-MODEL RADIO SETS

Present-day radio transmission is limited to 5000 cycles. Magnificent tone lies within this range. Most radio sets in the hands of the public fall far short of utilizing this facility. Most small table sets are incapable of reproducing *music* in the true sense of the word, but do well in transmitting speech and rhythm. Their very size is a limitation. Thus far it has been as physically impossible to reproduce the more essential tones of music through a box hardly 1000 cubic inches in size as it would be to generate cello tones on an instrument of miniature violin size. While it does not follow that the tone quality of a reproducing instrument is directly proportionate to its size, it does eliminate the midget radio from serious consideration as a reproducer of music.

Although the physical form factor is a starting-point in estimating the musical capabilities of a set, it should not be taken too seriously as a yardstick of quality. Acceptable music can be reproduced through a table model containing a volume of about one and one half cubic feet under the most favorable conditions of good engineering and the use of good components. The loud-speaker—which is, after all, the "voice of the instrument" and the most important single element in the reproduction of acceptable tone—should be at least seven inches in diameter or, if elliptical, should have a cone surface of about twenty-five square inches. The radio receiver or amplifier therein should be capable of furnishing at least three watts of undistorted power through the speaker. Such a set should be capable of reproducing a tonal range of approximately 100 to 4000 cycles with fairly good definition and harmonious tone. It is physically possible to extend the upper range, although such sets have not been commercially available, due perhaps to the economic factor.

Good music is so cheap nowadays in relation to the great joy it brings to the average music lover—being free on radio and only moderately costly on records—that a set incapable of reproducing it fairly well is a poor investment. It does not mean that the enjoyment of good music in the home is limited to those who have several hundred dollars available for an instrument, although instruments capable of rendering the best reproduction are relatively costly. When only modest sums are available, the buyer should be particularly cautious in selecting an instrument that is free from gadgets of questionable value, because he will get more for his money in buying the primary requirements which make for good tone—namely, a set with a good speaker and amplifier in it.

RADIO-PHONOGRAPHS ANALYZED

In analyzing the console type of set, radio-phonograph combinations only will be considered, as most modern sets over table-model size are of that type. A radio-phonograph combination selling for less than $250 should have a tone range extending from 75 to at least 5000 cycles. Regardless of the flowery claims on the part of the salesmen, sets in the past were far short of achieving this. Their effective range extended to about only 3500 cycles with "one note" bass at the bottom end. Such sets had a characteristic boomy response that not only lacked definition but also blurred out the middle and upper ranges.

An instrument costing upward of $200 should give excellent reproduction and cover a range extending from 60 to approximately 7500 cycles without distortion. If the response to the ear is relatively uniform over this range, the full beauty of the original rendition should be well preserved. Extending beyond this range under the most ideal conditions contributes very little to the quality of music and, under practical conditions, is usually detrimental because of injected noises. Standard or AM broadcasting extends to only 5000 cycles. However, some of the newest phonograph records, only recently available, are reproducible to approximately 7500 cycles—with, incidentally, very noticeable improvement over older recordings. The extended frequency range (to 7500 cycles) is conspicuously useful in reception of FM broadcasting, which is not limited as is AM broadcasting.

Unfortunately frequency range cannot be used as an exclusive criterion of tone quality. Within the ideal reproducing range there can be considerable distortion. Bass distortion is a common ailment, easily recognizable by the boomy character of reproduction. The difference in the timbre of string bass and horn bass should be easily distinguishable.

An instrument capable of reproducing bass notes reasonably well enables the listener to define each separate tone of the bass viol as the player draws his bow across the string. Another method of distinguishing between good and bad bass reproduction is to observe the natural decadence of the bass note. If the tone "hangs on" instead of rapidly dying down, it will blur out other bass notes and most of the middle register as well. Although an instrument may cover the range in question when single frequencies (pure tones) are reproduced through it, masking effect and overemphasis of any part of the middle or bass range will ruin definition and blanket out minute overtones in the upper range, limiting the response to a substantial degree.

OBSERVING EFFECTIVE TONE RANGE

It is all very well to describe the required range for best reproduction, but determining what the instrument actually does in this direction is quite another matter for the average person. The final decision and choice should again rest largely on how the reproduced music sounds to the listener. Chances are that if the tone is beautiful and each instrument in the orchestra is easily distinguishable—that is, there is good definition—the instrument has a good range.

Frequency records now available for testing phonographs can be used as a crude scientific test. Frequencies are usually defined in steps of ten cycles from 50 to 200; 50-cycle steps to 1000 cycles; and 100-cycle steps to 5000, to 7000, or sometimes 10,000 cycles. Playing each frequency, observe that each pure tone has approximately the same volume, using 1000 cycles as a reference. Such a test will show the limited range and also resonance points in both the low-frequency range (from 50 to 250 cycles) and the middle range extending to 3500 cycles. If the tones are perceptible in the range above 3500 cycles, but very soft, they will be masked by the much stronger tones in the middle and bass range and will actually not be heard when music is played.

The frequency response of a reproducing instrument is determined by a number of elements within the set, the speaker being the most important. In the best-engineered sets all the elements, including the acoustical properties of the cabinet, are blended together to give the desired over-all effect. It is obvious that the best instrument can be no better than the loud-speaker which reproduces the sound. It is also true that the loud-speaker in itself might be incapable of producing the desired result, unless the associated elements, including the amplifier, the RF section of the radio, and the phonograph pickup, are properly co-ordinated with it in the acoustical chamber or cabinet in which it is housed. Secondary in importance is the amount of audio power available in the amplifier to operate the speaker. About five watts is desirable in a good table model and at least ten watts in a console model, with twenty watts or more satisfactory for a large instrument.

The efficiency of the speaker and its ability to convert electrical energy into sound are also directly associated with the power factor. That is, a speaker of half the normal efficiency will require twice as much power, or forty instead of twenty watts, to produce the same results. In roughly estimating the relative efficiency, size and sometimes weight can be the determining factor. The size of the cone or diaphragm of the speaker varies from twelve to fifteen inches in diameter. The size of the cone is a factor in the efficiency only in the bass range—in fact, the larger cones are inefficient in extreme treble range and may require a supplementary small speaker to cover this range effectively. Flux density of the magnetic circuit largely determines the over-all efficiency. Therefore the magnet size of either electrodynamic (coil type) or permanent-magnet type is a good physical indication. The larger the field structure (magnet), the more efficient is the speaker.

Available power and the efficiency of the speaker are directly related to the intensity of sound. Although directly related, they do not solely determine the loudness of the set. Adequate power is required to reproduce low tones at normal room volume and is also essential to the prevention of transient distortion. About 80 per cent of the available power in a good instrument is required to reproduce frequencies below 200 cycles. A small table model with only a fraction of a watt of power may sound as loud as the large set having twenty times the power, because the former does not reproduce bass and has most of its sensitivity in the 3000-cycle range, where the sensitivity of the human ear is several thousand times greater than at the low frequencies.

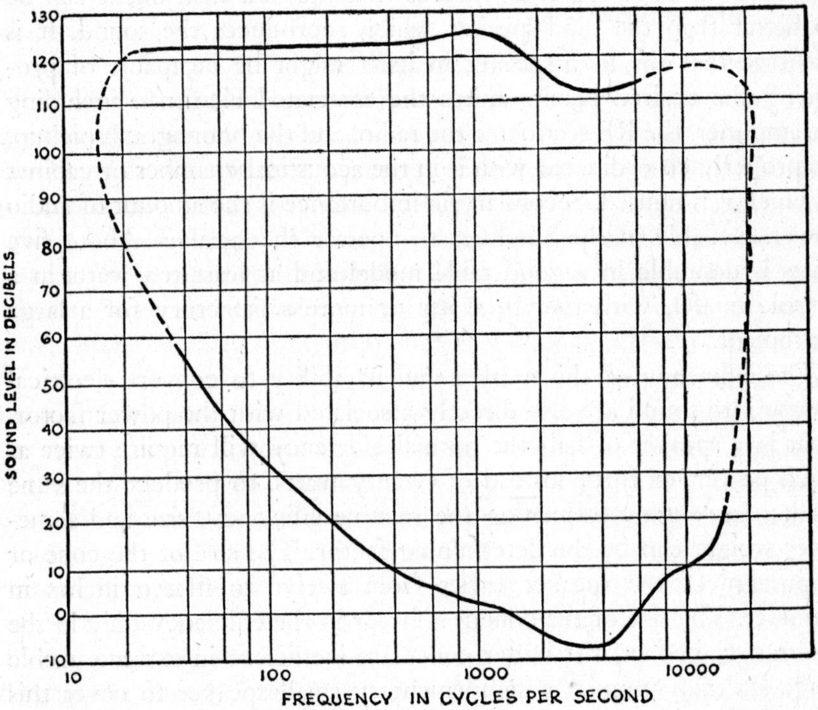

NOTE:
SOUND LEVEL IS INTENSITY LEVEL IN DECIBELS, MEASURED FROM 10^{-16} WATT PER SQUARE CENTIMETER.

*Figure II**—Solid lower curve shows relative sensitivity of the human ear to sounds of various frequencies. Lowest number indicates highest ear sensitivity, 2500 cycles being the point of greatest sensitivity.

*Redrawn from *Psychology of Music,* by Carl E. Seashore, by permission of McGraw-Hill Book Company, Inc., and courtesy of Western Electric Company.

At sound levels normally reproduced in the home, one thousand times more sound intensity is required at 50 cycles than at 3000 cycles to produce the same apparent loudness and ten thousand times as much at 20 cycles. Figure II shows the relative sensitivity of the human ear to various frequencies as calibrated in decibel sound units. A practical illustration is the triangle in an orchestra, which, when struck, can be heard just as distinctly as a bass drum, although the latter generates about twenty-five hundred times as much acoustic power.

RECORD CHANGERS

In recent years an automatic record changer has become an integral part of the radio-phonograph combination. The quality of these mechanisms has improved from year to year, as manufacturers have gained knowledge from past experience. Most record changers are now quite reliable, although the changer, being by requirement a precision mechanism with numerous moving parts, is the element that requires most of the service attention. Simplicity of design, with the least moving parts, is a desirable feature, provided the mechanism is reliable in operation, convenient to load and unload, and does not injure the records by frequent playings.

The drop type of record changer is the most economical and most popular. About ten records can be played at one time in proper sequence, thus furnishing about forty minutes of playing time (for twelve-inch records), at which time the stack is turned over and the second sides played. Of course, in the playing of complete symphonies or operas, the loading is limited to the number of records in the set. For example, five records are played on one side; the record stack is then turned over and the other five sides are played. In purchasing albums of records, the "DM" series should be specified for the "drop" type of changer.

There are several types of "drop changers." All are designed to drop one record at a time from the bottom of a stack of records. They are divided into two types—one supporting the records on a spindle through the center hole in the record, the other supporting the records at their edges. In the use of the spindle type, the bottom record is pushed off the ledge in the spindle in proper sequence; in the latter, revolving blades hold up the stack while the bottom record is dropped to the turntable. The principle of operation is equally good in both types, the quality of performance and dependability depending on how well these mechanisms are designed and made. Shoddy construction will lead to troublesome operation.

Other features are an automatic stop, which will shut off the motor after the last record is played (a highly desirable feature), and intermixing ten- and twelve-inch records automatically. The automatic intermixing feature is less important and, in some cases, undesirable, as it makes for more mechanism and a greater chance of its getting out of adjustment. It is very seldom necessary to play ten- and twelve-inch records on a single loading.

The convenience feature of the more costly changers which play both sides of a record to provide a continuity of music for several hours is an expensive premium, but desirable if the funds are available. Such mechanisms are subject to more frequent service attention because of their more elaborate machinery.

In selecting an instrument, an important consideration is the absence of "pitch waver." Records are recorded at the rate of seventy-eight revolutions of the turntable per minute. To reproduce the music with exact pitch, the records must be revolved at the same speed. The motor and turntable must, therefore, be a precision mechanism capable of running at the precise speed regardless of power-line voltage variation. A mechanism may fluctuate in speed, causing the pitch of reproduced music to waver or "tremble," with very annoying effects, particularly when a sustained note is played. Vibrations in the motor turntable mechanism will cause tone "flutter" and objectionable low rumbling in the reproduced music.

PERMANENT NEEDLES

The advent of permanent needles has eliminated the annoyance of frequent needle changes. No doubt most modern instruments will incorporate nonremovable needles which will play several thousand records before the cartridge is replaced at a modest cost. The theory that records will last longer when a "soft" needle is used is not valid. Carefully handled records can be played several hundred times, without detrimental wear, with a properly designed needle and pickup.

A permanent needle should not be used in an instrument designed for the old-style removable needle, as damage to records and needle may result, unless the weight at the end of the pick-up arm is less than 1½ ounces.

NEW RECORDS

In the past there has been a marked difference in the quality of records made for radio transcription and those sold for home consumption, the former being vastly superior in both tonal range and absence of surface noise. Records of comparable quality for home use are now appearing on the market. This will greatly add to the enjoyment of listening. These records have a fine-grained surface, minimizing surface noise to a point where it is hardly noticeable—in some instances eliminating it entirely through the use of vinylite or other plastic surface. In purchasing new records, request new releases and test them for surface noise, as "new releases" are sometimes old pressings warmed up in a new package.

VERTICAL VS. LATERAL RECORDINGS

All records sold for home use are laterally cut. They are recorded and reproduced at 78 RPM. Radio transcriptions are recorded both laterally and vertically (sometimes called "hill and dale"). These records are recorded and reproduced at a speed of 33 1/3 RPM. Due to the slower speed of rotation, a record of comparable diameter will play approximately 2.3 times as long. Thus a twelve-inch record rotated at 33 1/3 RPM will provide approximately nine minutes of music as compared with four minutes at 78 RPM. Most transcription records are sixteen inches in diameter and play fifteen minutes.

Vertically recorded records have the undulations running "hill and dale" instead of sideways or laterally across the grooves. The latter can be cut to a depth of approximately half the wall thickness of the grooves. The hill-and-dale method is not so restricted and therefore makes possible a greater volume range, from softest pianissimo to loudest fortissimo. There are other advantages in the hill-and-dale type of recording which may eventually induce record manufacturers and instrument manufacturers to make this method available for home use. The difference in realizable quality is, however, relatively small, and the advances made in the recording technique of 78 RPM records are steadily narrowing this gap.

WIRE RECORDINGS

The extensive publicity which accompanied the introduction of "recording on wire" for military applications has given rise to considerable speculation as to the possibility of such media replacing the conventional disc records. Wire recorders will undoubtedly be incorporated in some home instruments as accessory devices for instantly recording radio programs and the voices of members of the family and friends. But this device is not likely to affect disc records for many years to come, if ever. The technique of recording on wire or tape was invented by Vandermeer Polson as early as 1900 and has been relatively dormant in its application for many years. Its advantages or merits have been somewhat colored by numerous writers, mainly in anticipation of "industrial revolutions." Its most effective use for some time to come will probably be in commercial fields rather than in the home.

FREQUENCY MODULATION

The newest development in radio broadcasting is Frequency Modulation. It offers two distinct advantages: first, the tone range is not restricted to the 5000-cycle ceiling of the conventional AM broadcasting; second, all forms of static, man-made and atmospheric, are completely eliminated under ideal conditions. The enthusiasm of the advertising copywriters extolling the FM revolution should be tempered with these facts, because while the improvement of fidelity is apparent under ideal conditions, the listening difference between the best in AM reception and the best in FM reception is not so great as the difference between poor or mediocre AM reception and really good AM reception. As pointed out previously, range of frequency response alone is not a criterion of good tone reproduction. A relatively perfect instrument, confined to a range of 70 to 5000 cycles, will give infinitely better quality than one reproducing from 70 to 10,000 cycles with poor balance and other forms of distortion.

Much greater improvement in fidelity is obtained by extending the reproducing range from 3500 cycles to 5000 cycles than the observable difference from 5000 to 10,000 cycles, all other things being equal. The point is that, to get the benefits of the extended range FM offers, an instrument must have the basic attributes of good quality on AM reception. Therefore, as far as fidelity and tone are concerned, very little improvement may be expected in small and low-priced sets. The potential purchaser would, therefore, make a better investment in putting the premium cost for FM into a better AM set, if his funds are limited.

Due to the limited transmission range of FM, limited theoretically to the line of sight, or a radius of fifty miles or less under favorable conditions, noise reduction is not obtained where it is needed most—that is, in the reception of stations one hundred miles or more away. Except for a very small minority of cases in apartment houses, located in the center of metropolitan areas, where the man-made static level may be unusually high, noiseless reception is now being obtained from powerful AM stations located within fifty miles of the receiver. Therefore the merits of static elimination may be somewhat discounted.

There is much enthusiasm for the future devolopment of FM broadcasting, which is, after all, now only in the development stage. It is expected, in years to come, that a great number of stations may offer additional program services that will not be available on the AM broadcasts. Currently, however, FM programs consist largely of radio transcriptions and regular home recordings, in addition to the simultaneous broadcasts of chain programs on AM as well as FM.

FM broadcasting was developed on the radio-frequency bands of 42 to 50 megacycles, with stations operating in relatively few scattered metropolitan areas. To provide "room" for hundreds of additional stations, with a minimum of interstation interference, FCC has reallocated the broadcast band into the higher frequency range of 88 to 106 megacycles. Although existing FM stations will continue to operate in the old band until new stations can be constructed, they will eventually be moved into the higher spectrum, thus, for all practical purposes, making obsolete the FM portions of the receivers now in the hands of the public. It is reasonable to believe that such a situation will not recur and therefore it should not be a deterrent to invest in a new FM set.

Radio-phonographs, as well as straight radio receivers, will be available with the FM band as an integral part of the AM receiver as well as a separate FM unit covering only the FM band, which is operated through the audio amplifier and speaker in the AM set. Both methods are good, with probably some additional merit for the separate FM band where it can be conveniently added to the same instrument without becoming an accessory outside the cabinet. It can be added at the owner's convenience when the new FM service becomes established in his particular community. While there is some slight manufacturing economy in combining the two in one chassis, there is also an operating economy in the instance of the separate FM chassis, as it can be turned off when the instrument is used for phonograph reproduction or AM reception.

GETTING THE MOST LISTENING PLEASURE

A good radio-phonograph usually becomes the focal point of family activity. It can offer endless hours of pleasure for all members of the family, and the selection of instrument and records should be made with this thought in mind.

As there is now a wide selection of models in good furniture styles, the radio-phonograph need no longer be relegated to some obscure corner of the home. The living room, for a variety of reasons, is usually the most appropriate location, unless a large library is available where the family spends most of its time. Unless an armchair model is selected, wall space is required for the average instrument for acoustical reasons as well as décor. Other than avoiding corners for acoustical reasons, the instrument can be fitted into the general decorative scheme just as any other cabinet furniture, with preference given, if possible, to obtaining the best sound coverage. That is, the instrument should preferably be placed against one of the narrow walls of an oblong room for the best distribution of sound.

For physiological reasons the greatest realism is obtained at relatively high sound levels of reproduction. However, because this is not always practical, the instrument to be purchased should be listened to at very low levels as well. Some instruments are fairly good at high levels but sound thin and distorted at low sound levels. Instruments which radiate mechanical noise from the phonograph mechanism should be avoided, as this noise, usually referred to as "pickup chatter," will interfere with the music reproduction when the instrument is played at low level.

Most people who acquire a radio-phonograph sooner or later accumulate a sizable library of records. Convenient storage and accessibility to these records should be a consideration. Don't be deceived by the sales appeal of a record compartment in the instrument. Record-storage compartments are valueless unless they provide space for at least a dozen albums. The overflow can be stored in a separate record cabinet in the same room or in a closet, as indicated in Dr. Spaeth's closing paragraphs.

Taking the line of least resistance by avoiding the installation of an antenna has become a common practice. The best reception is obtained with an adequate antenna installation, rather than by depending on the self-contained antenna in the set. This is particularly true of large, high-quality sets, which require the benefit of a strong signal because of the wider tone-reproduction capability of such instruments. They will also produce more static than instruments with a limited range. This, of course, can be offset by reducing the reproducing range of the instrument through turning back the tone control. In this process the fidelity of reproduction is also reduced. It does *not* hold that the owner of a good instrument, who finds it impossible to install an antenna, cannot depend on good reception. The lack of an outside antenna will, however, frequently limit noiseless reception to a few powerful local stations.

If these suggestions have been absorbed, it should be possible for anyone to select a radio-phonograph that will prove completely satisfactory, especially as regards tone quality. With the help of Sigmund Spaeth's interesting and informative discussions of the world's great music, the finest concerts may now be enjoyed to the utmost, right in your own home.

GREAT COMPOSERS IN A NUTSHELL

JOHANN SEBASTIAN BACH, b. Eisenach, March 21, 1685, d. Leipzig, July 28, 1750. The father of music as it is known today, and one of the greatest composers of all time. Organist, conductor and creator of such masterpieces as the *Grand Mass in B minor*, *The Passion according to St. Matthew*, *Christmas Oratorio*, over 200 *Cantatas*, six *French Suites*, six *English Suites*, the *Brandenburg Concertos*, *Sonatas*, *Fugues*, etc., *Inventions* in two and three parts and *The Well-Tempered Clavier* (48 *Preludes* and *Fugues* in all keys).

LUDWIG VAN BEETHOVEN, b. Bonn, Dec. 16, 1770, d. Vienna, March 26, 1827. Second of the "three B's" and the first great Romantic composer, master of the symphonic and sonata form. Revolutionary and dramatic in methods and results. Nine *Symphonies*, many *Sonatas* for violin, piano, etc., five *Piano Concertos* and one supreme *Violin Concerto*, *Overtures* to *Coriolanus*, *Egmont*, etc., the *Opera*, *Fidelio* (with four *Overtures*, three known as *Leonore*), *Missa Solemnis*, *Songs*, *String Quartets*, *Trios*, etc.

VINCENZO BELLINI, b. Catania, Sicily, Nov. 3, 1801, d. Paris, Sept. 23, 1835. Important composer of operas, of which *Norma* (1831) is considered his greatest, although it is seldom heard because of the enormous demands of the title rôle. His earliest success, *La Sonnambula*, is also dated 1831, and three years later he wrote *I Puritani*, both of which are heard occasionally.

HECTOR BERLIOZ, b. Côte St. André, Dec. 11, 1803, d. Paris, March 9, 1869. Pioneer in Program Music and elaborate orchestration, with results not always up to his spectacular ideas. Three important *Symphonies*, called *Harold in Italy*, *Romeo and Juliet* and *Fantastic; Oratorio*, *The Damnation of Faust; Opera*, *Benvenuto Cellini; Overture*, *Carnaval Romain*, etc.

GEORGES BIZET, b. Paris, Oct. 25, 1838, d. Bougival, June 3, 1875. Brilliant and popular French composer, best known by his *Opera*, *Carmen*, but also by *The Pearl Fishers* and the incidental music to *L'Arlesienne* (in two Suites).

JOHANNES BRAHMS, b. Hamburg, May 7, 1833, d. Vienna, April 3, 1897. Third of the "three B's," and now ranked as the equal of Bach and Beethoven in the field of absolute music. The perfect combination of the classic and romantic, balancing mastery of form with great melodic invention. Four *Symphonies*, two *Piano Concertos*, one *Violin Concerto*, many *Sonatas, String Quartets, Trios*, a *Quintet, Double Concerto* for violin, cello and orchestra, *Tragic* and *Academic Festival Overtures, Piano Music, Hungarian Dances*, many fine *Songs, Choral Works*, etc.

ANTON BRUCKNER, b. Ausfelden, Sept. 4, 1824, d. Vienna, Oct. 11, 1896. Composer of nine *Symphonies*, whose beauty and musical value are just beginning to be appreciated.

FRANCOIS FRÉDÉRIC CHOPIN, b. Warsaw, Feb. 22, 1810, d. Paris, Oct. 17, 1849. The most popular of all composers for the piano, and a pioneer in modern harmony and tone color, as well as a great concert pianist and individual personality. Four *Ballades*, a *Barcarolle, Berceuse*, three *Ecossaises*, 27 *Etudes*, four *Fantasies, Fantasie-Impromptu*, three *Impromptus, Funeral March*, 52 *Mazurkas*, 19 *Nocturnes*, 11 *Polonaises*, 25 *Preludes*, three *Rondos*, four *Scherzos*, three *Sonatas*, two *Concertos*, 13 *Waltzes, Variations*, all for piano, as well as *Songs* and other music.

CLAUDE ACHILLE DEBUSSY, b. Paris, 1862, d. Paris, March 26, 1918. Generally considered the founder of the modern school of composition, and the leading impressionist of music. One unique *Opera, Pelléas and Mélisande*, two *Cantatas*, orchestral *Prelude, The Afternoon of a Faun*, tone poems, *La Mer, Iberia; Nocturnes, Nuages, Fêtes*, and *Sirens*, many fine *Songs, Piano Pieces*, etc.

GAETANO DONIZETTI, b. Bergamo, Italy, Nov. 25, 1797, d. there April 8, 1848. Popular operatic composer, best known by his *Lucia di Lammermoor* (1835), a favorite vehicle for coloratura sopranos, containing the famous *Mad Scene* and *Sextet*. But he also wrote three lighter operas which have remained in the repertoire: *L'Elisir d'Amore* (1832), whose *Una Furtiva Lagrima* was immortalized by Caruso, *La Fille du Régiment* (1840), sung by Lily Pons and others, and *Don Pasquale* (1843), one of the masterpieces of comic opera (*buffa*).

ANTON DVORAK, b. Mühlhausen, Sept. 8, 1841, d. Prague, May 1, 1904. Outstanding Czech composer, residing for a time in America. Best known by his *Symphony, From the New World*, containing Negro themes, and also by his *American Quartet, Carnival Overture, Slavonic Dances, Stabat Mater, Chamber Music, Songs*, etc.

Edward Elgar, b. Broadheath, June 2, 1857, d. London, Feb. 23, 1934. England's best-known and most popular composer. *Enigma Variations, The Dream of Gerontius,* six *Marches, Pomp and Circumstance, Chamber Music, Songs,* etc.

Stephen Collins Foster, b. Lawrenceville, Pa., July 4, 1826, d. New York, Jan. 13, 1864. America's most popular composer, creating both words and music of many immortal songs. Among 160, the best known are *Old Folks at Home, Old Black Joe, My Old Kentucky Home, Oh, Susanna, Camptown Races, Massa's in de Cold, Cold Ground, Beautiful Dreamer, Jeanie with the Light Brown Hair, Old Dog Tray,* etc.

César Franck, b. Liége, Dec. 10, 1822, d. Paris, Nov. 8, 1890. Belgium's most important composer, combining the classic and modern styles. *Symphony in D minor, The Beatitudes,* two *Symphonic Poems, Sonatas, Chamber Music, Organ Music, Songs.*

Robert Franz, b. Halle, Germany, June 28, 1815, d. there Oct. 24, 1892. One of the outstanding masters of the German *Lied,* to which he devoted practically all his creative efforts. His real name, Knauth, was changed by royal permission. Among his best-known songs are *Widmung (Dedication), Stille Sicherheit (Quiet Confidence)* and *Es hat die Rose sich beklagt (The Rose Complained).*

George Gershwin, b. Brooklyn, Sept. 26, 1898, d. Hollywood, July 12, 1937. America's most important composer, combining the serious and popular styles. *Opera, Porgy and Bess; Piano Concerto in F, Rhapsody in Blue, An American in Paris, Preludes, Operettas,* many popular *Songs,* etc.

Alexander Glazounoff, b. St. Petersburg, Russia, Aug. 10, 1865, d. Paris, March 21, 1936. A successor to the Russian group of five, who revived folk-music, pupil of Rimsky-Korsakoff. His Ballet, *The Seasons,* has won popularity, particularly the *Bacchanale,* as danced by the great Pavlowa. A *Violin Concerto* in A minor is also well known and melodically appealing. He wrote eight symphonies, five *Suites,* four *Overtures,* the Symphonic Poem, *Stenka Razin* (1885), *Scènes de Ballet, Chamber Music,* etc.

Michail Glinka, b. Novospaskoi, June 1, 1804, d. Berlin, Feb. 15, 1857. Important Russian composer, founder of the nationalistic school. *Operas, A Life for the Czar, Russlan and Ludmilla; Orchestral Works, Chamber Music, Songs,* etc.

Christoph Willibald von Gluck, b. Weidenwang, July 2, 1714, d. Vienna, Nov. 25, 1787. Revolutionary composer of *Opera* in the classic style. *Alceste, Orpheus and Eurydice, Iphigenia in Aulis, Iphigenia in Tauris,* etc.

Charles Francois Gounod, b. Paris, June 17, 1818, d. Oct. 17, 1893. Popular French composer, best known by his *Operas, Faust* and *Romeo and Juliet*. Much *Church Music, Songs*, etc.

Edvard Grieg, b. Bergen, June 15, 1843, d. Bergen, Sept. 4, 1907. Outstanding Norwegian composer, with strongly nationalistic style, influenced by native folk-music. *Peer Gynt Suites, Piano Concerto, Violin Sonatas; Overture, In Autumn*, many fine *Songs* and *Piano Pieces*.

George Frederick Handel, b. Halle, Feb. 23, 1685, d. London, April 14, 1759. Master of the *Oratorio*, best known by his *Messiah*, but also composer of many *Operas, Concertos, Sonatas, Organ Music*, etc.

Franz Josef Haydn, b. Rohrau, March 31, 1742, d. Vienna, May 31, 1809. Father of the *Symphony* and pioneer in Sonata Form. *Oratorios, The Creation* and *The Seasons*, 125 *Symphonies*, 51 *Concertos*, 77 *String Quartets*, 14 *Masses*, four *Operas* and many other works.

Ruggiero Leoncavallo, b. Naples, Italy, March 8, 1858, d. Montecatini, near Florence, Aug. 9, 1919. His reputation rests almost entirely on one opera, *I Pagliacci* (The Clowns), produced in Milan in 1892, with Arturo Toscanini conducting the première. This short work, usually paired with Mascagni's *Cavalleria Rusticana*, is a permanently established success, with immense dramatic and musical appeal. The *Prologue* (baritone), *Bird Song* or *Ballatella* (soprano) and *Vesti la Giubba* (tenor) are all favorites with audiences. Leoncavallo's *Zaza* (1900) has also had some success, serving as a vehicle for Geraldine Farrar, and containing a popular baritone aria (*Zaza, piccola Zingara*).

Franz Liszt, b. Raiding, Oct. 22, 1811, d. Bayreuth, July 31, 1886. Most brilliant of all pianists and a successful composer in many forms. *Symphonic Poems, Les Préludes, Tasso*, etc., two *Symphonies*, 15 *Hungarian Rhapsodies, Nocturnes*, including *Liebestraum, Piano Etudes, Sonatas, Oratorio, St. Elizabeth, Songs, Church Music*, etc.

Edward MacDowell, b. New York, Dec. 18, 1861, d. New York, Jan. 23, 1908. America's best-known composer of serious music. *Indian Suite, Piano Concertos, Sonatas, Songs, Piano Music*, etc.

Gustav Mahler, b. Kalischt, July 7, 1860, d. Vienna, May 18, 1911. Conductor and composer of *Symphonies, Cantatas, Opera, Songs*, etc.

Pietro Mascagni, b. Leghorn, Italy, Dec. 7, 1863, d. Rome, Aug. 2, 1945. Known chiefly for one opera, *Cavalleria Rusticana*, "Heavenly Twin" of Leoncavallo's *I Pagliacci*, and winner of a prize offered by the publisher Sonzogno (1890). Its famous *Intermezzo* keeps it technically within one act. Santuzza's aria, *Voi lo sapete*, is also well known. Other operas by Mascagni are *Iris* and *L'Amico Fritz*.

Jules Massenet, b. Montreaux, May 12, 1842, d. Paris, Aug. 13, 1912.

Popular French composer of *Operas. Manon, Werther, Thais, Le Jongleur de Notre Dame*, etc. *Overtures, Piano Music, Songs*, etc.

FELIX MENDELSSOHN-BARTHOLDY, b. Hamburg, Feb. 3, 1809, d. Leipzig, Nov. 4, 1847. Prodigiously gifted composer in many forms. *Oratorio, Elijah; Overtures, A Midsummer Night's Dream, Fingal's Cave*, etc., four *Symphonies, Violin Concerto, Songs Without Words* (piano), *Chamber Music, Songs*, etc.

GIACOMO MEYERBEER, b. Berlin, Sept. 5, 1791, d. Paris, May 2, 1864. Composer of spectacular operas, with considerable influence on Wagner. His real name was Jakob Liebmann Beer. His best-known works are *Robert le Diable* (1831), *Les Huguenots* (1836), *Le Prophète* (1849) and *L'Africaine*, produced in 1865. The *Coronation March* from *Le Prophète* is often heard.

MODEST MOUSSORGSKY, b. March 21, 1839, d. St. Petersburg, March 28, 1881. Most nationalistic of Russian composers, and one of the greatest. *Operas, Boris Godounoff*, etc. *Pictures at an Exposition, Night on Bald Mountain, Songs*, etc.

WOLFGANG AMADEUS MOZART, b. Salzburg, Jan. 27, 1756, d. Vienna, Dec. 5, 1791. Possibly the greatest natural genius in all music, and a prolific composer in many forms. *Operas, The Marriage of Figaro, Don Giovanni, The Magic Flute*, etc., 41 *Symphonies*, 42 *Violin Sonatas, Piano Sonatas, Concertos, Chamber Music, Church Music, Requiem, Songs*, etc.

JACQUES OFFENBACH, b. Cologne, Germany, June 21, 1819, d. Paris, Oct. 5, 1880. Outstanding composer of opéra comique, best known today by his last and most serious work, *The Tales of Hoffmann*, first produced in 1881. Many popular tunes have been supplied by his *Orpheus in the Nether World* (*Can-Can*), *La Belle Hélène, La Vie Parisienne* and *La Grande Duchesse*. The tune of the *Marines' Hymn* came from his less-known *Genevieve of Brabant*.

GIOVANNI PIERLUIGI DA PALESTRINA, b. Palestrina, 1514, d. Rome, Feb. 2, 1594. Father of church music and master of the polyphonic style. 262 *Motets*, 92 *Masses*, 68 *Offertories*, 45 *Hymns*, etc.

GIACOMO PUCCINI, b. Lucca, Dec. 23, 1858, d. Brussels, Nov. 29, 1924. Popular Italian composer of *Operas. La Tosca, Madame Butterfly, La Bohème, Manon Lescaut*, etc.

HENRY PURCELL, b. London, 1658, d. Westminster, Nov. 21, 1695. England's most famous composer, with the opera, *Dido and Aeneas* (1690) considered his greatest work. He wrote much instrumental and vocal music, some of which is still heard, mostly in modern arrangements. One of his most popular songs is the setting of Shakespeare's *Come unto these yellow sands*.

Sergei Rachmaninoff, b. Onega, April 2, 1873, d. California, March 28, 1943. Outstanding contemporary Russian composer and pianist. *Symphonies, Piano Concertos, Operas, Choral Works, Preludes, Songs; Symphonic Poem, The Island of the Dead,* etc.

Maurice Ravel, b. Ciboure, March 7, 1875, d. Paris, Dec. 28, 1937. Important modern French composer, best known by his popular *Bolero. Opera, L'Heure Espagnole; Orchestral Pieces, La Valse, Daphnis and Chloë, Mother Goose; Piano Music, Pavane,* etc., *String Quartet, Trio* and other *Chamber Music.*

Nikolai Rimsky-Korsakoff, b. Tikhvin, May 21, 1844, d. Liubensk, June 21, 1908. Colorful Russian composer, of nationalistic style, strongly influenced by Orientalism. *Operas, The Snow Maiden, Coq d'Or, Sadko,* etc., three *Symphonies, Symphonic Suite, Scheherazade,* etc.

Gioacchino Rossini, b. Pesaro, Feb. 29, 1792, d. Ruelle, Nov. 13, 1868. Successful composer of Italian *Operas, William Tell, The Barber of Seville,* etc., much *Church Music,* including a popular *Stabat Mater.*

Anton Rubinstein, b. Bessarabia, Nov. 30, 1830, d. Peterhof, Nov. 20, 1894. Brilliant pianist and popular Russian composer. Six *Symphonies, Operas, The Demon,* etc., 100 *Songs, Cantatas, Concertos, Sonatas,* etc.

Camille Saint-Saëns, b. Paris, Oct. 9, 1835, d. Algiers, Dec. 16, 1921. Distinguished French composer. *Operas, Samson and Delilah,* etc., *Symphonies, Symphonic Poems, Danse Macabre,* etc., *Violin* and *Piano Concertos, Suite Algerienne, Carnival of the Animals, Songs, Piano Music.*

Franz Peter Schubert, b. Lichtenthal, Jan. 31, 1797, d. Vienna, Nov. 19, 1828. Musical genius of the greatest natural gifts, and a prolific composer in many forms. Ten *Symphonies,* over 600 *Songs, Operas, Masses, Chamber Music, Piano Pieces,* including *Impromptus, Moments Musicals,* etc.

Robert Schumann, b. Zwickau, June 8, 1810, d. Endenich, July 29, 1856. Outstanding Romantic composer and critic. Four *Symphonies,* much fine *Piano Music,* including *Papillons, Carnaval, Kreisleriana, Novelettes, Sonatas, Scenes from Childhood, Album for the Young,* many great *Songs, Overtures, Chamber Music,* etc.

Alexander Scriabin, b. Moscow, Jan. 10, 1872, d. there April 14, 1915. Russian mystic of importance in the development of modernism. His *Divine Poem, Poem of Ecstasy* and *Color Symphony* (*Prometheus*) are important orchestral works, and he also wrote much significant music for the piano.

Jean Sibelius, b. Tavastehus, Dec. 8, 1865. Most important contemporary composer, and Finland's greatest. Seven *Symphonies, Tone Poems,* including *Finlandia, The Swan of Tuonela, Songs, Piano Music, Valse Triste,* etc.

Johann Strauss, b. Vienna, Oct. 25, 1825, d. June 3, 1899. "The Waltz King." *Light Operas, Die Fledermaus,* etc. 400 *Waltzes* and other dance music, including the popular *Blue Danube, Artists' Life, Tales from the Vienna Woods,* etc.

Richard Strauss, b. Munich, June 11, 1864. One of the greatest of contemporary composers. *Operas, Elektra, Salome, Der Rosenkavalier,* etc. *Tone Poems, Don Juan, Don Quixote, Ein Heldenleben, Till Eulenspiegel, Death and Transfiguration, Symphonies, Sonatas, Chamber Music, Ballets,* many fine *Songs.*

Igor Stravinsky, b. Oranienbaum, June 17, 1882. Russia's leader among the modern composers. *Ballets, Petrouschka, The Fire Bird, Rites of Spring,* etc. *Symphony of Psalms, Oedipus Rex, Piano Concertos, Orchestral Music, Songs.*

Sir Arthur Sullivan, b. London, May 14, 1842, d. there Nov. 22, 1900. Popular English composer, best known for his light operas, written with Sir William S. Gilbert as librettist: *The Mikado, Pinafore, Patience, Iolanthe, The Pirates of Penzance, The Gondoliers, The Yeomen of the Guard, Princess Ida, Ruddigore, Trial by Jury,* etc. He also wrote the cantata, *The Golden Legend* (1886) and other choral works, the great hymn tune, *Onward, Christian Soldiers,* and many songs, of which the best known is *The Lost Chord.*

Peter Ilitch Tschaikowsky, b. Wotinsk, Dec. 25, 1840, d. St. Petersburg, Nov. 6, 1893. Most popular of the Russian composers. Six *Symphonies,* eleven *Operas, Eugen Onegin, Pique Dame,* etc., *Overtures, Romeo and Juliet,* 1812, *Francesca da Rimini, Nutcracker Suite,* etc., *Marche Slave, Violin* and *Piano Concertos, Songs, Chamber Music, Piano Pieces.*

Giuseppe Verdi, b. Le Roncole, Oct. 9, 1813, d. Milan, Jan. 27, 1901. Italy's greatest composer of *Operas, Aida, La Forza del Destino, Rigoletto, Il Trovatore, La Traviata, Otello, Falstaff, Un Ballo in Maschera, Simon Boccanegra,* etc., also the *Manzoni Requiem.*

Richard Wagner, b. Leipzig, May 22, 1813, d. Venice, Feb. 13, 1883. Greatest of dramatic composers, and creator of the music-drama, successor to old-fashioned opera. *Rienzi, The Flying Dutchman, Tannhäuser, Lohengrin, Das Rheingold, Die Walküre, Siegfried, Götterdämmerung, Tristan und Isolde, Die Meistersinger, Parsifal,* a *Faust Overture, Songs,* etc.

Carl Maria von Weber, b. Eutin, Dec. 18, 1786, d. London, June 5, 1826. Gifted pioneer of the Romantic school, important in the development of opera. *Der Freischütz, Oberon, Euryanthe, Piano Concertos, Concertstück, Invitation to the Dance, Symphonies, Songs,* etc.

SPECIAL RECORDS FOR CHILDREN

COLUMBIA

The Adventures of Bubble and Squeak, COLUMBIA MUSIC STORY GROUP, J-10.

Captain Kidd's Cats, CHILDREN'S MUSIC STORY GROUP, J-2.

Cherub the Chick, VERNON CRANE, J-4.

Christmas Fantasie, THIRZO-ALTIERI, J-22.

The Con Moto Rhythmic Series, DAVID BEANSON, J-16.

Edward, the Dignified Monkey, VERNON CRANE, J-13.

Folk Dances, CONDUCTED BY ARNOLD FOSTER AND VICTOR OLAF, J-21.

Great Surprise of Spring, VERNON CRANE, J-24.

Herman the Littlest Locomotive, VERNON CRANE, J-3.

How the Man in the Moon Lost His Face, THIRZO-ALTIERI, J-1.

Lullabies, BETTY MARTIN AND QUARTET, J-17.

Merry Music, BETTY MARTIN AND S. R. LEWIS, J-15.

Mike, the Tough Little Tugboat, VERNON CRANE, J-11.

Music Fairy Stories, YVONNE RAVELL AND HAROLD LEAMAN, J-19, 20, 23.

Nonsense Alphabet Suite, LEAR-NAGINSKI, J-12.

The Nursery, MOUSSORGSKY, J-14.

Our Songs, BETTY MARTIN AND S. R. LEWIS, J-8.

The Rollicking Roller Skates, VERNON CRANE, J-18.

Sugar Cookie Flats, VERNON CRANE, J-5.

DECCA

French Folk-Songs for Children. Vol. 1, LOUIS CHARTIER, BARITONE, A-4.

French Folk-Songs for Children. Vol. 2, LOUIS CHARTIER, BARITONE, A-24.

Tchaikowsky: Nutcracker Suite, SMALLENS, DECCA LITTLE SYM. ORCH., A-23.

Patriotic Songs for Children, BING CROSBY, FRANK LUTHER & CENTURY QUARTET, A-50.

The Wizard of Oz, JUDY GARLAND WITH VICTOR YOUNG & HIS ORCHESTRA, A-74.

Insect Pictures in Music, Decca Little Symphony Orch., Cesare Sodero, Conductor, A-84.

Animal Pictures in Music, Decca Little Symphony Orch., Cesare Sodero, Conductor, A-85.

The Symphony Orchestra, String Family, Decca Little Symphony Orch., under dir. of David Mendoza, A-90.

The Symphony Orchestra, Woodwind Family, A-91.

The Symphony Orchestra, Brass Family, A-92.

The Symphony Orchestra, Percussion Family, A-93.

Gulliver's Travels, Victor Young & His Orchestra with Soloists and Max Terr's Choristers, A-100.

The Song Hits from Walt Disney's "Pinocchio," Cliff Edwards with Victor Young & Orchestra, Ken Darby Singers, A-110.

An Album of Lullabies, Sung by Ireene Wicker, A-127.

Peter and the Wolf, Prokofieff, Decca Symphony Orchestra, Alexander Smallens, Conductor, Frank Luther, Narrator, A-130.

Novelty and Instrumental Selections for Children, Victor Young, Louis Katzman, Jack Hylton, Ted Fio Rito & Dick Robertson Orchestras, A-146.

Christmas Songs for Children, Harry Reser Orch., Men About Town, Dick Robertson Orch., Frank Luther, A-161.

Walt Disney, Best Remembered Songs from Shorts and Full Length Feature Cartoons. Played by Nat Brandywynne and His Orchestra, A-243.

School Days, Favorite songs of Childhood sung by Moylan Sisters, A-251.

Play Party Games, Vocal Square Dance Songs Sung by Frank Luther with the American Square Dance Orchestra, A-278.

Uncle Remus Stories, Three of the Joel Chandler Harris stories adapted by Edith and Tom McKnight. Narrated by Sterling Holloway, A-282.

Rounds and Jingles, Sung by King's Men. Male Quartet with Piano Acc., A-287.

A Christmas Carol, Ronald Colman as Scrooge, Supporting Cast, etc., A-290.

Sterling Holloway, Relating humorous stories of Ferdinand the Bull, Horace the Bear and Mulberry Street, A-309.

Rolito, Armando-Cleary, Songs and stories about the life and adventures of a little Mexican boy, told and sung in English and Spanish by Frank Luther and Llopis de Olivares. Jesse Crawford at the Organ, A-313.

Hans Christian Andersen Fairy Tales, Narrated by Jean Hersholt with Supporting Cast and Sound Effects. Jesse Crawford at the Organ, A-327.

The Count of Monte Cristo, Dumas. Adapted and directed

BY GEO. WELLS, HERBERT MARSHALL AS EDMOND DANTÈS WITH A SUPPORTING CAST, SOUND EFFECTS AND MUSIC. VICTOR YOUNG, MUSICAL DIRECTOR, A-337.

A Christmas Gift, The Story of the Juggler of Our Lady, AS TOLD BY JOHN NESBITT, NARRATION WITH CHOIR, A-357.

Snow White and the Seven Dwarfs, SELECTIONS FROM WALT DISNEY'S FEATURE PRODUCTION. MUSIC BY FRANK CHURCHILL. LYRICS BY LARRY MOREY. LYN MURRAY AND HIS ORCHESTRA AND CHORUS WITH EVELYN KNIGHT, HARRISON KNOX, AUDREY MARSH, ELIZABETH MULLINER, ANDY LOVE FOUR, A-368.

The Three Caballeros, MUSIC FROM THE WALT DISNEY PRODUCTION. PLAYED BY CHARLES WOLCOTT AND HIS ORCHESTRA, A-373.

Alice in Wonderland, STORY BY LEWIS CARROLL ADAPTED BY GEORGE WELLS WITH SONGS BY LEWIS CARROLL AND FRANK LUTHER. SOUND EFFECTS AND MUSIC. MUSICAL SCORE COMPOSED AND DIRECTED BY VICTOR YOUNG. GINGER ROGERS AS ALICE AND A SUPPORTING CAST. DIRECTED BY GEORGE WELLS, DA-376.

Mr. Pickwick's Christmas, (DICKENS) AS TOLD BY CHARLES LAUGHTON. WITH ORIGINAL MUSICAL ACC. COMPOSED AND CONDUCTED BY HANNS EISLER, DA-379.

Mother Goose Rhymes, FRANK LUTHER, K-1.

Nursery Rhymes, FRANK LUTHER, K-2.

Fairy Tales, FRANK LUTHER AND CO., K-3.

Tuneful Tales, FRANK LUTHER, K-4.

Bible Stories for Children, LUTHER, K-5.

Holidays, FRANK LUTHER, K-6.

Alice in Wonderland, FRANK LUTHER, K-7.

Babar Stories, FRANK LUTHER, K-8.

More Tuneful Tales, FRANK LUTHER, K-9.

Thirty-Two Children's Songs, LUTHER, K-10.

Children's Songs, SYBIL JASON, K-11.

Winnie the Pooh and *Christopher Robin*, FRANK LUTHER, K-12.

Hansel and Gretel and *The Sleeping Beauty*, TOLD BY IREENE WICKER, K-13.

Home on The Range, LUTHER & TRIO, K-14.

More Winnie the Pooh and *Christopher Robin*, FRANK LUTHER, K-15.

The Gay Nineties, FRANK LUTHER, ZORA LAYMAN AND THE CENTURY QUARTET, K-16.

Snow White and the Seven Dwarfs, FRANK LUTHER WITH ZORA LAYMAN, THE CLUBMEN AND BOB MACGIMSEY, K-17.

Raggedy Ann's Sunny and Joyful Songs, FRANK LUTHER, K-18.

Singing Game for Young Children, DECCA ORCHESTRA, K-19.

Songs of Safety, FRANK LUTHER, K-20.

Aesop's Fables in Song, FRANK LUTHER, K-21.

A Child's Garden of Verses, LUTHER, K-22.

More Babar Stories, FRANK LUTHER, K-23.

Minnie the Tired Trolley Car, Busybody Brothers, FRANK LUTHER, K-24.

Little Patriots, FRANK LUTHER, K-25.

Tarzan of the Apes, TARZAN PLAYERS, K-26.

More Mother Goose Rhymes, LUTHER, K-27.

Superman's Christmas Adventure, SUPERMAN PLAYERS DIR. JACK JOHNSTONE, K-28.

Tarzan and the Little Black Boy, TARZAN PLAYERS, K-29.

VICTOR

From the Book of Mother Goose, JAMES HARKINS, LOUIS JAMES, CLIFFORD JOHNS, JOSEPHINE THERESE, MARILYN MILLER AND BOBBY HASTINGS, B-5102, BK-2, 3, 4, B-7851, V-22135, V-22134, B-6159, V-22133, B-585-7, B-5270.

Uncle Mac's Nursery Rhymes, UNCLE MAC AND CHORUS, B-518-20.

Jolly Songs for Jack and Jean, VAUGHN DE LEATH, B-576-8.

Singing and Guessing Games, B-7901-2, B-573-5.

A Child's Garden of Verse, STEVENSON-MYERS, B-543-5.

Lullabies of Many Lands, LOLA MAE FLYNN, B-567-9.

Winnie the Pooh, Christopher Robin, MILNE-SIMPSON-LUTHER, J-2, J-6.

Raggedy Ann Songs, GRUELLE-WOODIN-LUTHER, J-1, J-4.

Songs from Shirley Temple Pictures, BK-1.

Little Black Sambo's Jungle Band, PAUL WING, BC-17.

The Magic Door, ALICE REMSEN, BC-5.

Mickey Mouse, WALT DISNEY, BC-3.

Mickey Mouse's Birthday Party, WAYNE KING, V-25419.

Pinocchio, WALT DISNEY, P-18.

Popeye, the Sailor, FLOYD BUCKLEY, B-6723-4.

Reg'lar Fellers at the Circus, IRVIN GRAHAM, BC-20.

Rumpelstiltskin, HELEN E. MYERS, BC-34.

Silly Symphony, WALT DISNEY, BC-2.

Songs Under the Sails, ERNEST LA PRADE, BC-8.

Snow White and the Seven Dwarfs, WALT DISNEY, J-8.

Uncle Ned's Stories, UNCLE NED, BC-13.

Winnie the Pooh Builds a House, MILNE-CRAIG MCDONNELL, BC-19.

Winnie the Pooh Goes Visiting, MILNE-CRAIG MCDONNELL, BC-7.

Hans Christian Andersen Stories, PAUL LEYSSAC, BC-10, 24, 32.

Androcles and the Lion, THE WONDERFUL PLAYERS, J-5.

East of the Sun and West of the Moon, SYLVIA JAMES, BC-28.

The Elephant's Child, KIPLING-PAUL WING, BC-15.

The 500 Hats of Bartholomew Cubbins, DR. SEUSS-PAUL WING, BC-26.

The Gingerbread Boy, MILTON CROSS, B-7937.

Little Black Sambo, PAUL WING, BC-6.

Little Red Riding Hood, MILTON CROSS, BC-4.

The Nutcracker of Nuremberg, HELENE M. CASKIN, BC-31.

Stories in Rhythm, THE KORALITES, BC-9.

Ferdinand and Wee Gillis, MUNRO LEAF-PAUL WING, BC-16.

Tinkle-Tonkle Town, ALICE REMSEN, BC-21.

BLUEBIRD CHILDREN'S RECORDS

The Three Little Pigs (WALT DISNEY) 39-3000

Uncle Mac's Nursery Rhymes, UNCLE MAC (DEREK MCCULLOCH OF THE B.B.C.) WITH STUART ROBERTSON, DOROTHY HELMRICH, CHILDREN'S CHORUS AND ORCHESTRA, 39-3001

Rock-a-Bye Parade (VAUGHN DE LEATH) 39-3002

Mother Goose Nursery Rhymes (JOSEPHINE THERESE, MARILYN MILLER AND BOBBY HASTINGS) 39-3003-39-3005

Let's Play (HELEN E. MYERS) 39-3006-39-3008

Singing Games (MADGE TUCKER-FRANK NOVAC) 39-3021

The Little Engine That Could (MABEL C. BRAGG-PAUL WING) 39-3023-39-3025

One String Fiddle (ERICK BERRY-LILLIAN WEBSTER) 39-3026-39-3028

Songs of the Zoo (JOHN AND LUCY ALLISON) 39-3029

Bertram and the Baby Dinosaur, Bertram and the Flying Horse (PAUL T. GILBERT) 39-3030-39-3032

The Sheep and the Pig Who Set Up Housekeeping (GUDRIN THORNE-THOMSEN) 39-3033

The Christmas Adventure of Billy and Betty (BARBARA AND ERNEST CHAPPELL) 39-3035-39-3037

Little Masters Records

MUSIC YOU ENJOY

1. *Blue Danube Waltz*, STRAUSS.
   Marche Militaire, SCHUBERT.
2. *Liebestraum*, LISZT.
   2nd. Hungarian Rhapsody, LISZT.
3. *Ride of the Valkyries*, WAGNER.
   Pizzicato Polka, DELIBES.
4. *Minuet*, MOZART.
   The Poet Speaks, SCHUMANN.
5. *Chinese Dance and Trepak*, From *Nutcracker Suite*, TSCHAIKOWSKY.
   Marche Slave, TSCHAIKOWSKY.
6. *Anitra's Dance*, GRIEG.
   In the Hall of the Mountain King, GRIEG.
7. *Tales from the Vienna Woods*, STRAUSS.
   March of the Dragoons, BIZET.
8. *Träumerei*, SCHUMANN.
   Pilgrims' Chorus, WAGNER.

9. *Minuet from Don Juan*, MOZART.
   Overture to *William Tell*, ROSSINI.

10. Prayer from *Hansel and Gretel*, HUMPERDINCK.
    Triumphal March from *Aida*, VERDI.

11. *Nocturne*, MENDELSSOHN.
    Dance of the Hours, PONCHIELLI.

12. *Aragonaise*, BIZET.
    Overture to *Carmen*, BIZET.

14. *Finlandia*, SIBELIUS.
    Salut D'Amour, ELGAR.

15. *Moment Musical*, SCHUBERT.
    Gavotte from *Mignon*, THOMAS.

16. *Londonderry Air* (IRISH TUNE).
    Gopak, MOUSSORGSKY.

17. Ballet Music from *Faust*, GOUNOD.
    Valse Triste, SIBELIUS.

18. Prelude to Act 3, *Lohengrin*, WAGNER.
    Rakoczy March, BERLIOZ.

19. *Coronation March*, MEYERBEER.
    Minuet in G, BEETHOVEN.

20. *Spanish Caprice*, RIMSKY-KORSAKOFF.
    Gigue, BACH.

21. *Prelude No. 20*, Opus 28, CHOPIN.
    Intermezzo from *Cavalleria Rusticana*, MASCAGNI.

22. Dance of the Toy Pipes (from *Nutcracker Suite*), TSCHAIKOWSKY.
    Turkish March, BEETHOVEN.

23. *Gavotte*, BACH.
    Bourrée in G, BACH.

24. *Country Dances* Nos. 1 & 7, BEETHOVEN.
    Country Dance No. 12, BEETHOVEN.

25. *La Traviata* Prelude, VERDI.
    Ballet Music from *Sylvia*, DELIBES.

Pied Piper Children's Records

MUSIC YOU ENJOY

1. Carry Me Back to Old Virginny
   Oh, Susanna
2. Skaters' Waltz
   Blue Danube
3. Waltz of the Flowers
   Schubert Waltz
4. March of a Marionette
   March of the Three Kings
5. Marche Lorraine
   President's March (Hail Columbia)
6. Marche Militaire
   Tramp, Tramp, Tramp, the Boys are Marching
7. March of the Dwarfs
   Marche Slave
8. Turkey in the Straw
   The Arkansas Traveler
9. Comin' Thru the Rye
   Old Folks at Home
10. Polka
    When They Played the Polka
11. The Irish Washerwoman
    La Cucaracha
12. Camptown Races
    Minuet

14. Farmer in the Dell
    A Tisket, A Tasket–Pussy Cat, Pussy Cat
15. London Bridge is Falling Down.
    Hi Diddle Diddle–Little Jack Horner
16. Twinkle, Twinkle, Little Star
    Sing a Song of Sixpence
17. Little Bo Peep
    Mary Had a Little Lamb
18. Jack and Jill
    All Around the Mulberry Bush
19. Home on the Range
    Wait for the Wagon
20. Git Along, Little Dogies
    Lone Prairie
21. Comin' Round the Mountain
    Good-bye, Old Paint
22. The Red River Valley
    The Chisholm Trail

Listen Look Picture Books

MUSIC YOU ENJOY

Little Red Riding Hood.
Little Black Sambo.
The Three Little Pigs.
Myrtle The Turtle.
Alice in Wonderland.
Cinderella.

Melodyland Record Book, (ORCHESTRA CONDUCTED BY ERNO RAPEE; NARRATION BY MILTON CROSS.) SIX MUSICAL FAIRY TALES IN EIGHT RECORDINGS: *Billy Bee; The Farmer in the Dell; The Silver Nutcracker; Old King Cole; The Ugly Duckling; The Wicked Witch.*

GLOSSARY OF COMMON MUSICAL TERMS

A—The first letter of the musical alphabet, representing a standard pitch of 440 vibrations per second. The letter is applied also to any octave above or below this pitch and to the diatonic major and minor scales beginning on that tone. It is the tone to which the orchestra tunes, invariably sounded by the oboe.

A—Italian preposition, by, from, to, at, in.

ABSOLUTE—Self-sufficient, as applied to music that requires no words or program.

ABSOLUTE PITCH—The ability to recognize or sound any pitch without the help of the keyboard.

ACCELERANDO—Growing faster.

ACCENT—The emphasis on a tone or beat, which may be either natural or artificial.

ACCIDENTAL—A sharp or flat turning up "accidentally," without being in the signature.

ACCOMPANIMENT—A secondary part added to a melody.

ACCORDION—A reed instrument played by a double bellows, with keys for the melody and buttons for the accompaniment.

ACOUSTICS—The science of sound.

ADAGIO—Slow; a slow movement or division of a symphony or sonata.

ADAPTATION—Arrangement or transcription.

AGITATO—Agitated.

AIR—Melody; aria.

ALBERTI BASS—An accompaniment of simple broken chords, named for its inventor.

ALLA BREVE—Doubling the time.

ALLEGRETTO—A little slower than allegro.

ALLEGRO—Literally happy, hence in rapid time.

ALLEMANDE—German dance, generally in triple time, used as a movement of the classic suite.

ALT—High; used of tones in the octave above the treble staff.

ALTER—To change a chord by the addition of one or more accidentals.

ALTO—Originally high (falsetto in men's voices) but now applied to the low female voice. A position of the C clef covering this range. A form of horn common in brass bands.

ANDANTE—Literally "going" or "walking," hence fairly slow.

ANDANTINO—A little faster than andante.

ANIMATO—With animation.

ANSWER—The second subject of a fugue.

ANTHEM—A piece of sacred music for several voices.

APPOGGIATURA—A grace-note.

ARABESQUE—A decoration. A graceful piece of music.

ARCO—The bow. (Used in contrast to *pizzicato* for stringed instruments when the bow resumes after plucking.)

ARIA—Air, song, melody, particularly in opera and oratorio.

ARPEGGIO—Played in the manner of a harp. (Generally applied to chords on the piano.)

ATTACK—The way voices or instruments strike the beginning of a phrase of music.

AUBADE—A morning song, opposite of a serenade.

AUGMENT—To increase a major interval by half a tone. A chord containing such an interval is called *augmented*.

AUTHENTIC—The notes between the tonic and the dominant above, those between the tonic and the dominant below being called *plagal*. The authentic modes are credited to St. Ambrose.

B—The second letter of the musical alphabet, a whole tone higher than A, with its octaves and major and minor scales. (The German B means B-flat, and our B they call H [Ha].)

BAGATELLE—A trifling piece.

BAGPIPE—An ancient wind instrument.

BALALAIKA—A Russian guitar of triangular shape.

BALLAD—A piece of music in ballad style.

BALLATA—A dance tune or simple song.

BALLET—An elaborate dance, or the performance of it. Also a form of glee (with the t sounded).

BAND—A group of instrumentalists.

BANJO—A stringed instrument with a drumlike body, popular among the Negroes.

BAR—A vertical line separating one measure from another, often incorrectly used of the measure itself.

BARD—A minstrel.

BARITONE (BARYTONE)—The male voice (or the singer himself) between the bass and tenor range.

BASE—The root of a chord.

BASS (BASSO)—The lowest part in a harmony, or the voice or instrument sounding that part. (Applied particularly to the lowest male voice, the bass-viol and the tuba.)

BASSOON—A double-reed instrument representing the bass of the woodwind.

BEAT—The pulse or measure of music, or the action of a conductor indicating it.

BEL—Beautiful, as in *bel canto,* "beautiful song."

BELL—A metallic instrument set in vibration by a clapper or hammer. Also the widening of a horn.

BEN—Well, good; as in *ben sostenuto,* well sustained.

BERCEUSE—Cradle song.

BERGERETTE—Shepherd song.

BOUCHÉ—Stopped or covered (used of horns and pipes).

BOURRÉE—An old dance, appearing in the classic suite.

BOW—A stick strung with horsehair for setting strings in vibration.

BRACE—The connection between two staves of music.

BRASS—The brass section of an orchestra.

BRAVURA—Showing brilliance.

BREVE—A long note (originally short) equal to two whole tones. *Alla breve,* doubling the time.

BRIDGE—The piece of wood holding up the strings of the viol family.

BRINDISI—A drinking song.

BRIO—Vigor, fire, as in *con brio,* with spirit.

BROKEN—Not played simultaneously (used of the notes in a chord).

BUFFA—Comic.

BUGLE—A military horn.

BURDEN—A recurrent refrain. A drone-bass.

BUTTON—The knob on a violin to which the strings are attached.

C—The third letter of the musical alphabet, representing the pitch of 256 vibrations per second (Middle C), and its octaves. The normal scale without sharps or flats (also called Do).

CADENCE—A close. The perfect or complete cadence consists of a dominant chord followed by a tonic; the imperfect or incomplete, of a tonic followed by a dominant. A plagal cadence is the subdominant chord followed by the tonic.

CANON—Literally "rule." A melody harmonizing with itself, in the same or a different key.

CANTABILE—In singing style.

CANTATA—Originally music to be sung rather than played (sonata). Later a form of sacred or secular music, similar to oratorio but shorter.

CANTO—Song, melody, voice, as in *col canto*, "with the voice." The art of singing.

CANTO FERMO, *see* Cantus firmus.

CANTOR—Singer, particularly a leader or soloist in ecclesiastical song.

CANTUS—Song, melody.

CANTUS FIRMUS—Plain-song. The chief melody in contrapuntal music.

CANZONA—Folk-song, part-song.

CAPO—The beginning, as in *da capo*, "from the beginning."

CAPO-DASTRO, or CAPOTASTO—A bar clamped over strings to change their pitch simultaneously.

CAPPELLA—Chapel. A band of musicians. *A cappella*—without instrumental accompaniment.

CAPRICE—A whimsical, capricious piece of music.

CARILLON—A set of bells on which tunes can be played.

CAROL—A song, particularly for Christmas.

CATCH—A round in which the singers catch up their lines.

CAVATINA—A melody of one strain.

CELESTA—A keyboard instrument producing tinkling sounds.

CÉLESTE—Celestial, applied to organ stops of soft, sweet tone.

CELLO—The common abbreviation of *violoncello*.

CEMBALO—Harpsichord, cymbal.

CHACONNE (CIACCONA)—A slow dance, in triple time, with a ground bass; similar to the *passacaglia*.

CHAMBER MUSIC—Music composed for a small room.

CHANSON—A song or ballad.

CHANT—Originally a song but now applying to the ecclesiastical type of song, repeating many syllables on a single note.

CHAPEL—Musicians in the retinue of a patron.

CHIME—A set of bells tuned to a special pattern.

CHOIR—A group of singers in a church. A section of the orchestra.

CHORAL—Pertaining to a choir or chorus.

CHORALE—Choral psalm or hymn, particularly the early German Protestant type of hymn.

CHORD—A combination of three or more tones in harmony.

CHORUS—A group of singers or the music composed for them. A refrain.

CHROMATIC—Literally "colored," referring to the addition of accidentals to chords or melodies. The chromatic scale is composed entirely of half-tones.

CLARINET—A popular wood-wind instrument with a single reed.

CLAVICHORD—An ancestor of the piano, with strings set in vibration by small brass wedges, called "tangents."

CLAVIER—The keyboard of a clavichord, also used for the instrument itself.

CLEF—A sign indicating the general pitch of the staff. The commonest clefs are the treble (G) and the bass (F). There is also a C clef, known as soprano, tenor, or alto, according to its position on the staff.

CLOSE—A cadence.

CLOSE HARMONY—Harmony in which the tones lie close together.

COLOR—Timbre; quality of tone.

COLORATURA—"Colored," hence brilliant, florid.

COMMA—A breathing-mark.

COMMON TIME—Four beats to a measure.

COMPOUND—Intervals beyond the octave. Used also of time that has subdivisions of the principal beats, as 9-8, 12-8.

CONCERT—A public performance of music.

CONCERT GRAND—The largest grand piano.

CONCERTINA—A small accordion.

CONCERTINO—A small concerto.

CONCERTMEISTER—Concertmaster. The leader of the first violins in an orchestra.

CONCERTO—A composition for one or more solo instruments with orchestral accompaniment.

CONCERTO GROSSO—A composition for full orchestra.

CONCERT PITCH—A pitch higher than standard.

CONCORD—Harmonious combination of tones.

CONDUCTOR—The director of a chorus or orchestra.

CONSECUTIVE—Following in immediate succession, as of intervals in harmony.

CONSONANCE—An agreeable combination of sounds.

CONSONANT CHORD—One without a dissonant interval.

CONTRA (CONTRE)—Literally, under or against, generally referring to a pitch an octave lower, as *contrabass.*

CONTRALTO—The lowest female voice (often called "alto").

CONTRAPUNTAL—Relating to counterpoint.

CONTREDANSE—A country dance in which the dancers stand opposite each other.

CORDA (CORD)—String; *una corda,* using one string (the soft pedal shifting the piano hammer from three strings to one). Vocal cord.

CORNET—Loosely used of *cornet à pistons.*

CORNET À PISTONS—A three-valved chromatic brass instrument of the trumpet family, popular in brass bands.

COUNT—A beat of time. To count time is to number the beats.

COUNTER(-)—Prefix indicating contrast. *Counter-tenor,* higher than the usual tenor; *counter-bass,* lower than the usual bass; *counter-subject,* the answering subject in a fugue.

COUNTERPOINT—Literally, note against note (point against point), a counter-melody. Also the art of combining melodies in harmony with each other.

COURANTE—Literally "running," an old dance in triple time, used in the classic suite.

CRESCENDO—Increasing in loudness.

CROTCHET—A quarter-note.

CSÁRDÁS—A Hungarian (Magyar) dance in duple time, composed of two parts, the *lassu* or slow movement, and the *friska* (friss) or fast movement.

CYMBALS—Metal plates used for a clashing sound.

CZYMBALOM—A Hungarian dulcimer played with drum-sticks.

D—The fourth letter in the musical alphabet, representing a whole tone above C, and its octaves.

DA—By, from, for, through, as in *da capo* (D.C.), from the beginning; *dal segno* (D.S.), from the sign.

DAMPER—A cushion which stops the vibrations of piano strings. It is raised by the *damper pedal* which permits the tone to continue and is hence called the "loud pedal."

DANSE (DANZA)—A dance.

DECRESCENDO—Decreasing in loudness.

DELICATO—Delicately.

DEMI—Half, as in demiquaver, half an eighth note (quaver).

DEMIQUAVER (or SEMIQUAVER)—A sixteenth note.

DEMISEMIQUAVER — A thirty-second note (half a sixteenth).

DERIVATIVE—The root of a chord. An inversion.

DESCANT—*See* Discant.

DESTRA—Right, as in *destra mano*, "right hand"; *colla destra*, "with the right hand."

DEVELOPMENT—Working out; free fantasy. The second section in sonata form.

DI—Of, with, for, from, by.

DIAPASON—An octave.

DIAPHONY—The earliest form of two-voiced harmony.

DIATONIC—The regular scale of any key, literally "going through" the tonality without any accidentals.

DIMINISHED—Used of intervals which are a semitone smaller than the minor or perfect intervals, and also of chords containing such intervals.

DIMINUENDO (DIM.)—Diminishing in loudness; *dim. molto*, "with extreme diminution of power."

DIMINUTION—Opposite of augmentation, meaning the repetition or imitation of a theme in shorter notes.

DISCANT (DISCANTUS)—In early counterpoint, the adding of parts to a melody, often extemporaneously. Also the highest voice in such a harmony.

DISSONANCE—Discord. Technically a combination of tones that require motion or resolution into some other chord, but not necessarily discordant.

DISSONANT—Not technically concordant.

DIVERTIMENTO (DIVERTISSEMENT)—A musical diversion. In a fugue, an episode.

DIVISI—Divided. Used of instruments playing two parts from the same music.

DIVISION—A variation. A long note divided into short notes. A series of notes sung on one syllable. A double bar.

DO—The syllable applied to the first note of a scale in the Solfa system.

DOLCE—Sweet, soft.

DOMINANT—The fifth tone of the diatonic scale.

DOPPIO—Double, as in *doppio movimento*, "twice as fast."

DOT—A point placed after a note to increase its duration by one half. A point placed above or below a note to indicate that it is to be played staccato.

DOUBLE—To add an octave to the tones of any part; to give the same tones to different instruments. Adjective, twofold, as in double flat or sharp (two flats or sharps), double reed (two reeds), double concerto (for two solo instruments), double quartet (eight voices).

DOUBLE-BASS—The bass-viol.

DOUBLE-BASSOON—An octave lower than the regular bassoon.

DOUBLE-COUNTERPOINT—Having parts that can be inverted.

DOUBLE-FUGUE—A fugue with two subjects.

DOUBLE-STOP—Two notes played simultaneously on a stringed instrument.

DOWN-BEAT—The accent in a measure, or the motion indicating this accent.

DRONE-BASS—Monotonous bass.

DRUM—The commonest instrument of percussion, having many forms. Bass-drum, the lowest sounding drum. Kettledrum, shaped like a kettle and having a distinct pitch. Side drum, snare drum, the small drum generally combined with the bass drum.

DUET—A composition for two singers, or instrumentalists.

DULCIMER—An ancient instrument played with hammers.

DUPLE TIME—Double time, consisting of two beats to the measure or four counted as two.

DURCHKOMPONIERT—Literally "composed through," as contrasted with the use of the same melody for each stanza of a song.

E—The fifth letter in the musical alphabet, representing a full tone above D, and its octaves.

E (ED)—And.

ECOSSAIS (E)—A Scottish dance.

EMBELLISHMENT—Ornament, decoration.

EMBOUCHURE—The mouthpiece of a wind instrument.

ENCORE—Again; demand for repetition.

ENGLISH HORN—The alto oboe (*cor anglais*).

ENHARMONIC—Literally, having more than the twelve intervals of the chromatic scale. Also used of a change of notation without change of sound (as C-sharp to D-flat).

ENSEMBLE—A group of musicians, or the effect of the whole.

ENTR'ACTE—Music played between the acts.

EPISODE—Incidental portion of a composition, as in a fugue.

ETUDE—A study.

EXPOSITION—The first section of sonata form, introducing the chief themes.

F—The sixth letter in the musical alphabet, half a tone above E, and its octaves.

FA (Fah)—The fourth of the syllables of the Solfa system.

FAGOT (FAGOTTO)—Bassoon.

FALSETTO—A high, artificial register of the human voice, having an unnatural, effeminate sound.

FANDANGO—A popular Spanish dance in triple time.

FANFARE—A trumpet flourish.

FANTASIA (FANTASIE)—Fantasy, caprice, a composition in free form. Free fantasia, or fantasy, the development section in sonata form.

FERMATA (E)—The symbol, sometimes called a "bird's-eye," to indicate that the note under it is to be held.

FIFE—Small flute.

FIFTH—The dominant, or fifth tone in the scale. An interval containing five tones, counting both top and bottom.

FIGURATION—The use of ornamental passages in the variation on a theme.

FIGURE—A pattern or design of notes. The number used to indicate the chord on a bass note. Part of a dance.

FINALE—The last part of a composition.

FINGERING—The manner of using the fingers on an instrument, or the symbols indicating this.

FIORITURA—Florid ornament.

FIRST—The highest part or voice. A unison.

FLAGEOLET—A small flute played through the end. A harmonic.

FLAT—A symbol lowering the note before which it is placed by half a tone; if in the signature, it affects every note occurring on its line or space. *Double flat* lowers the note two half-tones. The word flat is also used of minor intervals.

FLORID—Embellished; ornamented.

FLUTE—An instrument of the woodwind family (though often made of metal). Also an organ-stop giving a similar tone.

FOLK-MUSIC—Music of the people.

FOLK-SONG—Vocal folk-music.

FORM—The organizing factor which creates a complete composition.

FORTE—Loud.
FORTISSIMO—Very loud.
FREE—Unrestrained by strict rules.
FRENCH HORN—The brass horn of the orchestra.
FRET—A ridge across the neck of stringed instruments to indicate the tones of the scale.
FRISKA (FRISS)—The fast movement in a Csárdás, or Hungarian rhapsody.
FUGUE—A composition in which one theme or subject is imitated by others, in the manner of a flight (*fuga*) and pursuit.
FULL—Complete, as in "full orchestra" and "full organ."
FUNDAMENTAL—The root of a chord. The basic tone to which overtones are added.
G—The seventh letter in the musical alphabet, a full tone above F, and its octaves.
GALLIARD—An old dance.
GAMUT—The scale.
GAVOTTE—An old French dance, appearing in the classic suite.
GEDACKT—Stopped (of organ pipes).
GIGUE—Jig; an old dance.
GLEE—Unaccompanied secular composition for three or more voices.
GRACE—A decorative note or combination of notes.
GRAND—Large, great, applied to pianos, operas, etc.
GRAZIA—Grace, elegance.
GREGORIAN—In the style of church music introduced by Pope Gregory.
GROSSO—Large, great, grand, full.
H—The German letter for B-natural. (The German B means B-flat.)
HAMMER—That part of the mechanism of a piano which strikes the strings and produces the tone.
HARMONIC—As an adjective, musical, concordant; harmonious, the opposite of melodic. The flageolet tone of a stringed instrument.
HARMONICA—A familiar reed instrument.
HARMONY—The organizing factor in music by which the tones are sounded simultaneously with pleasing effect.
HARP—A familiar stringed instrument, of great antiquity.
HARPSICHORD — Forerunner of the piano, with the tones produced by quills instead of hammers.
HAUTBOIS—The oboe.
HOLD—A fermata or "bird's-eye."
HOMOPHONIC—Emphasizing a single melody, with accompaniment.
HORN—A general term covering most wind instruments of metal. Also used specifically of the French horn (*Waldhorn*).
HYMN—A sacred song.
IMITATION—The repetition of a theme or subject by another voice, either note for note (canon) or with slight changes (augmentation, diminution, etc).
IMPERFECT—Not perfect, incomplete. *See* Perfect.
IMPROVISATION—Literally, extemporaneous performance, hence also a composition of informal style.
IMPROVISE—To make music extemporaneously.
INSTRUMENTATION—The art or manner of writing music for instruments.
INTERVAL—The distance between two tones, counting both top and bottom.
INTONATION—Pitch of sound.
INTRODUCTION—Preliminary music.
INVENTION—A contrapuntal study with one theme.
INVERSION—Transposition of the notes of a chord, interval, theme, or of parts in harmony.
KEY—The starting point of a scale (tonic) or the foundation of a harmony. The visible representative of each tone of a piano or organ.
KEYBOARD—The set of keys on a piano or organ.
KEYNOTE—The tonic.

LA—The sixth interval in the Solfa system.

LÄNDLER—Ancestor of the waltz.

LARGAMENTE—Broadly.

LARGHETTO—Not quite so slow as largo.

LARGO—Slow, broad. Usually taken as slower than *lento*.

LEAD—The leading part. (A voice or instrument.)

LEADER—Conductor, director.

LEADING—Guiding, predominant. *Leading tone*, the seventh step in the scale (leading into the tonic).

LEADING-MOTIVE—See Leitmotif.

LEGER (LEDGER) LINE—A short line above or below the staff.

LEGATO—Literally "bound," hence in a smooth, connected manner.

LEGGERAMENTE—Lightly.

LEGNO—Wood, as in *col legno*, played with the wood of the bow.

LEITMOTIF—Leading-motive. Wagner's musical label for a character, episode, etc., consisting generally of only a few tones, easily recognized.

LENTO—Very slow.

LIBRETTO—Text of an opera or oratorio.

LIED—German for song. Specifically, the German type of art-song.

LOURE—An old French dance.

LUTE—An ancient stringed instrument similar to the mandolin and guitar.

LYRE—Perhaps the oldest of all stringed instruments.

LYRIC—Songlike. Also used loosely of the words of a popular song.

MAESTRO—Master.

MAJOR—Literally "greater," as opposed to minor. Applying to intervals greater than the minor.

MANDOLIN—A popular stringed instrument descended from the lute.

MANUAL—Keyboard of an organ.

MARCH (MARCHE, MARCIA, MARSCH)—A composition to accompany marching, actually or theoretically.

MASS—Part of the Roman Catholic service, consisting of the Kyrie, Gloria, Credo, Sanctus, Benedictus, and Agnus Dei, creating an elaborate form of vocal music.

ME (MI)—The third interval in the Solfa system.

MEASURE—The unit of rhythm, including the notes between two bars, containing one major accent.

MEDIANT—The third note of the scale.

MEDLEY—A mixture of tunes.

MELODEON—An American organ.

MELODIC—Having to do with melody as opposed to harmony.

MELODY—Tune. A logical progression of tones, organized as to pitch. The leading part.

MENO—Less; as in *meno mosso*, "not so fast."

MENUET (MENUETTO)—*See* Minuet.

METER (METRE)—The arrangement of rhythmic units, or measures.

METHOD—System of instruction.

METRONOME—An instrument produced by Maelzel for sounding the beat of music.

MEZZO—Half, as in *mezza voce*, "half voice"; *mezzo soprano*, "medium soprano"; *mezzo piano* or *forte*, "medium soft" or "loud."

MIDDLE C—The C nearest the middle of the piano keyboard.

MINOR—Literally "smaller," hence intervals smaller than major.

MINSTREL—An itinerant singer.

MINUET—A stately dance in triple time. *Minuetto*, a little faster.

MISSA—A Mass; *Missa brevis*, short Mass.

MIXED—Composed of male and female voices.

MIXTURE—A compound organ stop.

MODERATO—Moderate in time.

MODE—An old word for scale, used in Greek and ecclesiastical music.

MODULATE—To change logically from one key to another.

MODULATION—Change of key.

MOLTO—Much, very.

MONOCHORD—An instrument of one string with a movable bridge for determining intervals and pitch.

MONODIC—With one voice predominating, as in a melody with accompaniment.

MONOTONE—Uniformity of pitch.

MORDANT (MORDENT)—A double grace-note, or short trill.

MOSSO—Literally "moved," hence rapid.

MOTET—A sacred madrigal.

MOTIF—Motive, subject, melodic pattern.

MOTION—Progression.

MOTIVE—A brief melodic phrase or pattern.

MOTO—Motion, speed; as in *con moto*.

MOVEMENT—Rate of speed. Style of rhythm. One of the chief divisions of a composition, generally complete in itself.

MUSE—One of the nine goddesses of art.

MUSETTA—A small oboe. A bagpipe. A short pastoral dance tune with a drone-bass.

MUSIC—The organization of sound toward beauty.

MUSIC-DRAMA—Opera of the Wagnerian type.

MUTE—A device for muffling tone.

NATURAL—The sign canceling a sharp or flat.

NINTH—The interval of an octave plus a second.

NOCTURNE (NOTTURNO)—A composition of dreamy, nocturnal mood, created by John Field and immortalized by Chopin.

NOTE—A character representing a musical tone. (Often used to mean the tone itself.)

NUANCE—Shade of expression.

NUMBER—A piece of music. A figure used for identifying such a piece.

OBBLIGATO—Literally "indispensable," hence a part which cannot be omitted, although now generally understood as an optional part, by an instrument accompanying a voice, etc.

OBOE—A double-reed instrument, of great importance among the wood-winds.

OCTAVE—The series of eight diatonic tones from one letter to its duplicate above or below, or the eighth tone itself.

OCTET—A composition for eight parts, or a group of eight musicians.

ODE—An elaborate song of dignified type.

OPEN—Unstopped (of a string), not closed at the top (of a pipe), with tones spread out (of a chord).

OPERA—The musical presentation of drama.

OPERA BUFFA (BOUFFE)—Low-comedy opera.

OPÉRA COMIQUE—Opera containing spoken words. *Grand opera*, the most elaborate type. *Light opera*, *operetta*, a less serious treatment.

OPUS (OP.)—Work, composition.

ORATORIO—Sacred opera, performed without action, costume, or scenery.

ORCHESTRA—The largest and most important group of instrumentalists. *Symphony orchestra*, one capable of playing symphonic music.

ORGAN—A wind instrument, with one or more keyboards.

ORGANUM—The earliest polyphonic music.

OSSIA (OSIA)—Or, otherwise.

OSTINATO—Literally "obstinate," hence continuous, as in *basso ostinato*, a ground-bass.

OVERTONE—Partial tone, blending inaudibly with the fundamental tone.

OVERTURE—The prelude to an opera or oratorio, sometimes an independent composition of this type.

P.—Abbreviation of *piano* (soft), and sometimes Pedal.

PARALLEL—Moving at an equal distance, as consecutive intervals.

PARAPHRASE—Free transcription.

PARLANDO (PARLANTE) — Literally "speaking," hence in a recitative manner.

PART—The music of an individual voice or instrument. Division of a composition.

PART-SONG—A song for three or more voices.

PARTIAL—A harmonic or overtone.

PARTITA—Variations, or a suite.

PARTITUR—A full score for voices or instruments.

PASSACAGLIA (PASSACAILLE)—A chaconne with a ground-bass.

PASSAGE—Phrase, section, figure, run.

PASSEPIED—A lively old French dance in triple time.

PASSING TONE—A brief dissonance.

PASSION—A musical setting of the Passion of Christ, in the style of oratorio.

PASTORAL—Rustic, having to do with shepherds.

PAUSA (PAUSE)—A rest; *lunga pausa,* "a long pause."

PAVANE—A grave, stately dance originally in triple time.

PEDAL—A device for controlling tone with the foot.

PEDAL-TONE (NOTE, or POINT)—A tone sustained by the pedal or some voice, usually the bass, while the other parts move independently.

PERCUSSION—Striking, as of drums, cymbals, etc.

PERFECT CADENCE—A close on the tonic from the dominant.

PERFECT INTERVAL—A fourth, fifth, or an octave.

PERIOD—A passage containing two or more phrases and some form of cadence.

PHRASE—The musical parallel to a phrase in speech.

PIACERE (A)—At pleasure.

PIANISSIMO (PP.)—Very soft.

PIANO (P.)—Soft.

PIANOFORTE—The familiar keyed percussion instrument playing "soft and loud," now abbreviated to piano.

PICCOLO—A small flute.

PICK—A plectrum.

PIECE—A composition. An instrument in an orchestra or band.

PIPE—A tone-producing tube of reed, wood, or metal.

PITCH—The relative height or depth of a tone.

PITCH PIPE—Small reed pipe, of fixed pitch.

PIÙ—More, as in *più mosso,* more speed.

PIZZICATO—Plucked, instead of bowed (of strings).

PLAGAL CADENCE—A close on the tonic from the subdominant.

PLAGAL MODE—One of the modes added by Gregory.

PLAIN-CHANT (PLAIN-SONG)—The old Gregorian church music, unaccompanied.

PLECTRUM—A pick.

PLUS—More.

POCO—A little; rather; somewhat. *Poco a poco,* little by little.

POINT—Dot; staccato-mark.

POLKA—A round dance in lively 2-4 time.

POLONAISE—Polish national dance in triple time.

PORTAMENTO—Gliding, with voice, or by sliding a finger on a stringed instrument.

POSITION—The placing of tones in a chord. The position of the left hand in violin-playing.

POT POURRI—Medley.

PRELUDE (PRELUDIO, PRAELUDIUM)—An introductory phrase, section or composition.

PREPARATION—A method of preparing the mind for a discord by previously introducing the dissonant note.

PRESTO (PRESTISSIMO)—Very fast.

PRIMA (PRIMO)—First, as in *tempo primo*, the original tempo.

PRIMA DONNA—First lady, hence leading singer; *prima ballerina*, "first dancer."

PROGRESSION—Movement, melodic or harmonic.

QUARTER (NOTE)—A crotchet, half of a half-note.

QUARTER-TONE—An interval of half a half-tone.

QUASI—As if.

QUAVER—An eighth note.

QUINTET (QUINTETTE, QUINTETTO)—A five-part composition, or the group of five musicians.

RANGE—Compass.

RE—The second syllable in the Solfa system.

RECITATIVE (RECIT., RECITATIVO)—An unrhythmical style of singing in the manner of a recitation or a declamation.

RECITAL—A musical performance given by one performer.

REED—A thin strip of wood or metal, set in vibration by a current of air.

REEL—A lively dance.

REFRAIN—A burden, or chorus.

REGISTER—A set of pipes, or the stop controlling them. Part of the range of a voice (upper, lower, etc.).

RELATION—An affinity of keys or chords.

REPEAT—A sign indicating the repetition of a passage.

REPRISE—Repetition or reappearance of a theme.

REQUIEM—Mass for the dead.

RESOLUTION—The dissolving of dissonance into concord.

RESONANCE—The reinforcement of tone.

REST—A rhythmic pause.

RHAPSODY—An informal composition of the rhapsodic type.

RHYTHM—The organizing factor of time.

RITARDANDO (RIT., RITARD.)—Becoming gradually slower.

RITENUTO (RITEN.)—Becoming suddenly slower.

ROLL—Trill on drum or tambourine.

ROMANCE (ROMANZA, ROMANZE)—A composition of romantic character.

RONDO (RONDEAU)—Originally a dance with alternating solos and chorus ensembles. Hence a form of music in which a principal theme alternates with others.

ROOT—Fundamental tone of a chord.

ROUND—An infinite canon, on the unison or octave. Also a round dance (roundelay).

ROUNDELAY (ROUNDEL)—Ballad with a recurrent refrain. Also a round dance.

RUBATO—Literally "robbed," hence applied to tempo deprived of its strict values.

RUN—A rapid succession of tones.

SALTANDO—Dancing, hence with bouncing bow.

SARABANDE (SARABAND)—A stately Spanish dance in slow, triple time, appearing in the classic suite.

SAXOPHONE—A brass clarinet, invented by Antoine Joseph Sax, shaped like a Dutchman's pipe, popular in dance bands.

SCALE—Literally "ladder," hence the steps in a logical succession of tones, as diatonic, chromatic, etc.

SCHERZO—Literally "jokingly," hence applied to a rapid, lighthearted tempo.

SCHOTTISCHE—Literally "Scottish," a dance in rather slow duple time.

SCORE—The music of a piece showing all the parts, or an arrangement.

SECCO—Dry, applied to recitative.

SECULAR MUSIC—Opposite of sacred music.

SEGNO—A sign, as in *al segno,* "return to the sign"; *dal segno* "repeat from the sign."

SEGUE—Follows, goes right ahead.

SEGUIDILLA—Spanish dance in triple time, usually slow and in minor.

SEMI—Half, as in semiquaver, sixteenth note, etc.

SEMPRE—Always.

SENTENCE—An interlude in sacred music; also a passage or phrase.

SENZA—Without.

SEPTET (SEPTUOR, SEPTETTO)—Composition for seven voices or instruments, or a combination of seven musicians.

SERENADE—Literally "evening music," hence a song or instrumental piece originally intended to be sung in the evening (usually outside a window).

SEXTET (SEXTUOR)—A composition for six voice parts or instruments, or a group of six musicians.

SFORZATO (SF)—Literally "forced," applying to a chord or a note to be suddenly emphasized.

SHADE—To give expression to music.

SHAKE—Trill.

SHARP—A character raising the pitch of the following note a half-tone. In the signature it raises every note on the line or space it occupies. A *double sharp* (x) raises the tone two half-steps. Also, too high in pitch.

SI (TI)—The seventh syllable in the Solfa system.

SICILIANA (SICILIENNE)—Sicilian peasant dance in slow time.

SIGNATURE—Group of sharps or flats at the start of a piece, to be used throughout. *Time signature,* the figures indicating the time (2–4, 3–4, etc.).

SING—To utter pleasant vocal sounds, with definite pitch.

SIXTEENTH—One-half of an eighth-note.

SIXTH—An interval in the scale or a chord employing that interval.

SIXTY-FOURTH—Half of a thirty-second note.

SLIDE—A movable tube used in the trombone and other instruments. A portamento.

SLUR—A curved line above or below two or more notes indicating that they are to be played *legato* or sung on one syllable. (If the notes are the same, the tone is continuous.)

SMORZANDO (SMORZ.) Dying away.

SOL—The fifth syllable in the Solfa system.

SOLFA—Solmisation. A system giving the tones of the absolute scale the syllables do (ut), re, mi, fa, sol, la, si, do.

SOLFEGGIO (SÒLFÈGE)—Exercise for the voice in solmisation (Solfa) or on one syllable.

SOLMISATION—Singing the syllables of the Solfa system.

SOLO—Alone, hence a passage or composition for a single voice or instrument, with or without accompaniment.

SONATA (SONATE)—Originally, music that was played (sounded) not sung. Now the name for the most elaborate form of absolute music, used for at least the first movement of sonatas, concertos, symphonies, etc. Specifically, a sonata is a composition for a solo instrument in sonata form, with no more than piano accompaniment.

SONATINA—A small sonata.

SONG—A vocal melody, or a lyric piece for an instrument.

SONG-FORM—A structure in three parts, A-B-A, used in actual songs but also in much instrumental music and the basis of sonata form.

SOPRANO—The highest female human voice.

SORDINE (SORDINO)—A mute. (*Con sordino,* with mute.)

SOUND-BOARD (SOUNDING-BOARD)—A resonant piece of wood which enlarges and enriches the tone of the strings stretched across it (as in pianos, violins, etc.).

STACCATO—Literally "detached," used of short, crisp notes.

STAFF (STAVE)—The five horizontal parallel lines on which the notes are written.

STEP—A progression to the adjoining note of the scale (whole-step or half-step).

STOP—Loosely the knob on an organ which is drawn out to let the real stop function. Actually the pipes or sets of pipes in an organ. Also, a fret on a stringed instrument or the pressure of the finger upon such a spot, to control pitch. *See* Double-stop. On wind instruments, the closing of a hole or key. Inserting the hand in the bell of a horn.

STRETTO — Literally "compressed," hence, in a fugue, a closing up of the subjects so as to overlap.

STRING—A vibrating cord, capable of musical tone.

STRING QUARTET (QUINTET, ETC.)—A group of players on stringed instruments or a composition for such a group.

STRINGENDO—Accelerating.

SUBDOMINANT—The fourth tone of the diatonic scale.

SUBITO (SUBITAMENTE)—Sudden(ly), immediate(ly).

SUBJECT—A melody or theme, particularly in a fugue or in sonata form.

SUITE—A set of pieces, originally dances, and a forerunner of the symphony.

SWELL—Gradual increase of sound, particularly the pedal of an organ and the mechanism for making such swelling of tone possible.

SYMPHONY (SYMPHONIE, SINFONIE)—A sonata for orchestra.

SYMPHONIC POEM—An orchestral piece of symphonic type but in one movement, usually programmatic.

SYNCOPATION—Distortion of rhythm by anticipating or delaying the natural accent.

SYRINX—Pan pipes.

TACET—Be silent.

TAMBOUR—Drum, drummer.

TAMBOURINE (TAMBOURIN)—A small drum with little bells in the rim, played by shaking and striking with the hand.

TARANTELLA (TARANTELLE)—An Italian dance, supposedly caused by the bite of the tarantula. A fast instrumental piece, usually in 6-8 time.

TECHNIC (TECHNIQUE)—The mechanics of musical performance.

TEMPERAMENT—A compromise system of tuning, so as to secure a practical scale. Used also of an artist's personal characteristics.

TEMPO—Time; rate of speed. Sometimes loosely used for rhythm in general.

TENOR (TENORE)—The highest natural male voice. (There is a distinction between lyric and dramatic tenors, chiefly of quality and style.)

TENTH—An interval of an octave plus a third.

TESSITURA—Literally "web," meaning the average pitch or range of a melody.

TETRACHORD—A four-stringed instrument. The interval of a fourth.

THEME (THEMA, TEMA)—An important melody. *Tema con variazioni*, "theme with variations."

THEORY—The science of music.

THIRD—An interval in the diatonic scale, also called the mediant.

THIRTY-SECOND—Half of a sixteenth note.

TIE—A slur.

TIMBRE—Tonal quality or color.

TIME—The most primitive organizing factor in music, representing the measure of tones, as to length or frequency, accent, and speed. Loosely used to mean both rhythm and tempo. (All time is either duple or triple, based upon multiples of two or three.)

TOCCATA—A brilliant piece, presenting a light, fast "touch."

TOMTOM—Primitive drum.

TONE—The basic material of music, created by vibrations of air and affected by pitch, quality, and time.

TONALITY—Key relationship.

TONIC—The keynote on which a scale begins and ends.

TONIC CHORD—Chord built on the keynote.

TONIC SOLFA—The system of teaching singing by syllables (Solmisation).

TOUCH—The act or manner of pressing the keys of an instrument (also applied to the response of the instrument itself).

TRANSCRIPTION—Rearrangement of a composition for a different instrument or instruments.

TRANSPOSE—To change the pitch of a composition throughout.

TREBLE—The highest voice or part. (Used also of the G clef.)

TREMOLO—Trembling (used of an organ stop and also effects on stringed instruments).

TRIAD—Chord of three tones.

TRIANGLE—A small steel rod bent into a triangle and tapped with a rod for tinkling, rhythmic effects.

TRILL—The rapid alternation of two adjacent tones.

TRIO—A composition for three instruments or voices. (Piano trio, written for violin, cello, and piano. String trio, for three stringed instruments.) Also a section of a composition, as in a minuet. Sometimes an added chorus.

TRIPLE—Threefold.

TRIPLET—A group of three equal notes.

TROMBONE—A trumpetlike brass instrument with valves or a slide for lengthening and shortening the tube.

TROUBADOUR (TROUVÈRE)—A musician of the Middle Ages, often of high rank, sometimes employing minstrels as assistants.

TRUMPET—A metal wind instrument fitted with crooks for variety of key and now also with valves for chromatic effects.

TUBA—The bass of the brass choir.

TUNE—Melody. Also, as a verb, to make the pitch of an instrument correct.

TURN—A decoration similar to a mordent but more elaborate.

TUTTA (TUTTO, TUTTE, TUTTI)—All, referring to the entire band, etc.

TYMPANI—Kettledrums.

UNISON—Identity of pitch.

UT—The old syllable for Do, still representing C in some countries.

VALVE—A device for giving natural brass instruments a chromatic scale.

VAMP—An improvised accompaniment or interlude.

VARIATION (VARIAZIONE)—The treatment of a melody in a decorative style or other change.

VERSE—Part of a song or hymn, with particular reference to the words.

VIBRATION—The shaking of an elastic body, creating sound waves.

VIBRATO—Vibrating.

VIOL—The family name of a familiar type of stringed instruments.

VIOLA—The alto, or tenor, violin. (Viola d'amore, viola da gamba are older types of viols.)

VIOLIN—The most popular of the viol family, representing the soprano voice.

VIOLONCELLO—The bass of the string quartet, generally abbreviated to cello.

VIRGINAL—A small spinet, popular in Elizabethan England.

VIRTUOSO—A performer of great skill.

VIVACE—Lively.

VOCAL—Relating to the voice.

VOCE—Italian for voice, as in *colla voce, mezza voce,* etc.

VOICE—The musical or articulate sound produced by human beings.

VOLUNTARY—An introductory organ piece.

VOX—Latin for voice. Used chiefly for organ stops, as *vox humana,* "human," *vox céleste,* "celestial."

WALTZ (WALZER, VALSE)—The most popular dance in triple time.

WELL-TEMPERED—Equally divided as to pitch.

WHISTLE—A small, shrill wind instrument. Also, as a verb, to play such an instrument or imitate it with the lips.

WIND—The instruments or music for a band of wind instruments. The band itself.

WOOD-WIND—In an orchestra the group of instruments presumably or actually made of wood.

XYLOPHONE—A percussion instrument producing different tones from strips of wood.

YODEL—To sing with a breaking of the voice into falsetto.

ZINGARESE (ZINGARESCA)—In gypsy style.

ZITHER—A stringed instrument plucked by the fingers or a pick.

INDEX

Index